Footprint Handbook

Bolivia

BEN BOX,
ROBERT & DAISY KUNSTAETTER

This is
Bolivia

Like its luminescent sky, Bolivia remains largely unpolluted and, in an age of rampant Disneyfication, stands out for its authenticity. There are over 17 million hectares of protected natural areas, but isolation is what best protects the intense and often bizarre beauty of Bolivia's landscapes. For the same reason, the cultural integrity of its peoples remains intact. Even though Evo Morales' government is bringing municipalities closer together, paving roads and building communal facilities, it takes time and patience to travel from one place to the next.

We (the authors) have travelled the length and breadth of Bolivia between us, but just when we might think that we have figured it out, it will catch us off guard. Some amazing new experience leaves us humbled and in awe of this remarkable country. Some of our favourites include a guide playing his charango in a cathedral-like cave near Torotoro; listening to the choir practise baroque music in San José de Chiquitos; walking all day without ever reaching the mirage-like shore of Lago Poopó; bathing in hot springs at Laguna Blanca and not wanting to get out because the air is almost zero; gliding down the River Yacuma being watched by countless caiman and cackled at by family after family of prehistoric hoatzin.

From the shores of Titicaca, the world's highest navigable lake, to the 'Lost World' table-lands of Noel Kempff Mercado National Park, following the footsteps of dinosaurs, bandits and revolutionaries, there are endless opportunities for off-the-beaten path exploration. Along the way are rest-stop cities and towns where travellers can indulge in creature comforts as well as tall tales of their adventures.

Ben Box, Robert & Daisy Kunstaetter

Best of
Bolivia

❶ La Paz

The capital city is building up its 21st-century credentials, but it still has its market streets where you can shop in the countless stores for multicoloured textiles and musical instruments, or head higher up into the indigenous area for produce and traditional items. Page 28.

❸ Lake Titicaca

The crystal-clear waters of the highest navigable lake in the world and, above, cloudless skies make this an essential place to visit. Don't stick to the shore, sail out to the Isla del Sol, birthplace of the Inca creation myth. Page 81.

❷ Tiwanaku

Just a short ride from La Paz, Tiwanaku contains the remnants and artefacts of one of the most important pre-Inca civilizations in South America. Page 77.

❹ Sorata

Just three hours from La Paz, this town has a beautiful setting and is an ideal centre for trekking in the Cordillera Real and for cycling in the mountains or down to the river ports which will take you to Rurrenabaque. Page 97.

❺ The 'world's most dangerous road'

The most famous downhill adrenalin rush on two wheels in the country from the heights near La Paz past waterfalls and dizzying drops to Coroico in the Yungas. Pages 110 and 111.

❻ Salar de Uyuni

This is a vast white salt plain interspersed with the occasional cactus-covered island. Tours from either Uyuni or Tupiza visit lakes of unimaginable colours, volcanic horizons and vast stretches of awe-inspiring emptiness. Page 149.

❼ Potosí

Silver from Potosí bankrolled the Spanish Empire. What remains in the highest city in the world is a fascinating mix of colonial opulence and the workings of poor miners gleaning what they can from the tunnels in the silver mountain. Page 184.

❽ Sucre

This attractive whitewashed colonial city is the seat of the republic's judiciary and a lively student culture. Take the Sauromóvil to see some of the 5000 dinosaur footprints at nearby Cal Orcko, or explore the traditional textiles of the Jalq'a communities. Page 169.

❾ Tarija

In the far south, Tarija is the centre of the Bolivian wine trade, as well as other fruits and vegetables. Away from the main tourist path it may be, but it's a charming small city and on a good route to or from neighbouring Argentina. Page 201.

❿ Torotoro National Park

In Potosí department, but most easily reached from Cochabamba by a road whose views change every 30 minutes, Torotoro is a geologist's paradise, with magnificent rock formations, fossils from the ocean bed and dinosaur tracks. Page 231.

⓫ Rurrenabaque

This is the starting point for tours upriver to community-based lodges in the jungles of Parque Nacional Madidi, or downriver to gallery forests and wetlands of the pampas. Expect to see plenty of wildlife on boat trips and hikes. Page 287.

⑫ Samaipata

A short drive from Santa Cruz, Samaipata was an outpost of the Incas, who took advantage of a huge carved rock for their easternmost fortress. As well as ruins, there are waterfalls, a relaxing town and, nearby, the Che Guevara Trail. Page 250.

⑬ Amboró National Park

At the convergence of the Amazon, the Andes, the dry Chaco plains and the Cerrado, Amboró's array of wildlife in its 11 recognized life zones is outstanding, and includes endangered cats and birds and more butterflies than anywhere else on earth. Page 259.

⑭ Chiquitania

UNESCO has recognized six surviving Jesuit mission churches as World Heritage Sites. Not only the beautiful architecture and decoration survives, but also the baroque music that was written and played here. Page 265.

⑮ Noel Kempff Mercado National Park

This remote wilderness near the Brazilian border has more ecosystems in a single place than anywhere else on the planet and its table-top mountains, waterfalls, forests and animal and plant species are considered by some to be the inspiration for Conan Doyle's *The Lost World*. Page 277.

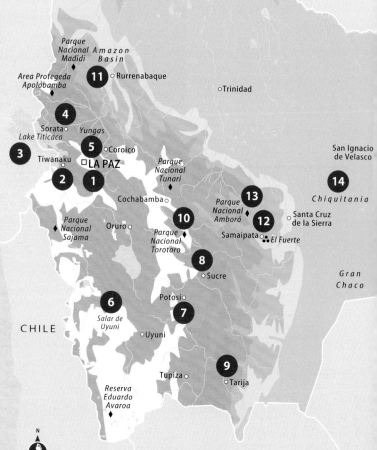

BRAZIL

PERU

Parque Nacional Madidi *Amazon Basin*

○ Rurrenabaque

○ Trinidad

11

4

○ Sorata
Yungas

Area Protegeda Apolóbamba

Lake Titicaca

3

○ Tiwanaku

2   **1**

□ LA PAZ

5 ○ Coroico

Parque Nacional Tunari

San Ignacio de Velasco

○ Cochabamba

13

Parque Nacional Amboró

14

Chiquitania

○ Oruro

Parque Nacional Sajama

10

Parque Nacional Torotoro

12

○ Santa Cruz de la Sierra

Samaipata ○•• *El Fuerte*

CHILE

8

○ Sucre

Gran Chaco

○ Potosí

7

6

Salar de Uyuni

○ Uyuni

9

○ Tupiza

○ Tarija

Reserva Eduardo Avaroa

N

ARGENTINA

100 km

100 miles

15
Parque Nacional
Noel Kempff
Mercado

○ Santa Ana
○ San Rafael

San José
○ de Chiquitos *Pantanal*

PARAGUAY

Route
planner

One to two weeks

base yourself in the capital

Your best bet is to stay within reach of **La Paz**, whose centre can be explored on foot in a couple of days. There are several worthwhile museums to visit, the warren of streets running uphill from El Prado lead you into a strange and fascinating world and the new cable cars to El Alto give a different perspective on the city. Trailheads of several good day walks can be reached by public transport and specialist tour companies can take you on short mountain-bike rides. An enlightening excursion from La Paz is the archaeological site of **Tiwanaku**. **Lake Titicaca** can also be visited in a day, but it is much more rewarding to stay overnight at the lakeside and visit Isla del Sol the following day. A day or two could easily be spent in the subtropical town of **Coroico**, 2½ hours from La Paz on a spectacular and hair-raising road. Three hours from La Paz is **Sorata**, another small town surrounded by beautiful mountain scenery and a major climbing, trekking and biking centre.

If you have a few more days, you might consider taking a four-day tour to either the **Salar de Uyuni** or to the jungle near **Rurrenabaque**.

Two to three weeks: Salar-Cochabamba circuit

salt lakes and colonial cities

After a couple of days in La Paz, making the most of the city while acclimatizing to the altitude, take a bus to Oruro. Continue by train to Uyuni or Tupiza. Either is a good place to start a tour to the **Salar de Uyuni** and its dramatic, volcanic surroundings. It takes at least four days to enjoy this world-class attraction properly, but you could easily spend more time in the vast and magnificent area. If short of time you can fly to Uyuni from La Paz. A paved road

Right: Oruro Carnival
Opposite page: La Paz

• 11

runs from Uyuni (or a soon-to-be-paved one from Tupiza) to **Potosí** to visit the mines and the Mint. From there buses and train run to **Sucre**, the nation's capital and most distinguished city. From Sucre you could fly or take a bus back to La Paz, or extend the circuit to **Cochabamba** by short flight or long bus journey, to enjoy the city, the surrounding colonial towns, nearby **Parque Nacional Tunari** and, if time permits, **Parque Nacional Torotoro** (four days). Both Sucre and Torotoro are great places to see dinosaur tracks.

Two to three weeks: Jesuit Missions and Samaipata

religious art and a cool resort

From **Santa Cruz de la Sierra**, one of Bolivia's international gateways, begin your travels by bus to San Javier, the closest of the Jesuit mission towns. The missions circuit needs at least five days and involves seven towns, six of which have UNESCO World-Heritage-status churches, perhaps the finest examples of religious art and craftsmanship in the country. From **San José de Chiquitos** you can return to Santa Cruz by bus or train. After the heat and dust of **Chiquitania**, head up to the refreshingly cool resort of **Samaipata**, only 2½ hours from Santa Cruz on a good paved road. It's a great place to relax and

nearby is **El Fuerte** archaeological site, once the easternmost stronghold of the Inca Empire. North of Samaipata is **Parque Nacional Amboró**, one of Bolivia's richest wildlife reserves, and southwest is the **Che Guevara Trail**, a significant element of recent Latin American history.

Above: Hoatzin birds
Left: Jesuit mission church, Concepción
Opposite page: Llamas on the altiplano

Two to three weeks: Yungas to Amazon

adrenalin fix and jungle trips

After a few days in La Paz, ride the infamous road down to Coroico by bike or minibus. Once you have recovered in the delightful surroundings of the **Yungas**, take a shared taxi to Caranavi where you can break your journey again before starting the rough 12-hour bus ride to **Rurrenabaque**. Alternative ways to get to Rurre are to fly in, or to go by mountain bike and boat from Sorata via Guanay (two hours from Caranavi) – tour operators offer this route. In Rurre, there are two types of tour: *selva* into the **Parque Nacional Madidi** and *pampas* into the **Beni lowlands**. Allow at least three days for each; there are many agencies to choose from. Instead of a marathon bus ride back to La Paz, consider flying and taking in the breathtaking views as you soar over the top of the Cordillera Real.

A month or more

taking it all in

The above can all be combined or extended. From **Potosí** you can go south to **Tarija** and the **Gran Chaco**, then loop back north to **Santa Cruz**. You can take a bus or train east to the Bolivian **Pantanal** on the border with Brazil. San Ignacio de Velasco offers the only road access to the wild and magnificent **Parque Nacional Noel Kempff Mercado**. From **Rurrenabaque** you can press on to **Trinidad** and then ever deeper into the heart of the Amazon jungle. Having plenty of time will allow you to experience the finest activity Bolivia has to offer – genuine exploration.

13

Best
parks
& reserves

Eduardo Avaroa

This 714,745-ha reserve protects a series of magnificently unusual coloured lakes, as well as high-altitude geysers and diverse fauna. Ninety-six species have been recorded here, including 69 types of bird. Most notable are the three species of flamingo, coots and the *suri* (rhea); all best seen from November to January. Among the mammals are the vicuña and the *titi* (Andean cat). The flora includes stands of *queñua* (polylepis) trees, yareta cushion plants, and tholar (an aromatic shrub). Page 152.

Madidi

Bolivia's premier jungle destination, Parque Nacional Madidi may be the most biodiverse of all the protected natural areas on earth. It is the variety of habitats that accounts for the array of flora and fauna in the park. In 1,895,750 ha, are an estimated 4750 species of plant, 900 bird species, 10 species of primate, five species of cat (with healthy populations of jaguar and puma), giant anteaters and many reptiles. Pages 288.

Sajama

Created in 1939, this is Bolivia's oldest national park. Ranging in altitude from 4200 m to over 6500 m above sea level, it protects 100,230 ha of high-Andean

Above: Tapir, Madidi
Left: Eduardo Avaroa

flora and fauna and is home to Nevado Sajama, the country's highest peak at 6542 m. The fauna includes vicuña, *quirquincho* (armadillo), puma, *suri* (rhea), condor, flamingo and coot. The scenery is magnificent: an impressive array of snow-capped volcanoes, as well as lakes, geysers and thermal springs. Page 136.

Torotoro

Parque Nacional Torotoro is highly recommended for adventurous travellers. It is a huge hanging valley (16,570 ha) at 2700 m, surrounded by 3500-m-high mountains. The park is riddled with dinosaur tracks and bones, and punctuated by dizzying drop-offs into deep canyons. You can climb down into one of the canyons and clamber over boulders along the river until a sunny swimming hole appears next to a shimmering waterfall. Geologists, palaeontologists, archaeologists and botanists have all carried out studies here. Page 231.

Apolobamba

Area Protegida Apolobamba is one of Bolivia's finest trekking venues as well as home to the famed Kallawayas, Bolivia's ancient medicine men. It contains the Cordillera Apolobamba, known for its snow-capped mountains, crystal-clear lakes and glaciers, and includes other ecological zones such as the altiplano,

grasslands, subtropical Yungas and unique Cela rainforest. Established to preserve dwindling herds of vicuña, it is also home to condors, as well as domestic alpacas and llamas. Page 105.

Noel Kempff Mercado

Parque Nacional Noel Kempff Mercado is remarkable for its Amazon forests, spectacular waterfalls and eerie-looking flat-topped mountain ranges called *mesetas* – thought to have inspired Arthur Conan Doyle's *The Lost World*. Seven ecosystems, with over 620 bird species have been identified here, which is approximately one-quarter of all the birds in the neotropics. Its impressive biodiversity has so far been protected by sheer isolation. Pages 277.

Top left: Sajama
Top right: Noel Kempff Mercado
Above: Pelechuco Pass, Cordillera Apolobamba

When to go

...and when not to

The dry season is May to September, July and August see the most tourists, while some of the best festivals, eg Carnaval and Holy Week, fall during the wet season – generally December to March. The country has four climatic zones:

The Puna and altiplano Average temperature, 10°C, but above 4000 m may drop as low as -30°C at night from June to August. By day, the tropical sun raises temperatures to above 20°C. Rainfall on the northern altiplano is 400-700 mm, much less further south. Little rain falls upon the western plateau between May and November, but the rest of the year can be wet.

The Yungas north of La Paz and Cochabamba Among the spurs of the Cordillera; altitude, 750-1500 m; average temperature 24°C. Rainfall in the Yungas is 700-800 mm a year, with high humidity.

The Valles The high valleys and basins gouged out by the rivers of the Puna; average temperature 19°C.

The tropical lowlands Altitude 150 m to 750 m; rainfall is high but seasonal (heaviest November to March, but can fall at any time); large areas suffer from alternate flooding and drought. The climate is hot, ranging from 23° to

Weather La Paz					
January	**February**	**March**	**April**	**May**	**June**
15°C 4°C 137mm	15°C 4°C 83mm	15°C 3°C 82mm	15°C 2°C 32mm	15°C -2°C 8mm	14°C -4°C 10mm
July	**August**	**September**	**October**	**November**	**December**
14°C -4°C 6mm	15°C -3°C 30mm	16°C -1°C 28mm	16°C 2°C 40mm	17°C 2°C 50mm	16°C 4°C 77mm

25°C in the south and to 30°C in the north. Occasional cold winds from the south, the *surazos*, can lower the temperature suddenly and considerably.

Festivals

Celebrated throughout the country and throughout the year, Bolivian festivals extend far beyond the legendary Carnaval de Oruro. A fiesta is at once a festival, a feast, a party, a holiday, a holy day, a day that is somehow marvellous and always out of the ordinary. It is a time to look forward to and prepare for; a moment in which to be very happy, very solemn or very patriotic. Most festivals are a rich and complex blend of indigenous and European cultural influences, Andean spirituality and Roman Catholic doctrine. The result is often so inscrutably authentic as to bewilder outsiders. Some visitors might also wonder how the country can get anything done amid so many prolonged celebrations. For most Bolivians, however, fiestas are not an interruption of the rhythm of life – they are its milestones. See also Festivals, page 367.

Alasitas

January One of the most intriguing items for sale in Bolivian markets is Ekeko, the god of good fortune and plenty and one of the most enduring and endearing of the Aymara gods and folk legends. He is a cheery, avuncular little chap, with a happy face to make children laugh, a pot belly due to his predilection for food and short legs so he can't run away. His image, usually in plaster of Paris, is laden with various household items, as well as sweets, confetti and streamers, food, and with a cigarette dangling from his lower lip. Believers say that these statues only bring luck if they are received as gifts.

Ekeko plays a central role in the festival of Alasitas, the Bolivian Feast of Plenty, which takes place in La Paz every January. Everything under the sun can be bought in miniature: houses, trucks, buses, tools, building materials, bolivianos, dollars and euros, suitcases, credit cards, cell phones, university diplomas and computers – you name it, you can find it here. The idea is to have your mini purchase blessed by a *yatiri* (an Aymara priest) or a Catholic priest and the real thing will be yours within the year.

Alasitas means different things to different people, but what they all share is the magic of dreaming that comes with Alasitas. See also page 61.

Carnaval de Oruro

February/March Held in Oruro in February or March, on the four days preceding Ash Wednesday, this is the best-known festival in Bolivia. It draws on indigenous traditions dating back to the pre-Inca Uru nation, as well as being part of the celebrations that are so common throughout Latin America and the Catholic world before Lent. Some 50 groups participate, ranging in size from 50 to 700 dancers and each is accompanied by brass bands, some with over 100 musicians. Eighteen different types of dances are performed, the most famous of which is La Diablada, the dance of the devils. La Diablada features grotesquely elaborate costumes and masks, some spewing fire. Yet despite its diabolical theme, participants in Oruro's carnival dance as an act of devotion to the Virgen del Socavón, patroness of the miners. The climax is at the church, which marks the end of the gruelling 4-km parade, where the most devout dancers approach the altar on their knees. See also page 128.

Carnaval de Santa Cruz
February/March Held in Santa Cruz in February or March, during the four days before Ash Wednesday, this Brazilian-style celebration is a wild and raucous time with music and dancing in the streets, parades, fancy dress and the coronation of a carnival queen. The main event is the *corso* parade, with over 300 groups participating. As with all Bolivian festivals at this time, there is plenty of water- (and even some paint-) throwing; nobody is spared.

Pujllay
March Held in Tarabuco, near Sucre, on the third Sunday of March, Pujllay is one of the best-known local festivals in the country. It celebrates the independence battle of Jumbate, when the native people defeated the Spaniards on 12 March 1816. Thousands of people from 30 rural communities, dressed in elaborate costumes, participate in this colourful celebration. Music is performed on native instruments and vigorous dancing invokes the souls of the fallen indigenous soldiers. Pujllay is just one of thousands of small-town fiestas held throughout Bolivia, all featuring music, dance, costumes, food and the obligatory *chicha*. See also page 179.

Festival de Música Renacentista y Barroca Americana
April Held in April every other year (next in 2016) in the city of Santa Cruz and the Jesuit mission towns of Chiquitania, this festival celebrates the wealth of sacred music written by European and indigenous composers in the 17th and 18th centuries. It has become an important international event with groups from all over the world participating during 10 days of concerts and choral presentations. The music and the venues, in the beautifully restored Jesuit churches, complement each other perfectly, making for an unforgettable experience. See also page 248.

Gran Poder

May/June Held in La Paz in May or June, Gran Poder is the liveliest and best attended event in the city's festival calendar. With music and dance similar to the Carnaval de Oruro, it was first celebrated in 1939 and has developed into a huge event in which tens of thousands of people take over the city centre. Its full name is Festividad de Nuestro Señor Jesús del Gran Poder and it pays homage to a venerated image of Jesus. It is also the festival of the cholos, La Paz's urban indigenous social class, who have worked their way up the social ladder as traders or craftsmen. The various prestes, or sponsors, enhance their social status by generously financing groups in the procession. See also page 61.

San Ignacio de Moxos

July/August Held in San Ignacio de Moxos, in the department of Beni, starting 30 July and lasting for a week, this is the most important and colourful festival in the Bolivian Amazon. Featuring elaborate feather headdresses, masked dancers and others with wooden machetes, drums and huge wind instruments, it is yet another delightfully authentic Bolivian fiesta.

Chutillos

August Held in Potosí and the nearby village of La Puerta around 24 August, Chutillos is a classic blend of Catholic and indigenous traditions that have merged to the point where they are indistinguishable from one another. It is both the feast day of San Bartolomé and the celebration of the saint's victory over Umphurruna, a native evil spirit who had kidnapped the sun and held her hostage in a dark cave. Participants visit the cave and thousands of parades and activities take place in the city throughout the month of August. See also page 195.

What to do

from legendary mountain biking to trekking a thousand curves

Birdwatching

Birdwatching is just getting underway in Bolivia as an organized activity. It offers great potential but requires considerable effort. The country is estimated to have over 1300 bird species, about 40% of the total found in South America, which range from macaws to condors, and hummingbirds to rheas. All national parks have opportunities for birdwatching, which can be combined with other tours. Parque Nacional Madidi has an estimated 900 bird species, and a couple of comfortable lodges. Parque Nacional Amboró has 850 species and is close to the resort towns of Samaipata and Buena Vista. Parque Nacional Tortoro is home to the rare red-fronted macaw.

Reserva Eduardo Avaroa, visited on most *salar* tours, has three species of flamingo as well almost 70 other bird species.

Climbing

Bolivia has nearly 1000 peaks over 5000 m (12 at or above 6000 m) in four cordilleras: the Real (the main area for mountaineering), Apolobamba, Quimza Cruz and Occidental. The climbing season is May-September.

In June-August the weather is better and more stable than in any other major mountaineering area in the world. Proper technical equipment, experience and/or a reputable guide are essential. A number of summits are achievable by acclimatized beginners with a competent guide and the correct equipment. Popular summits include: Huayna Potosí (6088 m; two days), Pequeño Alpamayo (5370 m; three days), Illimani (6439 m; four days) and Bolivia's highest mountain, Sajama (6542 m; four to five days). Other peaks of 6000 m or over are: Ancohuma (6427 m), Illampu (6368 m), Chearoco (6104 m) and Chachacomani (6000 m).

Mountain biking

Experienced, fit and acclimatized riders can choose from a huge range of possibilities in Bolivia, with unlimited scope for exploration. At the same time, a single tourist ride – dubbed the 'world's most dangerous road' – has

ON THE ROAD

Las mil curvas

One of the highlights of the Charazani–Pelechuco hike in the Cordillera Apolobamba is a 4600-m pass reached by an intimidatingly steep slope.

Climbing 500 m over loose stones in 1 km, the ascent is rendered a bit easier by a zigzag trail aptly nicknamed 'las mil curvas', the thousand curves. Reaching the top brings quite a feeling of accomplishment, but don't be too embarrassed if you are passed by a heavily laden little donkey carrying miners' supplies. He does it all the time.

become so popular with mainstream visitors as to spawn an industry of its own. And for good reason, as this legendary route is spectacular. Beginning at La Cumbre, a mountain pass above La Paz at 4725 m where there is often snow, it drops more than 3600 m in around four hours and 64 km to the subtropical jungle near Coroico. For most of the route the road is little more than a bumpy, rocky ledge carved into the rock face of the mountains. It lives up to its reputation for danger, so make sure you sign up with a reputable operator; check all equipment carefully before heading out and ride carefully. Some operators also offer newer, more innovative (or less hazardous) rides in the La Paz area, as well as other parts of the country. A demanding multi-day bike trip runs from Sorata to Charazani or Rurrenabaque, combining mountain biking, jeep and river travel. One- or two-day biking trips are also offered from Sucre and Tarija.

Trekking

Of the many off-the-beaten-path travel opportunities in Bolivia, none is as extensive or enticing as back-country trekking. There is hardly a better venue in all of South America for the experienced, well-equipped and self-sufficient trekker who wants to explore new routes. In addition, there are various established trails that have long been popular with independent trekkers and tour agencies. Most of the latter are based in La Paz, but there are others in places such as Potosí, Sucre and Tupiza.

Where to stay

from boutique hotel to wilderness camping

Hotels and hostales

Hotels must display prices by law, but often do not. The number of stars awarded each hotel is also regulated, but not always accurate. The following terms likewise reflect the size and quality of an establishment (from largest and best, to smallest and simplest): *hotel, hostal, residencial, alojamiento* and *casa de huéspedes*. A *pensión* is a simple restaurant and may double as a place to sleep in smaller towns. For a selection of boutique hotels and resorts, see www.bolivianboutiquehotels.com.

Camping

Camping is best suited to the wilderness areas of Bolivia, away from towns, and people. Organized campsites, car or trailer camping does not exist here. Because of the abundance of cheap hotels you should never have to camp in populated areas

Youth hostels

Youth hostels or self-styled 'backpackers' are not necessarily cheaper than hotels. A number of mid-range *residenciales* are affiliated to **Hostelling International** (HI) ① *www.hihostels.com/destinations/bo/hostels*; some others just say they are. Another website listing hostels is www.boliviahostels.com, but they are not necessarily affiliated to HI.

Price codes

Where to stay	Restaurants
$$$$ over US$150	$$$ over US$12
$$$ US$66-150	$$ US$7-12
$$ US$30-65	$ US$6 and under
$ under US$30	

Price for a double room in high season, including taxes.

Price for a two-course meal for one person, excluding drinks or service charge.

ON THE ROAD
Checking in

- Always take a look at the room before checking in. Hotel owners will often attempt to rent out the worst rooms first – feel free to ask for a better room or bargain politely for a reduced rate if you are not happy.

- In cities, rooms away from the main street will be less noisy.

- Air conditioning (a/c) is only required in the lowlands and jungle. If you want an a/c room it will add approximately 30% to the price.

- The electric showers in cheaper places should be treated with respect. Always wear rubber sandals to avoid an unwelcome shock.

- Taller travellers (over 1.8 m) should check out the length of beds, especially in highland areas.

- A torch or candles are advisable in more remote areas and jungle lodges, where electricity may only be supplied during certain hours.

- Upmarket hotels will usually have their own restaurant, while more modest places may only serve a simple breakfast.

- Some hotels charge per room and not per bed, so if travelling alone, it may be cheaper to share with others.

- The cheapest and nastiest hotels are usually found near bus and train stations and markets. In small towns, better accommodation can often be found around the main plaza.

- Be sure that taxi drivers take you to the hotel you want rather than the one that pays the highest commission or is owned by their cousin.

Food
& drink

salteñas, emapanadas and a glass of fermented chicha

Food

Bolivian highland cooking is usually tasty and *picante* (spicy). Recommended local specialities include *empanadas* (cheese pasties) and *humintas* (maize pies); *pukacapas* are *picante* cheese pies. Recommended main dishes include *sajta de pollo*, hot spicy chicken with onion, fresh potatoes and *chuño* (dehydrated potatoes), *parrillada* (mixed grill), *fricase* (juicy pork with *chuño*), *silpancho* (very thin fried breaded meat with eggs, rice and bananas), and *ají de lengua*, ox-tongue with hot peppers, potatoes and *chuño* or *tunta* (another kind of dehydrated potato). *Pique macho*, roast meat, sausage, chips, onion and pepper is especially popular with Bolivians and travellers alike. Near Lake Titicaca fish becomes an important part of the local diet and trout, though not native, is usually delicious. Bolivian soups are usually hearty and warming, including *chairo* made of meat, vegetables and *chuño*. *Salteñas* are very popular meat or chicken pasties eaten as a mid-morning snack, the trick is to avoid spilling the gravy all over yourself.

In the lowland Oriente region, the food usually comes with cooked banana, yucca and rice. This area also has good savoury snacks, such as *cuñapés* (cheese bread made with manioc flour). In the northern lowlands, many types of wild meat are served in tourist restaurants and on jungle tours. Bear in mind that the turtles whose eggs are eaten are endangered and that other species not yet endangered soon will be if they stay on the tourist menu.

Ají is hot pepper, frequently used in cooking. *Locoto* is an even hotter variety (with black seeds), sometimes served as a garnish and best avoided by the uninitiated. *Llajua* is a hot pepper sauce present on every Bolivian table. Its potency varies greatly so try a little bit before applying dollops to your food.

Bolivia's temperate and tropical fruits are excellent and abundant. Don't miss the luscious grapes and peaches in season (February-April). Brazil nuts, called *almendras* or *castañas*, are produced in the northern jungle department of Pando and sold throughout the country.

The popular tourist destinations have a profusion of cafés and restaurants catering to the gringo market. Some offer decent international cuisine at reasonable prices, but many seem convinced that foreigners eat only mediocre pizza and vegetarian omelettes. There must be a hundred 'Pizzerías Italianas' in Bolivia's tourist towns.

Drink

The several makes of local lager-type **beer** are recommendable; *Paceña*, *Huari*, *Taquiña* and *Ducal* are the best-known brands. There are also microbrews in La Paz (see page 52). *Singani*, the national spirit, is distilled from grapes, and is cheap and strong. *Chuflay* is *singani* and a fizzy mixer, usually 7-Up. Good **wines** are produced by several vineyards near Tarija (tours are available, see page 210). *Chicha* is a fermented maize drink, popular in Cochabamba. The hot maize drink, *api* (with cloves, cinnamon, lemon and sugar), is good on cold mornings. **Bottled water** is readily available. Tap, stream and well water should never be drunk without first being purified.

Restaurants in Bolivia

Most restaurants do not open early but many hotels include breakfast, which is also served in markets (see below). In *pensiones* and cheaper restaurants a basic lunch (*almuerzo* – usually finished by 1300) and dinner (*cena*) are normally available. The *comida del día* is the best value in any class of restaurant. Breakfast and lunch can also be found in markets, but eat only what is cooked in front of you. Dishes cooked in the street are not safe. Llama meat contains parasites, so make sure it has been properly cooked, and be especially careful of raw salads as many tourists experience gastrointestinal upsets.

ON THE ROAD
Fruit salad

Treat your palate to some of Bolivia's exquisite temperate and tropical fruits. They are great on their own, as *ensalada de frutas*, or make delicious *refrescos* (fruit juices). Always make sure these are prepared with purified water and preferably without ice. Temperate fruit season is generally February to April. Dried fruits are available in markets and make good provisions for trekking.

Chirimoya Custard apple. A very special treat, soft when ripe but check for tiny holes in the skin which usually mean worms inside.

Carambola Star fruit. Not for eating plain, but makes an excellent tangy juice.

Copoazú An exquisite fruit from the northern jungle, the frozen pulp is available in health food shops in La Paz; worth looking for.

Duraznos Peaches. The season is February-April and quality can be very good.

Higos or **brevas** Fresh figs are abundant, inexpensive and delicious, but best enjoyed in moderation as they are a mild laxative.

Pacay Ice cream bean. Large pod with sweet white pulp around hard black seeds.

Peras Pears. Gigantic ones are grown in the Luribay valley, in the department of La Paz.

Tumbo Banana passion fruit. Peel open the thin skin and slurp the fruit without chewing the seeds. Also makes a popular *refresco*.

Tuna Prickly pear. Sweet and tasty (some are blood-red) but never pick them with bare hands. Tiny blond spines hurt your hands and mouth unless they are carefully removed first.

Uvas Luscious grapes are possibly Bolivia's best-kept secret. The season is long, January-May, and the best are grown in the department of Tarija.

La Paz & around

the world's highest capital will take your breath away

La Paz is arguably the most fascinating metropolis in all of South America. Architecturally, the city is no beauty, nor does it have many classic tourist attractions, but what sets it apart are the sights, sounds and smells of the streets and the phenomenal views of the encircling mountains.

Airborne visitors touch down at the highest commercial airport in the world, in the rapidly expanding city of El Alto. Choked streets lead to the lip of the huge canyon down which La Paz snakes from over 3500 to under 3000 m. Colonial terracotta, modern red-brick and high-rise blocks with glass in rainbow hues press together, metamorphosing at night into a canyon of stars as the lights come on.

Much of old La Paz appears to be one gigantic street market. Every square inch of pavement is taken up by Aymara women in traditional bowler hats and voluminous skirts selling their wares. There is a vast array of handicrafts, markets devoted to food, drink and bags of coca leaves, even a Witches' Market for talismans, cure-alls and spells.

A dramatic descent from the altiplano leads to the subtropical Yungas, forested valleys that are rich in fruit and coffee and an ideal place to catch your breath before heading back to the heights or onwards to the Amazon lowlands.

Best for
Markets ▪ Museums ▪ Tours

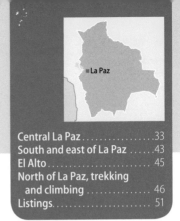

Footprint
picks

★ **Calle Jaén**, page 36
Picturesque colonial street with good views and museums.

★ **San Francisco church and monastery**, page 37
Fine colonial architecture and treasures.

★ **Browse the markets**, pages 39 and 45
From small neighbourhood markets to the massive twice-weekly Feria 16 de Julio in El Alto.

★ **Museo Nacional de Arqueología**, page 39
Good collections of arts and crafts from ancient Tiwanaku.

★ **Sopocachi**, page 40
The place to head for a night on the town.

★ **El Montículo and Parque Laikakota**, pages 40 and 42
The best places to take in the views and admire La Paz's unique setting.

★ **Ride the Teleférico**, page 40
The red and yellow lines give a spectacular overview of La Paz (but can be very busy on Sunday).

Essential La Paz

Finding your feet

Airport La Paz has the highest commercial airport in the world, high above the city at El Alto. A taxi from the airport to or from the centre takes between 30 minutes and one hour.

Bus station There are three main bus terminals: the bus station at **Plaza Antofagasta**, the **cemetery district** for Sorata, Copacabana and Tiwanaku, and **Minasa** bus station in Villa Fátima for the Yungas, including Coroico, and northern jungle.

Getting around

A system of cable cars (*teléfericos*) is under construction. Three lines were in operation at the time of writing, the red line, between El Alto and Vita, west of the main bus station, the yellow line from Sopocachi to Ciudad Satélite, and the green line, which continues from Sopocachi to Obrajes. There are three

types of city bus: *puma katari* (a fleet of new buses operating since March 2014), *micros* (small, old buses) and faster, more plentiful minibuses. *Trufis* are fixed-route collective taxis, with a sign with their route on the windscreen. Taxis come in three types: regular honest taxis, fake taxis and radio taxis, the safest, which have a dome light and number.

The city's main street runs from **Plaza San Francisco** as Avenida Mariscal Santa Cruz, then changes to Avenida 16 de Julio (more commonly known as El Prado) and ends at **Plaza del Estudiante**. The business quarter, government offices, central university (UMSA) and many of the main hotels and restaurants are in this area. Banks and exchange houses are clustered on Calle Camacho, between Loayza and Colón, not far from **Plaza Murillo**, the traditional heart of the city. From the Plaza del Estudiante, Avenida Villazón splits into Avenida Arce, which runs southeast towards the wealthier residential districts of **Zona Sur**, in the valley,15 minutes away; and Avenida 6 de Agosto which runs through **Sopocachi**, an area full of restaurants, bars and clubs. Zona Sur has shopping centres, supermarkets with imported

Best view

Nothing can beat the view of triple-peaked Illimani, with its snow-caps ignited a blazing orange by the setting sun.

Weather La Paz

January	February	March	April	May	June
15°C 4°C 137mm	15°C 4°C 83mm	15°C 3°C 82mm	15°C 2°C 32mm	15°C -2°C 8mm	14°C -4°C 10mm

July	August	September	October	November	December
14°C -4°C 6mm	15°C -3°C 30mm	16°C -1°C 28mm	16°C 2°C 40mm	17°C 2°C 50mm	16°C 4°C 77mm

Tip...

Travellers arriving in La Paz, especially when flying directly from sea level, may experience mild altitude sickness. If your symptoms are severe, consult a physician. See Health, page 368.

items and some of the best restaurants and bars in La Paz (see page 57).

Safety

La Paz is in general a safe city, but like any metropolis it is not crime-free. Areas where you must take care are around Plaza Murillo and the Cemetery neighbourhood where local buses serve Copacabana and Tiwanaku. **Tourist police** (T222 5016) now patrol these bus stops during the daytime, but caution is still advised. **Warning for ATM users**: scams to get card numbers and PINs have flourished, especially in La Paz. The tourist police post warnings in hotels. See also Safety, page 372.

When to go

It is good to visit La Paz at any time. The weather is cool all year; locals say that the city experiences all the seasons in one day. The sun is strong, but the moment you go into the shade, the temperature falls. From December-March, the summer, it rains most afternoons, making it feel colder than it actually is. Temperatures are even lower in winter, June-August, when the sky is always clear. The two most important festivals, when the city gets particularly busy, are **Alasitas** (last week of January and first week of February) and **Festividad del Señor del Gran Poder** (end May/early June). See Festivals, page 61.

Time required

Two to three days to acclimatize to the altitude and see the city's highlights; one to two weeks for excursions and treks.

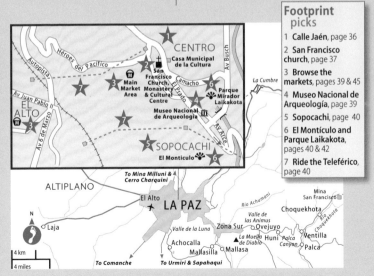

Footprint picks

The ideal La Paz day is a slow one with plenty of time for appreciative wandering through its stall- and people-laden streets and with café breaks for high-altitude recuperation.

After a good start to the day with breakfast in a café on Linares or Sagárnaga, check out the **Witches' Market** along Calle Linares, note the aroma of the medicinal herbs and ask the vendors about the use of the special items sold here. If you need to purchase souvenirs or a warm alpaca sweater, you are in the right area; Sagárnaga and Linares are full of shops selling all sorts of handicrafts. If you want to get a feel for a more authentic market, continue uphill along Sagárnaga, the area becomes much less touristy and stalls sell fruit, traditional dresses, bits of engines and hats.

Back down Sagárnaga, at Plaza San Francisco you reach the church of the same name. To see this impressive colonial church and the art treasures it holds, take a tour of the **Centro Cultural Museo San Francisco**. If you would rather focus on pre-colonial treasures, wander down El Prado, the city's main thoroughfare, towards the **Museo Nacional de Arqueología** and marvel at the Inca and Tiwanaku artefacts and mummies. Along the way, be sure to join locals in the mid-morning tradition of having a *salteña* and hot drink.

Weather permitting, the one thing not to miss in La Paz is the view of Illimani; walk along **Puente de las Américas**, the bridge joining Sopocahi and Miraflores, and you will be rewarded. For great views of the city, **Parque Laikakota** is nearby. By now you are surely tired and hungry. Many of the best lunch places are back near Sagárnaga, where you will find Bolivian fare and a choice of Middle Eastern, Indian, Chinese and other options. Most offices and shops close until 1500, so you can catch your breath until then.

After lunch you could have a look at the fascinating history of the famous leaf in the **Museo de la Coca** or head straight across to the eastern side of El Prado to the heart of the city, **Plaza Murillo**, a good place to sit, people-watch and admire the public buildings. Around you are the cathedral, the **Palacio Presidencial** and the **Congreso Nacional**. North of here is **Calle Jaén**, a small street with much of the city's notable colonial architecture and several interesting little museums.

After a rest at your hotel, get ready for a night out in **Sopocachi**, one of La Paz's trendy eating and drinking areas. Take a taxi to Plaza Avaroa and have a look around the plaza and on neighbouring streets. Eating options are plentiful and international.

This is also a good area for evening entertainment – the Thelonius Jazz Bar is on Avenida 20 de Octubre, or if you prefer rock, **Equinoccio** is on Sánchez Lima. Alternatively, if you fancy your music and drink mixed with other fellow travellers, try **Mongo's** before heading home for a well-earned rest.

Sights
La Paz

Central La Paz *Colour map 2, B2.*

the old city has lively markets and some worthwhile museums

There are few colonial buildings left in La Paz; probably the best examples are in **Calle Jaén** (see below). Late 19th- and early 20th-century architecture, often displaying European influence, can be found in the streets around Plaza Murillo, but much of La Paz is modern. The **Plaza del Estudiante** (Plaza Franz Tamayo), or a bit above it, marks a contrast between old and new styles, between the commercial and the more elegant. **El Prado** itself is lined with high-rise blocks dating from the 1960s and 1970s.

1 La Paz orientation

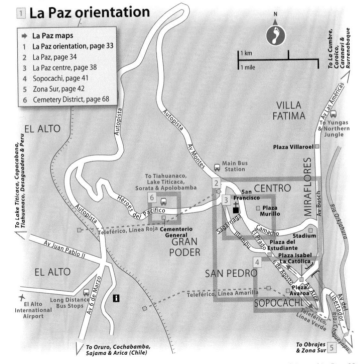

➜ La Paz maps
1 La Paz orientation, page 33
2 La Paz, page 34
3 La Paz centre, page 38
4 Sopocachi, page 41
5 Zona Sur, page 42
6 Cemetery District, page 68

La Paz

Where to stay 🛏
1 Adventure Brew B&B *A2*
2 Adventure Brew Hostel *A2*
3 Arthy's Guesthouse *A2*
4 Bacoo *A3*
5 Casa Fusión *E5*
6 Casa Prado *C4*
7 El Rey Palace *D4*
8 Estrella Andina *B2*
9 Europa *C4*
10 Hostal Copacabana *B2*
11 Hostal República *B4*
12 La Joya *B1*
13 La Loge & La Comedie Restaurant *E5*
14 Mitru La Paz *E5*
15 Onkel Inn 1886 *C3*
16 Rosario *B2*
17 Stannum *E5*
18 Tambo de Oro *A3*
19 Wild Rover Backpackers Hostel *B4*

Restaurants 🍴
1 Alexander Coffee *C4, E5*
2 Arco Iris *E4*
3 Armonía *E5*
4 Beatrice *E4*
5 Café Soho *A3*
6 Café Urbano *C4*
7 El Consulado *C4*
8 Fridolin *E5*
9 Ken-Chan *D4*
10 Kuchen Stube *E5*
11 La Terraza *E5*
12 Maphrao On *E6*
13 Mongo's *E5*
14 Olive Tree *E6*
15 Paladar *C6*
16 Potokos *A6*
17 Reineke Fuchs *E5*
18 Rendezvous *E5*
19 Suma Uru *E5*
20 Vienna *D4*

Bars & clubs 🍸
21 Equinoccio *E4*
22 Etno Café *A3*
23 Thelonius Jazz Bar *E4*

N

100 metres
100 yards

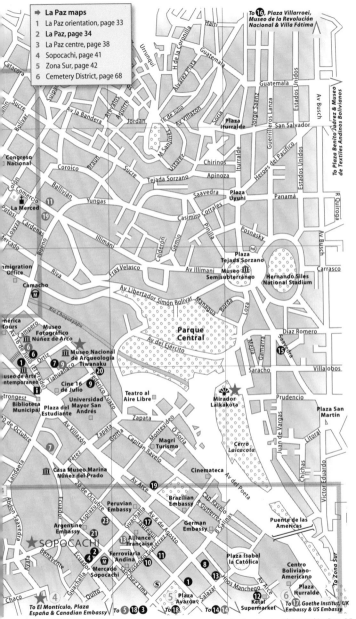

Around Plaza Murillo

Plaza Murillo Three blocks north of El Prado, this is the traditional centre. Facing its formal gardens are the **Cathedral**, the **Palacio Presidencial** in Italian Renaissance style, known as the **Palacio Quemado** (burnt palace) twice gutted by fire in its stormy 130-year history, and, on the east side, the **Congreso Nacional**. In front of the Palacio Quemado is a statue of former President Gualberto Villarroel who was dragged into the plaza by a mob and hanged in 1946.

Across from the Cathedral on Calle Socabaya is the **Palacio de los Condes de Arana** (built 1775), with beautiful exterior and patio. It houses the **Museo Nacional de Arte** ⓘ *T02-240 8600, www.mna.org.bo, Tue-Fri 0930-1230, 1500-1900, Sat 1000-1730, Sun 1000-1330, US$2.15.* It has a fine collection of colonial paintings including many works by Melchor Pérez Holguín, considered one of the masters of Andean colonial art, and which also exhibits the works of contemporary local artists. Calle Comercio, running east-west across the Plaza, has most of the s tores and shops.

West of Plaza Murillo, at Ingavi 916, in the palace of the Marqueses de Villaverde is the **Museo Nacional de Etnografía y Folklore** ⓘ *T02-240 8640, www.musef.org. bo, Mon-Fri 0900-1230, 1500-1900, Sat 0900-1630, Sun 0900-1430, US$3, filming costs US$6.* Various sections show the cultural richness of Bolivia by region through textiles and other items. It has a *videoteca*.

★**Calle Jaén** Northwest of Plaza Murillo is Calle Jaén, a picturesque colonial street with a café, craft shops, good views and four museums (known as **Museos Municipales** ⓘ *Tue-Fri 0930-1230, 1500-1900, Sat 1000-1700, Sun 0900-1330, US$1.50 each*) housed in colonial buildings. **Museo Costumbrista Juan de Vargas** ⓘ *on Plaza Riosinio, at the top of Jaén, T02-228 0758, US$0.60,* has miniature displays depicting incidents in the history of La Paz and well-known Paceños, as well as miniature replicas of reed rafts used by the Norwegian Thor Heyerdahl, and the Spaniard Kitin Muñoz, to prove their theories of ancient migrations. **Museo del Litoral Boliviano** ⓘ *T02-228 0758,* has artefacts of the War of the Pacific, and interesting selection of old maps. **Museo de Metales Preciosos** ⓘ *T02-228 0329,* is well set out with Inca gold artefacts in basement vaults, also ceramics and archaeological exhibits, and **Museo Casa Murillo** ⓘ *T02-228 0553,* the erstwhile home of Pedro Domingo Murillo, one of the martyrs of the La Paz independence movement of 16 July 1809, has a good collection of paintings, furniture and national costumes. In addition to the Museos Municipales and also in a colonial house is the **Museo de Instrumentos Musicales** ⓘ *C Jaén 711 e Indaburo, T02-240 8177, Tue-Fri 0930-1230, 1500-1900; Sat-Sun 1000-1300 US$1.40,* founded by Ernesto Cavour and based on 30 years of research. The International Charango Association is based here and lessons are available.

Museo Tambo Quirquincho ⓘ *C Evaristo Valle, south of Jaén, Plaza Alonso de Mendoza, T02-239 0969, Tue-Fri, 0930-1230, 1500-1900, Sat-Sun, 0900-1300, US$1.20,* displays modern painting and sculpture, carnival masks, silver, early 20th-century photography and city plans, and is recommended.

BACKGROUND

La Paz

The Spaniards originally founded La Paz on the altiplano in what is now Laja, a small town 30 km west on the way to Desaguadero. In 1548 they moved down to the valley of the Río Choqueyapu to escape the cold winds of the altiplano and get closer to the alluvial gold in the river whose name in Aymara means God of Gold , today mostly underground and polluted beyond recognition. The city of Nuestra Señora de La Paz was founded on 20 October 1548, conveniently located between recently discovered silver mines of Potosí and Lima, capital of the Spanish colony.

The official capital of Bolivia is Sucre, but La Paz became the country s biggest city after the decline of Potosí in the 17th century. While the Supreme Court is still based in Sucre, most other branches of government were moved to La Paz after a civil war in 1899. Although La Paz remains an important commercial centre, its economic superiority has been surpassed by Santa Cruz. In terms of population, in 2008 it was estimated to be third after Santa Cruz and El Alto.

Since colonial times, the centre of La Paz has been around Plaza Murillo. The first real suburbs were San Pedro and Sopocachi, west of El Prado, and Miraflores, on a ridge to the east. The spread down to what is now Obrajes and beyond, to the Zona Sur, began during the early 20th century. At the same time the slopes of the canyon have filled with houses and working-class areas have spread out further and further from the centre. The major pole of growth since the 1970s, however, has been the bleak altiplano surrounding the canyon where El Alto (see page 45) has become a city in its own right. At the time of the 2012 census, the population of La Paz was 764,617, whereas that of El Alto was 848,840.

Plaza San Francisco up to the cemetery district

★**Church and monastery of San Francisco** ① *Plaza San Francisco, open for Mass at 0700, 0900, 1100 and 1900, Mon-Sat, and also at 0800, 1000 and 1200 on Sun.* At the upper end of Avenida Mcal Santa Cruz, this church and monastery, dating from 1549, is one of the finest examples of colonial religious architecture in South America and well worth seeing. The church is richly decorated using native religious themes; the mestizo baroque façade clearly displays how the traditional baroque vine motif is transformed into an array of animals, birds and plants. The interior contains huge, square columns and gilt altars.

Centro Cultural Museo San Francisco ① *Plaza San Francisco 503, T02-231 8472, Mon-Sat 0900-1800, US$2.80, allow 1½-2 hrs, free guides available. but tip appreciated, some speak English and French.* The cultural center offers access to various areas of the church and convent including the choir, crypt (open 1400-1730), roof, various chapels and gardens. Fine art includes religious paintings from the 17th, 18th and 19th centuries, plus visiting exhibits and a hall devoted to the works of Tito Yupanqui, the indigenous sculptor of the Virgen de Copacabana. There is a pricey but good café at entrance. Behind the San Francisco church a network of narrow cobbled streets rise steeply up the canyon walls.

3 La Paz centre

➡ **La Paz maps**
1 La Paz orientation, page 33
2 La Paz, page 34
3 La Paz centre, page 38
4 Sopocachi, page 41
5 Zona Sur, page 42
6 Cemetery District, page 68

N

100 metres
100 yards

Where to stay
1 Arcabucero C1
2 Casa de Piedra B2
3 El Solario B1
4 Fuentes C1
5 Gloria B2
6 Hosp Milenio A3
7 Hostal Naira C2
8 La Casona B2
9 La Posada de la Abuela Obdulia C1
10 Loki A1
11 Milton D1
12 Muzungu B1
13 Posada El Carretero A3
14 Presidente & La Kantuta Restaurant B2
15 Sagárnaga C1
16 Torino B3

Restaurants
1 100% Natural C1
2 Alexander Coffee B3
3 A Lo Cubano C1
4 Angelo Colonial C1
5 Banais B2
6 Café del Mundo C1
7 Café Illampu & Gravity Bolivia C1
8 Café Pepe's C1
9 Colonial Pot C1
10 K'umara C1
11 La Cueva C2
12 Pizzería Italia C1
13 Sol y Luna C2
14 Star of India C2
15 Steakhouse C2

Bars & clubs
16 Hard Rock Café B1
17 Oliver's English Tavern C2
18 Peña Parnaso C2
19 Peña Huari C1

West of Plaza San Francisco ★**Street market** covers much of this area. Handicraft shops, travel agencies, hotels and restaurants line the lower part of **Calle Sagárnaga** (here you find the highest concentration of tourists and pick-pockets). The **Mercado de Brujas**, 'witchcraft market', on Calles Melchor Jiménez and Linares, which cross Santa Cruz above San Francisco, sells charms, herbs and more gruesome items like llama foetuses. The small **Museo de la Coca** ⓘ *Linares 906, T02-231 1998, Mon-Sat 1000-1900, Sun 1000-1600, US$2.15, www.cocamuseum.com, shop with coca products for sale*, is devoted to the coca plant, its history, cultural significance, medical values and political implications. A guidebook in English is available.

Further up, from Illampu to Rodríguez and in neighbouring streets, is the produce-based **Rodríguez market** ⓘ *daily, but best on Sun morning*. Turning right on Max Paredes, heading north, is **Avenida Buenos Aires**, where small workshops turn out the costumes and masks for the Gran Poder festival, and with great views of Illimani, especially at sunset. Continuing west along Max Paredes towards the **cemetery district**, the streets are crammed with stalls selling every imaginable item. Transport converges on the cemetery district (for more information see page 68). See also Safety, page 372.

El Prado, Sopocachi, Miraflores and Zona Sur

museums, nightlife and some of the city's best views

El Prado

The **Museo de Arte Contemporáneo Plaza** ⓘ *Av 16 de Julio 1698, T02-233 5905, daily 0900-2100, US$2.20*, in a 19th-century house that has been declared a national monument, exhibits a selection of contemporary art from national and international artists.

Nearby, the ★**Museo Nacional de Arqueología** or **Tiwanacu** ⓘ *Tiwanacu 93 entre Bravo y F Zuazo, T02-231 1621, www.bolivianet.com/tiwanacu*, just off El Prado (down the flight of stairs near the Maria Auxiliadora church), contains good collections of the arts and crafts of ancient Tiwanaku and items from the eastern jungles. It also has an exhibition of gold statuettes and objects found in Lake Titicaca. Further north, on Avenida Libertador Simón Bolívar, from where there are views of Mount Illimani, is the modern **Mercado Camacho** produce market.

Towards the southeast, Avenida Camacho turns to Avenida Simón Bolívar, one of the accesses to the district of Miraflores. Where the two avenues meet is an entrance to the **Parque Central Urbano**, a linear park along the shores of the Río Choqueyapu. The river runs in culverts under the park, which has an open-air theatre and sports fields and is the scene of the Alasitas festival.

West of Avenida 16 de Julio (El Prado) in the residential district of San Pedro is the pleasant **Plaza Sucre**. Here, at Avenida 20 de Octubre y Colombia, is the church of **San Pedro**. Also on Plaza Sucre is the notorious **San Pedro Prison**, once one of La Paz's most unusual tourist attractions and made famous by Rusty Young's book, *Marching Powder* (Sidgwick & Jackson, 2003). In 2013 the authorities announced that the prison would close, but in early 2015 it was still functioning.

ON THE ROAD
La Chola Paceña

The traveller arriving in La Paz will be struck by the distinctive dress of the *chola paceña*, native women who wear full skirts and a bowler, or derby, hat.

There is some disagreement as to the origin of the term *cholo*, which is used to refer to indigenous peoples who have abandoned the traditional rural life and moved to cities and towns. One version is that the word comes from the Aymara word *chhulu*, which means mestizo, someone born of native and Spanish parents. Another is that the term derives from the Spanish word *chulo*, still used to refer to people from the lower-class areas of Madrid.

It is said that the style of dress of the *chola paceña* was influenced by the women of 17th-century Toledo. The most distinctive garment of the chola is her voluminous skirt known as a *pollera*. This comes from the Spanish word *pollo* (chicken), so *pollera* translates as some kind of cage for chickens. Up until 1920 *polleras* were made of silk, velvet, taffeta and brocade in bright colours. Today, for practical as well as economic reasons, polyester and other synthetic fabrics are used.

The long-fringed *manta* (shawl) has not changed in shape since originally worn by the *cholas* in the 16th century. It is similar to that worn by the women of Salamanca in Spain, the only difference being that the *chola* wears it folded in a rectangular shape, in keeping with the tradition of the *llijlla*, which was worn by the *ñustas*, the princesses of the Inca empire.

The hat of the *chola paceña* has changed in shape and in the materials used since its original design. The felt hat of today appeared only after 1925. Its origin is something of a mystery, though one theory is that a merchant mistakenly imported this kind of derby hat. Not knowing what to do with them, he passed them off as ladies' hats, which turned out to be a very lucrative move. In the 1930s the Italian firm of Borsalino began to mass produce the derby hat for export to Bolivia. Today the felt is imported from Brazil, Portugal and Italy, and the hats are made locally.

A quality outfit is a sign of status and keeping up the tradition does not come cheap. The purchase of a top-quality Borsalino alone represents one month's salary, not to mention the cost of the *pollera* and the *manta*.

★Sopocachi

To the south of Plaza del Estudiante, Sopocachi is a combination of older stately homes (many now house shops or offices) and high-rise buildings. **Plaza Avaroa**, where a number of the city's cultural activities take place, is the centre of the neighbourhood. Uphill from Plaza Avaroa is the smaller **Plaza España**, near which is the link station for the yellow and green lines of the ★**Teleférico**, and next to it ★**El Montículo**, a lovely park with more great views of the city. From Plaza España, Avenida Ecuador leads north towards San Pedro and downtown. Along it is the **Casa Museo Marina Núñez del Prado** ⓘ *Ecuador 2034, T02-242 4175, www.*

bolivian.com/cmnp, daily 0930-1300, Tue-Fri 1500-1900 (may be closed afternoons and weekends), US$0.75, students US$0.30, which houses an excellent collection of Marina Núñez's sculptures in the family mansion.

Miraflores

Downhill from Plaza Avaroa along Calle Pedro Salazar, at the intersection with Avenida Arce, is **Plaza Isabel La Católica**. Nearby are several embassies and hotels. Avenida Arce leads to the Zona Sur, the continuation of Salazar leads to Miraflores via the **Puente de las Américas**, which offers more excellent views of Illimani.

In the residential district of Miraflores, east of the centre, on Plaza Tejada Sorzano, outside the Hernán Siles national football stadium is the **Museo Semisubterráneo**, a sunken garden full of replicas of statues and artefacts from Tiwanaku, but difficult to get to because of the traffic. At the north end of Avenida Busch are Plaza Villarroel and **Museo del la Revolución Nacional** ① *Tue-Fri 0930-1200,*

④ Sopocachi

Where to stay	2 Arco Iris	12 Mongo's
1 Casa Fusión	3 Armonía	13 Olive Tree
2 La Loge	4 Beatrice	14 Rendezvous
3 Landscape B&B	5 Café Urbano	15 Sancho Panza
4 Mitru La Paz	6 Chez Moustache	
5 Rendezvous	7 El Arriero	**Bars & clubs**
6 Stannum	8 Fridolín	16 Equinoccio
	9 Kuchen Stube	17 Glam
Restaurants	10 La Comédie	18 Hallwright's
1 Alexander Coffee	11 Maphrao On	19 Thelonius Jazz Bar

➡ **La Paz maps**
1 La Paz orientation, page 33
2 La Paz, page 34
3 La Paz centre, page 38
4 **Sopocachi, page 41**
5 Zona Sur, page 42
6 Cemetery District, page 68

1500-1800, Sat-Sun 1000-1200, US$0.15, a memorial of the 1952 revolution and a mausoleum with tombs of former presidents. East of Avenida Busch, on Calles Cuba and Guatemala, are Plaza Benito Juárez and the **Museo de Textiles Andinos Bolivianos** ① *Plaza Benito Juárez 488, T02-224 3601, Mon-Sat 0930-1200, 1500-1800, Sun 1000-1230, US$1.25,* with good displays of textiles from around the country, detailed explanations and a knowledgeable owner. Southeast of the stadium are the **Botanical Gardens** ① *C Lucas Jaimes, between H Palacios and Villalobos, T02-241 1692, Tue-Sun 0900-1800,* with flora from the altiplano and Yungas valleys.

★**Parque Mirador Laikakota** ① *US$0.50,* to the southwest of the stadium along Avenida del Ejército, is a lookout with wonderful views of the city and a children's playground.

Zona Sur

The Zona Sur, in the valley 15 minutes south of the city, includes the wealthier suburbs of La Paz. Home to some of the diplomatic and expat community, it has shopping centres, supermarkets stocked with imported items, a few exclusive hotels, and some of the smartest restaurants and bars of the city. **Obrajes** is the first suburb reached after a steep descent from the city; it is the terminus of the green Teleférico line. From the centre take any minibus (US$0.35) or *trufi* (US$0.45) marked Calacoto, San Miguel, Achumani or Chasquipampa.

At the entrance to the district of **Calacoto**, by Plaza Humboldt, is the attractive **Parque La Florida**, with exhibitions of local art work most Sundays and kiosks selling cheap snacks. On the opposite side of the road is the **Jardín Japonés**,

⑤ Zona Sur

To Obrajes & City Centre / Jardín Japonés / Influentes / To Irpavi
To ② Aranjuez, Mallasa & Valle de la Luna
Parque La Florida / Plaza Humboldt / Arce / Kennedy / Lincoln / Ballivián / Sánchez Bustamante / **CALACOTO** / Xanamui / Lincoln / Patino / Arequma / Av Costanera / Los Sauces / Prudencio / Gonzales / Montenegro / Mendoza / Moreno / Peñaranda / Aliaga / Monroy / M Zalles
Murillo / Torre Ketal / San Miguel / **SAN MIGUEL** / Sudamér / BNB / Villanueva
To Achumani & Alto Irpavi
To ② Cota Cota, Muela del Diablo, Ovejuyo, Koani & Palca

N
Not to scale

La Paz maps
1 La Paz orientation, page 33
2 La Paz, page 34
3 La Paz centre, page 38
4 Sopocachi, page 41
5 Zona Sur, page 42
6 Cemetery District, page 68

Where to stay 🛏
1 Casa Grande
2 Oberland

Restaurants 🍴
1 Alexander Coffee
2 Chalet La Suisse
3 Fridolín
4 Gigibontá
 -Rinascimento
5 Gustu
6 Reineke Fuchs

another nice park. The main road, Avenida Ballivián, begins here at Calle 8 and continues up the hill to the modern church of San Miguel on Calle 21 (about a 20-minute walk). The shopping district of **San Miguel** comes alive in the evening, when the streets are crammed with La Paz's affluent youth and the city's expats.

East of San Miguel is the fancy district of **Achumani** and to the south of San Miguel is **Cota Cota**, with a second campus of the Universidad San Andrés and the **Museo de Historia Natural**. Just before Calacoto the road splits, the right branch leads to the districts of **Mallasa** and **Río Abajo**, favourite spots for weekend outings among *paceños*, see Around La Paz, page 43.

South and east of La Paz

day trips from the capital once you've acclimatized

In addition to the trips detailed below, many of the places described in the Lake Titicaca and the Cordilleras chapter can be visited as an excursion out of La Paz. For all outings keep in mind the high altitude and intense sun radiation, take protective dark glasses (especially in blinding snows), sunscreen, a hooded windbreaker, a plastic bag for picnic refuse, bottled water, and of course, comfortable shoes with good grip. For transport information for all excursions, see page 67.

Mallasa and Valle de la Luna

To the south of the city, in the district of **Mallasa** are several attractions that can be visited on a day trip or you can stay there in a much warmer climate than that of the city (10-25°C). The road that turns to the right just before Calacoto in the Zona Sur follows the river past Aranjuez to the Mallasa area. As you descend, more and more striking eroded cliffs come into view.

The **Cactario**, is a pleasant terraced cactus garden worth walking through. Further downhill and about 3 km from the bridge at Calacoto the road forks; sharp right leads to Club de Caza y Pesca and Mallasilla Golf Course. Near the turn-off and to the east of the main road is the entrance to **Valle de la Luna** ① *US$3*, a lunar landscape of eroded cliffs. The vistas can be inspirational, but beware that armed robberies have taken place, do not go alone or take valuables. Most of the local travel agents organize tours to the Valle de la Luna. Some are a brief, five-minute stop for photos in a US$15 tour of La Paz and surroundings, but longer tours are available.

Just past the Valle de la Luna is **Mallasa**, where there are several small roadside restaurants and cafés and the **Hotel Oberland** (see page 55). Beyond Mallasa is **Río Abajo** with more restaurants, by the river of the same name, which cuts through the Andes to split the Cordillera Real from the Cordillera Quimza Cruz.

La Muela del Diablo

Of all the eroded formations located to the south of La Paz, most impressive is La Muela del Diablo, a huge, tooth-shaped rock that stands above the other ridges and can be seen from parts of the city and from the Valle de la Luna road. It is located to the south of the Zona Sur and accessed through the peripheral neighbourhood of El Pedregal. Cross the river and climb through the village to the cemetery; then it is 1½-hour climb. It is impressive, especially if the wind is blowing. Travel agents run tours here for about US$15.

Illimani Lookout, Valle de las Animas and Palca Canyon

To the southeast of the Zona Sur the land rises to a ridge, which stands like a balcony right in front of Illimani and offers wonderful views. From Cota Cota in the Zona Sur, a road goes to the peripheral neighbourhoods of Chasquipampa and Ovejuyo. At the transit control (*tranca* or *garita*) in **Ovejuyo** the road splits, the right branch goes towards Illimani and Viloco, the left branch to Huni, Palca, Ventilla, Mururata, Illimani and beyond. Along the latter road, by the pass between Ovejuyo and Huni is the **Illimani Lookout**. You can walk in 30 minutes from Ovejuyo or about 45 minutes from Chasquipampa, look for the small Laguna las Animas to the right of the road (a favourite picnic area among *paceños*), from the hill just above the pond you will have breathtaking views of Illimani and Mururata. If you take a bus to Huni or Palca, get off at the pond. It takes 25 minutes to walk down from the lookout to **Huni**, a small village.

Between Ovejuyo and Huni (to the left of the road) stretches the **Valle de las Animas**, impressive eroded cliffs which look like enormous organ pipes. A nice trail goes through a valley amid the cliffs. To walk between Ovejuyo and Huni through the canyon takes four to five hours; the views of Illimani from the ridge above Huni are wonderful. **Pampa Koani** is a valley that lies below the lookout and also has excellent views of the *cordillera*, here is **Hotel Allkamari** (see Where to stay, page 56). Its access is along a road that branches to the right between the pass and Huni, opposite Iglesia de las Animas, a modern church at the base of the Animas cliffs.

Palca is a pleasant village 14 km from Ovejuyo. It is often full at weekends, but quiet the rest of the week, it has limited accommodation and many shops. Between Huni and Palca is the **Palca Canyon**, an amazing eroded valley surrounded by steep mud walls and pinnacles. The route follows the bed of the Quebrada Chua Kheri, a tributary of the Río Abajo, and should not be attempted in the wet season. In Huni look out for a broad road leading down to the right and follow it down, past the school and onwards. The path turns into prehispanic stone paving and leads down to the canyon floor. Walk through the canyon for two hours until it opens out. Follow the path up and left to Palca which will take you another 30 minutes. Sunday is a good day for this walk since there are hourly minibuses going through to La Paz; other days there are a few buses. Map IGM Palca 6044 III covers the trail but is not really necessary.

Urmiri *Altitude: 3426 m.*

Due south of the city, in a beautiful setting at the bottom of an isolated narrow canyon are the **Urmiri thermal baths** ⓘ *day use for pools and sauna US$5, massage US$14, hotel contact information on page 52.* The complex, part of the **Hotel Gloria** group, includes several hot pools, a couple of saunas, a hot waterfall, massage service and a hotel, built in 1933 and faithful to the style of that era, despite some modern additions. The water comes out of the ground at 72°C (it takes two to three minutes to boil an egg) and is cooled in several tanks amid pleasant gardens. It gets quite busy with families on weekends and holidays. There are nice walks including an 8-km downhill walk to the village of Sapahaqui, though getting back can be a challenge, there is little traffic on the road (there is transport Sapahaqui–El Alto along a different road).

Access is along the road from La Paz south to Oruro. At Km 70, **Villa Loza** (or El Tholar), a dairy-producing village, a dirt road goes east towards **Sapahaqui**, 25 km along this road is a turn-off to the right. A steep 3-km scenic descent on narrow, hair-raising hairpins (dangerous in the wet season), leads to the complex.

El Alto

take the cable car for views across La Paz

Until the 1940s, there was nothing more than a train station on the barren altiplano surrounding La Paz. Following the construction of the airport, the small poor district of El Alto sprung up and, fuelled by migration from rural areas, grew at a rate of 12% per year between 1976 and 1996 – the fastest-growing city in South America. Although the rate of growth declined, El Alto is now the second largest city in Bolivia after Santa Cruz (with a population of 848,840, according to the 2012 census). Its population is mostly indigenous, predominantly Aymara, with a small percentage of Quechua.

In 1985 El Alto separated from the municipality of La Paz, developed its own character and became a political force to be reckoned with throughout Bolivia. It boasts its own university, a symphony orchestra and three theatres. It is a large flat city sprawling over the altiplano, with only tall church steeples and a few garish high-rises to break the monotony. The views of the snow-capped peaks of the Cordillera Real are excellent. The wind blowing off the ice contributes to making it a very cold place, the mean temperature is 7°C and there is frost at night throughout the winter.

El Alto is a city of commerce, the ★**Feria 16 de Julio**, where on Thursdays and Sundays you can find everything from a sewing needle to the latest model car, is the largest market in the department of La Paz, occupying 5 sq km. You will see *alteño* traders all over Bolivia. El Alto is also a transport hub and, if you are short of time, you can change buses here instead of going down to La Paz. There are a couple of hotels, restaurants and banks, but it is less attractive than La Paz and less safe at night.

The municipality of El Alto is trying to attract visitors. Every second Sunday, a **tourist train** ⓘ *C 8, 3 blocks from Av 6 de Marzo, by Cuartel Ingavi, departs 0800, returns 1320, US$5.60, office in Sopocachi, Av Sánchez Lima 2199 y F Guachalla, T02-241 9770, www.fca.com.bo*, runs from El Alto to Guaqui, with a 1½-hour stop at Tiwanaku and two hours at Guaqui station. The **Chulpares de Kaque Marka**, 20 minutes from town on the road to Oruro, are funerary structures in an area of eroded rock formations. The ravines here are rich in vegetation and bird life, parrots (*kaque* in Aymara) might even be seen. Huayna Potosí and Chacaltaya in the Cordillera Real are also within El Alto's jurisdiction. Further information from the **Unidad de Turismo** ⓘ *M Sempertegui between Calles 3 y 4 Villa Dolores, near Plaza Juana Azurduy de Padilla (also at international arrivals at the airport), T02-282 9356, turismo.elalto on Facebook, Mon-Fri 0800-1200, 1400-1800.*

North of La Paz, trekking and climbing

spectacular high Andean scenery within easy reach of the city

Day walks around La Cumbre

To the north of La Paz, the road that leads to the subtropical Yungas (see page 109) climbs gradually out of the city canyon towards the Cordillera Real. At 4660 m it reaches a pass at La Cumbre. There is a lake to the left of the road and many possibilities for walking in the area. Views are wonderful, it is close to La Paz and transport is easy.

Valeriani
For an easy walk, to the right (east) of the paved road at La Cumbre, follow a rutted jeep track that that climbs gradually via hairpin turns to a telephone station at the top of Valeriani (5000 m). It should take you 1¼ hours to reach the top. You will see no other human being along the way, unless one of the occasional jeeps is bumping up to or down from the telephone relay station. What you will see are untended herds of alpaca, and to your right, near the top, a fresh lake. You re well above the tree line, so there's no shade. Patches of rough grass and diminutive yellow and purple butterflies break up the stony decor. Once at the level of the telephone station, there is a rock formation that will take you to the peak. Scaling these rocks in five or ten minutes is the only difficult part of this hike. The views from the top are awesome, straight down to the highway (a distant ribbon winding its way to Unduavi 1200 m below) and brilliant glaciers on the craggy face of several imposing mountains, staring you in the face. To say these mountains tower above the highway would be an understatement. Their jagged vertical rock formations, with brilliant patches of snow, announce to the most intrepid human beings: Here no one will ever climb.

Twin peaks
A more difficult hike takes you to some twin peaks (5200 m) to the left (west) of the road. Starting at the La Cumbre lake, follow the trail that winds to the right of the lake, then switches back left and uphill. You'll hear what sounds like a waterfall (about 20 minutes into the hike), simultaneous to a fork in the trail. Keep left at the fork, with the creek running below to your left. In another 10 minutes you'll reach a pair of lakes with a natural causeway in between. You should be able to spot two jagged 'teeth' looming above, these are the twin peaks. From here you are about one hour and ten minutes from either one of the peaks. (A conservative estimate

is to allow two hours from La Cumbre to the top of either of these peaks.) Resting at the causeway between the two lakes, you can hear the brook water slurping into the lake. Ten minutes to the left of the lake, not on the route of this hike, there is a geyser.

Enjoy the total silence. Follow the footprints in the snow that are heading for Abra Chacura, the trailhead of the Cumbre–Coroico trek (see below). Soon, the trail reaches a fork. Up and right on a rounded hill is Abra Chacura. To the left, you dip down slightly over some (usually firm) bogs by a small stream. Be tentative with each step. After you cross the trickling stream, the footpath divides (a) left and lateral, or (b) right and up. You want right and up. The two jagged 'teeth' now become more striking. The one to the right is a slightly easier climb. Both are above and to the left of Abra Chacura. If you choose the left of the two 'teeth', you should be especially careful of slippery ledges with unstable snow. For either of the two peaks, the climb becomes steeper as you near the top. Under the snow patches are shavings of shale with good traction. But approaching the top, every step must be measured.

Sitting on the rocky point of either of the twin teeth, with the shiny glacier of Wila Mankilisani, the most attractive mountain of the cordillera, to the left and the plunging olive green gash of the Cumbre–Coroico trail straight below, the view is memorable. Take great care when you leave on the way down. The early part of the descent can be treacherous if you don't contemplate each and every step.

The Yungas

If you are willing to give up the top-of-the-world views in exchange for green surroundings, waterfalls, and the caressing warm air, walking along the dirt roads to Yungas will give you a chance to experience the change in vegetation, from above tree line *puna* to subtropical cloudforest, and climate, from less than 10° C to nearly 30°C, in a few hours walking. One option, requiring four to five hours, is along the road to Chulumani (Sud-Yungas). It starts at **Unduavi** at 3800 m, 15 minutes beyond and down from La Cumbre, and goes to **Velo de la Novia** (the Bride's Veil), a slender waterfall plunging from a towering green ridge, above the village of **Chaco** (see page 116). Another option is along the famous 'world's most dangerous road' or 'road of death', so popular for cycling. It begins at **Cotapata** (3400 m), 15 minutes past Unduavi, where the old and new roads to Nor-Yungas separate, and follows the old dirt road to **Yolosa** (1150 m), near Coroico. The hike takes about seven hours and you will share the road with many cyclists, their support vehicles and a few other vans and trucks kicking up dust. At Yolosa you can catch a pick-up truck that will take you the 600 m up to Coroico (US$0.70). At least an overnight stay is recommended in the charming hillside town of Coroico (see page 112).

Trekking near La Paz

Four prehispanic roads, referred to as 'Inca Trails', link the altiplano with the Yungas, taking you from the high Andes to the subtropics, with dramatic changes in weather, temperature and vegetation. Each has excellent sections of stonework and they vary in difficulty from relatively straightforward to quite hard going. In the rainy season, going can be particularly tough.

For details of how to reach the starting point of each trail, see Transport, page 72. Take water whenever you have the opportunity as there are dry sections. These walks are popular and littering is an issue, don't contribute to the problem. A brief description follows, more details can be found in *Trekking in Bolivia,* by Yossi Brain and *Caminos Precolombinos Departamento de La Paz,* by Montaño et al.

Takesi Trail

IGM maps: Palca 6044 III (for Ventilla to Mina San Francisco, not indispensable) and Chojlla 6044 IV, Fundación Pueblo, Yanacachi, T02-212 4413, www.fundacionpueblo. org, has information and cleans the trail each year.

Start at **Ventilla** (3200 m), 19 km from Ovejuyo, walk up the valley for about three hours passing the village of Choquekhota (mules with muleteers can be hired here) and ford the river. Above town and to the right of the road, there is a falling-down brick wall with a map painted on it. The Takesi and Alto Takesi trails start here, following the path to the right of the wall. The road continues to Mina San Francisco 30 minutes away. Climb to the pass (4630 m) in about one hour along excellent stone paving which is either Inca or pre-Inca, depending on who you believe. The paving continues on the descent to Estancia Takesi one hour beyond. There are camping possibilities by small lakes below the pass and above the *estancia* and near the village of Kakapi, 30 minutes from the estancia, you can sleep at an albergue either camping or in a shelter. The unpleasant mining settlement of Chojlla is the next landmark (there may be transport to La Paz from there, or from La Florida 1½ hours further on), then a descent to Yanacachi, before which is a gate where it is necessary to register and often pay a small fee. Be prepared for bridges to be washed away periodically. **Yanacachi** has a number of good places to stay, see page 116. Buy a minibus ticket on arrival in Yanacachi (they fill quickly) or walk 45 minutes down to the La Paz–Chulumani road for transport. The trek can be done in one long day, especially if you organize a jeep to the start of the trail, but is more relaxing in two or three. **Alto Takesi** is a higher and more difficult trail, which sees little traffic and is therefore overgrown in parts. It leaves the regular route about 35 minutes past the pass and rejoins it below Kakapi, requiring at least two days.

La Reconquistada Trail

A two- to three-day alternative to Takesi (same map as above) is from **Mina San Francisco** (3½ hours from Ventilla) to El Castillo and the village of **Chaco** on the La Paz–Chulumani road. The first three hours to the village of Totor Pata are along a paved path. After this section the Khala Khalani River must be crossed hopping on boulders, this may be problematic if the river is high. Laguna Khellhuani is the next landmark before reaching the abandoned Mina La Reconquistada, above where you must follow a 200-m disused mining tunnel, which requires caution because it descends 15 m and, immediately before the descent, there is a shaft on the left dropping steeply down (take a good torch). After the tunnel you climb to a pass at 4080 m before a long descent to the road at 1950 m.

Choro Trail (La Cumbre to Coroico)
IGM maps: Milluni 5945 II and Unduavi 6045 III.

Start by the lake to the left of the road at La Cumbre (4660 m), where cloud and bad weather are normal. A jeep track leads to the trail head, the narrow pass of Abra Chacura (or Apacheta Chucura 4850 m). You have to sign in at the Guardaparque post on the way to the pass. See the description for the day walk to the twin peaks, page 46. The well-built prehispanic trail descends steeply to Samaña Pampa (small shop, sign in again, camping), Chucura (or Achura, pay US$1.20 fee, another shop, camping), Challapampa (camping possible, US$1.20, small shop), the Choro bridge and the Río Jacun'Manini (fill up with water at both river crossings). Next is Sandillani where there is a community lodge ($$-$). A Japanese man, Tamiji Hanamura, used to welcome passing travellers here. Sadly, he died in 2013. There is good paving down to Villa Esmeralda, after which is Chairo (1260 m, lodging and camping), about 4 km from the new road. It takes three days to trek from La Cumbre to Chairo, from where you can get transport to Puente Yolosita, the turn-off for Coroico on the new road. From Yolosita pickup trucks run uphill to Coroico when they fill, US$0.80, 15 minutes.

Yunga Cruz (Chuñavi to Chulumani)
IGM maps: Lambate 6044 II and Chulumani 6044 I.

The best, but hardest of the four 'Inca' trails: from Chuñavi (3710 m) follow the path left (east) and contour gently up. Camping is possible after two hours. Continue along the path staying on left hand side of the ridge to reach Cerro Khala Ciudad (literally, Stone City Mountain, you'll see why). Good paving brings you round the hill to join a path coming from Quircoma (on your right); continue, heading north, to Cerro Cuchillatuca and then Cerro Yunga Cruz, where there is water and camping is possible. After this point water and camping are difficult and normally impossible until you get down to **Sikilini** (1850 m). The last water and camping possibilities are all within the next hour, take advantage of them. Each person should have at least two litres of water in bottles. There are some clearances on the way down but no water. *Colectivos* run from Sikilini to Chulumani. Starting in Chuñavi the trek takes about three days. Add two days if starting in Lambate.

Zongo Valley

The Zongo Valley lies at the foot of Huayna Potosí (6088 m) and goes from the Zongo Dam to Huaji in Yungas. Access is along a road that starts by the ex Milluni tin mine and the colourful but polluted Lago Milluni, in El Alto (the municipality promotes both as tourist areas). The valley starts at the end of a steep but scenic ride past several lakes (dams for La Paz's power plants) and an aqueduct on the left. Keep left at each junction en route. About 20 minutes past the mine, you come to the Zongo Dam and, on the right, a guard house (4750 m), this is the starting point for climbing Huayna Potosí (see below).

From the Zongo Dam, the road drops over 3000 m in some 40 km to Huaji, and is popular with mountain bikers as an alternative to the so-called 'most dangerous road in the world' to Coroico (see Cycling, in What to do, page 111). As you descend into the Yungas, the vegetation gets green and lush. It is quite safe to drive yourself (in a suitable vehicle) and to hike; you have to return the same way as the road is a dead end.

If you would rather hike towards the glaciers, get off by the guard house. Global warming has completely destroyed the ice cave, which used to be the main attraction here, but you can still reach the ice. Walk up and over the small hill on the right-hand side of the road until you meet the aqueduct again. Follow it for 45 minutes, taking special care as it is cut into the side of a sheer cliff in places with some spectacular drops, then cross it and walk up to reach the base of the Charquini glacier. Do not go onto the glacier unless you have crampons and are roped. At the end of the bridge, turn right uphill to a stone cairn. Continue over the hill, cross a stream and go straight up the next hill to another cairn. From the top of the hill, it is only a few minutes down to the site of the former ice cave. It's about 1¼ hours walk in total.

Several La Paz operators offer full-day tours which combine a visit to Chacaltaya (see page 64), followed by a walk up to the Huayna Potosí base camp, for US$60 per person based on two passengers, including transport, guide and box lunch.

Huayna Potosí

The most frequently climbed peak is Huayna Potosí (6088 m), which requires two days, with one night camped on a glacier at 5600 m. Experience on ice is essential. There are four shelters: a community-run shelter 10 minutes up from the pass, one by the lake, very cold; **Refugio Huayna Potosí** at 4780 m, with toilets and shower, run by the tour operator of the same name, and a basic shelter at 5300 m owned by the same operator. Average cost is US$110 per person for a two-day tour for three people including all equipment except sleeping bag, US$135 for three days. **Refugio Huayna Potosí** charges US$130 for two days, US$150 for three days with exclusive use of its base camp. Park entrance fee of US$2.10 is not included. The starting point for the normal route is at Zongo, see above.

Chacaltaya

Quite close to La Paz, Chacaltaya (5345 m) is a mountain that has lost its glaciers due to global warming. When it gets snow (in the rainy season) keen skiers still go to its slopes. The views of other peaks in the cordillera, the altiplano and La Paz in the distance are fantastic. The **Club Andino Boliviano** (www.bolivianmountainguides. com) has a mountain shelter on Chacaltaya and may arrange transport. It is a pleasant downhill mountain-bike ride first to the altiplano, then relatively flat to El Alto and steep down to La Paz, for a total descent of 2000 m.

Other climbs near La Paz

The Cordilleras Real and Quimsa Cruz offer wonderful opportunities for climbers with a number of peaks over 6000 m. Make sure you are acclimatized before attempting a climb and go with a reputable guide.

Illimani

Due to its difficult access, four days are required to climb the magnificent five-peaked Illimani (6439 m). Going with a certified guide is recommended for this climb. It is not the most difficult technical climb, but the altitude makes it harder and there is one unforgiving spot that has claimed several lives.

Condoriri

This is a group of 13 mountains, 5100-5700 m, including Pequeño Alpamayo, which is beautiful and not technically difficult. Non-climbers can go to the mirador for fantastic views of the surrounding peaks, including Huayna Potosí. The access is from Tuni Dam, but there is no public transport.

Listings La Paz and around *maps p33, p34, p38, p41, p42 and p68*

Tourist information

Gobierno Municipal de La Paz

Bus terminal
T02-228 5858. Mon-Fri 0830-1200, 1430-1900, Sat-Sun 1000-1400, holidays 0800-1200, 1600-2000.

El Prado InfoTur
Mariscal Santa Cruz y Colombia, T02-265 1677, www.discoverlapaz.com. Mon-Fri 0830-1900, Sat-Sun 0930-1300.

Plaza del Estudiante
Lower end of El Prado between 16 de Julio and México, T02-237 1044. Mon-Fri 0830-1200, 1430-1900, Sat-Sun 0900-1300.
Very helpful, English and French spoken.

Plaza Pérez Velasco
Opposite San Francisco, under the

pedestrian walkway. Mon-Fri 0830-1200, 1430-1900.

Tomás Katari
Av Bautista y José María Aliaga, by the cemetery. Mon-Fri 0900-1630, Sat-Sun 1000-1800.

Boltur (Boliviano de Turismo)
Plaza Murillo 551, T800-107060 or 02-212 5099, www.boltur.gob.bo.
State tourism agency, offering a limited number of tours throughout the country. Specifically for tourists going to and from Tiwanaku and Titicaca. It has a luggage store.

There are also information booths at the **Plaza Alonso de Mendoza, Angelo Colonial**, on C Linares, at the **Casa de** la Cultura and **Parque Metropolitano Laikacota.**

Useful websites and publications
www.lapaz.bo
www.turismolapaz.com
http://lapaz.metro-blog.com
www.bolivianexpress.org For news and information pick up a copy of the free *Bolivian Express* magazine.

Tourist police
Plaza Stadium, Edif Olimpya, Miraflores, next to Love City Chinese restaurant, T800-140081, 0900-1800, or in office hours T02-222 5016. Open 0830-1800.
For police report for insurance claims after theft.

Where to stay

Around Plaza Murillo

$$$$ Presidente
Potosí 920 y Sanjines, T02-240 6666, www.hotelpresidente-bo.com.
The "highest 5-star in the world". Excellent service, comfortable, heating, good food, gym and sauna, pool, all open to non-residents, bar. See also **Urban Rush**, under What to do, below.

$$$ Casa de Piedra
Sanjinés 451, T02-290 6674, http://casadepiedrahb.com.
In a historic posada in the centre, wooden floors, beautiful ceilings above the inner balcony, objets d'art, 16 rooms with heating and all facilities, restaurant open 0700-2300, new in 2014.

$$$ Gloria
Potosí 909, T02-240 7070, www.hotelgloria.com.bo.
Modern, central, includes buffet breakfast, 2 restaurants (1 is vegetarian), good food and service, runs **Gloria Tours** (www.gloria tours.com.bo) and also owns **Gloria Urmiri** resort, 2 hrs from La Paz. Recommended.

$$-$ Hostal República
Comercio 1455, T02-220 2742, www.hostalrepublica.com.
Old house of former president, more expensive in apartment, with and without bath, hot water, good café, quiet garden, book ahead and ask for room on upper floor.

$ Adventure Brew Bed & Breakfast
Av Montes 533, T02-291 5896, www.theadventurebrewhostel.com.
Mostly private rooms with bath, cheaper in dorms for 8, includes pancake breakfast, use of kitchen, free beer from microbrewery every night, rooftop bar with great views and spa, nightly BBQs, good value, popular meeting place.

$ Adventure Brew Hostel
Av Montes 504, T02-291 5896, www.theadventurebrewhostel.com.
More economical than B&B, above, 8- to 12-bed dorms, with shared hot showers, includes pancake breakfast and a free beer every night, rooftop terrace with great views of the city and Illimani, basement bar, travel agency and bank, lively young crowd, convenient to the bus station, associated with **Gravity Bolivia** (see What to do, page 66).

$ Arthy's Guesthouse
Montes 693, T02-228 1439, http://arthyshouse.tripod.com.
Shared bath, warm water, safe, helpful, popular with bikers, English spoken, 2400 curfew.

$ Bacoo
Calle Alto de la Alianza 693, T02-228 0679, www.bacoohostel.com.

Some rooms with private bath, cheaper in dorm, jacuzzi, restaurant and bar, garden, ping-pong and pool, arrange tours.

$ Hospedaje Milenio
Yanacocha 860, T02-228 1263, hospedajemilenio@hotmail.com.
Economical, shared bath, electric shower, basic, family house, homely and welcoming, popular, helpful owner, quiet, kitchen, breakfast extra, security boxes, great value.

$ Loki
Av América 120, esq Plaza Alonso de Mendoza, T245 7300, www.lokihostel.com.
Members of a chain of popular party hostels. Private double rooms and dorms, TV room, computer room, bar (meals available), tour operator.

$ Posada El Carretero
Catacora 1056, entre Yanacocha y Junín, T228 5271, El-Carretero on Facebook.
Very economical single and double rooms (cheaper with shared bath), also dorms, hot showers, helpful staff, good atmosphere and value.

$ Tambo de Oro
Armentia 367, T02-228 1565.
Near bus station, cheaper with shared bath, hot showers, good value if a bit run down, safe for luggage.

$ Torino
Socabaya 457, T02-240 6003, www.hoteltorino.com.bo.
Ask for better rooms in new section, older ones are run-down, cheaper without bath. Old backpackers' haunt, free book exchange, cultural centre, travel agency, good service. Restaurant next door for breakfast and good-value lunch (Mon-Fri 1200-1500).

$ Wild Rover Backpackers Hostel
Comercio 1476, T02-211 6903, http://wildroverhostels.com.
Party hostel in renovated colonial-style house with courtyard and high-ceilings, dorms with 4-10 beds with shared bath, Irish bar, TV room, book exchange, meals available, helpful staff speak English.

Plaza San Francisco up to the cemetery district

$$$ La Casona
Av Mcal Santa Cruz 938, T02-290 0505, www.lacasonahotelboutique.com.
Boutique hotel in beautifully restored former San Francisco convent dating to 1860, nice rooms (those in front get street noise), suites have jacuzzi, includes buffet breakfast and some museum entry fees, heating, safe box, terrace and cupola with nice views, very good restaurant.

$$$ Rosario
Illampu 704, T02-245 1658, www.gruporosario.com.
Tasteful rooms, laundry, internet café (free for guests, great view), good restaurant with buffet breakfast, stores luggage, no smoking, very helpful staff. Highly recommended. **Turisbus** travel agency downstairs (see Tour operators, page 67), **Cultural Interpretation Centre** explains items for sale in nearby 'witches' market'.

$$ Estrella Andina
Illampu 716, T02-245 6421, juapame_2000@hotmail.com.
Cheaper in low season, all rooms have a safe and are decorated individually, English spoken, family-run, comfortable, tidy, helpful, roof terrace, heaters, money exchange, very nice. Also owns **$ Cruz de los Andes**, Aroma 216, T245 1401,

same style but shares premises with a car garage.

$$ Fuentes
Linares 888, T02-231 3966,
www.hotelfuentes.com.bo.
Cheaper without bath, hot water, variety of rooms and prices, nice colonial style, comfortable, sauna, good value, family-run.

$$ Hostal Naira
Sagárnaga 161, T02-235 5645,
www.hostalnaira.com.
Hot water, comfortable but pricey, rooms around courtyard, some are dark, price includes good buffet breakfast in **Café Banais**, safety deposit boxes.

$$ La Posada de la Abuela Obdulia
C Linares 947, T02-233 2285,
http://hostalabuelaposada.com.
Very pleasant inn in a courtyard in an early 20th-century building on this popular shopping street, rooms for 2-4 people, café, terrace with city view.

$$ Milton
Illampu 1126-1130, T02-236 8003,
www.hotelmiltonbolivia.com.
Hot water, psychedelic 1970s-style wallpaper in many rooms, restaurant, laundry, excellent views from roof, popular.

$ Arcabucero
C Viluyo 307 y Linares, T02-231 3473,
arcabucero-bolivia@hotmail.com.
Price rises in high season, pleasant new rooms in converted colonial house, excellent value but check the beds, breakfast extra.

$ El Solario
Murillo 776, T02-236 7963.
Central, shared bath, medical services, taxi and travel agency, good value, gets crowded.

$ La Joya
Max Paredes 541, T02-245 3841,
www.hotelajoya.com.
Cheaper without bath, modern and comfy, lift, area unsafe at night but provides transfers.

$ Muzungu Hostel
Illampu 441, T02-2451640,
muzunguhostel@hotmail.com.
Rooms with 1-4 beds, with and without bath and cheaper rate for dorms, several common areas, good restaurant (closed Sun) and bar, breakfast and 1 drink per day included.

$ Onkel Inn 1886
Colombia 257, T02-249 0456,
www.onkelinn.com.
Hostel in a remodelled 19th-century house, rooms with and without bath, doubles, triples and bunks. Jacuzzi, laundry facilities, café and bar, HI affiliated. Also in Copacabana.

$ Sagárnaga
Sagárnaga 326, T02-235 0252,
www.hotel-sagarnaga.com.
Cheaper in plain rooms without TV, solar hot water, 2 ATMs, English spoken, *peña*, popular with tour groups, helpful owner.

El Prado, Sopocachi, Miraflores and Zona Sur

$$$$ Casa Grande
Av Ballivián 1000 y C 17, T02-279 5511,
and C 16 8009, T02-277 4000, both in
Calacoto, www.casa-grande.com.bo.
Beautiful, top-quality apartments on Ballivián and hotel suites under a greenhouse dome on C16, buffet breakfast, pool and spa, airport transfers at night only, restaurants, very good service.

$$$$ Europa
Tiahuanacu 64, T02-231 5656,
www.hoteleuropa.com.bo.
Next to the Museo Nacional de
Arqueología. Excellent facilities and
plenty of frills, health club, several
restaurants, parking. Recommended.

$$$$ Stannum
Av Arce 2631, Torre Multicine, p 12 , T02-
214 8393, www.stannumhotels.com.
Boutique hotel on the 12th floor of an
office building with lovely views of
Illimani and the city, above mall and
cinema complex. Comfortable rooms
with minimalist decor, includes breakfast,
bathtub, heating, a/c, fridge, restaurant,
bar, gym, spa, airport transfers, no
smoking anywhere on the premises.

$$$ El Rey Palace
Av 20 de Octubre 1947, Sopocachi, T02-
241 8541, www.hotelreypalace.com.
Large suites with heating, excellent
restaurant, stylish.

$$$ Mitru La Paz
6 de Agosto 2628, Edif Torre Girasoles,
T02-243 2242, www.hotelmitrulapaz.com.
Modern hotel on the first 3 floors of the
highest building in La Paz (37 storeys).
Includes breakfast and complimentary
hot drinks, comfortable, bright ample
rooms most with bathtubs, heating,
safe boxes, fridge, convenient location
for Sopocachi dining, excellent value
for its price category, helpful staff.
Recommended.

$$$-$$ Casa Fusión
Miguel de Cervantes 2725, Sopocachi,
T02-214 0933, www.casafusion.com.bo.
Lovely hotel with modern comfortable
rooms, predominantly white, good
fittings, includes buffet breakfast,
heating, good value, no smoking.
Near Plaza España Teleférico station.

$$$-$$ Casa Prado
Av 16 de Julio (El Prado) 1615, entre
Campero y Ortiz, T02-231 2094,
www.casapradolapaz.com.bo.
In a renovated old building, 'boutique'-
style, plain rooms with colourful
furnishings, suites and standard
rooms, café for breakfast, airport
transfer arranged.

$$$-$$ La Loge
Pasaje Medinacelli 2234,
Sopocachi, T02-242 3561,
www.lacomedie-lapaz.com/es/loge.
Above, and owned by, **La Comédie**
restaurant, elegant apart-hotel rooms,
a good option with all services.

$$ Rendezvous
Sargento Carranza 461, side street at the
end of Sánchez Lima, Sopocachi, T02-
291 2459, www.rendezvouslapaz.com
(unavailable at time of writing).
Delightful rooms in small hotel above
the restaurant of the same name (see
below), family atmosphere, roof terrace
with good view, communal area with
DVD library, kitchen, laundry service,
safe. Recommended.

$ Landscape B&B
Reseguín 1945 entre Aspiazu y Harington,
Sopocachi, T7066 0542, Facebook:
landscape.bolivia.
Reserve through Booking.com or AirBnB.
Like a family home, use whatever you like
except the washing machine, 5 rooms,
shared bath, with breakfast, popular.
Also has another house at Reseguín 1981
and an apartment in the city centre.

South of La Paz

$$$ Oberland
Mallasa, Av Florida, C 2, Mallasa, 12 km
from La Paz centre, T02-274 5040,
www.h-oberland.com.

A Swiss-owned, chalet-style restaurant (excellent, not cheap) and hotel (also good) with older resort facilities, lovely gardens, spa, sauna, covered pool (open to public – US$4.25-5.65 – very hot water), volleyball, tennis. Welcomes camping with or without vehicle. Recommended.

$$ Allkamari
near Valle de las Animas, 30 mins from town on the road to Palca, T02-279 1742, www.boliviamistica.com.
Reservations required, cabins for up to 8 in a lovely valley between the Palca and La Animas canyons, a place to relax and star-gaze, **$** pp in dorm, solar heating, jacuzzi included, meals on request, lots of packages available, horse and bike rentals, massage, shamanic rituals, taxi from Calacoto US$7, bus No 42 from the cemetery to within 1 km.

$$-$ Colibrí Camping
C 4, Jupapina, near Mallasa, 30 mins from La Paz, T7629 5658, http:// colibricamping.com.
Cabins, teepee, tents and sleeping bags for hire or set up your own tent for US$7 pp, nice views, details about transport on their website.

El Alto

$$-$ Alexander Palace
Av Jorge Carrasco 61 y C 3, Ceja, Zona 12 de Octubre, T02-282 3376, hotelalexander2011@hotmail.com.
Modern, with breakfast, **$** pp in dorm, parking, disco.

$ Orquídea
C Dos 22 y Av 6 de Marzo, Villa Bolívar A, near bus terminals, T02-282 6487.
Comfortable heated rooms, cheaper with shared bath, electric showers, good value. Better than others in the area.

Around Plaza Murillo

$$ La Kantuta
In Hotel Presidente, Potosí 920, T02-240 6666.
Excellent food, good service. **La Bella Vista** on the top floor is fancier.

Cafés

Alexander Coffee
Potosí 1091.
Part of a chain (see below), sandwiches, salads, coffee, pastries.

Café Soho
Jaén 747. Mon-Sun 0930-2300.
Cosy café with small courtyard, inside and outside seating, local artwork.

Plaza San Francisco up to the cemetery district

$$$-$$ Steakhouse
Psje Tarija 243B, T02-214 8864, www.4cornerslapaz.com. Daily 1500-2300.
Good cuts of meat, large variety of sauces and a great salad bar in a modern environment.

$$ La Cueva
Tarija 210B, T02-231 4523, www.4cornerslapaz.com. Daily 1130-late.
Small cosy Mexican restaurant, quick service, wide selection of tequilas.

$$ Pizzería Italia
Illampu 840, T02-246 3152, and 809, 2nd floor, T02-245 0714.
Thin-crust pizza, and pasta.

$$-$ A Lo Cubano
Sagárnaga 357, entre Linares y Illampu, T02-245 1797. Mon-Sat 1200-2200.
Almuerzo for US$3.65, but it runs out fast,

also other choices of good Cuban food, good value.

$$-$ Angelo Colonial
Linares 922, T02-215 9633. Open early for breakfast.
Vegetarian options, good music, internet, can get busy with slow service. Has a *hostal* at Av Santa Cruz 1058.

$$-$ Colonial Pot
Linares 906 y Sagárnaga.
Bolivian dishes and a variety of main courses including vegetarian, set meal US$4.35 and à la carte, pastries, snacks, hot and cold drinks, quiet, homely, music, exceptional value.

$$-$ Sol y Luna
Murillo y Cochabamba, T02-211 5323, www.solyluna-lapaz.com. Open daily from 0900.
Dutch-run, breakfast, *almuerzo* and international menu, coffees and teas, full wine and cocktail list, live music Mon and Thu, movies, Wi-Fi, guide books for sale, book exchange, salsa lessons.

$$-$ Star of India
Cochabamba 170, T02-211 4409.
British-run Indian curry house, will deliver, including to hotels.

$$-$ Tambo Colonial
In Hotel Rosario (see above).
Excellent local and international cuisine, good salad bar, buffet breakfast, *peña* at the weekend.

$ 100% Natural
Sagárnaga 345.
Range of healthy, tasty fast foods ranging from salads to burgers and llama meat, good breakfasts.

Cafés

Banais
Sagárnaga 161, same entrance as Hostal Naira.
Coffee, sandwiches and juices, buffet breakfast, set lunch, laid-back music and computer room.

Café del Mundo
Sagárnaga 324, www.cafe-delmundo.com.
Swedish-owned, breakfasts, pancakes, waffles, sandwiches, coffees, teas and chocolate.

Café Illampu
Linares 940, upstairs. Mon-Sat 0800-2000, Sun 0930-1700.
La Paz branch of the Swiss-run Sorata café known for its sandwiches, bread and cakes. Also salads, llama sausages, and European specialities such as *rösti* and *spätzle*. Recommended.

Café Pepe's
Pasaje Jiménez 894, off Linares.
All-day breakfasts, sandwiches, omelettes, tables outside, cards and dominoes, magazines and guidebooks.

K'umara
Pasaje Tarija casi Linares.
Small café serving breakfasts, cereals, juices, sandwiches, omelettes, soups and drinks, organic produce, Wi-Fi.

El Prado, Sopocachi, Miraflores and Zona Sur

$$$ Chalet la Suisse
Av Muñoz Reyes 1710, Cota Cota, T02-279 3160, www.chaletlasuisse.com. Open 1900-2400, booking is essential on Fri.
Serves excellent fondue, steaks.

$$$ Gustu
C 10 No 300, Calacoto, T02-211 7491, www.restaurantgustu.com.
Upmarket restaurant with remarkable food and cookery school. Part of the Nordic cuisine pioneers, aimed at stimulating Bolivian gastronomy and giving opportunities to vulnerable people through the **MeltingPot Foundation**, www.meltingpot-bolivia.org. Also has a street food tour, **Suma Phayata**.

$$$-$$ El Arriero
F Guachalla 319 entre Av 6 de Agosto y 20 de Octubre, and Pinilla 273 entre Av 6 de Agosto y Arce, T02-244 0844, elarrierobolivia on Facebook. Daily 1130-2330.
Argentine meat dishes, excellent parrillada, also has salad bar, wine list, good service.

$$$-$$ La Comédie
Pasaje Medinacelli 2234, Sopocachi, T02-242 3561. Mon-Fri 1200-1500, 1900-2300, Sat-Sun from 1900.
'Art café restaurant', contemporary, French menu, good salads, wine list and cocktails. For website, see **La Loge** under Where to stay, above.

$$ Beatrice
Guachalla y Ecuador, opposite Sopocachi market. Open 1200-2200, closed Tue.
Excellent home-made pasta, good value and very popular with locals.

$$ Chez Moustache
F Guachalla esq Av 20 de Octubre, at Alliance Française, Chez-Moustache on Facebook.
French restaurant with good food, extensive wine list and fun atmosphere.

$$ El Consulado
Bravo 299 (by Hotel Europa), T02-211 7706. Open 0900-2000.
Serves lunch and coffee and drinks in the evening. In gorgeous setting with outdoor seating and covered terrace, includes high-end handicraft store, book exchange, Wi-Fi, photo gallery, organic coffee and food, pricey but worth it.

$$ Maphrao On
Hnos Manchego 2586, near Plaza Isabel La Católica, T02-243 4682. Open 1200-1400, 1900-2400.
Thai and Southeast Asian food, warm atmosphere, good music.

$$ Paladar
F Guachalla 359, Sopocachi, T02-244 4929, Av Saavedra 1948, Edif Cristembo, Miraflores, T02-224 1520, and in San Miguel. Open 1200-1530, 1900-2230.
Brazilian dishes, daily specials, popular and good value.

$$ Reineke Fuchs
Pje Jáuregui 2241, Sopocachi, T02-244 2979. Mon-Fri 1200-1500 and from 1900, Sat from 1900 only.
Also Av Montenegro y C 18, San Miguel, T02-277 2103. Mon-Fri from 1800, Sat and Sun from 1200, www.reinekefuchs. com. German-style bar/restaurant, many imported German beers, also set lunch from US$5.

$$ Suma Uru
Av Arce 2177 in Radisson Plaza Hotel, T02-244 1111.
Almuerzo Mon-Fri for US$8 and excellent buffet, in 5-star setting on Sun 1200-1500, US$11.60. Friendly to backpackers.

$$-$ Ken-Chan
Bat Colorados 98 y F Suazo, p 2 of Japanese Cultural Centre, T02-244 2292. Open 1130-1500, 1830-2230, closed Sun.
Japanese restaurant with wide variety of dishes, popular.

$$-$ Mongo's
Hnos Manchego 2444, near Plaza Isabel La Católica, T02-244 0714. Open 1830-0300, live music Tue, club after midnight.
Excellent Mexican fare and steaks, open fires, bar (cocktails can be pricey), popular with gringos and locals.

$$-$ Potokos
Costa Rica 1346, T02-224 4306, Potokos on Facebook. Weekends.
Open at weekends only for *potosino* food, traditional dishes, very good.

$$-$ Rendezvous
Sargento Carranza 461, end of Sánchez Lima, Sopocachi, T7913 8566, rendezvouslapaz on Facebook. Mon-Sat 1830-2230.
Classic French cuisine, excellent variety and quality, remodelled with new chef and menu in 2014.

$$-$ Sancho Panza
Av Ecuador 738 y Gutiérrez, T02-242 6490, Sopocachi. Tue-Sat 1200-1500, 1900-2300, Sun 1200-1500.
Mediterranean and Spanish tapas, tablas and daily specials, also good-value set lunches (no credit cards or US dollars).

$$-$ Vienna
Federico Zuazo 1905, T02-244 1660, www. restaurantvienna.com. Mon-Fri 1200-1400, 1830-2200, Sun 1200-1430.
Excellent German, Austrian and local food, great atmosphere and service, live piano music, popular.

$ Armonía
Av Ecuador 2286, above bookstore. Mon-Sat 1230-1400.
Nice varied vegetarian buffet with organic produce from proprietors' farm. Recommended.

$ Olive Tree
Campos 334, Edificio Iturri, T02-243 1552. Mon-Fri 1100-2200, Sat 1100-1500.
Good salads, soups and sandwiches, attentive service.

Cafés

Alexander Coffee
Av 16 de Julio 1832, also at 20 de Octubre 2463 Plaza Avaroa, Av Arce 2631 (Multicine), Av Montenegro 1336, San Miguel, and at the airport (16 branches in all). Open Mon-Sat 0730-2400, till 2200 on Sun.
Excellent coffee, smoothies, muffins, cakes and good salads and sandwiches, Wi-Fi.

Arco Iris
F Guachalla 554 y Sánchez Lima, Sopocachi.
Also in Achumani, C 16 by the market. Bakery and handicraft outlet of **Fundación Arco Iris** (www.arcoirisbolivia.org), which works with street children, good variety of breads, pastries, meats and cheeses.

Café Urbano
16 de Julio 1615, and 20 de Octubre 2331, Sopocachi, Mon-Sat 0800-2400, Sun 0900-2100.
Excellent sandwiches and coffee, pancakes, breakfasts, Wi-Fi.

Fridolín
Av 6 de Agosto 2415; and Prolongación Montenegro, San Miguel. Daily 0800-2200.
Empanadas, tamales, savoury and sweet (Austrian) pastries, coffee, breakfast, Wi-Fi.

Gigibontá-Rinascimento
Claudio Aliaga 1202, San Miguel, see gigibonta.bolivia on Facebook.
Authentic Italian ice creams, delicious flavours.

Kuchen Stube
Rosendo Gutiérrez 461, Sopocachi. Mon-Fri 0800-2000, Sat-Sun 0800-1900.
Excellent cakes, coffee and German specialities, also *almuerzo* Mon-Fri.

Bars and clubs

The epicentre for nightlife in La Paz is currently **Plaza Avaroa** in Sopocachi. Clubs are clustered around here and crowds gather Fri and Sat nights.

Around Plaza Murillo
Etno Café
Jaén 722, T02-228 0343. Mon-Sat 1930-0300.
Small café/bar with cultural programmes including readings, concerts, movies, popular, serves artisanal and fair trade drinks (alcoholic or not).

Plaza San Francisco up to the cemetery district

Hard Rock Café
Santa Cruz 399 e Illampu, T02-211 9318, www.hardrockcafebolivia.lobopages. com.
Serves Hard Rock fair, turns into nightclub around 2400, popular with locals and tourists, especially on Sun.

Oliver's English Tavern
Murillo y Cochabamba, olivers.english on Facebook.
Fake English pub serving breakfast from 0600, curries, sandwiches, fish and chips, pasta, sports channels, music, dress-up parties and more. Pub crawl tours start here (see What to do, below).

El Prado, Sopocachi, Miraflores and Zona Sur
Equinoccio
Sánchez Lima 2191, Sopocachi. Thu-Sat, cover charge US$2.10, or more for popular bands.
Top venue for live rock music and bar.

Glam
Sánchez Lima 2237, next to Ferroviaria Andina. Thu-Sat from 2100.
Good place to go dancing, live salsa on Fri, electronic music on Sat.

Hallwrights
Sánchez Lima 2235, next to Glam. Mon-Sat 1700-2400.
The only wine bar in La Paz.

Thelonius Jazz Bar
20 de Octubre 2172, Sopocachi, T02-242 4405. Wed-Sat shows start at 2200.
Renowned for jazz, cover charge US$3-5.

Entertainment

For current information on cinemas and shows, check *La Prensa* or *La Razón* on Fri, or visit www.laprensa.com.bo or www.la-razon.com. Also look for *Bolivian Express* (in English) and *Mañana*, both free monthly magazines with listings of concerts, exhibits, festivals, etc.

Cinemas
Films mainly in English with Spanish subtitles cost around US$3.50-4. See www.cinecenter.com.bo, http://megacenter.irpavi.com and www.multicine.com.bo; the latter has the most comfortable halls.
Cinemateca Boliviana, *Oscar Soria (prolong Federico Zuazo) y Rosendo Gutiérrez, T02-244 4090, www.cinematecaboliviana.org.* Municipal theatre with emphasis on independent productions.

Peñas and live musicc

Bocaisapo, *Indaburo 654 y Jaén. Thu-Fri 1900-0300.* Live music in a bar; no cover charge, popular.

Huari, *Sagárnaga 339, T02-231 6225.* Good shows of traditional music and dance, also serves food and drink.

Parnaso, *Sagárnaga 189, T02-231 6827.* Daily peña starting at 2030, meals available, purely for tourists but a good way to see local costumes and dancing.

Theatre

Teatro Municipal Alberto Saavedra Pérez, *Sanjinés e Indaburo, T02-240 6183.* Has a regular schedule of plays, opera, ballet and classical concerts, at The National Symphony Orchestra is very good and gives inexpensive concerts. Next door is the **Teatro Municipal de Cámara**, which shows dance, drama, music and poetry.

Casa Municipal de la Cultura 'Franz Tamayo', *almost opposite Plaza San Francisco*, hosts a variety of exhibitions, paintings, sculpture, photography, etc, mostly free. Free monthly guide to cultural events at information desk at entrance.

Palacio Chico, *Ayacucho y Potosí, in old Correo, Mon-Fri 0900-1230, 1500-1900.* Operated by the Secretaría Nacional de Cultura, also has free exhibitions (good for modern art), concerts and ballet.

Festivals

For a list of festivals outside La Paz, see page 18.

24 Jan-Feb Particularly impressive is the **Alasitas Fair** held 24 Jan at noon in the Parque Central, Plaza Sucre in San Pedro and several other plazas. It is most striking at the Parque Central because of its magnitude and the variety of miniatures on offer including minute bread rolls and other food. At the park the fair continues for 2 weeks. See also page 39.

Feb/Mar Carnival in La Paz is quite lively. Although the parades here are not as formal or grandiose as those of Oruro, they have their own flavour. Water-throwing is rampant everywhere. Sat is the Corso Infantil, a children's parade; Sun for the main parade, *pepinos* dressed as clowns are the main characters of the *comparsas*, blocks of friends that get together to parade and have a good time; Mon is the **Jisk'a Anata**, perhaps the most interesting of the parades, with the participation of groups from rural communities around La Paz; Tue is **Martes de Ch'alla** with a traditional offering to the Pachamama (Mother Earth) at Plaza Murillo and a day families gather for thanksgiving ceremonies. The **Carnaval Andino** in El Alto features native Andean music.

Mar/Apr A 6-hr-long **Easter** procession makes its way by 9 churches in El Alto.

May/Jun Festividad de Nuestro Señor Jesús del Gran Poder (generally known simply as the 'Gran Poder'), the most important festival of the year, with a huge procession (16 hrs) of costumed and masked dancers, held on the 3rd Sat after Trinity. It has the flare of the Oruro carnival (without the water) and the same dances (see description on page 20). The *morenada* is the main dance of this festival, colourful *diabladas* and *caporales* are also common and you also find more unusual ones like the *waka tokoris*, which derives from the disdain and reproach for the Spanish bullfight. For information about the history of the festival, visit www.granpoder.bo.

Jun Corpus Christi, important Catholic celebration on Thu after Trinity Sun.

21 and 24 Jun The winter solstice and **Aymara New Year** (see Wallkakuti Festival, page 79) and **San Juan** are a time to let off fireworks.

Jul Fiestas de Julio, a month of concerts and performances at the Teatro Municipal with a wide variety of music, including the University Folkloric Festival.

16 Jul Virgen del Carmen, is the main festival in El Alto.

6 Aug Independence Day is marked by a very loud gun salute at 0630 which can be heard all over the centre of the city.

8 Dec A **festival** is held around Plaza España. It's not very large, but is very colourful and noisy.

31 Dec On **New Year's Eve** fireworks are let off and make a spectacular sight – and din – best viewed from a high vantage point.

Shopping

Camping equipment

Kerosene for pressure stoves is available from a pump in Plaza Alexander, Pando e Inca.

Ayni Sport Bolivia, *Jiménez 806, open Mon-Sun 1030-2100*. Rents and sometimes sells camping equipment and mountain gear (trekking shoes, fleeces, climbing equipment etc).

Caza y Pesca, *Edif Handal Center, No 9, Av Mcal Santa Cruz y Socabaya, T02-240 9209*. English spoken.

The Spitting Llama, *Linares 947 (inside Hostal La Posada de la Abuela), T02-298 6248, www.thespittingllama.com*. Sell camping gear including GPS units, used books, guidebooks, issue ISIC cards, English spoken, helpful; branches in Cochabamba and Copacabana.

Tatoo Bolivia, *Illampu 828, T02-245 1265, www.tatoo.ws*. Tatoo clothing plus outdoor equipment including backpacks, shoes, etc. English and Dutch spoken, closed Sun. For camping stove fuel enquire at **Emita Tours** on Sagárnaga.

Handicrafts

Above **Plaza San Francisco** (see page 39), up **Sagárnaga**, by the side of San Francisco church (behind which are many handicraft stalls in the Mercado Artesanal), are booths and small stores with interesting local items of all sorts. The lower end of Sagárnaga is best for antiques.

Alpaca Style, *C 22 No 14, T02-271 1233, Achumani*. Upmarket shop selling alpaca and leather clothing.

Arte y Diseño, *Illampu 833*. Makes typical clothing to your own specifications in 24 hrs. The shop at Illampu 857 sells *tejidos* (material) by the metre.

Artesanía Sorata, *Sagárnaga 303 y Linares, T02-245 4728, and Sagárnaga 363, www.artesaniasorata.com*. Specializes in dolls, sweaters and weavings.

Ayni, *Illampu 704, www.aynibolivia.com*. Fair trade shop in Hotel Rosario, featuring Aymara work.

Comart Tukuypaj, *Linares 958, T02-231 2686, in Galería Doryan (see above) and C 21, Galería Centro de Moda, Local 4B, Calacoto, www.comart-tukuypaj.com*. High-quality textiles from an artisan community association.

Galería Doryan, *Sagárnaga 177*. An entire gallery of handicraft shops; includes **Tejidos Wari**, unit 12, for high-quality alpaca goods, will make to measure, English spoken. On Linares, between Sagárnaga and Santa Cruz, high-quality alpaca goods are priced in US$. Also in this area are many places making fleece jackets, gloves and hats, but shop around for value and service.

Jiwitaki Art Shop, *Jaén 705, T7725 4042. Mon-Fri 1100-1300, 1500-1800*. Run by local artists selling sketches, paintings, sculptures, literature, etc.
LAM shops *on Sagárnaga and Linares*. Good quality alpaca goods.
Millma, *Sagárnaga 225, T02-231 1338, and Claudio Aliaga 1202, Bloque L-1, San Miguel, closed Sat afternoon and Sun*. High-quality alpaca knitwear and woven items and, in the San Miguel shop, a permanent exhibition of ceremonial 19th- and 20th-century Aymara and Quechua textiles (free).
Mistura, *Sagárnaga 163, www.misturabolivia.com*. Clothing, hats, bags, wine and other produce, jewellery and scents, high-end design incorporating traditional features.
Mother Earth, *Linares 870, T02-239 1911. 0930-1930 daily*. High-quality alpaca sweaters with natural dyes.
Toshy *on Sagárnaga*. Top-quality knitwear.

Jewellery
Good jewellery stores with native and modern designs include **King's**, *Loayza 261, between Camacho and Mercado also at Torre Ketal, C 15, Calacoto* and **Mi Joyita**, *Av Mariscal Santa Cruz 1351, El Prado*.

Maps
IGM, *head office at Estado Mayor, Av Saavedra 2303, Miraflores, T02-214 9484, Mon-Thu 0900-1200, 1500-1800, Fri 0900-1200*. Also in *Edif Murillo, Final Rodríguez y Juan XXIII, T02-237 0116, Mon-Fri 0830-1230, 1430-1830*. Take passport to buy maps. The Edif Murillo office stores some stock or will get maps from HQ in 24 hrs.
Librería IMAS, *Av Mcal Santa Cruz entre Loayza y Colón, Edif Colón, T02-235 8234*.

Ask to see the map collection. Maps are also sold in the Post Office on the stalls opposite the Poste Restante counter.

Markets
In addition to those mentioned in the Plaza San Francisco section (page 39), **Mercado Sopocachi**, Guachalla y Ecuador, a well-stocked covered market selling foodstuffs, kitchen supplies, etc, closes 1400 on Sun.

Musical instruments
Many shops on Pasaje Linares, the stairs off C Linares, also on Sagárnaga/Linares, for example **Walata 855**.

What to do

City tours
The red and yellow lines of the **Teleférico** give a spectacular overview of La Paz (see Transport). See also **La Paz On Foot** under Tour operators, below.
Sightseeing, *www.lapazcitytour.net*, city tours on a double-decker bus, 2 circuits, downtown and Zona Sur with Valle de la Luna (1 morning and 1 afternoon departure to each), departs from Plaza Isabel La Católica and can hop on at Plaza San Francisco, tour recorded in 7 languages, US$8.50 for both circuits, daily at 0900 and 1500 (city), 1030 and 1330 (Zona Sur).
Red C&P, *T7628 5738, www.redcap walkingtours.com, 1100 and 1400 every day from Plaza San Pedro, 2½ hrs*. Free walking tours of La Paz. They also offer pub crawl starting from Oliver's Tavern (see above) Tue-Sat 2030, US$1, local food tours, US$30, extended tours off the beaten track and, on Sun, to El Alto to see the market and Wrestling Cholitas (see **Andean Secrets**, below), US$25.

Climbing, hiking and trekking

Guides must be hired through a tour company. There is a mountain rescue group, **Socorro Andino Boliviano**, Calle 40 Villa Aérea, T02-246 5879.

Altitud 6000, *Sagárnaga 389, T02-245 3945, www.altitud6000.com*. Climbing tours in Bolivia, Argentina, Chile, Ecuador and Peru. Well organized, very good guides and excellent food.

Andean Summits, *Muñoz Cornejo 1009 y Sotomayor, Sopocachi, T02-242 2106, www.andeansummits.com. Mon-Fri 0900-1200, 1500-1900.* For mountaineering and other trips off the beaten track, contact in advance.

Bolivian Mountain Guides, *Sagárnaga 348, T7526 3820, www.bolivianmountainguides.com.* For climbs and treks in the Cordillera and around La Paz.

Bolivian Mountains, *Rigoberto Paredes 1401 y Colombia, p 3, San Pedro, T02-249 2775, www.bolivianmountains.com (in UK T01273-746545).* High-quality mountaineering with experienced guides and good equipment, not cheap.

Climbing South America, *Linares 940, T02-297 1543, www.climbingsouthamerica.com. Mon-Fri 0900-1900, Sat 0900-1300.* Climbing, trekking, hiking and multi-activity trips, 4WD and cultural tours, Australian-run.

Refugio Huayna Potosí, *Sagárnaga 308 e Illampu, T02-231 7324, www.huayna-potosi.com. Mon-Fri 0900-1200, 1300-1900, Sat 0900-1500.* Climbing and trekking tours, run 2 mountain shelters on Huayna Potosí and a climbing school. Check equipment before using.

Football

Popular and played on Wed and Sun at the **Siles Stadium** in Miraflores (Micro A), which is shared by both La Paz's main teams, Bolívar and The Strongest. There are reserved seats.

Golf

Mallasilla is the world's highest golf course, at 3318 m. Non-members can play here on weekdays, US$85.

Language schools

Instituto Exclusivo (IE), *Av 20 de Octubre 2315, Edif Mechita, T02-242 1072, www.instituto-exclusivo.com.* Spanish lessons for individual and groups, accredited by Ministry of Education.

Speak Easy Institute, *Av Arce 2047, between Goitía and Montevideo, T02-244 1779, speakeasyinstitute@yahoo.com.* US$6 for one-to-one private lessons, cheaper for groups and couples, Spanish and English taught.

Private Spanish lessons

Enrique Eduardo Patzy, *Méndez Arcos 1060, Sopocachi, T02-241 5501 or T776-22210, epatzy@hotmail.com.* US$6 an hr one-to-one tuition, speaks English and Japanese. Recommended.

Tour operators

America Tours, *Av 16 de Julio 1490 (El Prado), Edificio Avenida pb, No 9, T02-237 4204, www.america-ecotours.com. Mon-Fri 0900-1800.* Cultural and ecotourism trips to many parts of the country, day tours in La Paz, rafting, climbing, trekking and horse riding. English spoken. Highly professional and recommended.

Andean Base Camp, *Illampu 863, T02-246 3782.* Overland tours throughout Bolivia, Swiss staff, good reports.

Andean Secrets, *General Gonzales 1314 y Almirante Grau, San Pedro, T7729 4590, quimsacruz_bolivia@hotmail.com, www.andean-secrets.com. Mon-Fri 1500-1900,*

Sat 0900-1730, Sun 1000-1400. Mountain guide Denys Sanjines specializes in the Cordillera Quimsa Cruz. She also arranges visits to El Alto to see the Wrestling Cholitas, themanager@cholitaswrestling. com. Arrange hotel pick-up, go on your own or book through a Red C&P Sunday tour (see above).

Barracuda Biking Company, *Linares 971, of 5*, T7672 8881, *info@barracudabiking. com. Mon-Fri 1100-1900, Sat 1000-1400.* Bike trips to Coroico at a lower price than the upmarket companies.

Bolivian Journeys, *Sagárnaga 363, p 2*, T7201 4900, *www.bolivianjourneys. org.* Camping, mountain bike tours, equipment rental, maps, English and French spoken, helpful.

Crillon Tours, *Camacho 1223*, T02-233 7533, *www.uyuni.travel. (In USA: 1450 Brickell Bay Drive, Suite 815, Miami, Florida 33131.) Mon-Fri 0900-1200, 1430-1830, Sat 0900-1200.* A company with over 50 years' experience. Joint scheduled tours with Lima arranged. Fixed departures and luxury camper service to Salar de Uyuni (www.uyuni.travel), trips throughout Bolivia, including the Yungas, Sajama and Lauca, community and adventure tourism and much more. ATM for cash. Recommended. Full details of their Lake Titicaca services on page 82. See www.alwa.travel for their deluxe overlanding scheme.

Deep Rainforest, *Galería Doryan of 9A, Sagárnaga 189 y Murillo*, T02-215 0385, *www.deep-rainforest.com. Mon-Fri 1000-1400, 1500-1900, Sat 1000-1800.* Off-the-beaten-track trekking, climbing, canoe trips from Guanay to Rurrenabaque, rainforest and pampas trips.

Enjoy Bolivia, *Plaza Isabel La Católica, Edif Presidente Bush, of 2*, T02-243 5162, *www.njboltravel.com.* Wide selection of tours and transport service. Transfers to bus terminal and airport (US$17), van service to Oruro (US$108 shared between 4-8 passengers).

Fremen Tours, *Av 20 de Octubre 2396, Edif María Haydee, p 10*, T02-242 1258, *www.andes-amazonia.com. Mon-Fri 0900-1200, 1430-1830, Sat 1000-1200.* Customized tours and special interest travel throughout Bolivia, including Salar de Uyuni and Reina de Enín riverboat.

Gloria Tours, *Potosí 909*, T02-240 7070, *www.gloriatours.com.bo. Mon-Fri 0900-1230, 1430-1900, Sat 0900-1300.* Good service for ½ to full-day city tours and excursions further afield. See **Hotel Gloria**, page 52.

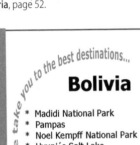

We take you to the best destinations...

Bolivia

* Madidi National Park
* Pampas
* Noel Kempff National Park
* Uyuni´s Salt Lake
* Titicaca & Isla del Sol
* Cordillera Real
* Sucre & Potosí
* Tupiza
* Jesuit Missions
* also Cusco, Inca Trail, and Machu Picchu

America Tours
Travel and Ecotourism Consultants

www.america-ecotours.com

AMERICA TOURS SRL.
Av. 16 de Julio (El Prado)
1490 Edificio Avenida PB Nº 9
La Paz-Bolivia
Tel.: (591) 2 2374204
Fax: (591) 2 2310023
info@america-ecotours.com

Gravity Bolivia, *Linares 940, p 1, T02-231 0218, Mon-Fri 0900-1900, Sat 1000-1500. Has a small office at Av 16 de Julio 1490 (El Prado), Edif Avenida, ground floor, of 10, T02-231 3849, www.gravitybolivia. com (book on website).* A wide variety of mountain-biking tours throughout Bolivia, including the world-famous downhill ride to Coroico. They offer a zipline at the end of the ride, or independently (www.ziplinebolivia. com). Also more challenging bike rides, including single-track and high-speed dirt roads, with coaching and safety equipment, and customized bike tours. Also have cycle spares, very knowledgeable service. Also has a new skiing and snowboard agency, **SnowRush**, *T7721 9634,* book in advance or by phone until 2200. Recommended.

Kanoo Tours, *Illampu 832 entre Sagárnaga y Santa Cruz, T02-246 0003, www.kanootours.com. Mon-Fri 1000-1830, Sat 1000-1700.* Also at **Adventure Brew Hostel**. Sells **Gravity Bolivia** tours (see above), plus Salar de Uyuni, Rurrenabaque jungle trips and Peru.

La Paz On Foot, *Indaburo 710 y Jaén, T7154 3918 (or Prol Posnanski 400, Miraflores, T02-224 8350), www. lapazonfoot.com.* Walking city tours, walking and sailing trips on Titicaca, tours to Salar de Uyuni, multi-day treks in the Yungas and Apolobamba and regional tours focused on Andean food and biodiversity, which also include Peru, northern Chile and Argentina. Also works with the **Tarapari Biodiversity Garden and Guesthouse** in Chulumani, www.tarapari.org, see page 120. Recommended.

Lipiko Tours, *Av Mariscal Santa Cruz 918 y Sagárnaga, Galería La República p 6, T02-231 5408, http://lipiko.com. Mon-Fri 0900-1700, Sat 0900-1300.* Tailor-made tours

for all budgets, 4WD tours, trekking, climbing and adventure sport, trips to Amazon and national parks. Also runs trips to Peru, Chile and Argentina.

Magri Turismo, *Capitán Ravelo 2101, T02-244 2727, www.magriturismo.com. Mon-Fri 0830-1215, 1430-1830, Sat 0900-1200.* Recommended for tours throughout Bolivia, flight tickets. Own **La Estancia** hotel on the Isla del Sol. They also have a city walking tour led by shoeshine boys.

Moto Andina, *Urb La Colina N°6 Calle 25, Calacoto, T7129 9329, www.moto-andina. com (in French).* Motorcycle tours of varying difficulty in Bolivia, contact Maurice Manco.

Mundo Quechua, *Av Circunvalación 43, Achumani, Zona Sur, T02-279 6145, www. mundoquechua.com.* Daily tours to the Cordillera Real, private transport in and around La Paz, custom-made climbing, trekking and 4WD tours throughout Bolivia. Also extensions to Peru and Argentina. English and French spoken, good service.

Peru Bolivian Tours, *Calle Capitán Ravelo 2097, esq Montevideo, Edif Paola Daniela, oficina 1-A, T02-244 5732, www. perubolivian.com. Mon-Fri 0900-1230, 1430-1830, Sat 0900-1200.* More than 20 years' experience, arranges special programmes throughout Bolivia and Peru.

Pure! Bolivia, *T02-243 4455 (6701 1344 24 hrs), info@bolivia-pure.com.* Member of the Pure! Travel Group, www.pure-travelgroup.com. Offering tailor-made, conventional, special interest and adventure tours in Bolivia.

Topas Travel, *Carlos Bravo 299 (behind Hotel Plaza), T02-211 1082, www.topas. bo. Mon-Fri 0830-1630, Sat 0900-1200.* Joint venture of **Akhamani Trek** (Bolivia), **Topas** (Denmark) and the Danish embassy, offering trekking, overland

truck trips, jungle trips and climbing, English spoken, restaurant and *pensión*.
Transturin, *Av Arce 2678, Sopocachi, T02-242 2222, www.transturin.com. Mon-Fri 0900-1300, 1400-1800, Sat 0900-1200.* Full travel services with tours in La Paz and throughout Bolivia. Details of their Lake Titicaca services on page 83.
Tupiza Tours, *Villalobos 625 y Av Saavedra, Edif Girasoles, ground floor, Miraflores, T02-224 5254, www.tupizatours. com. Mon-Fri 0900-1230, 1500-1830.* La Paz office of the Tupiza agency. Specialize in the Salar and southwest Bolivia, but also offer tours around La Paz and throughout the country.
Turisbus, *Av Illampu 704, T02-245 1341, also C 10 y Av Costanera 501, Calacoto, www.gruporosario.com. Mon-Fri 0900-1200, 1500-2000, Sat 0900-1300.* Lake Titicaca and Isla del Sol, Salar de Uyuni, Rurrenbaque, trekking and Bolivian tours. Also tours and tickets to Puno and Cuzco.
Turismo Balsa, *Av 6 de Agosto y Pinilla, Pje Pascoe 3, Sopocachi, T02-244 0620, www.turismobalsa.com.* City and tours throughout Bolivia. Owns **Hotel Las Balsas**, in beautiful lakeside setting at Puerto Pérez on Lake Titicaca, T02-289 5147, 72 km from La Paz, with excellent restaurant.
Urban Rush, *T7628 5738, www.urbanrush bolivia.com.* Go to **Hotel Presidente**, 17th floor, 1300-1800 for abseiling or rap jumping from one of the tallest buildings in La Paz, US$21 for first jump, US$10 for each extra jump.

La Paz
Air
La Paz has the highest commercial **airport** in the world, at El Alto (4061 m); T02-215 7300, www.sabsa.aero. **Cotranstur** minibuses, T02-231 2032, white with 'Cotranstur' and 'Aeropuerto' written on the side and back, go from Plaza Isabel La Católica, stopping all along El Prado and Av Mcal Santa Cruz to the airport, 0610-2130, US$1 (allow about 1 hr), best to buy an extra seat for your luggage, departures every 4 mins. Shared transport from Plaza Isabel La Católica, US$3.55 pp, carrying 4 passengers, also private transfers from **Enjoy Bolivia**, see Tour operators, page 65. Radio-taxi is US$7-10 to centre and Sopocachi, US$8.50-15 to Zona Sur. Prices are displayed at the airport terminal exit. There is an **Info Tur** office in arrivals with a *casa de cambio* next to it (dollars, euros cash and TCs, poor rates; open 0530-1300, 1700-0300, closed Sun evening). Several ATMs in the departures hall. There are also food outlets and shops (prices of handicrafts in the duty-free area are ridiculously high). The international and domestic departures hall is the main concourse, with all check-in desks. There are separate domestic and international arrivals. The airport was expanded in late 2014. For details of air services, see under destinations.

Bus
City buses There are 3 types of city bus: the modern *puma katari*, with 3 lines along different routes, mostly from El Alto through the centre to the Zona Sur, US$0.25-0.30 depending on route, additional lines will be added (www. lapazbus.bo); *micros* (small, old buses),

which charge US$0.20 a journey; and minibuses (small vans), US$0.20-0.35 depending on the journey. *Trufis* are fixed-route collective taxis, with a sign with their route on the windscreen, US$0.45 pp in the centre, US$0.55 outside.

Long distance For information, T02-228 5858. Buses to: **Oruro**, **Potosí**, **Sucre**, **Cochabamba**, **Santa Cruz**, **Tarija**, **Uyuni**, **Tupiza** and **Villazón**, leave from the main terminal at Plaza Antofagasta (micros 2, M, CH or 130), see under each destination for details. Taxi to central hotels should be US$1.50-2.50 and US3-4 to hotels in Sopocachi and Zona Sur. Take Taxi Terminal, or Taxi Magnífico for best service. The terminal (open 0400-2300) has a tourist booth by the main entrance, ATMs, internet, a post office, **Entel**, restaurant, luggage store and travel agencies. Touts find passengers the most convenient bus and are paid commission by the bus company. To **Oruro** van

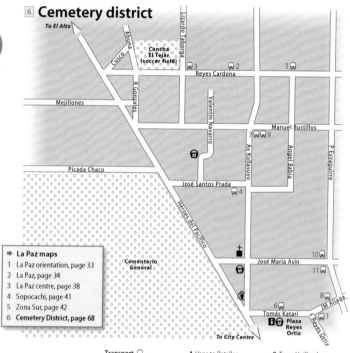

⑥ Cemetery district

To El Alto

Cancha El Tejar (soccer field)

Reyes Cardona

Mejillones

Manuel Bustillos

Picada Chaco

José Santos Prada

Cementerio General

José María Asín

Tomás Katari

Plaza Reyes Ortiz

To City Centre

Streets: Abuna, Cuzco, Lizardo Taborga, R. Gonzales, Valentín Navarro, Av Kollasuyo, Angel Babia, P. Eyzaguirre, Héroes del Pacífico, JM Aliaga, E. Reyes Ortiz

50 metres
50 yards

Transport 🚐
1 2 de Febrero to Copacabana
2 Trans Altiplano to Charazani
3 Provincias del Norte to Charazani & buses to Puerto Acosta
4 Vans to Batallas
5 Trans Altiplano to Apolo
6 Manco Capac to Copacabana
7 Trans Titicaca to Huatajata
8 Trans Tours to Tiwanaku
9 Trans Unificada to Sorata
10 Vans to Tiwanaku & Guaqui
11 Vans to Desaguadero

service with **Enjoy Bolivia**, see Tour operators, page 65, US$13 pp shared, US$90 private. To **Copacabana**, several bus companies (tourist service) pick-up travellers at their hotels (in the centre) and also stop at the main terminal, tickets from booths at the terminal (cheaper) or agencies in town. They all leave about 0800 (**Titicaca Bolivia** also at 1400), 3½ hrs, US$3.60-4.50 one way, return from Copacabana about 1330. When there are not enough passengers for each company, they pool them. **Diana Tours**, T02-235 0252, **Titicaca Bolivia**, T02-246 2655, **Turisbus**, T02-245 1341 (more expensive), many others. You can also book this service all the way to Puno, US$7.

Public buses to **Copacabana**, **Tiwanaku**, **Desaguadero** (border with Peru) and **Sorata**, leave from the Cemetery district. To get there, take any bus or minibus marked 'Cementerio' going up C Santa Cruz (US$0.15-0.22). On Plaza Reyes Ortiz are **Manco Capac**, and **2 de Febrero** for **Copacabana** and **Tiquina**. From the Plaza go up Av Kollasuyo and at the 2nd street on the right (Manuel Bustillos) is the terminal for minibuses to **Achacachi**, **Huatajata** and **Huarina**, as well as **Trans Unificada** and **Flor del Illampu** minibuses for **Sorata**. Several micros (20, J, 10) and minibuses (223, 252, 270, 7) go up Kollasuyo. Taxi US$2 from downtown, US$4.30 from Zona Sur.

Buses to **Coroico, the Yungas and northern jungle** leave from Terminal Minasa in Villa Fátima (25 mins by micros B, V, X, K, 131, 135, or 136, or *trufis* 2 or 9, which pass Pérez Velasco coming down from Plaza Mendoza, and get off at Minasa terminal, Puente Minasa). See Safety, page 31.

International buses From main bus terminal: to **Puno** and **Cuzco**, luxury and indirect services, see under Lake Titicaca, page 88. Also **Bolivia Hop**, www.boliviahop.com, which runs a hop-on, hop-off service from La Paz to Cuzco via Copacabana and Puno, Mon, Tue, Wed and Fri 0630, 1700 from Copacabana, packages start at US$39. Direct to Cuzco, 12 hrs with **Litoral**, US$23 via Desaguadero and Puno (5 hrs, US$8).

To **Lima**, Ormeño daily at 1430, US$90, 27 hrs; **Nuevo Continente** at 0830, US$88, 26 hrs, via Desaguadero, change to **Cial** in Puno.

To **Buenos Aires**, US$102, 2 a week with **Ormeño**, T02-228 1141, 54 hrs via Santa Cruz and Yacuiba; via Villazón with **Río Paraguay**, 3 a week, US$75, or **Trans Americano**, US$85. Alternatively, go to Villazón and change buses in Argentina.

To **Arica** via the frontier at Tambo Quemado and Chungará, **Pullmanbus** at 0630 (good), **Cuevas** at 0700, **Zuleta** at 0600, **Nuevo Continente** at 1230 except Sat, **Litoral**, T02-228 1920, Sun-Thu 1230, US$26.

The main route to **Chile** is via Tambo Quemado (see page 139), but an alternative route, on which there are no trucks, is to go by good road direct from La Paz via Viacha to **Santiago de Machaco** (130 km, petrol); then 120 km on a very bad road to the border at **Charaña** (basic **Alojamiento Aranda**; immigration behind railway station). From Visviri, on the Chilean side of the frontier (no services), a regular road runs to Putre. A motorized railway car also runs from Viacha to Charaña on Mon and Thu at 0800 (4 hrs, US$4.30), returning Tue and Fri at 1200. There is no train service on the Chilean side.

Cable car

Teleférico A system of 3 lines of cable cars (www.miteleferico.bo) joining neighbourhoods along the edge of the altiplano, including El Alto, with the centre of the city and the Zona Sur, was inaugurated in 2014. The lines are: **Línea Roja** (red line) from La Ceja, El Alto, to the old train station, 3 blocks above Plaza Eguino, in an area known as Vita in the northwest of the city; **Línea Amarilla** (yellow line) from Ciudad Satélite in El Alto, to Puente Holguín in Alto Obrajes, via Av Buenos Aires and Plaza España in Sopocachi; **Línea Verde** (green line) from Puente Holguín to Irpavi, via 17 de Obrajes in the Zona Sur. Each ride costs US$0.45, but for frequent use you can buy a card for US$2.10, which can then be topped up. 5 more lines are planned.

Car hire

Imbex, *C11, No 7896, Calacoto, T02-212 1012, www.imbex.com*. Wide range of well-maintained vehicles; Suzuki jeeps from US$60 per day, including 200 km free for 4-person 4WD. Also office in Santa Cruz, T03-3111001. Recommended.
Kolla Motors, *Rosendo Gutiérrez 502 y Ecuador, Sopocachi, T02-241 9141, www.kollamotors.com*. 6-seater 4WD Toyota jeeps, insurance and gasoline extra.
Petita Rent-a-car, *Valentín Abecia 2031, Sopocachi Alto, T02-242 0329, www.rentacarpetita.com*. Swiss owners Ernesto Hug and Aldo Rezzonico. Recommended for personalized service and well-maintained 4WD jeeps, minimum rental 1 week. Their vehicles can also be taken outside Bolivia. Also offer adventure tours (German, French, English spoken). Ernesto has a highly recommended garage for VW and other makes, Av Jaimes Freyre 2326, T02-241 5264.

Taxi

Taxis are often, but not always, white. Taxi drivers are not tipped. There are 3 types: **standard taxis**, which may take several passengers at once (US$0.45-1.75 for short trips within city limits), **fake taxis**, which have been involved in robberies, and **radio taxis**, which take only one group of passengers at a time. Since it is impossible to distinguish between the first two, it is best to pay a bit more for a radio taxi, especially at night. These have a dome light, a unique number (note this when getting in) and radio communication (eg **Servisur**, T02-279 9999; Taxi Terminal at the bus station; Taxi Magnífico; Taxi Diplomático T02-222 4343). They charge US$1.50-2.50 in the centre, more to suburbs and at night. Taxi ranks outside malls, cinemas, etc operate with radio taxis and are more expensive than the ones you flag down on the street, but are good places to find the safer option.

Train

Ferroviaria Andina *(FCA), Sánchez Lima 2199 y Fernando Guachalla, Sopocachi, T02-241 9770, www.fca.com. bo, Mon-Fri 0800-1600*. Sells tickets for the **Oruro–Uyuni–Tupiza–Villazón** line; see schedule and fares under Oruro Transport (page 134). Tickets for *ejecutivo* class sold up to 2 weeks in advance; for *salón* 1 week. Must show passport to buy tickets. Every second Sun, FCA runs a **tourist train** from El Alto to Guaqui, with a 1½-hr stop at Tiwanaku and 2 hrs at Guaqui. The station is at C 8, 3 blocks from Av 6 de Marzo, by Cuartel Ingavi, departs 0800, returns 1320, arrives in El Alto 1915, US$11.50 ejecutivo, US$3 salón, tickets from office in Sopocachi, as above. Confirm all details in advance.

Mallasa and Valle de la Luna
Minibus
Nos 231, 273 and 902 can be caught on
C México, El Prado or Av 6 de Agosto.
Also Micro 11 ('Aranjuez' large, not
small bus) or ones that say 'Mallasa' or
'Mallasilla' along El Prado and Av 6 de
Agosto, US$0.65. They pass **Valle de la
Luna** on the way to **Mallasa**.

La Muela del Diablo
Minibus
Take No 288, 207 or Micro R towards
Chiaraque, along C México, El Prado and
Av 6 de Agosto, and ask to be let off at
El Pedregal.

Illimani Lookout, Valle de las
Animas and Palca Canyon
Minibus
Micro 42 starts at the cemetery district,
goes along El Prado, Av 6 de Agosto,
Zona Sur, Ovejuyo and Huni, 9 a day
from 0700 to 1900 weekdays, hourly
on weekends starting at 0700, US$0.65,
1-1½ hrs, it returns right away. Also
along El Prado and Av 6 de Agosto,
minibus 385 goes to Ovejuyo, 243 to
Chasquipampa. **Trans Río Abajo** goes
to **Palca** from C Romualdo Herrera y
Venacio Burgoa, San Pedro, Tue, Fri and
Sat 1400, US$1, 2 hrs. On Sun hourly

minibuses, see also Transport to Ventilla
for Takesi trek, it also goes through Palca.

Urmiri
Bus
Micro A micro runs to Urmiri on Mon at
0700 from Av Franco Valle y Calle 3 (by
Pollos Imba), Ceja, El Alto; it returns at
1500 if there are 5 passengers, otherwise
it returns right away.

Minibus Those with stamina for
an 8-km steep uphill walk can take a
minibus to **Sapahaqui** and walk to
Urmiri. They leave from C Demetrio
Moscoso y C 5, Villa Dolores, El Alto,
every 30 mins daily 0700-1900, US$1.75,
2½ hrs. The trail starts in Kahata, outside
Sapahaqui.

Hotel Gloria (see Where to stay)
runs transport every day at 0800 with
a minimum of 7 people, US$6.50 per
person return, 2 ½ hrs; return to La Paz
at 1600.

El Alto
El Alto is connected to La Paz by the
new Teleférico and by a motorway (toll
US$0.25) and by a road to Obrajes and
the Zona Sur. Minibuses from Plaza
Eguino leave regularly for Plaza 16 de
Julio, El Alto, more leave from Plaza Pérez
Velasco for La Ceja, the edge of El Alto.

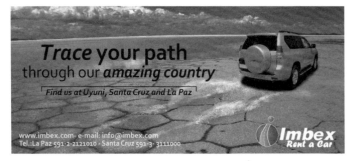

Day walks around La Cumbre
Bus/minbus
Those going from Villa Fátima to Coroico or Chulumani, see page 117, go through La Cumbre, US$3, and Unduavi; only transport going to Coroico goes through Cotapata. Be sure to tell the driver where you are going, some companies charge the full fare to Coroico US$4.25, even if you go part of the way. A taxi to La Cumbre takes 45 mins, US$20.

Trekking near La Paz
Takesi Trail
Bus Take a **Líneas Ingavi** bus from C Gral Luis Lara esq Venacio Burgoa near Plaza Líbano, San Pedro, going to **Pariguaya** (2 hrs past Chuñavi), several daily, US$3.55, 2 hrs. On Sun, also minibuses from C Gral Luis Lara y Boquerón, hourly 0700-1500. To **Mina San Francisco**: hire a **jeep** from La Paz; US$85, takes about 2 hrs. **Veloz del Norte** (T02-221 8279) leaves from Ocabaya 495 in Villa Fátima, T02-221 8279, 0900 daily, and 1400 Thu-Sun, US$3.55, 3½ hrs, continuing to Chojlla. From Chojlla to La Paz daily at 0500, 1300 also on Thu-Sun, passing **Yanacachi** 15 mins later. You can also catch a bus to La Paz from La Florida on the main Yungas road, US$3.55.

La Reconquistada To **Mina San Francisco**: hire a **jeep** from La Paz; US$85, 2 hrs or walk from Ventilla.

For the return, **Veloz del Norte** goes to Yanacachi and Chojlla leaves from Ocobaya 495 y Av Las Américas, Villa Fátima, T02-221 8279, 0900 daily, also 1400 Thu-Sun;US$3.55, 3½ hrs. From Chojlla to La Paz daily at 0500, Thu-Sun also at 1300, passes Yanacachi about 15 mins later.

Choro For transport to La Cumbre, see Day walks around La Cumbre above.

Yunga Cruz Líneas Ingavi from C Gral Luis Lara esq Venacio Burgoa near Plaza Líbano, San Pedro, **bus** to **Pariguaya** (2 hrs past Chuñavi) Mon-Sat at 0800, US$3.50, 6 hrs to Chuñavi, US$4; 6½ hrs to Lambate. It's not possible to buy tickets in advance, be there at 0700. Also **Trans Río Abajo**, C Gral Luis Lara y Romualdo Herrera, San Pedro, to **Lambate**, daily 0700-0800.

Zongo Valley
Bus
Trans Zongo bus from Av Chacaltaya y C Ingavi, Ballivián, El Alto, daily at 0600, US$2, 2½ hrs, to Zongo, US$3, 6½ hrs to **Huaji** (check with them for return time). A trip with a tour operator costs about US$100, a taxi US$45.

Minibus There are also minibuses that go from the Ballivián area in El Alto as they fill (few on Sun), they often return full, but you may get lucky and return with them.

Lake Titicaca, the Cordilleras & Yungas

Within striking distance of La Paz are an enormous variety of landscapes, extraordinary historical sites and potential for adventure. The most popular excursion is to the remarkable site of Tiwanaku, 72 km west of the city. Rising out of the vast flatness of the altiplano are the remains of pyramids and temples, of a great civilization that predated the Incas by a thousand years.

No visit to Bolivia would be complete without seeing the sapphire-blue waters of mystical Lake Titicaca and its beautiful islands. Covering 8000 sq km, Titicaca is the highest navigable lake in the world at over 3800 m above sea level.

Hidden in the mountains of the magnificent Cordillera Real, to the east of the lake, the colonial town of Sorata is a natural base for climbers, trekkers and day-hikers. Further north, the Cordillera Apolobamba has more fantastic trekking and wildlife territory.

A dramatic descent from the altiplano leads to the subtropical Yungas, an ideal place to catch your breath before heading back to the heights or onwards to the Amazon lowlands.

Best for
Archaeology ▪ Cycling ▪ Islands ▪ Trekking ▪ Wildlife

Footprint
picks

★ **Tiwanaku ruins**, page 77
Bolivia's best-known archaeological site.

★ **Delicious fish dishes in Copacabana**, page 88
Fresh trout from Lake Titicaca flash fried to perfection.

★ **Isla del Sol**, page 90
Titicaca's largest island and an ancient holy Inca site.

★ **Illampu Circuit**, page 99
Challenging high-altitude trek with impressive scenery.

★ **Area Protegida Apolobamba**, page 105
Popular hiking trails and thousands of vicuñas.

★ **The Yungas**, page 109
Walking, relaxing and enjoying the warm climate.

★ **Ride to Coroico**, page 110
The world's 'most dangerous road'.

PERU

◆ *Parque Nacional Madidi*

Puerto Salinas

Reyes

San Buenaventura ✈ Rurrenabaque

Rio Tuichi

Rio Amantola

○ Puina

Chaupi Orco (6044m) ▲ ○ Queara

Apolo ○

Rio Atén

Suches

○ Suches ○ Pelechuco

Antaquilla ☆ ◆ *Area Protegida Apolobamba*
Hichocolo

Ulla Ulla ○ Hilo Hilo

○ Canisaya

Aten ○

Rio Camata

○ Curva

Charazani ○

∴ *Iskanwaya*

Chuma ○ ○ Aucapata

○ Consata

Mapiri ○

Rio Llica

Rio Mapiri

Teoponte ○

Santa Ana ○

Guanay ○

Puerto Linares ○ ○ Palos Blancos

○ Puerto Acosta

Rio Tipuani

Tipuani ○

Sapecho ○ ○

San Miguel de Huachi

○ Escoma

Ancoma ○ ○ Ocara

Llipi ○

Ticumbaya ○

Alcoche ○

Carabuco ○

Cordillera Muñecas

Rio San Cristobal

Sorata ☆

Illampu (6380m) ▲

Rio Challana

Caranavi ○

Rio Zongo

Rio Alto Beni

Lake Titicaca (Chucuito)

Ancoraimes ○

Ancohuma (6427m) ▲

NOR YUNGAS

Rio Boopi

Warisata ○

○ Challana

San Pedro ○

Isla del Sol
☆ *Isla de la Luna*

Achacachi ○

Cordillera Real de los Andes

○ Challa

Yampupata ○

Straits of Tiquina

San Pablo ○

Condoriri ▲

Zongo ○

El Choro ○

Coroico ○ ☆
Yolosa ○

Arapata ☆

Copacabana ○ ☆

Huatajata ○

Huayna Potosi (6088m) ▲

Unduavi ○

Coripata ○

San Pedro ○
Lago Huiñamarca

Huarina ○

Pata Manta ○

Chacaltaya ▲

Yanacachi ○

☆

○ Chulumani ☆

PERU

Puerto Pérez ○

Pucarani ○

La Cumbre

Puente Villa ○

Chicaloma ○ ○ Irupana

Taraco ○

Tiwanaku ○

Laja ○

LA PAZ ✈

Ventilla ○

Chuñavi ○

Lambate ○

Desaguadero ○

Guaqui ○

Tambillo ○

Viacha ○

Tiwanaku ∴ ☆

Mallasa ○

Palca ○

Mururata ▲

Illimani (6402m) ▲

Las Juntas ○

Rio La Paz

LA PAZ

Tirate ○

N

Collana ○

Sapahaqui ○

Cordillera Quimza Cruz

20 km
20 miles

Vilchaya ○

Caquiviri ○

Comanche ○

Ballivian ○

Calamarca ○

Ayo Ayo ○

Urmiri ○

Luribay ○

Caxata ○

Corocoro ○

Topohoco ○

Tiwanaku

At first sight, there's not much to recommend Pampa Koani, a cold, bleak, windswept valley near Lake Titicaca's southeastern edge. But a few kilometres west was the centre of one of South America's greatest and longest-surviving civilizations, Tiwanaku (the preferred local name and that used by UNESCO) or Tiahuanaco.

The site *Colour map 2, B1.*

Bolivia's best-known archaeological site is a 'must see' excursion

★This remarkable archaeological site, 72 km west of La Paz, near the southern end of Lake Titicaca, takes its name from one of the most important pre-Columbian civilizations in South America. It is the most popular excursion from La Paz, with good facilities for the visitor.

Many archaeologists believe that Tiwanaku existed as early as 1200 BC, while the complex visible today probably dates from the eight to the 10th centuries AD. The site may have been a ceremonial complex and political centre, the nucleus of an empire which is thought to have covered most of Bolivia, southern Peru, northern Chile and northwest Argentina. It was also a hub of trans-Andean trade. The demise of the Tiwanaku civilization remains a mystery, but heading the list of

Tiwanaku ruins

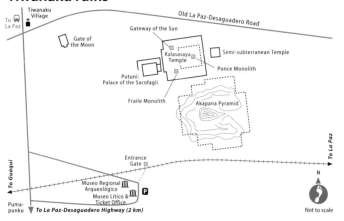

Essential Tiwanaku

Finding your feet

La Paz airport at El Alto, west of the city centre, is the closest.

Tiwanaku village, Copacabana, Sorata and other towns in the area are all linked by bus from La Paz.

If not on a tour take any **micro** marked 'Cementerio' in La Paz, get out at Plaza Félix Reyes Ortiz, on Mariano Bautista (north side of cemetery), go north up Aliaga, one block east of Asín to find Tiwanaku micros, US$2, 1½ hours, every 30 minutes, 0600 to 1500. Tickets can be bought in advance. **Taxis** cost US$30-55 return (shop around), with two hours at the site. Some **buses** go on from Tiwanaku to Desaguadero; virtually all Desaguadero buses stop at the access road to Tiwanaku, a 20-minute walk from the site. Return buses (last back 1700) leave from south side of the Plaza in village. Minibuses (vans) toDesaguadero, from José María Asín y P Eyzaguirre (Cemetery district) US$2, two hours, most movement on Tuesday and Friday when there is a market at the border.

Site information

The site is open 0900-1700, US$12, including entry to museums. Allow four hours to see the ruins and village. Organized tours to Tiwanaku cost US$10-12, not including the site's entry fee.

Guides

Written material is difficult to come by; hiring a guide costs US$25 for two hours, some speak English but don't be bullied into taking one if you prefer to go on your own. Locals sell copies of Tiwanaku figures; cheaper here than in La Paz.

Safety

When returning from Tiwanaku (ruins or village) to La Paz, do not take an empty minibus. We have received reports of travellers being taken to El Alto and robbed at gun point. Wait for a public bus with paying passengers in it.

Time required

One day to visit the village and ruins.

theories is that some form of major change in the climate, most probably drought, meant that the area's extensive system of raised fields (sukakollu), which at one stage were capable of sustaining many thousands of people, failed to feed the population and, more importantly, the elites. As a result, some time around 1000-1100 AD the main culture collapsed and disappeared. The Pumapunku section, 1 km south of the main complex, may have been a port, as the waters of the lake used to be much higher than they are today. The raised field system is once again being used in parts of the Titicaca area.

One of the main structures is the **Kalasasaya**, meaning 'standing stones', referring to the statues found in that part: two of them, the Ponce monolith (centre of inner patio) and the Fraile monolith (southwest corner), have been re-erected. In the northwest corner is the Puerta del Sol, originally at Pumapunku. Its carvings are thought to be either a depiction of the creator god, or a calendar. The motifs are exactly the same as those around the Ponce monolith. The **Templo Semisubterráneo** is a sunken temple whose walls are lined with faces, all different. According to some theories they depict states of health, the temple being a house of healing; another theory is that the faces display all the ethnicities of the world. The **Akapana**, originally a pyramid (said to have been the second largest in the world, covering over 28,000 sq m), still has some ruins on it. Plastering of the Akapana's walls was halted in 2009 when UNESCO, among others, declared it inappropriate. A natural disaster may have put a sudden end to the construction at **Pumapunku** before it was finished; some of the blocks here weigh between 100 and 150 tonnes. There is a small **Museo Lítico** at the ticket office, with several large stone pieces and, at the site, the **Museo Regional Arqueológico**, contains a well-illustrated explanation of the raised field system of agriculture. Many other artefacts are in the **Museo Nacional de Arqueología** in La Paz.

Nearby **Tiwanaku village**, with several basic hotels and eateries, still has remnants from the time of independence and the 16th-century church was built using pre-Columbian masonry. In fact, Tiwanaku for a long while was the 'quarry' for the altiplano. For the **Willkakuti**, winter solstice festival on 21 June, there is an all-night vigil and colourful dances. There is also a colourful local festival on the Sunday after Carnaval.

BACKGROUND
Tiwanaku culture

There remains much to learn about the Tiwanku culture, not least the reasons for its demise. What has been gleaned from continuing excavations and studies at the looted and severely damaged site is that it grew from a small, self-sufficient settlement in the pre-Christian era to the capital of a significant empire by 550 AD. The development of an abundant agricultural system nurtured a society revolving around an elite which conducted the affairs of state and the sacred rituals. A skilled artisan class also flourished. Income from trade in wool, copper, ceramics, textiles and other items funded monumental constructions – pyramids, temples, courtyards, gateways and monoliths – some decorated with detailed religious iconography. The empire expanded, absorbing other cities, until its influence spread from Titicaca to southern Peru, northern Chile and northwest Argentina.

Most recent estimates claim that at its height in the 8th-10th centuries AD as many as 1.4 million people could have been supported by the crops produced on the fields and ditches that covered nearly 50 sq km of Pampa Koani.

Without doubt, the greatest of all the accomplishments of the Tiwanaku culture was its elaborate and unparalleled system of raised fields, *sukakollu*, so carefully built that many remain intact today. The fields are massive constructions, over 1 m high, with planting surfaces up to 15 m wide and 200 m long. Each is a carefully layered structure with a thick stone base, which is covered with a layer of impermeable clay. Over the clay is a layer of coarse gravel and then another layer of finer gravel. Over all that sits the topsoil. The raised fields lie parallel, separated by deep, 3-m-wide irrigation channels running in straight lines or graceful curves that form precise geometric patterns. The irrigation ditches provided water in times of drought and the elevated fields protected crops in times of flooding.

The layer of clay at the base of the fields prevented the brackish water of nearby Lake Titicaca from seeping up into the topsoil. The exact positioning of the fields and ditches was designed to take advantage of the fierce Andean sun. The heated water in the ditches protected the fields from frost during the bitterly cold nights and also promoted the rapid growth of algae that fed fish. Furthermore, it attracted a resident population of ducks which entered the local diet as meat and eggs. Duck droppings, decayed algae and fish remains were then used as fertilizer.

There is some evidence to show that the empire's far-flung outposts came to a violent end. On the altiplano, however, drought (or some other catastrophic natural event) appears to have expedited Tiwanaku's decline which took place some 50-100 years after 950 AD. Isolated pockets of the culture survived, eventually to be incorporated into the Inca Empire. The city effectively vanished until the Spanish conquistador Pedro Cieza de León described its ruins in 1549, marvelling at the size of the structures and reporting that he was told that the Incas copied the style for their own monuments in Cuzco. They even, he said, thought of building their own city at 'Tiaguanaco'.

Lake Titicaca

Lake Titicaca is two lakes joined by the Straits of Tiquina: the larger, northern lake (Lago Mayor, or Chucuito) contains the Isla del Sol and Isla de la Luna; the smaller lake (Lago Menor, or Huiñamarca) has several small islands. The waters are a beautiful blue, reflecting the hills and the distant cordillera in the shallows of Huiñamarca, mirroring the sky in the rarified air and changing colour when it is cloudy or raining. A boat trip on the lake should not be missed.

La Paz to Copacabana

superb views, altiplano life and trips on the lake

Puerto Pérez *Colour map 2, B1.*
Puerto Pérez (population 17,600, altitude 4000 m) is the closest point to La Paz on Lake Titicaca, only 72 km. The views of the lake and mountains are superb and the sunsets here are spectacular. Because of the winds off the lake, the town enjoys almost permanently clear skies. As a result it is very hot during the day, but bitterly cold at night. The port was the original harbour for La Paz, founded in the 19th century by British navigators for the first steam boat on the lake. The vessel was assembled in Puno, Peru.

The large plaza is fronted by brightly painted houses and the town has appeared to benefit from the influx of tourists who come to the Hotel Las Balsas (see Where to stay, page 67).

The road to Puerto Pérez turns off the main La Paz Copacabana road at **Batallas** (population 19,900), a typical altiplano market town so named because of the battles between the Spanish commanders Almagro and Pizarro. It provides an insight into life on the altiplano and makes a pleasant walk (two to three hours).

Huatajata
At Huarina, 25 km north of Batallas, the road forks: north to Achacachi (with a branch to Sorata) and Puerto Acosta; and west beside the lake to the Staits of Tiquina. Along the northeast shore of the lake is Huatajata, with **Yacht Club Boliviano** and **Crillon Tours' International Hydroharbour** and **Inca Utama Hotel** (see below). Reed boats are still built and occasionally sail here for the tourist trade. There are several small but interesting exhibits of reed boats that were used

Essential Lake Titicaca

Finding your feet

A paved road runs from La Paz to the southeastern shore of the lake. One branch continues north along the eastern shore, another branch goes to the Straits of Tiquina (114 km El Alto–San Pablo) and Copacabana. A third road goes to Guaqui and Desaguadero on the southwestern shore. Ferries cross the Straits of See also Transport, page 78.

Getting around

Copacabana, Tiwanaku village, Sorata and other towns in the area are all linked by bus from La Paz.

Tours

Crillon Tours, www.crillontours. com and www.uyuni.travel, see also La Paz, Tour operators, page 65. A very experienced and consistently recommended company which runs a hydrofoil service on Lake Titicaca with excellent bilingual guides. Tours stop at their Andean Roots cultural complex at **Inca Utama** (see page 84). The hydrofoil trips include visits to Andean Roots complex, Copacabana, Isla del Sol and Isla de la Luna, Straits of Tiquina and the Cocotoni community. See Isla del Sol, page 92, for **La Posada del Inca**. Crillon has a sustainable tourism project with Urus-Iruitos people from the Río Desaguadero area on floating islands by the Isla Quewaya. Trips can be arranged to/from Puno and Juli (bus and hydrofoil excursion to Isla del Sol) and from Copacabana via Isla del Sol to Cuzco and Machu Picchu. Other combinations of hydrofoil and land-based excursions can be arranged (also highland, eastern lowland, jungle and adventure tours). All facilities and modes of transport are connected by radio.

Weather Copacabana

January	February	March	April	May	June
16°C	16°C	16°C	17°C	16°C	16°C
4°C	4°C	3°C	1°C	-2°C	-4°C
117mm	81mm	72mm	36mm	3mm	3mm

July	August	September	October	November	December
16°C	16°C	17°C	18°C	17°C	17°C
-6°C	-4°C	-1°C	1°C	2°C	3°C
0mm	9mm	12mm	24mm	45mm	51mm

Transturin, www.transturin.com, see also La Paz, Tour operators, page 67). Runs catamarans on Lake Titicaca, either for sightseeing or on the La Paz–Puno route. The catamarans are more leisurely than the **Crillon** hydrofoils, so there is more room and time for on-board meals and entertainment, with bar, video and sun deck. From their dock at Chúa, catamarans run full-day and two-day/one-night cruises starting either in La Paz or Copacabana. Puno may also be the starting point for trips. Overnight cruises involve staying in a cabin on the catamaran, moored at the Isla del Sol, with lots of activities. On the island, Transturin has the Inti Wata cultural complex which has restored Inca terraces, an Aymara house, the underground Ekeko museum and cultural demonstrations and activities. There is also a 30-passenger totora reed boat for trips to the Pilcocaina Inca palace. All island-based activities are community-led and for catamaran clients only. **Transturin** runs through services to Puno without many of the formalities at the border. It also offers last-minute programmes in Puno, Cuzco and La Paz, if booked six days prior to departure only. You can book by phone or by email, but ask first, as availability depends on date.

Turisbus, www.gruporosario.com/turisbus-tours, see La Paz, Tour operators page 67, **Hotel Rosario**, La Paz, and **Rosario del Lago**, Copacabana. Full-day guided tours in the fast launches *Titicaca Explorer I* (28 passengers) and *II* (eight passengers) to the Isla del Sol, and two-day tours with an overnight at **Hotel Rosario del Lago** and the option to include Isla de la Luna.

Time required

You will need to spend at least two to four days in and around Copacabana.

on long ocean voyages. Beyond here is **Chúa**, where there is fishing, sailing and Transturin's catamaran dock (see box, page 83).

Islands of Lago Huiñamarca

On **Suriqui** (one hour from Huatajata) in Lake Huiñamarca, a southeasterly extension of Lake Titicaca, you can see reed *artesanías*. The late Thor Heyerdahl's *Ra II*, which sailed from Morocco to Barbados in 1970, his *Tigris* reed boat, and the balloon gondola for the Nazca (Peru) flight experiment (see the Nazca Lines in the Peru chapter), were also constructed by the craftsmen of Suriqui. Reed boats are still made on Suriqui, probably the last place where the art survives. On **Kalahuta** there are *chullpas* (burial towers), old buildings and the uninhabited town of Kewaya. On **Pariti** there is Inca terracing and the **Museo Señor de los Patos**, with weavings and Tiwanku-era ceramics.

From Chúa the main road reaches the east side of the Straits of Tiquina at **San Pablo** (clean restaurant in blue building, toilets at both sides of the crossing). On the west side is San Pedro, the main Bolivian naval base, from where a paved road goes to Copacabana and the border. Vehicles are transported across on barges, US$5. Passengers cross separately, US$0.20 (not included in bus fares) and passports and visas may be checked (do not leave your documents on the bus or in your hotel in La Paz). Expect delays during rough weather, when it can get very cold.

Listings La Paz to Copacabana

Where to stay

$$$ Inca Utama Hotel and Spa
Huatajata. Reservations through Crillon Tours in La Paz (see page 65).
Rooms are comfortable, with heating, electric blankets, good service, bar, restaurant, Wi-Fi. The health spa is based on natural remedies and Kallawaya medicine. There is also an observatory (*alajpacha*) with 2 telescopes and retractable roof for viewing the night sky, an altiplano museum, a floating restaurant and bar on the lake (**La Choza Náutica**), a 252-sq-m floating island and examples of different altiplano cultures. Health, astronomical, mystic and ecological programmes are offered. See also page 65.

$$ Hotel Titicaca
between Huatajata and Huarina, Km 80 from La Paz, T02-289 5180 (in La Paz T02-290 7000).
Beautiful views, sauna, pool, good restaurant. It's very quiet during the week.

$ Máximo Catari's Inti Karka Hotel
on the lakeshore, T7197 8959, erikcatari@hotmail.com.
Rooms are cheaper with shared bath. Also restaurant, open daily, average prices.

Restaurants

$$-$ Inti Raymi
next to Inca Utama hotel, Huatajata.
With fresh fish and boat trips. There are

other restaurants of varying standard, most lively at weekends and in the high season.

Huatajata
Bus
La Paz–Huatajata, US$1, frequent minibuses from Bustillos y Kollasuyo,

Cementerio district, daily 0400-1800, continuing to Tiquina.

Islands of Lago Huiñamarca
Boat
Máximo Catari (see Where to stay, above) and Paulino Esteban (east end of town, T7196 7383) arrange trips to the islands in Lago Huiñamarca for US$15 per hr.

Copacabana *Colour map 2, B1.*

popular lakeside resort town and base for great trekking

★A popular little resort town on Lake Titicaca, 158 km from La Paz by paved road, Copacabana (population 5515, altitude 3850 m) is set on a lovely bay and surrounded by scenic hills. On major holidays (Holy Week, 3 May and 6 August) the town fills with visitors. It can also be busy at weekends and in the high season (June to August).

Copacabana has a heavily restored, Moorish-style **basilica** ⓘ *open 0700-2000; minimum 5 people at a time to visit museum, Tue-Sat 1000-1100, 1500-1600, Sun*

Copacabana

Lake Titicaca

To Cerro Calvario

Capitanía de Puerto

Michel Pérez

Transportes 2 de Febrero

Jáuregui

La Paz

Tito Yupanqui

Plaza Sucre

Transportes Manco Capac

Plaza 2 de Febrero

To La Paz   To Kasani

Av 6 de Agosto

Bus/Tour Agencies

Prodem

Av Busch

Basílica

Manuel Mejía

Potosí

Rigoberto Paredes

To Kasani & Yunguyo (Peru)

To Horca del Inca

To La Paz

To 1 (2 km)

N

200 metres
200 yards

Where to stay		Restaurants
1 Ecolodge	8 Leyenda	1 Aransaya
2 Emperador	9 Rosario del Lago	2 Café Bistrot Copacabana
3 Gloria Copacabana	10 Sonia	3 El Cóndor & The Eagle
4 Kantutas	11 Utama	4 La Orilla
5 Kotha Kahuaña	12 Wendy Mar	5 Mauraz
6 La Cúpula		6 Snack 6 de Agosto
7 Las Olas		7 Sujna Wasi

1000-1100, US$1.50, no photos allowed. It contains a famous 16th-century miracle-working Virgen Morena (Black Madonna), also known as the Virgen de Candelaria, one of the patron saints of Bolivia. The basilica is clean, white, with coloured tiles decorating the exterior arches, cupolas and chapels. It is notable for its spacious atrium with four small chapels; the main chapel has one of the finest gilt altars in Bolivia. There are 17th- and 18th-century paintings and statues in the sanctuary. Vehicles decorated with flowers and confetti are blessed (Bendición de las Movilidades) in front of the church at weekends and other special days (eg Semana Santa).

On the headland which overlooks the town and port, **Cerro Calvario**, are the Stations of the Cross (a steep 45-minute climb – leave plenty of time if going to see the sunset). On any day, but especially Sundays and holidays, the faithful follow the stations to the summit, but also to receive both Catholic and native religious blessings for tasks they will undertake and plans they hope to achieve in the year ahead. On the hill behind the town is the **Horca del Inca**, two pillars of rock with another laid across them; probably a solar calendar, the Inti Watana, now covered in graffiti. There is a path marked by arrows; boys will offer to guide you, but fix a price in advance if you want their help. There are three unreliable ATMs in town; best take some cash.

Listings Copacabana *map p85*

Tourist information

Centro de Información Turística
16 de Julio y 6 de Agosto, T7251 6220, Mon-Sat 0800-1330, 1600-1900.
English is spoken; they have pamphlets and maps of Copacabana and Isla del Sol.

Red de Turismo Comunitario
6 de Agosto y 16 de Julio, T7729 9088, Mon-Sat 0800-1230, 1300-1900.
Can arrange tours to nearby communities.

Where to stay

$$$ Rosario del Lago
Rigoberto Paredes y Av Costanera, T02-862 2141, reservations La Paz T02-244 1756, www.hotelrosario.com/lago.
Comfortable rooms with lake views, beautifully furnished, good restaurant,

small museum, **Turisbus** office (see Transport, below), parking. Efficient.

$$ Ecolodge
2 km south along the lakeshore, T02-862 2500 (or T02-245 1626, Hostal Copacabana, La Paz).
Small comfortable cabins in a quiet out-of-the-way location, nice grounds. Only breakfast available, solar hot water, helpful owner.

$$ Gloria Copacabana
16 de Julio y Manuel Mejía, T02-862 2094, La Paz T02-240 7070, www.hotelgloria.com.bo.
On the lakeshore. Full board available, bar, café and restaurant with international and vegetarian food, gardens, parking. Same group as **Gloria** in La Paz.

$$ Las Olas
lake-end of Pje Michel Pérez
past La Cúpula, T7250 8668,
www.hostallasolas.com.
Tastefully decorated suites, each in its
own style. All have kitchenettes, heaters,
lovely grounds and views, outdoor
solar-heated jacuzzi, a special treat.
Warmly recommended.

$$ Utama
Michel Pérez, T02-862 2013,
www.utamahotel.com.
Comfortable rooms, hot water, good
showers, restaurant, book exchange.

$$ Wendy Mar
Av 16 de Julio, opposite Gloria, T02-862
2124, www.hotelwendymar.com.
Very clean, light rooms in pastel colours,
large modern building, conveniently
placed, terrace, cheaper in low season.

$$-$ La Cúpula
Pje Michel Pérez 1-3, 5 mins'
walk from centre, T6708 8464,
www.hotelcupula.com.
Variety of rooms and prices from suite
with jacuzzi to comfortable rooms with
shared bath, reliable hot water, sitting
room with TV and video, fully equipped
kitchen, library, book exchange, attentive

service, excellent restaurant ($$ with
vegetarian options, great breakfast).
Popular, advance booking advised.
Highly recommended.

$$-$ Leyenda
Av Costanera y Germán Busch, T7067
4097, hostel.leyenda@gmail.com.
Lakeshore hotel with eclectic decor,
rooms elaborately decorated with local
motifs, electric shower.

$ Emperador
C Murillo 235, T02-862 2083.
Very economical, even cheaper
without bath, electric showers, newer
rooms at the back, popular, helpful,
tours arranged.

$ Kantutas
Av Jaúregui esq Bolívar, on Plaza Sucre,
T02-862 2093, hostalkantutas@entel.bo.
Good rooms, a decent option in the
middle price range, convenient location
for transport, includes breakfast.

$ Kotha Kahuaña
Av Busch 15, T7652 3760,
juandediosab@gmail.com.
Very economical, cheaper without
bath, simple kitchen facilities, quiet,
hospitable, basic but good value, new
management in 2014.

$ Sonia
Murillo 253, T7196 8441.
Rooms are cheaper without bath, good beds, big windows, roof terrace, laundry facilities, breakfast in bed on request, very helpful, good value. Recommended.

Restaurants

Excellent restaurants at hotels **Rosario del Lago** and **La Cúpula**. Many touristy places on Av 6 de Agosto toward the lakeshore, all similar.

$$ Café Bistrot Copacabana
Cabo Zapana y 6 de Agosto, upstairs. Daily 0730-2100.
Varied menu, international dishes, vegetarian options, French and English spoken.

$$-$ Mauraz
Av 6 de Agosto, opposite La Orilla.
A good choice for food (pizza, fast food, breakfasts) and drinks, has a happy hour, music, open 0730-2230.

$$-$ La Orilla
Av 6 de Agosto, close to lake. Daily 1000-2200 (usually).
Warm, atmospheric, tasty food with local and international choices.

$ Aransaya
Av 6 de Agosto 121.
Good restaurant and café serving local dishes, including trout.

$ El Cóndor & The Eagle
Av 6 de Agosto, p 1, one block from Plaza Sucre in Residencial París.
Only open for breakfast, good food, also sandwiches, cakes, teas and coffee, friendly, English spoken.

$ Snack 6 de Agosto
Av 6 de Agosto, 2 branches.
Good trout, big portions, some vegetarian dishes, serves breakfast.

$ Sujna Wasi
Jaúregui 127. Daily 0730-2300.
Serves breakfast, vegetarian lunch, wide range of books on Bolivia, slow service.

Festivals

Note At these times hotel prices quadruple.
24 Jan Alacitas, held on Cerro Calvario and at Plaza Colquepata, is when miniature houses, cars and the like are sold and blessed.
1-3 Feb Virgen de la Candelaria, massive procession, dancing, fireworks, bullfights.
Mar/Apr Easter, with candlelight procession on Good Friday.
2-5 May Fiesta del Señor de la Cruz de Colquepata, very colourful with dances in typical costumes.
21 Jun Aymara New Year, celebrated throughout the Titicaca region.
4-6 Aug La Virgen de la Candelaria, again with processions, dancing, fireworks; coincides with Bolivian Independence Day.

What to do

Copacabana town is filled with tour agencies, all offering excursions to floating islands on imitation reed vessels, and tours to Isla del Sol (see Transport, below). Kayak and pedal-boat rentals on the beach, US$3 per hr.

Transport

If arriving in Bolivia at Copacabana and going to La Paz, it is best to arrive in the city before dark.

Bus

To/from **La Paz**, US$2.15 plus US$0.30 for Tiquina crossing, 4 hrs, throughout the day with **Manco Capac, 2 de Febrero**. Both have offices on Copacabana's main plaza (but leave from Plaza Sucre) and in La Paz at Plaza Reyes Ortiz, opposite entrance to cemetery. Buy ticket in advance at weekends and on holidays. Tourist bus services are run by Vicuña Travel, Turbus/Trans Titicaca (www. titicacabolivia.com), **Diana Tours** and others daily from Plaza Sucre, 16 de Julio y 6 de Agosto, US$3.50-4.50; they take you to Sagárnaga e Illampu in the tourist district, but will not drop you off at your hotel. (See also Border with Peru via Copacabana, below.)

Hiking near Copacabana   *Colour map 2, B1.*
caves, a shrine, a prehispanic route and awe-inspiring views

This is a beautiful location for trekking and day-walking. All the nearby hills invite you to climb and there are superb views of the lake and distant cordilleras. Near the village of **Copacati Alto**, 3 km toward the border, are petroglyphs including an ancient whipala-like design called Inca Banderani, the Inca flag. (The whipala is a multicoloured flag adopted in contemporary times by the continent's indigenous political movements.) Visits can be arranged by Sonia (see Where to stay, page 88).

Yampupata Peninsula

A good longer walk is to the fishing village of Yampupata, at the tip of the eponymous peninsula. It is 17 km along the side of the peninsula from Copacabana to Yampupata and takes between four and six hours. There are three small streams for water, but this must be purified.

From Copacabana head down and northeast out of town to the little-used lakeside road. After about 45 minutes the road climbs around the first headland. Half an hour later the road rises again, around a second headland. An hour and a half from Copacabana, the road forks – take the lower (left) fork, which crosses a concrete bridge over a stream. Either head immediately right, which follows the left bank of the stream and soon becomes a paved Inca road running uphill, or take the steps up

Yampupata Peninsula

to a cave and shrine (the Gruta de Lourdes), then head right along a path through eucalyptus trees to join the Inca road.

After a 25-minute climb the steep Inca road rejoins the main road. Bear left here to head down to the lake again. The road continues beside the lake, through **Titicachi** to **Sicuani**, where you can buy refreshments at Hostal Yampu. There are also signs advertising reed-boat trips. Three hours from Copacabana you go around another headland, a long slow climb of half an hour or so, before descending again around a beautiful small bay with a patchwork of fields and a few houses.

About four hours from Copacabana (for the quickest of walkers), you arrive at Yampupata. From the end of the road a path heads left across the beach to where you can find someone to take you across the straits by motor- or rowing boat to the south end of Isla del Sol. There is also an infrequent micro back from Yampupata to Copacabana.

From the tip of Isla del Sol, Las Mil Gradas (the Inca steps by the main boat terminal) is about 30 minutes' walk away. The last boats leave the island at 1600, so leave plenty of time if you plan to return to Copacabana the same day. It's a good idea to set off before 0900.

You can trek to Yampupata from the Straits of Tiquina and follow a prehispanic road through Parquipujio, Chisi (which has some ancient ruins), the stone village of Sampaya and other villages. This particular version of the trek takes two to three days and is not very common but gives fantastic views of the Cordillera Real across the lake. Sampaya, which has a community-run *hospedaje* ($ including breakfast and guiding) overlooking the village and lake, is 14 km from Copacabana. Boats can be hired from Sampaya to Isla de la Luna (see Transport, below).

Isla del Sol and around *Colour map 2, B1.*

an overnight stay is recommended to fully appreciate the island

★The site of the main Inca creation myth (there are other versions) is a place of exceptional natural beauty and spiritual interest. Legend has it that Viracocha, the creator god, had his children, Manco Kapac and Mama Ocllo, spring from the waters of the lake to found Cuzco and the Inca dynasty.

La Roca Sagrada (sacred rock) at the island's northwest end is worshipped as their birthplace. Near the rock are the impressive ruins of **Chincana**, the labyrinth, a 25-minute walk from the village of **Challapampa**, with a basic **Museo de Oro** ⓘ *US$1.45 includes landing fee and entry to Chincana*. Challampa is beautifully set along two sandy bays, separated by an isthmus. Near the centre of the island is the community of Challa on a secluded bay with an **ethnographic museum** ⓘ *US$2.15, includes trail fees*. Towards the south end of the island is the **Fuente del Inca**, a spring reached by Inca steps, Las Mil Gradas, leading up from the lake and continuing up to Yumani. The village is spread out along a steep slope between the port and a ridge 200 m above. Near the southeast tip of the island, 2 km from the spring, are the ruins of **Pilcocaina** ⓘ *US$0.75 include landing fees*, the Temple of the Sun, a two-storey building with false domes and nice views over the water. You must pay the fees even if you don't visit the museums or ruins. Keep all entry tickets, you may be asked for them at other locations. Several restored pre-Columbian roads cross the island from north to south.

The three communities are along the east shore of the island. All have electricity (Yumani also has internet), accommodation and simple places to eat. The island is heavily touristed and gets crowded in high season. Touts and beggars can be persistent, especially in Yumani. Tour operators in Copacabana offer half- and full-day 'tours' (many are just transport, see page 88) but an overnight stay at least is recommended to appreciate fully the island and to enjoy the spectacular walk from north to south (or vice-versa), about 11 km, at a comfortable pace. In a day trip, you will barely have time for a quick look at Chincana and you will see Pilcocaina from the boat. Note that it is a steep climb from the pier to the town of Yumani. Local guides are available in Challapampa and Yumani.

Isla de la Luna

Southeast of Isla del Sol is the smaller Isla de la Luna (or Coati), which may also be visited. The community of Coati is located on the west shore, the ruins of the Inca **Palacio de Iña Kuyu** ⓘ *US$1.45 community fee for ruins and landing,* on the east

Isla del Sol

ON THE ROAD

The sacred lake

The name Titicaca may derive from the Aymara word *titi*, a small mountain cat, and the Quechua word *caca*, meaning rock or cliff. The rock is said to refer to the Sacred Rock at Chincana on the Isla del Sol which was worshipped by the pre-Incan people on the island. Legend has it that they saw the eyes of a mountain cat gleaming in the Sacred Rock and so named it Titicaca, or Rock of the Mountain Cat.

Another legend tells of an underwater city lying between the islands of Koa and Pallala, near the Isla del Sol. This city was said to exist before there was a lake. In the city was a temple which could only be entered by women dedicated to the sun. Each day these women would go to fill their water jars at a spring located in the ruins of Chincana, near the Sacred Rock. One day two men followed the women and surprised one of them who dropped her water jar, breaking it. Due to the power of the Inca god Viracocha, the water continued to flow, creating the lake.

The above are but two examples of the important role that Titicaca has long played in Andean beliefs. Tiwanaku ceremonial sites were built along its shores 2000 years ago and the Inca's central creation myth is also intimately tied to the lake. It tells how Manco Capac and his sister, Mama Ocllo, arose from the azure waters to found Cuzco and the Inca Dynasty.

In addition to inspiring such tales of the supernatural, Lake Titicaca is also home to a great many natural wonders. It has long been called the highest navigable lake in the world, although the large Lago Junín, in the central

shore. The island is very peaceful, ideal for getting away from the mainstream tourist route. Boats stop only at the ruins and only for an hour, which doesn't give enough time to visit the village as well. If you wish to stay overnight there is an Albergue Familiar in Coati village ($, private or shared bath) and an **Albergue Comunitario** at the entrance to the ruins (also $, shared bath and solar-heated water).

Listings Isla del Sol *map p91*

Where to stay

La Posada del Inca, a restored colonial hacienda, owned by **Crillon Tours**, is only available as part of a tour with Crillon, see pages 65 and 82. **Magri Turismo** also owns a hotel on the island, **La Estancia** (www.ecolodge-laketiticaca. com). See La Paz, Tour operators on page 64. See also **Transturin's** overnight options on page 67.

Yumani

The majority of posadas are in the south of the island, most in the upper part of Yumani. For those unable to walk a long way up the steps there are hostales and cabañas between Yumani

highlands of Peru, is almost 200 m higher. The exact level of Titicaca has fluctuated between 3806 m and 3812 m above sea level, over the past century.

The traditional totora-reed boats, so emblematic of Titicaca, are today restricted to the tourist trade. A reed boat lasts seven to eight months, while a wooden boat lasts seven to eight years. Reed vessels built by the craftsmen of Titicaca have nonetheless sailed the world's oceans. During the 19th and early 20th centuries, iron-hulled steamships, brought up in pieces from Pacific ports and painstakingly re-assembled, sailed Titicaca's waters, the forerunners of today's hydrofoils and catamarans.

The waters of Titicaca are not fed by any large rivers, only local rain, and they never reach the sea; 94% is lost through evaporation, 5% leaves via the Río Desaguadero, which empties into equally landlocked Lago Poopó, and the remainder filters into surrounding aquifers.

The moderating effect of Titicaca's waters creates microclimates in the surrounding valleys. Orchards on the northeast shore produce peaches and other crops that would not normally survive the harsh conditions of the altiplano.

The trout farmed in the lake and served in so many restaurants is not native. Endemic fish species include the tiny *ispi* and *karachi*, which can be seen for sale in local markets. The lake is also home to a great many birds, including coots, ducks and grebes.

Growing population around the lake means increased water pollution, endangering these species and Titicaca's unique natural beauty. Today, a determined effort is required of both Peru and Bolivia in order to protect the sacred lake. For details see www.alt-perubolivia.org.

port and higher up the village. Quality varies; ignore the touts and shop around for yourself. Please conserve water, it is hauled up the steep hill by donkeys.

$$ Palla Khasa
600 m north of town on the main trail to Challapampa, T7321 1585, pallakhasa@gmail.com.
Includes good breakfast, nice cabins, large rooms, good beds, restaurant with fine views, nice location and grounds, family-run, solar electricity, changes US$ and other currencies. Book in advance.

$ Casa de la Luna
Halfway down from Inti Kala towards Hostal Imperio del Sol, T7190 8040.
More expensive than some, spacious

rooms, breakfast included, also has a restaurant.

$ Hostal Utama
Almost at the top of the hill, T7300 3268.
In a pleasant location, rooms with or without bath, breakfast and restaurant, small garden, helpful and good value.

$ Inti Kala
At the top of the hill, T7194 4013, javierintikala@hotmail.com.
With bath, electric shower, terrace, lake views, serves breakfast in dining area.

$ Mirador del Inca
Access from the port along the steps to the south of the main Inca steps, at the same level as the Fuente del Inca.
Simple but nice hostel with lake views,

cheaper rooms with shared bath, electric showers, breakfast extra.

$ Templo del Sol
At the top of the hill, T7351 8970.
Comfortable rooms, cheaper without bath, electric shower, great views, comfy beds, meals available on request, good value.

Challa

Located mid-island on the east shore, about 200 m below the main north-south trail. Most hostels are on the beach, the town is uphill.

$ Inca Beach
On the beach, T7353 0309.
Simple rooms with bath, electric shower, kitchen and laundry facilities, meals available, nice common area, camping possible, good value.

$ Qhumpuri
On hillside above beach, T7472 6525.
Simple 2-room units with nice views, private toilet, shared electric shower, tasty meals available.

Challapampa

$ Cultural
1 block from beach, T7190 0272.
Clean rooms, cheaper without bath, nice terrace, does not include breakfast, helpful owners, good value.

$ Manco Kapac
By the dock, T7128 8443.
Basic clean rooms, shared bath, electric shower, camping possible, does not include breakfast.

$ Mirador del Sol
At the north end of southern bay, past the docks, T7370 6536.
Simple rooms with great views, shared bath, electric shower, no breakfast.

Camping is permitted along the beach of the northern bay.

Restaurants

$$ Las Velas
Yumani, near the top of the hill behind a eucalyptus grove, follow the signs.
Great views, especially at sunset, take a torch for the way back. Lovely candle-lit atmosphere, small choice of excellent meals, all freshly prepared, slow service, but worth the wait.

Transport

Boat

Boat companies have ticket booths at the beach, by the bottom of Av 6 de Agosto; there are also agencies selling boat and bus tickets along Av 6 de Agosto. All departures are at 0830, unless otherwise noted, and boats arrive back at Copacabana around 1730. The crossing from Copacabana to Yumani takes about 1½ hrs, to Challpampa 2 hrs. Return tickets are only valid on the same day, get a one way fare if you plan to stay overnight. **Andes Amazonía** run full-day trips Copacabana–Challapampa–Yumani–Copacabana, US$5. If you wish to walk, you can be dropped off at Challapampa around 1030-1100 and picked up at Yumani at 1530 (boats leave punctually, so you will have to walk quickly to see the ruins in the north and then hike south to Yumani and down to the pier). They also have a 1330 departure to Yumani, returning 1600, with a 10-min stop at Pilcocaina on the way back. **Unión Marinos**, run Copacabana–Challapampa–Copacabana, US$4.25 (US$3.50 one way); they depart for Challapampa at 0830 and 1330. **Titicaca Tours** run Copacabana–Coati (Isla de la

Luna)–Yumani–Copacabana, US$5.65 return, US$4.25 Copacabana–Coati–Yumani, US$2.80 Copacabana–Yumani; they leave for Coati and Yumani at 0830, with a stop for 1 hr at Coati; they depart at 1330 for Yumani only. They depart from Yumani at 1530. Wilka boats also run from Challa to Copacabana Wed, Sat, Sun at 0700, returning 1330, US$2.80 one way.

From **Yampupata** to Yumani by motorboat, US$15 per boat (US$5 pp by rowing boat). To Isla de la Luna from the village of Sampaya, US$21 for a motorboat, US$14 for a rowing boat. **Taxi** Copacabana–Sampaya US$11.50 or take Yampupata transport and get out at the turn-off, 4 km before the village.

Border with Peru *Colour map 2, B1.*

a choice of three routes

West side of Lake Titicaca
The road goes from La Paz 91 km west to the former port of **Guaqui** (passports may be inspected at the military checkpoint here and at other spots along the road). The road crosses the border at **Desaguadero**, 22 km further west, and runs along the shore of the lake to Puno. Bolivian immigration is just before the bridge, open 0800-2030 (0700-1930 Peruvian time, one hour earlier than Bolivia). Get an exit stamp, walk 200 m across the bridge then get an entrance stamp on the other side. Peruvian visas should be arranged in La Paz. There are a few hotels and restaurants on both sides of the border; very basic in Bolivia, slightly better in Peru. Money changers on the Peruvian side give reasonable rates. Market days are Friday and Tuesday, otherwise the town is dead.

Via Copacabana
From Copacabana a paved road leads 8 km south to the frontier at Kasani, then to Yunguyo, Peru. Do not photograph the border area. For La Paz tourist agency services on this route, see International buses, page 88, and Essential Lake Titicaca, page 82. The border is open 0800-1930 Bolivian time (0700-1830 Peruvian time). International tourist buses stop at both sides of the border; if using local transport walk 300 m between the two posts. Do not be fooled into paying any unnecessary charges to police or immigration. Going to Peru, money can be changed at the Peruvian side of the border. Coming into Bolivia, the best rates are at Copacabana.

East side of Lake Titicaca
From Huarina, a road heads northwest to Achacachi (Sunday market; fiesta 14 September). Here, one road goes north across a tremendous marsh to **Warisata**, then crosses the altiplano to Sorata (see below). At Achacachi, another road runs roughly parallel to the shore of Lake Titicaca, through **Ancoraimes** (Sunday market, the church hosts a community project making dolls and alpaca sweaters, also has dorms), **Carabuco** (with a colonial church), **Escoma** (which has an Aymara market every Sunday morning) to **Puerto Acosta**, 10 km from the Peruvian border. It is a pleasant, friendly town with a large plaza and several simple places to stay and eat. The area around Puerto Acosta is good walking country. From La Paz to

Puerto Acosta the road is paved as far as Escoma, then good until Puerto Acosta (best in the dry season, approximately May to October). North of Puerto Acosta towards Peru the road deteriorates and should not be attempted except in the dry season. There is a smugglers' market at the border on Wednesday and Saturday, the only days when transport is plentiful. You should get an exit stamp in La Paz before heading to this border (only preliminary entrance stamps are given here). There is a Peruvian customs post 2 km from the border and 2 km before Tilali, but Peruvian immigration is in Puno.

Listings Border with Peru

Transport

West side of Lake Titicaca
Bus via Guaqui and Desaguadero
Road paved all the way to Peru. Buses from La Paz to Guaqui and Desaguadero depart from J M Asín y P Eyzaguirre, Cementerio, from 0500, US$1.50, shared taxi US$3, 2 hrs. From Desaguadero to **La Paz** buses depart 4 blocks from bridge, last vehicle 2000.

Via Copacabana
Bus
Several agencies go from La Paz to **Puno**, with a change of bus and stop for lunch at Copacabana, or with an open ticket for continuing to Puno later. They charge US$8 and depart La Paz 0800, pick-up from hotel. From Copacabana they continue to the Peruvian border at Kasani and on to Puno, stopping for immigration formalities and changing money (better rates in Puno). Both **Crillon Tours** (page 82) and **Transturin** (page 83) have direct services to Puno without a change of bus at the border. From Copacabana to Puno, with connection to Cuzco, **Trans Titicaca** (www.titicacabolivia. com) at 0900, 1330, 1830 and other agencies at 1330, offices on 6 de Agosto, US$4-5, 3 hrs. Also **Turisbus** (www. gruporosario.com) to Puno from Hotel

Rosario del Lago at 1330, US$9, and services La Paz–Copacabana–Cuzco–Machu Picchu. Also Bolivia Hop, www. boliviahop.com, hop-on, hop-off service La Paz–Copacabana–Puno–Cuzco 4 days a week. To go to **Cuzco**, you will have to change in Puno where the tour company arranges connections, which may involve a long wait, check details (US$14-22 La Paz–Cuzco). In high season, book at least a day in advance. It is always cheaper, if less convenient, to buy only the next segment of your journey directly from local bus companies and cross the border on your own. Colectivo taxi Copacabana (Plaza Sucre)–**Kasani** US$0.55 pp, minivan US$0.45, 15 mins, Kasani–**Yunguyo**, where Peruvian buses start, US$0.30 pp.

East side of Lake Titicaca
Bus
La Paz (Reyes Cardona 772, Cancha Tejar, Cementerio district, T02-238 2239)–**Puerto Acosta**, 5 hrs, US$4, Tue-Sun 0500. Transport past Puerto Acosta only operates on market days, Wed and Sat, and is mostly cargo trucks. Bus Puerto Acosta–La Paz at about 1500. There are frequent minivans to La Paz from **Escoma**, 25 km from Puerto Acosta; trucks from the border may take you this far.

good views, marshland and wide open spaces

The road from La Paz heads northwest to the shores of Lake Titicaca before branching off at Huarina towards the village of **Achacachi** (population 79,000), where there is a military checkpoint; have your passport at hand. There are good views of Lake Titicaca from the church up the hill from the plaza. There's a market behind the main plaza on Sundays and a local fiesta is celebrated on 14 September. From Achacachi the road continues north to **Warisata**, passing through a vast marsh of water and dykes, with farms, huge numbers of birds, and snow-capped peaks in the distance. It then reaches the wide open spaces of the altiplano and climbs to a pass before beginning its descent through a series of tight bends. At the bottom of a valley it crosses a bridge and climbs up from the river to Sorata.

charming laid-back town with a comfortable climate and great trekking

This beautiful colonial town, 163 km from La Paz along a paved road, is nestled at the foot of Mount Illampu; all around it are views over steep lush valleys. Sorata (population 2523, altitude 2700 m) has long been a trade and transport centre for coca, quinine, rubber and gold, produced in the lowland areas to which it provides access. More recently, the town has become a popular tourist destination offering superb hiking and trekking as well as being a great place to wander around and relax. It has a pleasant laid-back atmosphere and an extremely comfortable climate. It is lower and noticeably warmer than La Paz, and higher and cooler than most Yungas towns.

The town has a charming plaza, named after General Enrique Peñaranda who was born in the nearby village of Chuchulaya in 1892 and was president of the country 1940-1943. On a clear day, through the giant palms, you can see Illampu (on the left) and Ancohuma (on the right). The view of the mountains is better from the smaller Plaza Obispo Bosque. The main fiesta is 14 September. There is no ATM in Sorata, take cash.

A popular excursion is to **San Pedro cave** ⓘ *0800-1700, US$3, toilets at entrance,* beyond the village of San Pedro. The cave is lit and has an underground lake (no swimming allowed). It is reached either by road, a 12-km walk (three hours each way), or by a path high above the Río San Cristóbal (about four hours, impassable during the rainy season and not easy at any time). Get clear directions before setting out and take sun protection, food, water, etc. Taxis and pickups from the plaza run 0600-2200, US$11 with a 30-minute wait. The **Mirador del Iminapi** (above the community of Laripata) offers excellent views of town and the Larecaja tropical valleys. It is a nice day-walk or take a taxi, 20 minutes, US$11 return.

Other day hikes include **Cerro Istipata**: either take a La Paz-bound bus to below the cross on Cerro Ulluni Tijja (US$0.50), and follow the ridge up and over Cerro

Lorockasini and on to Cerro Istipata, or walk the whole way from Sorata. To walk, follow the La Paz road until just before the YPFB garage. Drop down right, cross the Río San Cristóbal and head up through the spread-out village of Atahuallani and then up to join the ridge between Cerro Lorockasini (on the right) and Cerro Istipata.

There is another one-day walk to **Lakathia**. Follow the old Spanish stone trail up, starting at the cemetery and following the ridge, and then descend the broad and well-used path back to Sorata. It takes four to six hours to get to Lakathia, which stands at a height of 4000 m, and two to three hours to descend to Sorata.

Trekking and climbing from Sorata

Sorata is the starting point for climbing **Illampu** and **Ancohuma**. All routes out of the town are difficult, owing to the number of paths in the area and the very steep

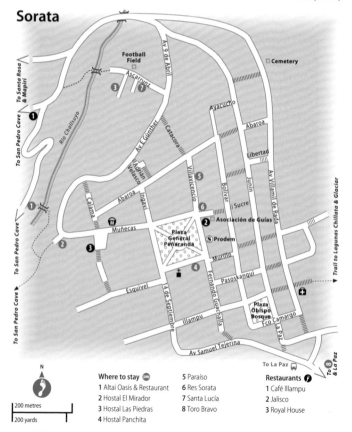

Sorata

Where to stay
1 Altai Oasis & Restaurant
2 Hostal El Mirador
3 Hostal Las Piedras
4 Hostal Panchita
5 Paraíso
6 Res Sorata
7 Santa Lucía
8 Toro Bravo

Restaurants
1 Café Illampu
2 Jalisco
3 Royal House

ascent. Experience and full equipment are necessary. You can hire trekking guides and mules (see What to do, page 100). The three- to four-day trek to **Lagunas Chillata and Glaciar** is the most common and gets busy during high season. Laguna Chillata can also be reached by road or on a long day-hike with light gear, but mind the difficult navigation and take warm clothing. Laguna Chillata has been heavily impacted by tourism (remove all trash, do not throw it in the pits around the lake) and groups frequently camp there. The ★**Illampu Circuit**, a six- to seven-day high-altitude trek (three passes over 4000 m, one over 5000 m) around Illampu, is excellent. It can get very cold and it is a hard walk, though very beautiful with nice campsites on the way. Some food can be bought in Cocoyo on the third day. You must be acclimatized before setting out. Another option is the **Trans-Cordillera Trek**, 10-12 days from Sorata to Huayna Potosí, or longer, all the way to Illimani at the opposite (south) end of the Cordillera Real. Some communities charge visitors fees along the way.

From Sorata to the jungle

There are two historic trails from Sorata to the jungle, both originally opened for the transport of natural resources out of the lowlands and both, for a while, difficult long treks. The **Mapiri Trail** was built to bring quinine out of the Mapiri area to Sorata. Over the years it was abandoned and re-opened several times and to trek was a very challenging eight days. Matthew Parris described it as a "trail of blood and tears" in *Inca Kola: a traveller's tale of Peru*. The **Camino de Oro** was a strenuous five- to seven-day trek from Ancoma on the Illampu Circuit to Guanay. Large parts of it have been swallowed up by gold mining operations. If tempted to embark on either trail, you must seek advice from a guide in Sorata. A much more common way to descend to the jungle these days is by mountain bike. For long-distance riders a good route is from the mountains and gold-mining communities above Sorata, down to the town of Consata and then on to Mapiri. From Mapiri the route continues by jeep or boat to Guanay, from where you can return to La Paz, or carry on by boat to Rurrenabaque. See **Gravity**, page 65, for a company offering this adventure by vehicle, bike and boat. Each year Sorata hosts the **Jacha Avalancha**, a two-day mountain-bike challenge.

Listings Sorata and around *map p330*

Where to stay

$$ Altai Oasis
T02-213 3895, www.altaioasis.com.
At the bottom of the valley in a beautiful setting, a 15-min steep downhill walk from town, or taxi US$2. Cabins, rooms with bath (cheaper with shared bath), dorms and camping (US$5 pp). Very

good restaurant ($$), bar, lovely grounds, pool, peaceful, very welcoming, family-run by the Resnikowskis, English and German spoken. Warmly recommended.

$ Hostal El Mirador
Muñecas 400, T7350 5453.
Cheaper with shared bath, hot water, kitchen, laundry facilities, terrace.

$ Hostal Las Piedras
Just off Ascarrunz, T7191 6341,
laspiedras2002@yahoo.de.
Rooms with and without bath, good
mattresses, electric shower, very nice,
good breakfast with home-made
products available, very helpful, English
and German spoken. Recommended.

$ Hostal Panchita
On the plaza, T02-213 4242.
Simple rooms, shared bath, electric
shower, sunny courtyard, washing
facilities, does not include breakfast,
good value.

$ Paraíso
Villavicencio 117.
With electric shower, basic rooms,
terrace, breakfast available.

$ Residencial Sorata
On the plaza, T02-213 6672.
Cheaper without bath, electric shower,
restaurant, large but scruffy grounds,
poor beds, a bit run-down overall but
still adequate.

$ Santa Lucía
Ascarrunz, T02-213 6686.
Rooms are cheaper with shared bath,
electric shower, carpeted rooms,
patio, does not include breakfast, not
always open.

$ Toro Bravo
Below petrol station at entrance to town,
T7725 5255.
With electric shower, ample grounds
and rooms (upstairs rooms are better),
small pool, restaurant, a bit faded but
good value.

Restaurants

There are several **$$-$** Italian places on
the plaza, all quite similar.

$$-$ Café Illampu
15 mins' walk on the way to San Pedro
cave.
Closed Tue and Dec-Mar. Excellent
sandwiches, bread and cakes, camping
possible. Offers tours with own
4WD vehicle, Swiss-run, English and
German spoken.

$$-$ Jalisco
On the plaza.
Mexican and Italian dishes,
sidewalk seating.

$ Royal House
Off Muñecas by the market.
Decent set lunch, friendly.

Festivals

14 Sep **Fiesta Patronal del Señor
de la Columna**, is the main festival.

What to do

Guides for trekking
It may be cheaper to go to Sorata and
arrange trekking there than to book
a trek with an agency in La Paz. Buy
necessary foods and supplies in La Paz,
Sorata shops have basic items.
Asociación de Guías, Sucre 302 y
Guachalla, leave message at **Residencial
Sorata** (T02-213 6672); hires guides,
porters and mules. Prices vary: guides
approximately US$30 per day, mules
US$15 per day. Porters take maximum
2 mules, remember you have to feed
your guide/porter.
Eduardo Chura, T7157 8671,
guiasorata@yahoo.com, is an
independent local trekking guide.

Transport

Bus

Minibuses throughout the day 0400-1800 from **La Paz** with **Trans Unificada** (C Manuel Bustillos 683 y Av Kollasuyo in the Cementerio district, T02-238 1693); also **Perla del Illampu** (Manuel Bustillos 615, T02-238 0548), US$2.50, 3½ hrs. Booking recommended on Fri. In Sorata they leave from C Samuel Tejerina, near the exit to La Paz. To or from **Copacabana** and **Peru**, change buses at Huarina but they are often full so start early and be prepared for a long wait.

Jeep

Jeeps run from La Paz (C Chorolque y Tarapacá, T02-245 0296, often full), via Sorata to **Santa Rosa** (US$15, 13 hrs), on the road to **Mapiri** and Guanay, a rough route with interesting vegetation and stunning scenery. Onward transport can be found in Santa Rosa. From Guanay private boats may be arranged to **Rurrenabaque**, and vehicles run to Caranavi and thence to Coroico.

Motorcycle

Sorata–Coroico by this route is excellent for off-road motorcycling. (See also Cycling, page 115.) If travelling by public transport it is easier to go La Paz–Coroico–Caranavi–Guanay–Santa Rosa–Sorata–La Paz, than vice versa.

Cordillera Apolobamba

North of Lake Titicaca and the Cordillera Real, near the Peruvian border, is the remote Cordillera Apolobamba. This is a wild land of incomparable natural beauty and home to the famed Kallawayas, Bolivia's ancient medicine men. You may hardly see another soul during a trek in this area, and the few that you do see might not speak Spanish as their first language. Here condors soar over the mountains, herds of vicuña run free and even the endangered spectacled bear occasionally makes an appearance.

The Cordillera Apolobamba stretches from Charazani north to Pelechuco and then on into Peru. The area has its own park, Area Natural de Manejo Integrado Nacional Apolobamba (ANMINA), more commonly known as the Area Protegida Apolobamba.

La Paz to Charazani *Colour map 2, B2-A1.*

scenic mountain route

Access to the Cordillera Apolobamba is via the northeast side of Lake Titicaca. From La Paz the road passes through Achacachi, Ancoraimes, Puerto Carabuco and Escoma. At Escoma it branches: northwest to Puerto Acosta (page 95); and north to Charazani (see below). The road is very scenic, climbing to 4500 m.

Charazani *Colour map 2, A1.*

With a population of 9950, Charazani (official name **Villa Juan J Pérez**) is the largest village in the region. At 3200 m it is noticeably warmer than La Paz and there are **thermal baths** ① by the river 10 mins below the village, US$0.75. Another local attraction is a three-day fiesta around 16 July, which is famous for having some of the best highland music, native costumes and non-stop dancing. There are basic places to stay (see Where to stay, below), some small shops and eateries around

ON THE ROAD
Saving the vicuña

The vicuña is the smallest representative of the South American camelids. It resembles the guanaco but is smaller and more slender and has a relatively long neck. They are strictly territorial, living in small herds of eight to 12, led by a single male. Young males are expelled from the breeding herd when eight to 10 months old and live together in bachelor groups often 100 strong. Their territorial boundaries are aggressively defended by the dominant male, which attacks intruders by biting or by spitting regurgitated food.

Vicuña wool is the finest and lightest in the world. During Inca times only royalty were allowed to wear vicuña robes. Vicuña refuse to breed in captivity and so have never been domesticated. However, they are rounded up once a year by some Andean communities and shorn for their wool. Unfortunately they are also hunted, despite the fact that it is illegal to do so.

Estimates suggest there were more than one million vicuñas in Bolivia during pre-Inca times. The first laws to protect vicuñas were passed in 1918, but by the 1950s numbers were down to 400,000 and in 1965 just 6000 were left. In 1965 there were 97 vicuñas in the area now covered by the Apolobamba reserve. There are now more than 10,000.

The vicuña protection programme in Apolobamba aims to provide local communities with a much-needed source of income from wool and textiles and, at the same time, help save this endangered species.

the plaza. In the plaza you'll also find an Entel office with sporadic telephone and internet service. There is also a medical post in the village.

From Charazani one road descends along steep river valleys to **Apolo** (population 13,600) in the subtropical valleys to the east, and another makes its roundabout way to the villages of **Lagunillas**, **Curva** and **Cañisaya**.

Listings La Paz to Charazani

Where to stay

There are also 2 basic residenciales, both $, both on the road to Curva: **Charazani** and **Inti Wasi**.

$ Hotel Akhamani
A block downhill from the plaza.
Clean rooms, some with private bath (cheaper with shared bath), small garden, parking, best in town.

Transport

Bus From La Paz Trans Altiplano (C Reyes Cardona 732, T02-283 0859, the more reliable of the 2 companies) and **Trans Provincias del Norte** (C Reyes Cardona 772, T02-238 2239), both near Cancha Tejar in the Cemetery district, daily, US$3.50, 8 hrs; check all departure times in advance as they change frequently. Return from Charazani around 1800. Also buses to Apolo (several a day from the same street in the Cemetery district) can drop you off at the crossroad just outside Charazani, but there may be no seats available back to La Paz.

Pelechuco *Colour map 2, A1.*

a base for trekking in the beautiful Area Protegida

Pelechuco (population 5400, altitude 3600 m) is set in the steep valley of the river of the same name on the eastern side of the Cordillera Apolobamba, bordered to the north by the snow-capped peaks of the Katantica and Matchu Suchi Cuchu mountain groups. The village's name comes from the Quechua puyu kuchu which means 'cloudy corner'. Founded in 1560, Pelechuco has a fine stone church and a few other colonial buildings. The main economic activity of the surrounding area is gold mining.

The village is basic, but there is a public phone on the plaza (ask around), electricity and a medical post which is often staffed. Shops and cafés selling and serving the basics are also found around the plaza. The biggest fiesta is held on the week around 25 July to celebrate the founding of the village, but there are fiestas every month, all of which are enthusiastically supported.

Buses to and from Pelechuco pass through the Area Protegida Apolobamba. The journey through the Río Pelechuco valley is spectacular and well worth doing in daylight. At night the journey across the altiplano in unheated buses can be bitterly cold, so dress as warmly as possible and also take your sleeping bag onto the bus. If you are returning from Pelechuco by private transport, you can visit the **Putina thermal baths**, two hours by jeep from Pelechuco near **Antaquilla**, followed by a daylight trip through the vicuña reserve of the Area Protegida Apolobamba.

Listings Pelechuco

Where to stay

$ Llajtaymanta on the plaza
T7195 3252 (La Paz).
2 nice rooms at the back share a hot shower, cheaper and simpler rooms with shared tepid electric shower. Basic meals may be available on request. Owner Reynaldo Vásquez is knowledgeable about the area and can organize trekking guides, etc.

Transport

From La Paz Trans Provincias del Norte, from Ex-Tranca de Río Seco in El Alto, most days, US$5, 10-12 hrs, via **Qutapampa** (7 hrs), **Ulla Ulla** and **Agua Blanca.** Tickets sometimes go on sale 24 hrs before departure at their office in the Cemetery district (see above). Return to La Paz from Pelechuco between 2400 and 0400 most days. Check all times in advance.

ON THE ROAD

Healers of the Andes

When a Bolivian is ill, he or she may be more likely to pay a visit to the local *curandero* (healer) than arrange an appointment with a doctor. In rural areas in particular, Western medicine is seen only as a last resort.

Traditional medicine is an integral part of Andean culture and, unlike Western practices, takes into account the patient's own perceptions of his or her illness and emotional condition. Healers believe that physical illnesses originate from the soul and are caused by the *ajaya* (life force) leaving the body. The healer's job is to coax the *ajaya* back into the body and restore the mind/body equilibrium.

The stars of Bolivian traditional medicine are the Kallawayas, the famous travelling healers of the Andes. With their bag of herbs, roots, ointments and amulets, the Kallawayas travel the length and breadth of the Andes from Ecuador to Argentina, dispensing spiritual wisdom and natural remedies.

Curiously, the Kallawayas all hail from the same region, a group of six small villages in the Apolobamba Mountains. Why this should be the case is something of a mystery, though one theory is that they are descendants of the Tiahuanaco culture. Something like a quarter of the residents of these villages are believed to possess considerable knowledge and healing powers. The Kallawayas' travels have given them access to and knowledge of as many as 1000 plants and herbs.

The Kallawayas pass their knowledge on to their sons, or occasionally apprentices. Women are traditionally not allowed to become Kallawayas, though they play an essential role as midwives and as healers of the female reproductive system.

Renewed interest in natural medicine has helped preserve the Kallawaya tradition, which was in danger of disappearing.

Area Protegida Apolobamba

one of Bolivia's many 'must see' parks

★The Area Protegida Apolobamba is next door to the western edge of Parque Nacional Madidi. Now at 483,744 ha, it is one of the few parks that has expanded in size. Created in 1972, it was named by UNESCO as a unique habitat in 1977, then re-named Reserva Nacional de Fauna de Ulla Ulla in 1983, before assuming its current designation in 1999. Established specifically to help preserve dwindling herds of vicuña, the reserve is also home to the more domesticated alpaca and llama.

Although remote, the Area Protegida Apolobamba is not all that difficult to reach. Located 180 km northwest of La Paz, it is on the road to Pelechuco, which has bus service most days. There are small communities within the reserve's borders, including **Hilo Hilo**, **Ulla Ulla** and **Pelechuco**. The official entrance, which is still free, is at La Cabaña (see below), just north of Ulla Ulla. Alternatively, you can simply get off the buses that run between Pelechuco and La Paz (they run through the southwest sector of the park) at one of the entry trails outside of Pelechuco in **Qutapampa**, **Soropata** or **Agua Blanca**. The park's western border is the international frontier with Peru, which, in addition to being a key ecological transition zone, makes it a politically strategic area.

Visiting the park

The reserve headquarters are at La Cabaña, 5 km outside the village of Ulla Ulla, where orphaned vicuñas are reared. For more information contact **SERNAP** ⓘ *Federico Suazo 1913, La Paz, T02-211 2149.*

Apolobamba is well known for its scenic beauty, owing to its impressive array of snow-capped mountains, crystal-clear lakes and glaciers (the impressive Chaupi Orcko is one of the largest intact glaciers on earth). The area is made up of several ecological zones, ranging from the mountainous and cold Cordillera Apolobamba to humid grasslands and subtropical Yungas. It also boasts the Cela rainforest, one of the most intact in South America.

Apolobamba is popular with trekkers, either travelling independently, with local community guides or with agencies from La Paz. The people of the area are therefore accustomed to seeing foreigners but not all villages are equally friendly. Responsible travel is especially important here, to protect both the natural and cultural environments.

There is much to see and do in the park. If you have your own transport, the wild vicuña herds can be observed at close range. During the day, especially in the dry season, the vicuñas graze in the marshy areas, in among the alpacas, but towards evening, when their domesticated cousins return home to their stone-walled corrals, the vicuñas wander off to more isolated pastures. It's a particularly beautiful sight to see these graceful animals grazing on the plains at dawn against a backdrop of snowy peaks.

This is also a primary habitat for condor, the national bird, and you may be fortunate to see flamingos during their winter migration. The terrain and altitude make it a trekker's paradise, although its primary purpose remains to preserve wildlife.

Trekking in the Cordillera Apolobamba

high mountain scenery rich in wildlife

Apolobamba South Trek

This four- to six-day mountain trek from Charazani or Curva/Lagunillas to Pelechuco is probably the best in Bolivia, passing through traditional villages and then up into the mountains of the southern Cordillera Apolobamba. The trek may also be done in the opposite direction, starting in Pelechuco, which allows you to enjoy the thermal baths outside Charazani at the end of the walk.

There is a local population between Charazani, Curva and Cañisaya, but further north you are unlikely to see more than a few people a day, often miners en route to and from their camps. For the few people there are, their first language is usually Quechua followed by Aymara and then Spanish.

The usual route is as follows: **Day 1** Charazani to beyond Curva. **Day 2** Curva to Incacancha. **Day 3** Incacancha to Sunchuli. **Day 4** Sunchuli to above Hilo Hilo. **Day 5** Hilo Hilo to Pelechuco. This trek is described in detail in *Trekking in Bolivia* by Yossi Brain (The Mountaineers, 1998). The northern part of the route is covered by Bolivian IGM sheet 3041 'Pelechuco', at 1:100,000. This map is hard to find but it does exist, try the kiosks inside the main La Paz post office.

Guides and pack animals can be hired at the hostels in Lagunillas (just outside Curva; see Where to stay, below) or Agua Blanca (5 km from Pelechuco). Guides, cooks and muleteers all charge about US$10 per day; pack animals cost US$8 per day. Each guide can look after a maximum of five trekkers, each muleteer maximum three animals; you must provide food for all your staff. In principle, anyone wishing to undertake the trek must be accompanied by a local guide recognized by the Apolobamba Eco-Tourism Association.

Pacha Trek

This four-day trek is offered as part of a community ecotourism project between three indigenous communities, of both Aymara and Quechua origin, with a focus on both the cultural and natural attractions of Apolobamba. Starting in Qutapampa, on the road from Charazani to Pelechuco, the route descends to Kaluyo before continuing on to Chacarapi, and finally to Charazani.

A walk of three to four hours each morning through spectacular scenery, accompanied by local guides, is followed by an afternoon of activities in the host community. Each village has an interpretive centre highlighting a different aspect of the area, from the national park and the vicuña protection program, to the Kallawaya, the herbal medicine men of the Andes and their natural remedies. There are opportunities to experience the music and dance of the area as well to take part in Kallawaya ceremonies, visit local alpaca farmers, village schools and handicraft centres where traditional weavings can be purchased.

Other treks

The Apolobamba region offers a great many other opportunities for independent self-sufficient trekkers, some of which are described in *Trekking in Bolivia* (see above). In addition to the above, there is virtually unlimited scope for exploration.

Where to stay

Apolobamba South Trek

$ Community Hostels
At Lagunillas (300 m from Curva) and Agua Blanca (5 km from Pelechuco).
Ample comfortable hostels with dorm acommodation, solar-heated showers (sometimes work), cooking facilities or meals on advance request. Guides and pack animals can be arranged.

Pacha Trek

$ Community Hostels
At Qutapampa, Kaluyo and Chacarapi.
Dorm accommodation.

What to do

La Paz on Foot, *contact Stephen Taranto, T7154 3918, www.lapazonfoot.com.*

US$160-325 depending on group size for Pacha Trek; other treks offered.
Reynaldo Vásquez, *see Llajtaymanta hostel in Pelechuco, above.*
All 6 agencies listed under La Paz, What to do, Climbing, hiking and trekking, offer trekking trips to Apolobamba (see page 64).

Transport

Bus

To make the Apolobamba South Trek a day shorter, some **Trans Altiplano** buses continue past Charazani 1½-2 hrs to **Lagunillas** and **Curva**. Schedules change constantly, enquire with the company office in La Paz.

The Yungas

Only a few hours from La Paz are the Yungas. These steep-sided, forested subtropical valleys are squeezed in between the high Cordillera and the vast green carpet of jungle that stretches east, providing a welcome escape from the breathless chill of the capital as well as a convenient stopping point on the arduous overland route to the jungle.

The comfortably warm climate of the Yungas is ideal for growing citrus fruit, bananas, coffee and coca leaves. The town of Coroico, in the Nor Yungas, is a favourite with visitors and the old road that winds its tortuous way down from the high mountains has achieved near-legendary status in South American travelling lore as 'the most dangerous in the world'. There is also a newer paved road, but many tourists opt for two wheels on gravel rather than four on asphalt, for the terrifying and spectacular 64-km downhill ride. For those who prefer using their own two feet, there are also several popular trekking routes from La Paz to the Yungas (see page 47). The lovely little town of Chulumani, in the Sud Yungas, is an equally attractive alternative and is a centre of both coca production and Afro-Bolivian culture.

a 3500-m drop to the green subtropical forest in 70 km

The roads from La Paz to Nor- and Sud-Yungas go via La Cumbre, a pass at 4725 m about one hour northeast of the city. The road out of La Paz circles cloudwards over La Cumbre; all around are towering snow-capped peaks.

The first village after the pass is **Unduavi**, where there is a checkpoint, a petrol station and roadside stalls. Beyond Unduavi an unpaved road branches right 75 km to Chulumani and the Sud-Yungas. Beyond Sud-Yungas, to the southeast, are the Yungas de Inquisivi, see Quime, page 135. The paved road continues to Cotapata, where it again divides: right is the old unpaved road to Yolosa, the junction 8 km from Coroico (this is the popular cycling route). To the left, the new paved road goes via Chuspipata and Puente Yolosita, where an unpaved road climbs steeply to Coroico. Between Yolosita and Yolosa (see below) is **Senda Verde** ⓘ *T7472 2825, www.sendaverde.com, open 1000-1700*, an animal refuge, ecolodge and restaurant with opportunities for volunteering. In addition, from Puente Villa on the Unduavi–Chulumani road, an unpaved road runs to Coripata and Coroico. For the La Cumbre–Coroico hike (Choro), see page 49.

For the La Cumbre–Coroico hike (Choro), see page 49.

Essential The Yungas

Getting around

Transport to the Yungas leaves La Paz from the Minasa Terminal in Villa Fátima. Services are mostly provided by minibus, which fan out to smaller communities from the main towns. There are also shared taxis. Onward travel to the jungle lowlands may mean finding a seat on an already full bus.

When to go

Subtropical, warm and damp all year, with most rain December to March. May to September are the drier months, but it can often be misty. High season is July to September.

Time required

A couple of days if on a down-and-up trip from La Paz, otherwise two to four days in Coroico, four or five days if visiting more than one town.

★All roads to Coroico drop some 3500 m to the green subtropical forest in 70 km. The best views are from May to June, when there is less chance of fog and rain. The old road, the so-called 'World's Most Dangerous Road', is steep, twisting, clinging to the side of sheer cliffs and slippery in the wet. It is a breathtaking descent (best not to look over the edge if you don't like heights) and its reputation for danger is more than matched by the beauty of the scenery. Many tourists go on a mountain-bike tour: it is your responsibility to choose top-quality bikes (with hydraulic disc brakes) and a reputable company which offers bilingual guides, helmet, gloves, vehicle support throughout the day (see La Paz, Tour operators, page 64). Many bike companies take riders back to La Paz the same day, but Coroico is worth more of your time. In Yolosa, at the end of the bike ride, is a three-segment zipline (total 1555 m) operated by **Gravity Bolivia** (see page 65 and www.

ON THE ROAD

The most dangerous road in the world?

Yes, it's true. The journey from La Paz to Coroico must be one of the most impressive in all Bolivia. It is also genuinely dangerous, an absolute must for adrenalin junkies but a definite no-no for those of a more nervous disposition. Beginning at La Cumbre, a mountain pass above La Paz at 4725 m where there is often snow, the bike ride drops more than 3600 m in around four hours and 64 km to the subtropical jungle by Yolosa, below Coroico. For most of this route the road is little more than a bumpy, rocky ledge carved into the rock face of the mountains, through streams and under waterfalls and often with a sheer drop of as much as 1000 m on the left-hand side. Almost every turn of the road seems to be punctuated with crosses for those that have died there. Into this mix should be added drivers who think nothing of the odd tipple or two before they set out and trucks who stop for nobody.

The claim that this counts as the most dangerous road in the world originally came from Inter-American Development Bank in 1995. Whether or not it still has genuine claim to the statistic, the biggest single road accident in history apparently happened here in the 1980s, when a lorry packed with almost 100 *campesinos* plunged over the edge.

The worrying accident rate can't be helped by the fact that, according to Bolivian road law, the vehicle going downhill should keep to the outside of the road, closest to the drop. (The opposite is the case however on the new paved road, drivers take note!)

Similarly, while hurtling downhill on two wheels trying not to look at the view, all your instincts will scream to keep away from the edge as a mammoth truck trundles up the road toward you.

Once you have done it, the dangers of the road to Coroico seem far outweighed by the thrill of the journey. The views are magnificent as you descend from the snows of the Cordillera to the humid subtropics. Not forgetting the considerable delights of Coroico itself. After a couple of days relaxing by the pool, enjoying a cold beer and the scenery, this trip won't seem so bad. Until of course, it's time to go back.

ziplinebolivia.com; T02-231 3849 or book through La Paz agencies). The road is especially dangerous when it is raining (mid-December to mid-February); be sure the bike is in top shape and be extra cautious.

Cotapata National Park

This tiny (583-sq-km) park is located just 20 km northeast of La Paz on a paved road. The old road from La Cumbre to Coroico passes through it (there is a US$3.55 community tax to pay), as do part of the Choro Trail (page 49) and the Takesi Trail (page 48).

The park is especially well known for its wealth of medicinal plants and vegetation. For such a small area, it has amazing biological diversity, with more than 1800 identified species and still others as yet unclassified.

As popular as it is, even given its proximity to La Paz, Cotapata is still largely unregulated and has no infrastructure, or accommodation. For further information contact SERNAP in Sopocachi, La Paz (page 351).

Coroico and Nor-Yungas *Colour map 2, B2.*

a good base for exploring the Yungas

The little town of Coroico (population 2903, altitude 1750 m), capital of the Nor-Yungas region, is perched on a hill amid beautiful scenery. The hillside is covered with orange and banana groves and coffee plantations. Coroico is a first-class place to relax with several good walks. A colourful four-day festival is held 19-22 October. On 2 November, All Souls' Day, the cemetery is festooned with black ribbons.

Coroico

Where to stay
1 Bella Vista
2 Don Quijote
3 El Cafetal
4 El Viejo Molino
5 Esmeralda
6 Gloria
8 Hostal Kory
10 Los Silbos
11 Matsu
12 Residencial de la Torre
13 Sol y Luna

Restaurants
1 Carla's Garden Pub & Pastelaería Aleman Back-stube
2 Bamboos
3 Pizzeria Italia

A good walk is up to the waterfalls, starting from **El Calvario**. Follow the stations of the cross by the cemetery, off Calle Julio Zuazo Cuenca, which leads steeply uphill from the plaza. Facing the chapel at El Calvario, with your back to the town, look for the path on your left. This leads to the falls which are the town's water supply (Toma de Agua) and, beyond, to two more falls. **Cerro Uchumachi**, the mountain behind El Calvario, can be climbed following the same stations of the cross, but then look for the faded red and white antenna behind the chapel. From there it's about two hours' steep walk to the top (take water). A third walk goes to the pools in the **Río Vagante**, 7 km off the road to Coripata; it takes about three hours. With the Yungas so close to La Paz, you get the chance to see the production of crops which cannot be grown at high altitude and some farms welcome visitors to their fruit, coffee or coca leaf plantations. In the interests of personal safety, women in particular should not hike alone in this area. There is a Banco Unión ATM on the plaza and the hospital is the best in the Yungas.

Caranavi

From the junction at Puente Yolosita, the paved road follows the river 11 km to Santa Bárbara, then becomes gravel for 65 km to Caranavi (population 21,883, altitude 600 m), an uninspiring town 156 km from La Paz. If staying overnight to wait for a bus, the plaza is pleasant enough for a stroll and there are good views from the bridge over the river. From here the road continues towards the settled area of the Alto Beni, at times following a picturesque gorge. Market days are Friday and Saturday. There is a range of hotels and *alojamientos* and buses from La Paz (Villa Fátima) to Rurrenabaque pass through. Paving of the road to Caranavi is due by end-2015. Beyond Caranavi, 70 km, is **Guanay** at the junction of the Tipuani and Mapiri rivers. When water levels allow, the Río Mapiri is navigable by motorized canoe upriver as far as Mapiri and downriver to Rurrenabaque and beyond. With increased road travel, however, there is no longer any regular public transport anywhere along the river, but this is becoming a popular route for tour companies taking people from Sorata to Rurrenabaque, or to La Paz. (Basic lodging in Guanay; see also under Sorata, page 100, What to do). The Caranavi–Guanay road is also scheduled to be improved.

Listings Coroico and Nor-Yungas

Tourist information

Tourist information
Gobernación, corner of the main plaza.
A good independent website is www.coroico.info.

Where to stay

Hotel rooms are hard to find at holiday weekends and prices are higher.

$$$-$$ El Viejo Molino
T02-278 3269 (Av 14 de Septiembre 4620, Obrajes, La Paz), www.hotelviejomolino.com.
2 km on road to Caranavi. Upmarket

hotel and spa with pool, gym, jacuzzi, games room, restaurant with set menu lunch and dinner.

$$$-$$ Gloria
C Kennedy 1, T02-289 5554,
www.hotelgloria.com.bo.
Traditional resort hotel, full board, pool, restaurant with set lunches and à la carte, internet, free transport from the plaza.

$$ Esmeralda
on the edge of town, 10 mins uphill from plaza (see website for transport), T02-213 6017, www.hotelesmeralda.com.
Most rooms include breakfast, cheaper in dorms, prices rise at weekends, hot showers, satellite TV and DVD, book exchange, good buffet restaurant, sauna, garden, pool, camping, can arrange local tours and transport to/from La Paz, free pick-up from Coroico bus stop or plaza.

$$ Sol y Luna
Apanto Alto, 15-20 mins beyond Hotel Esmeralda, T7156 1626, La Paz contact: Maison de la Bolivie, 6 de Agosto 2464, Ed Jardines, T244 0588, www.solyluna-bolivia.com.
Excellent accommodation in fully equipped cabins, apartments and rooms with and without bath, splendid views, restaurant (vegetarian specialities), camping US$5 pp (not suitable for cars), garden, pool, hot tub US$11.50, shiatsu massage and yoga available, good value, Sigrid (owner) speaks English, French, German, Spanish.

$$-$ Bella Vista
C Héroes del Chaco 7 (2 blocks from main plaza), T02-213 6059, www. coroicobellavista.blogspot.com.
Beautiful rooms and views, includes

breakfast, cheaper without bath, 2 racquetball courts, terrace, bike hire, restaurant, pool.

$$-$ Hostal Kory
at top of steps leading down from the plaza, T02-243 1234/7156 4050, info@hostalkory.com.
Rooms with shared bath are cheaper, electric showers, restaurant, huge pool, terrace, good value but basic, helpful.

$ Don Quijote
500 m out of town, on road to Coripata, T02-213 6007, hoteldonquijote@hotmail.com.
Economical, electric shower, pool, quiet, nice views.

$ El Cafetal
Miranda, 10-min walk from town, T7193 3979, http://elcafetal.coroico.info.
Rooms with and without bath, very nice, great views, restaurant with excellent French/Indian/vegetarian cuisine, French-run, a good choice.

$ Los Silbos
Iturralde 4043, T7350 0081/7199 7818.
Cheap simple rooms with shared bath, electric showers, good value.

$ Matsu
1 km from town on road to El Calvario (call for free pick-up, taxi US$2), T7069 2219, ecolodgematsu@hotmail.com.
Economical, has restaurant, pool, views, quiet, helpful.

$ Residencial de la Torre
Julio Zuazo Cuenca, ½ block from plaza, T02-289 5542.
Welcoming place with courtyard, cheap sparse rooms, no alcoholic drinks allowed.

Restaurants

$$ Bamboos
Iturralde y Ortiz.
Good Mexican food and pleasant
atmosphere, live music some nights with
cover charge. Happy hour 1800-1900.

**$$-$ Carla's Garden Pub and
Pastelería Alemana Back-stube**
*Pasaje Adalid Linares, 50 m from the
main plaza, T7207 5620. Wed-Thu 1200-
2300, Fri-Sat 1200-0200, Sun 1200-2100.*
Sandwiches, snacks, pasta and
international food, vegetarian options,
German dishes, coffee, groups catered
for. Lots of music, live music at weekends.
Garden, hammocks, games, terrace with
panoramic views, nice atmosphere.

$ Pizzería Italia
*2 with same name on the plaza.
Daily 1000-2300.*
Pizza, pasta, snacks.

What to do

Coffee production
Café Munaipata, *Camino a Carmen
Pampa Km 4, T7204 2824, www.
cafemunaipata.com.* Visits to a finca
producing high-altitude coffee.
Recommended. They also have an
outlet in La Paz, **MagicK**, Presbiterio
Medina 2526, Sopocachi, T7755 3535,
MagickCafe on Facebook.

Cycling
CXC, *T7157 3015, cxc_mtb@yahoo.com,
www.cxccoroico.lobopages.com.* Contact
2 days in advance by phone or email.
Good bikes, US$25 for 6 hrs including
packed lunch, a bit disorganized but
good fun and helpful, English and
German spoken.

Horse riding
El Relincho, *Don Reynaldo, T7191 3675,
100 m past Hotel Esmeralda (enquire here).*
Rides from 2 hrs to 2 days; average price
US$30 for 4 hrs.

Language classes
Siria León Domínguez, *T7195 5431.*
US$5 per hr, also rents rooms and makes
silver jewellery, excellent English.

Transport

Bus From La Paz all companies are at
Minasa terminal, Puente Minasa, in Villa
Fátima: minibuses and buses (less often)
leave throughout the day US$3-4.50,
2½ hrs on the paved road: **Turbus Totaí,
Palmeras, Yungueña** and several others.
Services return to La Paz from the small
terminal down the hill in Coroico, across
from the fooball field. All are heavily
booked at weekends and on holidays.

To **Rurrenabaque**: take a pick-up
from the small mirador at Pacheco
y Sagárnaga go to **Puente Yolosita**,
15 mins, US$0.70. Here you can try to
catch a bus, but they are usually full. Ask
at **Turbus Totaí** or others in the Coroico
terminal if you can reserve a seat to Rurre
(US$9). There are also *trufis* (US$3.25) and
trucks from Yolosita to **Caranavi**, where
La Paz–Rurre buses pass through in the
evening, often full. After Caranavi the
road goes to Sapecho and then Yucumo,
from where *trufis* go to Rurre. Caranavi–
Rurre 12 hrs minimum, US$7, **Flota
Yungueña**, at 1800-1900, **Turbus Totaí**
2100-2200, and others. See also Gravity
and **Deep Rainforest**, La Paz (page 65).
For Guanay to **Sorata** via **Mapiri** and
Santa Rosa, see page 99.

Coroico to Chulumani

There is no direct bus service between the two main centres of the Nor- and Sud-Yungas. You can take a bus from Coroico to La Paz and get off at Unduavi, not far from La Cumbre, and then wait for the next bus from La Paz to Chulumani – hoping it will have room. Alternatively, it is possible to travel from Coroico to Chulumani via the mining town of **Coripata** (population 12,400, basic *alojamientos*). Taxis from Coroico to Coripata charge about US$40, negotiable, and there may be buses passing through from La Paz, enquire locally. This has also been recommended as a cycling route. From Coripata there are a couple of buses daily to La Paz via **Puente Villa**, where you can change to a bus from La Paz to Chulumani.

> **Tip...**
> There is no ATM in Chulumani; take cash.

To Chulumani and Sud-Yungas from La Paz

The road from Unduavi to Chulumani is less nerve-wracking than the road to Coroico, but nevertheless is a scenically rewarding trip following the steep-sided valley of the Río Unduavi. Along the way is the beautiful **Velo de la Novia** (Bridal Veil) waterfall (views from the left side of the bus). The first settlement after Unduavi is **Chaco**, which is 1 km before the end of La Reconquistada Trail (see page 48). Here are several hiking trails to waterfalls and a suspension bridge over the river. A few kilometres further on is Florida, where a signed dirt road turns off to the right to the attractive colonial village of Yanacachi.

Yanacachi

This tiny colonial village (population 4400) is the ideal place to get away from it all. It lies at the end of the Takesi Trail (page 48). Yanacachi stands in a commanding position overlooking two major river valleys and there are great views over the village and surrounding areas from the bell tower of the village church, one of the oldest in the Yungas, dating from the 16th century. It has a couple of *alojamientos*, **Tommy** (T7308 1291), and **Hostal Takesi** (T7371 3586, see yanacachi on Facebook).

Yanacachi also offers various activities and several small hiking trails. You can help out in the local orphanage for the day, enquire at **Fundación Pueblo** ① *on the plaza, T02-212 4413, www.fundacionpueblo.org, daily 0800-1230, 1430-1830,* which also has maps and local information. The foundation itself is interesting for its community development programmes to prevent people migrating to the cities in search of jobs. You can hike the three-hour trail down to the river and swim in one of the delightful pools below the waterfall. Or, from the northeast side of Yanacachi, you can walk the one-hour prehispanic trail down to **Sakha Waya**.

You can also hike the often-ignored final day of the Takesi Trail. From the bottom of Yanacachi, this prehispanic trail continues on the south side of the ridge, past several small ruins and communities, and Villa Aspiazu, to the crossroads settlement of **Puente Villa**.

Chulumani

The main road goes through **Puente Villa**, where the above-mentioned road runs north to Coroico through Coripata. The capital of Sud Yungas is Chulumani, a small town (population 3650, altitude 1750 m), 124 km from La Paz, with beautiful views across the valley to the forest of Apa Apa and the villages of Chicaloma and Irupana. There are many coca plantations in the area. There are many birds in the area. The **Fiesta de San Bartolomé** (24 August) lasts 10 days and there is a lively market every weekend when Afro-Bolivians come dressed in traditional costume. **Tourist office** ⓘ *in the main plaza, open irregular hours, mostly weekends.*

Near Chulumani is the village of **Sikilini**, which is at the end of the Yunga Cruz Trail (see page 49).

Chulumani

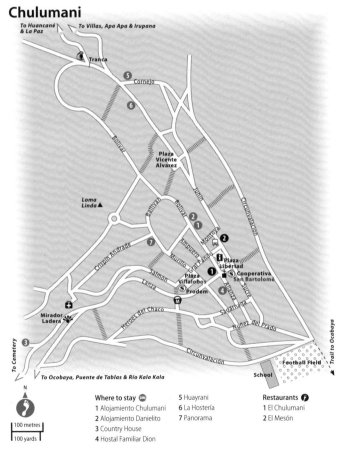

Where to stay 🛏	Restaurants 🍴
1 Alojamiento Chulumani	1 El Chulumani
2 Alojamiento Danielito	2 El Mesón
3 Country House	
4 Hostal Familiar Dion	
5 Huayrani	
6 La Hostería	
7 Panorama	

From Africa to the Yungas

One of the more incongruous sights in the tropical Yungas are the black *cholas*, women of African origin wearing the traditional Aymara bowler hat and pollera skirts. Some 17,000 descendants of black African slaves live in Bolivia. Originally from Angola and the Congo, they were brought via Peru and Argentina to work in the silver mines of Potosí. But they could not adapt to the harsh climate 4000 m up on the altiplano and were subsequently moved to the Yungas to work on coca plantations.

Slaves that spoke the same language were separated to prevent them conspiring against their owners. But they learned Spanish and developed a dialect that could not be understood by the colonial rulers or indigenous people. Bolivian blacks still speak these dialects, which include African words. Many of them also speak Aymara.

Slavery was officially abolished in the 1850s but it was not until a century later, after the 1952 revolution, that the lives of Afro-Bolivians began to change. Many have migrated to the lowlands in the department of Santa Cruz. Others remain in small communities like Tocaña, Mururata and Chijchipa in Nor-Yungas, and especially Chicaloma in Sud-Yungas.

Today, Afro-Bolivians represent less than 1% of the country's population. They have, however, made their mark on the nation's culture. La Morenada is one of the most famous of Bolivia's folkloric dances, performed at the Oruro carnival and many other festivals. In it, dancers wear masks to represent black slaves and caricature their bosses. More recently, the Saya, an Afro-Bolivian dance originally from Chicaloma, has become nationally and internationally famous.

Hikes from Chulumani

There are many day walks from Chulumani. **El Paraíso** is a one-hour trek. Take the left road up from the hospital. After 30 minutes you come to a tennis club (left) and water tanks (right). Climb up to the right here on any one of the many paths for a 20-minute detour to **Loma Linda**, a large cross with 180-degree views over the valleys. Otherwise continue along the path 20 minutes more through a pine forest until you fork right, about 300 m before La Granja, a former Jesuit mission that is now an agricultural school run by the army. After five or 10 minutes the road ends at El Paraíso where trails lead into cloudforest. From here it's a three-hour hike (it is best to have a guide) to **Chirca**, a 500-year-old village with a Spanish feel, a sanctuary church and a setting high on the ridge with great views. From Chirca it's a half-hour walk down to the main road, where you can take an afternoon bus back to Chulumani.

To get to **Río Kala Kala**, take the lower road at the Mirador Ladera and down to the Puente de Tablas, downstream from here there are natural swimming pools and forest.

Another hike is to the village of **Ocabaya**, to visit its ancient church. Ocabaya is also where the 1952 revolution began. From the football field at the southeast end of Chulumani, a trail leads to the Río Misquimayo and then up to Hacienda Tiquimpaya, 1 km from Ocabaya. The hike takes 2½ hours. For all these trips carry plenty of water, a packed lunch and start early as it gets pretty hot and dry in the valleys.

Apa Apa Ecological Park
5 km from town on road to Irupana, then walk 20 mins uphill from turn-off, or taxi from Chulumani US$3.50, T7254 7770, La Paz T02-213 9640, apapayungas@hotmail.com.

The main road to Irupana passes the turn-off to Apa Apa, a protected forest of 800 ha. This is the last original subtropical Yungas forest in the area with plenty of interesting wildlife, such as small deer, agoutis, hoachi, nocturnal monkeys and many birds including parrots and hummingbirds. Even porcupines, pumas and the rare Andean spectacled bear are sometimes seen here. The flora includes many orchids and giant leche-leche trees which have a small 'cave' in the trunk.

The park is managed by Ramiro Portugal and his US-born wife, Tildi. Ramiro was born locally and knows the area well; he also speaks English. Their home is an 18th-century hacienda that runs as a working dairy farm and has simple accommodation for two or three people ($ private bath, hot water, delicious meals available, home-made ice cream, pool). Near the house is a campsite with bathrooms and campers can buy food from the farm. There are hiking trails in the park. Day trips can be arranged including transport and a guide.

Irupana
This friendly little colonial village (altitude 1900 m, irupana.bolivia on Facebook), is 31 km east of Chulmani (minibus or shared taxi US$2) and has a lovely location, delightful climate, more good walking and birdwatching, and a couple of very nice places to stay. Three hours beyond Irupana by truck (one leaves twice a week – check in advance for times) are the seldom-visited Inca ruins and terraces of **Pastogrande** with a beautiful river flowing below.

Another road to Irupana goes via the village of Ocabaya (2½ hours away, see above), also passing through the Afro-Bolivian community of **Chicaloma**, where the Saya, a traditional and now famous Afro-Bolivian dance, was born (see box, page 118). This village hosts its Santísima Trinidad festival on 16 July and you can see the dancing at its Corpus Christi celebrations in late May. This road is less direct and used less often, and transport from the tranca in Chulumani is infrequent, so ask around.

From Irupana an unmade road goes to Quime (see page 135), via Circuata, Licoma, Iquisivi and the Yungas of that name.

Chulumani

Chulumani suffers from water shortages, check if your hotel has a reserve tank.

$ Country House
400 m out of town on road to cemetery, T7528 2212, La Paz T02-274 5584, countryhouse.chulumani on Facebook.
With electric shower, lovely tranquil setting, pool and gardens, library, breakfast and other home-cooked meals available, family-run. Enthusiastic owner Xavier Sarabia is hospitable and offers hiking advice and tours, English spoken.

$ Hostal Familiar Dion
Alianza, ½ block below plaza, T02-289 6034.
Cheaper without bath, electric shower, very well maintained, restaurant, attentive.

$ Huayrani
Junín y Cornejo, uphill from centre near bus stops, T02-213 6351/7658 6486.
Electric shower, nice views, pool, parking.

$ Tarapari
On the outskirts, 10 mins' walk from centre, T7154 3918, www.tarapari.org.
Guesthouse in a biodiversity garden, butterfly sanctuary and organic coffee farm, 3 rooms, shared bath, price is per person, breakfast included, use of kitchen extra, also tours, workshops and treks. Base of **La Paz on Foot**'s Sud Yungas tours (see www.lapazonfoot.com and La Paz, What to do, page 66).

Irupana

$ Bougainville Hotel
Near the centre of town, T02-213 6155.
Modern rooms, electric shower, pizzeria, pool, family-run, good value.

$ Nirvana Inn
Uphill at the edge of town past the football field, T02-213 6154, www.posadanirvanainn.com.
Comfortable cabins on beautiful grounds with great views, pool, parking, flower and orchid gardens lovingly tended by the owners. Includes breakfast, other meals on request.

Restaurants

$ La Cabaña Yungeña
C Sucre 2 blocks below plaza. Tue-Sun.
Simple set lunch and dinner.

There are a couple of other places around the plaza, all closed Mon. Basic eateries up the hill by bus stops.

Transport

Bus From **La Paz**, several companies from Virgen del Carmen y San Borja, Villa Fátima, leave when full, US$4, 4 hrs: eg **San Cristóbal** and 24 de Agosto, both also go to Irupana. In Chulumani most buses leave from the top of the hill by the petrol station; minibuses and taxis to local villages from plaza.

Southwest Bolivia

dazzling salt flats and multicoloured lakes

The high desert of southwestern Bolivia, stretching from the mining centre of Oruro to the borders of Chile and Argentina, is home to some of the country's greatest visual delights.

Oruro, the main city of the region, explodes into one of Latin America's greatest celebrations during carnival. In this internationally acclaimed folklore experience, thousands of spectacularly attired dancers driven by their faith in the Virgen del Socavón, outdo each other during two days of tireless action.

The region has two of Bolivia's finest protected natural areas. Parque Nacional Sajama contains the perfect cone of Sajama, the country's highest peak at 6542 m. Further south, Reserva Eduardo Avaroa has a unique landscape of eroded rock formations interrupted by sparkling soda lakes of jade, blue and scarlet; home to three species of flamingo and many other birds. Between these two protected areas lie the magical *salares* of Uyuni and Coipasa, inconceivably vast expanses of blinding-white salt flats, which become immense mirrors after rain.

En route to the Argentine border and surrounded by fantastic canyonlands is Tupiza, gateway to many of the region's attractions and the last hideout of Butch Cassidy and the Sundance Kid.

Best for
Adventure tours ▪ Fiestas ▪ Salt flats ▪ Wildlife

Footprint picks

★ **La Diablada festival**, page 128
Dance with the devil at Oruru's world-renowned carnival.

★ **Parque Nacional Sajama**, page 136
High-altitude desert plain with Bolivia's highest peak.

★ **Lago Poopó**, page 140
Green saltwater lake and a sanctuary for birds.

★ **Salar de Uyuni**, page 150
The largest and highest salt lake in the world.

★ **Laguna Colorada**, page 154
Thousands of flamingos on a blood-red lagoon.

★ **Canyonlands of Tupiza**, page 158
Rainbow-coloured ravines dotted with cacti.

PERU

LA PAZ

Viacha
Tirate
Las Juntas
Collana
Sapahaqui
Quime
Santiago de
Machaco
Urmiri
Caxata
Comanche
Ayo Ayo
Cavari
Cerro Tunari
(5200m)
Corani
Achiri
Calacoto
Cañaviri
Patacamaya
Morochata
Sacaba
Inola
Gral Campero
Umala
Sica Sica
Konani
Caracollo
Paria
Cochabamba
Tapacari
Tirque
Charaña
Ulloma
Chacarilla
Soledad
Challa
Arque
Cliza
Arani
Parque
Nacional
Sajama
Curahuara
de Carangas
Papelpampa
Capachos
Sacaca
2
Sajama
Totora
Oruro
1
Lagunas
Tambo Quemado
Turco
Toledo
Machacamarca
Corque
Llallagua
Sacabaya
Andamarca
Poopó
Uncia
Calacala
Huachacalla
San Juan
de Kala
3
Pazña
Huancané
Ocuri
Escara
Lago Poopó
Macha
Sabaya
Chipaya
Concepción
Challapata
Ventilla
Pisiga
Coipasa
Quillaca
Huari
Tinguipaya
Lago
Coipasa
Tambillo
Sevaruyo
Tarapaya
Potosí
Chacoma
Salinas
de Garci
Mendoza
Río Mulatos
Charquilla
Ingenio
Cucho
Llica
Volcán
Tunupa
Colcha
Opoco
Visicia
Caiza
Chita
Tomava
4
Salar de Uyuni
Yura
Canquella
Incahuasi
Colchani
Ticatica
Sinalco
Pulcayo
San Pedro
de Quemez
Villa Martín
(Colcha K)
Uyuni
Ubina
San Pablo
de Napa
Tolampampa
Cotagaita
San Juan
Río Grande
Cerdas
Quechisia
Julaca
San
Cristóbal
Atocha
Oro
Ingenio
Chiguana
San Vicente
Ollagüe
Avaroa
POTOSÍ
Tupiza
6
Volcán
Ollagüe
Villa Alota
Galera
Chuqui
Soniquera
San Pablo
de López
Villazón
5
Laguna
Colorada
Quetena
Chico
La Quiaca
Reserva de Fauna
Andina Eduardo
Avaroa
Cerro Uturuncu
(6008m)
Laguna
Chalviri
Volcán
Licancábur
(5868m)
Laguna
Verde
Hito
Cajones
ARGENTINA

CHILE

ORURO

Footprint
picks
1 **Oruro carnival**, page 128
2 **Parque Nacional Sajama**, page 136
3 **Lago Poopó**, page 140
4 **Salar de Uyuni**, page 150
5 **Laguna Colorada**, page 154
6 **Canyonlands of Tupiza**, page 158

N

50 km
50 miles

Oruro & around

Oruro is surrounded by barren altiplano where the hardy inhabitants manage to eke out a meagre existence by herding llamas and growing potatoes and quinoa, the only crops that will survive in such a harsh environment. Yet this desolate region has many hidden gems for the visitor.

Scenery is magnificent in Parque Nacional Sajama, to the west of Oruro, a must for nature lovers, trekkers and climbers. The park is rich in high Andean flora and fauna, including several endemic species. South of Sajama, the Río Lauca area has lakes and unique coloured *chullpas* (funerary towers). South of Oruro is Lago Poopó, a bird sanctuary and, southwest of Poopó, the very beautiful Salar de Coipasa, smaller than the better known Salar de Uyuni and linked to it by the Ruta Intersalar. Archaeological sites and villages lost in time are scattered along the way.

The Oruro countryside is inhabited mainly by Aymara people, but it is also home to the Carangas in the Sajama area and the Chipaya around the lake and river basins. The latter is the oldest ethnic group in Bolivia, with its own language. Today it struggles to survive.

Oruro *Colour map 3, A2.*

The mining town of Oruro is the gateway to the altiplano of southwest Bolivia. It's a somewhat drab, dirty, functional place.

Although Oruro became famous as a mining town, there are no longer any working mines of importance. It is, however, a railway terminus and the commercial centre for the mining communities of the altiplano, as well as hosting the country's best-known carnival (see La Diablada, page 131).

Essential Southwest Bolivia

Getting around

The only airport serving the region is at Uyuni, with flights to/from La Paz. The road from La Paz to Oruro is a dual carriageway, which has paved connections to Cochabamba and Chile and from Oruro to Potosí. South of Oruro roads aren't so good and south of Uyuni they are worse still, although there is a good paved road from Uyuni to Potosí. Buses do run on the north–south route, but the train Oruro–Uyuni–Tupiza–Villazón is usually a better option.

When to go

The Altiplano can be bitterly cold at night, especially in the drier months of May to September. Sunny days can be dazzling and warm and protection against the sun is needed. The rainy season is November to March, when travel can be disrupted. The high season is June to August, but in the wet season there is a popular market for rapid tours to see the Salar de Uyuni as a mirror, in and out in a day.

Time required

Except at carnival time, Oruro itself requires a day or two, but once you head south into the salares, the minimum you should spend is four days. Most tours of the Salar de Uyuni area are this long, but you can easily extend this for further exploration. If you continue to Tupiza, add another two or three days, but bear in mind the time required for transport into and out of the region.

Weather Oruro

January	February	March	April	May	June
19°C	19°C	19°C	19°C	17°C	15°C
6°C	5°C	4°C	1°C	-4°C	-7°C
85mm	79mm	43mm	13mm	3mm	5mm

July	August	September	October	November	December
16°C	17°C	18°C	20°C	20°C	20°C
-7°C	-4°C	-1°C	2°C	3°C	3°C
4mm	9mm	14mm	17mm	32mm	43mm

Sites

The Plaza 10 de Febrero and surroundings are well maintained and several buildings in the centre hint at the city's former importance. The **Museo Simón Patiño** ⓘ *Soria Galvarro 5755, Mon-Fri 0830-1130, 1430-1800, Sat 0900-1500, US$1*, was built as a mansion by the tin baron Simón Patiño, it is now run by the Universidad Técnica de Oruro in the Casa de Cultura and contains European furniture and temporary exhibitions.

Oruro

Where to stay 🛏	7 Res Gloria *D2*	3 Govinda *D2*
1 Alojamiento La Paz II *C3*	8 Res Gran Boston *C3*	5 La Casona *C2*
2 El Lucero *A3*	9 Villa Real San Felipe *D2*	6 Las Retamas *D1*
3 Flores Plaza *C2*		7 Nayjama *D3*
4 Gran Sucre *D2*	Restaurants 🍴	8 Panadería Doña Filo *D2*
5 La Fontana *D2*	1 Ardentia *C2*	9 Sergio's *C2*
6 Repostero *D3*	2 Café Sur *D2*	

There is a view from the Cerro Corazón de Jesús, near the church of the Virgen del Socavón, which is five blocks west of Plaza 10 de Febrero at the end of Calle Mier. The **Museo Sacro, Folklórico, Arqueológico y Minero** ① *inside the Church of the Virgen del Socavón, T02-525 0616, entry via the church daily 0900-1145, 1500-1800, US$1.50, guided tours every 45 mins*, contain religious art, clothing and jewellery and, after passing through old mining tunnels and displays of mining techniques, a representation of *El Tío* (the god of the underworld).

The **San José mine**, worked for over 450 years for silver, tin and other minerals, lies 3 km west of the city. Visits can be arranged with the Asociación de Guías Mineros, or a tour operator (see What to do on page 134). Micro D goes to the mine.

Museo Antropológico Eduardo López Rivas ① *south of centre on Av España y Urquidi, T02-527 4020, daily 0800-1200, 1400-1800, US$0.75, guide mandatory, getting there: take micro A heading south or any trufi going south*. It has a unique collection of stone llama heads as well as impressive carnival masks. The **Museo Mineralógico y Geológico** ① *part of the University, T02-526 1250, Mon-Sat 0800-1200, 1400-1900, US$0.70, getting there: take micro A south of the Ciudad Universitaria*, has mineral specimens and fossils. **Casa Arte Taller Cardozo Velásquez** ① *Junín 738 y Arica, east of the centre, T02-527 5245, http://catcarve.blogspot.co.uk, Mon-Sat 1000-1200, 1500-1800, US$1*. Contemporary Bolivian painting and sculpture is displayed in the Cardozo Velásquez home, a family of artists.

★Oruro carnival

The normally cold, austere city of Oruro undergoes a complete transformation during its carnival. It is a UNESCO World Heritage event, a fascinating insight into local folk legends, a blend of native beliefs going back to the Uru nation and Catholic doctrine and a chance to enjoy some of the finest Bolivian dance. Starting on the Saturday before Ash Wednesday, Los Carnavales de Oruro include the famous **Diablada** ceremony in homage to the miraculous Virgen del Socavón, patroness of miners, and in gratitude to Pachamama, the Earth Mother. The Diablada was traditionally performed by indigenous miners, but several other guilds have taken up the custom. The variety of dances has also increased and around 50 *fraternidades*, dance companies from all over the country, take part. The size of the companies ranges from 50 dancers up to 700 – so you can imagine the massive scale of the parades. Leading each company is the cargamento, a vehicle covered with fine embroidery and silverware, with a statue or image of the Virgin. Each group is accompanied by one or more brass bands, the larger ones have more than 100 musicians.

There is much partying and water-throwing and foam-spraying; this is an opportunity for visitors to share the experience with Bolivians.

The main parade
The **Sábado de Peregrinación** starts its 5-km route through the town at 0700, finishing at the Sanctuary of the Virgen del Socavón, and continues into the early hours of Sunday. There the dancers invoke blessings and ask for pardon.

ON THE ROAD

Invoking blessings

The *cha'lla* is an inherent part of Bolivian life, most noticeable on the Tuesday of carnival. It is a term you are likely to hear. Although there is no precise translation, it can relate to blessing a person or an object or, used more loosely, it can refer to almost any celebration. The blessed object is sprinkled with alcohol and adorned with confetti and streamers. It is a way of inviting good luck and abundance.

A related ceremony, prevalent among Aymara people is the Khoa. On the first Friday of every month (except Good Friday), *mesas*, paper trays with coca leaves, sweets, incense and at times a *sullyo* (llama feotus) are burned in hot coals. This is a sacrifice to the Pacha Mama (Mother Earth) to ensure prosperity.

This is how the protection of the gods of plenty is invoked and respect shown to them.

At dawn on Sunday, **El Alba** is a competition of all participating musicians at Plaza del Folklore near the Santuario, an amazing battle of the bands. The **Gran Corso** or **La Entrada** starts at 0800 on the Sunday, a more informal parade (many leave their masks off) along the same route.

Monday is **El Día del Diablo y del Moreno** in which the Diablos and Morenos, with their bands, bid farewell to the Virgin. Arches decorated with colourful woven cloths and silverware are set up on the road leading to the Santuario, where a Mass is held. In the morning, at Avenida Cívica, the Diablada companies participate in a play of the Seven Deadly Sins. This is followed by a play about the meeting of the Inca Atahualpa with Pizarro. On Tuesday, **Martes de Chall'a**, families get together, with *ch'alla* rituals to invoke ancestors, unite with Pachamama and bless personal possessions. The Friday before Carnaval, traditional miners' ceremonies are held at mines, including the sacrifice of a llama. Visitors may only attend with advance permission.

Preparations for Carnaval begin four months before the actual event, on the first Sunday of November, the Primer Convite (First Invitation), and rehearsals are held every Sunday until one week before Carnaval, the Ultimo Convite (Final Invitation), when a plain clothes rehearsal takes place, preceded by a Mass for participants.

The dances

Eighteen different dances are part of Oruro's carnival. **La Diablada** is the most representative of these and La Diablada Auténtica, the oldest dance company dating to 1904, always opens the parade. The procession is led by a condor and a pack of frolicking bears. Then follows a group of masked dancers, led by two masqueraders representing Lucifer and Satan who wear scarlet cloaks and carry a serpent twisted around one arm and a trident. The Archangel Michael urges on hundreds of leaping dancers in ferocious diabolical costumes. Prancing seductively at the head of columns of demons, a band of female dancers, wearing red wigs and masks, represents China Supay, Lucifer's consort, who plays the role of carnal temptress. A mighty brass band drives on the great team of devils.

The costumes, designed anew each year, always feature a heavy, gruesome mask modelled in plaster, with a toad or snake on top, huge glass eyes, triangular glass teeth, a horsehair wig and pointed, vibrating ears; some even breathe fire. Tied around the neck is a large, silk shawl embroidered with snakes or other figures, and the dancer also has a jewelled, fringed breastplate. Over his white shirt and tights he wears a sash trimmed with coins and from it hang the four flaps of his native skirt, embroidered in gold and silver thread and loaded with precious stones. Special boots equipped with spurs complete the elaborate outfit.

Another important dance, very much an Oruro tradition since 1913, is **La Morenada**, a satire of the lives of black slaves, the *morenos* brought to South America and led off in chains to work in the mines and haciendas. The group is led by the Rey Moreno (Black King) and the caporal (foreman). The richly decorated costumes of the participants represent the wealth of the slave owners, while the protruding eyes and tongue of the masks convey the fatigue of the slaves and their suffering. Following the same theme are the dance of **Los Negritos**, honouring the Afro-Bolivian slaves, with brightly coloured outfits and percussion bands, and the energetic dance of **Los Caporales**, which satirizes the slaves who were forced to act as foremen controlling and whipping their own people. **Los Doctorcitos** ridicule the pompous lawyers of colonial times.

The dance of **Los Incas** tells the myth of the origins of the Inca Empire and of historical events until the time of the Spanish conquest. The **Kallawayas** represent the medicine men moving with their bag of herbs from one community to another.

Some of the dances give a glimpse of life in the altiplano. The colourful **Llamerada** shows the herdsmen driving their llamas with whips. **Los Zamponeros** play their panpipes and dance to celebrate planting and harvesting in honour of the Pacha Mama. **La Cullaguada** is the dance of spinners and weavers, while **Los Potolos** display a courtship dance while fetching water.

Different regions of Bolivia are also represented in dances such as the energetic **Tobas**, from the eastern lowlands; performers wear large feather headdresses and carry lances. The **Tinku** represents the fighting rituals of communities in northern Potosí and southern Oruro, while the **Pujllay**, a celebration from near Sucre, commemorates the victory of ill-prepared natives against Spanish troops.

Practicalities

Seating Stands are erected along the entire route. Tickets are for Saturday and Sunday, there is no discount if you stay only one day. Some stands have a cover for shade or rain. A prime location is around Plaza 10 de Febrero where the companies perform in front of the authorities. Along Avenida 6 de Agosto, a sought-after location by TV cameras, is where performers put on their best. Seats cost US$35-70.

Where to stay During Carnaval, accommodation costs as much as five times more than normal and must be booked well in advance. Hotels charge for Friday, Saturday and Sunday nights. You can stay for only one night, but you'll be

ON THE ROAD

La Diablada

The best known and perhaps the most impressive part of Oruro's carnival is La Diablada, the Dance of the Devils. It dates back to the 12th century and the region of Catalonia in Spain, where the Dance of the Devils as well as the Dance of the Seven Deadly Sins was performed. It was subsequently adopted by the miners of Oruro who combined it with their own ancestral mythology. La Diablada incorporates the forces of evil as represented by Lucifer, his female consort China Supay, and the seven deadly sins; as well as the forces of good represented by the Archangel Michael. The condor and the bear, both ancient Andean symbols, also take part. According to legend, when the Spanish introduced Christianity, the Uru god Huari sent plagues to punish his people for abandoning him: a large frog from the north, a snake from the south, ants from the west and a cayman from the east. A ñusta (native princess) whose image today blends with that of the Virgin, saved them by turning these animals to stone. The petrified creatures can reportedly still be seen in and around Oruro. The defeated Huari retreated underground and now lives in the caves and mines. This may be the origin of Supay or El Tío, from the Uru word 'Tiw' which means protector. He is lord of the rich mineral seams running through the cordillera. He must be honoured with offerings, so he will in turn protect the miners and give them gifts from the mines. This concept of El Tío is distinct from the European devil, the incarnation of evil, but the two have become blurred in La Diablada.

charged for three. Locals also offer places to stay in their homes, expect to pay at least US$12 per person per night.

Transport When demand is at its peak, posted prices are ignored and buses from La Paz charge three or more times the usual fare. Buses fill quickly, starting Friday, and tickets are not sold in advance. Many agencies in La Paz organize day-trips for the Saturday parade. They leave around 0430 and return late. Trips in 2015 cost US$120-140 for transport, breakfast, box lunch, drinks and seats for the parade.

Other practicalities Do not take unnecessary valuables. Take a cushion and rain poncho even if it is sunny, as you are bound to get wet; also water bombs if you want to join in the mayhem. All these items are sold in abundance by street vendors. See www.carnavaldeoruroacfo.org or http://orurocarnaval.com for information in Spanish and photos.

Around Oruro

There are thermal baths outside town at **Obrajes** ⓘ *23 km from Oruro, minibuses leave from Caro y Av 6 de Agosto, US$1, 45 mins; baths open 0700-1800, US$1.50, Oruro office: Murgía 1815 y Camacho, T02-525 0646*. There are also baths at **Capachos**,

12 km from the city on the same road. Both have long been visited for the medicinal properties of the thermal waters and have covered swimming pools, but Obrajes is the better of the two. There is a choice of private baths or swimming pool. There's also a hotel at Obrajes ($$) and a disappointing restaurant.

The **Qala Qala (Cala Cala) cave paintings** ⓘ *20 km to the southeast of Oruro, entrance US$1.50*, have pictures and carvings mainly of llamas and are thought to date from the Wankarani period, 800 BC-AD 400. Buses leave 0700-1100 from Calle Brasil y Ejército; tour operators also offer this destination.

Listings Oruro *map p127*

Tourist information

Tourist office (*Bolívar y Montes 6072, Plaza 10 de Febrero, T02-525 0144, Mon-Fri 0800-1200, 1430-1830*) is helpful and informative. The **Prefectura** and the **Policía de Turismo** jointly run information booths in front of the **Terminal de Buses** (*T02-528 7774, Mon-Fri 0800-1200, 1430-1830, Sat 0830-1200*); and opposite the **railway station** (*T02-525 7881*), same hours. The **Immigration office** (*S Galvarro 5744 entre Ayacucho y Cochabamba, T02-527 0239, Mon-Fri 0830-1230, 1430-1830*) is across from Museo Simón Patiño.

Where to stay

$$ Flores Plaza
Adolfo Mier 735 at Plaza 10 de Febrero, T02-525 2561, www.floresplazahotel.com.
Comfortable carpeted rooms, central location.

$$ Gran Sucre
Sucre 510 esq 6 de Octubre, T02-525 4100, hotelsucreoruro@entelnet.bo.
Refurbished old building (faded elegance), rooms and newer suites, heaters on request, internet in lobby, helpful staff.

$$ Samay Wasi
Av Brasil 232 opposite the bus terminal, T02-527 6737, www.hotelessamaywasi.com.
Carpeted rooms, discount for IYHF members, has a 2nd branch in Uyuni (Av Potosí 965).

$$ Villa Real San Felip
San Felipe 678 y La Plata, south of the centre, T02-525 4993, sanfelipehotel@entelnet.bo.
Quaint hotel, nicely furnished but small rooms, heating, buffet breakfast, sauna and whirlpool, restaurant, tour operator.

$$-$ Repostero
Sucre 370 y Pagador, T02-525 8001.
Hot water, parking, restaurant serves set lunch. Renovated carpeted rooms are more expensive but better value than their old rooms.

$ El Lucero
21 de Enero 106 y Brasil, opposite the terminal, T02-527 9468, www.hotelbernal-lucero.com.bo.
Multi-storey hotel, reliable hot water, front rooms noisy, good value.

$ Residencial Gran Boston
Pagador 1159 y Cochabamba, T02-527 4708.
Refurbished house, rooms around a

covered patio, cheaper with shared bath, good value.

Restaurants

$$ Nayjama
Aldana 1880.
Good regional specialities, very popular for lunch, huge portions.

$$-$ Las Retamas
Murguía 930 esq Washington. Mon-Sat 0930-2330, Sun 0930-1430.
Excellent quality and value for set lunches ($), Bolivian and international dishes à la carte, very good pastries at **Kuchen Haus**, pleasant atmosphere, attentive service, a bit out of the way but well worth the trip. Recommended.

$ Ardentia
Sorria Galvarro y Junín, open 1900-2200.
Home cooking, tasty pasta and meat dishes.

$ La Casona
Pres Montes 5970, opposite Post Office.
Salteñas in the morning, closed midday. Good *pizzería* at night.

$ Govinda
6 de Octubre 6071. Mon-Sat 0900-2130.
Excellent vegetarian.

$ Sergio's
La Plata y Mier, at Plaza 10 de Febrero.
Very good pizza, hamburgers, snacks; also pastries in the afternoon, good service.

Cafés

Café Sur
Arce 163 entre Velasco y 6 de Agosto, near train station. Tue-Sat.
Live entertainment, seminars, films, good place to meet local students.

Panadería Doña Filo
6 de Octubre esq Sucre.
Closed Sun. Excellent savoury snacks and sweets, takeaway only.

Bars and clubs

Bravo
Montesinos y Pagador. Open 2100-0300.
Varied music.

Imagine
6 de Octubre y Junín. Open 2200-0400.
Latin and other music.

Shopping

Camping equipment Camping Oruro, *Pagador 1660, T02-528 1829, camping_ oruro@hotmail.com.*
Crafts On Av La Paz the blocks between León and Belzu are largely given over to workshops producing masks and costumes for Carnaval. **Artesanías Oruro**, *A Mier 599, esq S Galvarro.* Lovely selection of regional handicrafts produced by 6 rural community cooperatives; nice sweaters, carpets, wall-hangings.
Markets Mercado Campero (*V Galvarro esq Bolívar*) sells everything, also *brujería* section for magical concoctions.
Mercado Fermín López (*C Ayacucho y Montes*) sells food and hardware.
Mercado Kantuta (*Tacna entre Beni y D, north of the bus terminal; take minibus from northeast corner of Plaza 10 de Febrero*) is a *campesino* market on Tue and Fri. **C Bolívar** is the main shopping street. **Global** (*Junín y La Plata*) is a well-stocked supermarket. **Irupana** (*S Galvarra y A Mier*) sells natural food and snacks.

What to do

Asociación de Guías Mineros, *contact Gustavo Peña, T02-523 2446.* Arranges visits to San José mine, US$7-10.
Freddy Barrón, *T02-527 6776, lufba@hotmail.com.* Custom-made tours and transport, speaks German and some English.

Transport

Bus
Bus terminal 10 blocks north of centre at Bakovic and Aroma, T02-527 5070/9554, US$0.25 terminal use fee, luggage store, ATMs. Micro 2 to centre, or any saying 'Plaza 10 de Febrero'. To **Challapata** and **Huari**: several companies go about every hour, US$1, 1¾ hrs, and Huari, US$1.25, 2 hrs, last bus back leaves Huari about 1630. You can also take a bus to Challapata and a shared taxi from there to Huari, US$0.30. Daily services to: **La Paz** at least every hour 0400-2200, US$4-5.35, 3-4 hrs; also tourist van service with **Enjoy Bolivia**, see La Paz Tour operators, page 65. In February 2015, the La Paz to Oruro highway was opened as a 4-lane motorway. **Cochabamba**, US$4.50-5.75, 4 hrs, frequent. **Potosí**, US$5.50-7.50, 5 hrs, several daily. **Sucre**, all buses around 2000, US$9-12, 9 hrs. **Tarija**, 2 departures at 2030, US$14.50, 14 hrs. **Uyuni**, several companies, all depart 1900-2100, US$7 regular, US$10.75 *semi-cama*, 7-8 hrs. **Todo Turismo**, offers a tourist bus departing from La Paz at 2100, arrange ahead for pick-up at midnight in Oruro, US$28, office Rodríguez 134 entre 6 de Agosto y Bakovic, T02-511 1889. To **Tupiza**, via Potosí, **Boquerón** at 1230,

Illimani at 1630 and 2000, US$13, 11-12 hrs, continuing to Villazón, US$14.50, 13-14 hrs. **Santa Cruz**, **Bolívar** at 2000, US$12, *bus-cama* at 2130, US$17, 11 hrs. To **Pisiga** (Chilean border), **Trans Pisiga**, Av Dehene y España, T02-526 2241, at 2000 and 2030, or with Iquique bound buses, US$5, 4-5 hrs.

International buses (US$2 to cross border): to **Iquique** via Pisiga, US$17, 8 hrs, buses leave around 1200 coming from Cochabamba. **Arica** via Patacamaya and Tambo Quemado, several companies daily around 1100-1300 and 2300, US$25 normal, US$30 *semi-cama*, US$37 *cama*, 8 hrs, some continue to Iquique, 12 hrs.

Train
The station is at Av Velasco Galvarro y Aldana, T02-527 4605, ticket office Mon-Fri 0800-1200, 1430-1800, Sun 0830-1120, 1530-1800. Tickets for *ejecutivo* class are sold up to 4 weeks in advance, 1 week for *salón*. Tickets can also be purchased in La Paz, see page 70. **Ferroviaria Andina** (FCA, www.fca.com.bo), runs services from Oruro to **Uyuni**, **Tupiza** and **Villazón**. **Expreso del Sur** runs Tue and Fri at 1530, arriving in Uyuni at 2220, and **Wara Wara** on Sun and Wed at 1900, arriving in Uyuni at 0220.

Fares Expreso del Sur to **Uyuni**, *Ejecutivo* US$15, *Salón* US$7.50; **Tupiza**, 12½ hrs: US$30, US$13.50; **Villazón**: 15½ hrs, US$34.75, US$15.75. **Wara Wara del Sur** to **Uyuni**: *Ejecutivo* US$13.50, *Salón* US$6; **Tupiza**, 13½-14 hrs: US$22.50, US$10 respectively; **Villazón**, 17 hrs: US$27.50, US$12.50.

Perched between the Quimsa Cruz (Tres Cruces) range and the Yungas, Quime gives access to both snow and ice and subtropics. There are a number of day hikes (a map is available at Rancho Colibrí; see Where to stay, below). There are also lots of birdwatching opportunities in the area.

North of Oruro, 2½ hours by bus (233 km, four hours south of La Paz) is the junction at Konani, where there are a few places to eat. From here a beautiful road, mostly paved, runs over the altiplano to the Tres Cruces pass (over 5000 m) before dropping a spectacular 2000 m to Quime (founded 1887, population 3000), a town in the Yungas de Inquisivi at the southern edge of the Cordillera Quimsa Cruz. It can also be reached along scenic secondary roads from Chulumani in Sud-Yungas and Cochabamba.

Excursions include to Aymara mining communities and waterfalls and mountain-biking trips, including a downhill from Tres Cruces. The main festival is 24-25 July (Apóstol Santiago). There are basic services, modem internet in the Biblioteca Municipal in the Alcaldía at the Plaza, but no ATMs.

The road back to Konani crosses the mountains. Take a surubí to Pongo B2 (10 minutes) and get out at the bridge for the path to **Lago Naranjani** (if the river is high stay on the minibus to Villa Carmen). It's a 1½-hour walk to the lake. A further hour leads to a peak with a 360° view of the Andes. Leave Quime at 0600 and choose a dry, sunny day. Further towards Konani is **Huañacota**, from which, three minutes by car, is an area of Puya raymondii plants. Higher into the mountains, there are snowboarding and skiing opportunities; contact an agency like **Addiction Xtreme Bolivia** ⓘ *T7052 0499, axbolivia on Facebook*.

Mining for tin and wolfram was important in the early 20th century. Benjamin Guggenheim, who died on the Titanic, had major interests here. Much of the industry vanished when prices collapsed but cooperatives still work some mines, which can be visited. There is an **Asociación de Guías,** which organizes tours for US$9.50 (including boots, lamp, hat and guide). Closest to Quime is **Mina Chambillaya**, a 3- to 4-km walk or you can go in the miners' truck. This enterprise is recuperating Quime's own historic mining. Many new mines are run by outsiders.

La Ruta el Oso is a walk into an area where spectacled bears (*jucumarini*) may be seen at certain times of year. On the way is Chichipata, with an old church (20 minutes) and there are great views, condors' nests and, further away, other communities that can be visited, eg Titi Amaya and Cochabambita (one or two days with camping).

On the way to the Sud-Yungas, 2½ to three hours beyond Quime is **Choquetanga Grande**. The **Villa San Juan** hot springs are a 1½-hour walk away (no facilities, free, but a small charge may be introduced). The route to Chulumani continues through a region known as the **Ruta del Mango** and then towns such as Inquisivi and Licoma, thence to Irupana (see page 119). The road passes through a huge range of topography and it's best to go in your own transport, 4WD or motorbike. A bus from La Paz to Cajuata goes some, but not all the way (0600, 1330 from El Alto, and 1600) There is a bus from Cajuata to Chulumani, but the two schedules don't coordinate. There is lodging in Cajuata and Licoma. Suri, near Cajuata, just off the route, is a very old Spanish village (ask if anyone has a bed for the night).

Listings Quime

Tourist information

Info Tur office
Av Bolívar, near Avaroa, 2 blocks from Plaza Principal, T02-213 5644, or 6813 0384, Turismo Quime Bolivia on Facebook.
Not open all the time, but very helpful.

Where to stay

$ Hostal Rancho Colibrí
4 steep blocks uphill from main plaza (ask directions or see website, it's not easy to spot), http://ranchocolibri.wordpress.com.
8 simple rooms with shared bath, breakfast extra but has a fully equipped kitchen, most guests do their own cooking. Under changed management (2015). Ask for printed information on the area (website is helpful).

$ Quime
close to Plaza Principal.
Big, basic place with shared bath, a couple of more expensive rooms have bath, TV, windows onto corridor, private rooms in a smaller block.

Various other basic, slightly cheaper *alojamientos* in town (eg of the **Helguero** family, in an old house, nice, clean; also **Santiago**).

Restaurants

2 doors from the **Info Tur** office is a good place for *almuerzo* (set lunch). Otherwise the only option, particularly at night, is fast food or fried chicken.

Transport

Bus
To get to Quime, take any bus from La Paz to Oruro or Cochabamba and get out at Konani, 2-3 hrs, US$2 (likewise get out at Konani coming from Oruro or Cochabamba). Change to a bus, minibus or taxi (wait till full) to Quime, 1½ hrs, US$3.75. Direct buses from La Paz to Quime, 5 hrs, are **Inquisivi** from the bus terminal (T282 4734) and **Apóstol Santiago** from El Alto (T259 7544), US$3.75. All transport stops on the Alameda in town.

Parque Nacional Sajama

high-altitude plain with stark dramatic scenery

★The park, established in 1939 and covering 100,230 ha, contains the world's highest forest, consisting mainly of the rare queñual tree (Polylepis tarapacana) which grows up to an altitude of 5500 m. Also of interest are the slow-growing cushion plants, such as the yareta (*Azorella compacta*), threatened because they are used as fuel. The fauna includes vicuñas, *quirquinchos* (armadillo), puma and among birds the *suri* (rhea), condor, flamingos and coots. The scenery is wonderful with views of several volcanoes, including Sajama – Bolivia's highest peak at 6542 m – Parinacota and Pomerape (jointly called Payachatas), Quisi Quisini, Condoriri and Anallajcha. You can trek in the park, with or without porters and mules, but once you move away from the Río Sajama or its major tributaries, lack of water is a problem. There is basic accommodation in Sajama village (see below) as well as a more comfortable and expensive option at Tomarapi on the north side of the mountain; see page 139.

Curahuara de Carangas

At Km 95 from Patacamaya is the access to Curahuara de Carangas, a small colonial town. Its impressive **Iglesia de Santiago** ① *entry US$1.40, caretaker José Hilario Nina can be found at the entrance to town*, completed in 1603, is so beautiful that it has been dubbed 'The Sixtine Chapel of the Altiplano'. Sincretism between native and Christian beliefs is seen in its 17th-century frescoes with Old and New Testament scenes mixed with deities, such as the sun and the moon, and images of the conversion of the natives. In colonial times this church was for the use of Spaniards and mestizos, while indigenous people attended the **Iglesia de Santa Bárbara** on the outskirts of town. Near town are the ruins of **Pucara de Monterani**, a fortress, and the **Marka Kullu** hill, as well as many *chullpas* (funerary towers) with pot shards scattered about.

145 km southwest of Patacamaya, a dirt road goes north and makes a circle around Nevado Sajama, rejoining the highway at Km 168. Along this road are several communities: 3 km north of the Km 168 junction is **Lagunas** and 8 km further the village of **Sajama** (three hours from Patacamaya). The community of **Caripe** is 12 km from the Km 145 junction and 3 km beyond is the **Tomarapi Ecolodge** (19 km from Sajama Village). Tambo Quemado on the Chilean border is 45 minutes from Sajama, 20 km along the paved highway past the Km 168 junction.

Essential Parque Nacional Sajama

Finding your feet

A one-day drive to the west of Oruro. The paved road from La Paz to Arica (Chile) passes through the park and provides the most direct access. At Patacamaya, 109 km southeast of La Paz and 130 km northwest of Oruro, is the turn-off for the road west to Sajama and the Chilean border. See also Transport, page 139.

Getting around

There is much to explore in and around the park so it is advisable to stay a few days. A private 4WD vehicle is an asset as the area is extensive, but there is much to see even on foot. La Paz and Oruro operators offer tours here and you can hire a basic vehicle with driver in the village of Sajama for about US$10-20 depending on the destination. The area is high, with the plains at 4200 m and the mountains going up from there.

Park information

Park headquarters in Sajama village, T02-513 5526 (in La Paz SERNAP T02-242 6268, or 252 8080), www.biobol. org. Entry fee US$4.25 payable to community of Sajama.

Visiting Parque Nacional Sajama

Nevado Sajama, or **Tata** (grandfather) **Sajama** as locals call it, is a prime climbing destination. This dormant volcano became in 1939 the last major peak scaled in South America. Crampons, ice axe and rope are needed for climbing this and other volcanoes in the park. Some gear can be hired in Sajama village, where local guides (not certified but experienced, US$50-70 per day) and pack animals (US$10 per day including muleteer) are also available. There are four routes to the summit. Climbing season is April to September.

> **Tip...**
> Be prepared for very cold and windy conditions and extreme sun exposure.

There is excellent trekking and wherever you go there are grand views. Both Sajama and Tomarapi are good bases for day walks, from either village you can easily reach the flanks of Sajama to see the queñual forests. At **Junthuma**, 8 km west of Sajama and 26 km from Tomarapi, are some 30 thermal springs and geysers. The **Manasaya thermal complex** with four pools are 6 km northwest of Sajama and 14 km southwest of Tomarapi, there are changing rooms by each pool and toilets at the northern and southern access points, entry US$4.25. **Laguna Huañacota** where birds and vicuña herds might be seen is 12 km north of Sajama and some 7 km from Tomarapi. The area has many *bofedales*, marshy valleys where camelids graze; the largest is in Caripe, 1.5 km northeast of Tomarapi. Patoco, another large *bofedal* in the north of the park, about 16 km from either Sajama or Tomarapi, is a good place to see vicuñas. From Tomarapi, a 5-km trail leads to the community's mountain shelter at 4793 m. A second trail leads in 6.5 km to Inca Marka, where religious rites took place in ancient times. Near Lagunas village are the remains of a *pucara*, a fortress, which was also used for ceremonies in honour of Sajama and affords very good views of the mountain and surroundings. There are also small colonial adobe churches in several places including Sajama, Tomarapi and Lagunas.

Sajama village

In Sajama village (population 500, altitude 4200 m) visitors are billeted in family-run *alojamientos* on a rotating basis (about US$4.50 per person). All are basic to very basic, especially the sanitary facilities; no showers or electricity, solar power for lighting only. *Alojamientos* may provide limited food, so take your own supplies. It can be very windy and cold at night; a good sleeping bag, gloves and hat are essential. Many villagers sell alpaca woolen items.

South of Parque Nacional Sajama, along the border with Chile, is another scenic region in the basin of the **Río Lauca**. The main attractions here are the unique polychrome *chullpas*, funerary structures from the Inca period. The red and white designs resemble those found in Inca textiles and are part of the adobe rather than being painted on. Nearby are the Macaya and Sakewa lagoons rich in birdlife, including three species of flamingo, Andean gulls, ducks and migratory birds. The communities of **Macaya**, **Sacabaya** and **Julo** have a community tourism project and offer meals and guiding in the area. La Paz and Oruro operators also offer tours. Macaya is 41 km south of Tambo Quemado. From Oruro, this area can also be reached via the road to Pisiga (see below), turning north at **Sabaya** (Km 180, simple lodgings), from where it is 80 km to Julo and another 15 km to Macaya. There is a market in Macaya every second Tuesday, when minivans from Tambo Quemado go there early in the morning and return around midday (not enough time to visit the attractions). It might be possible to stay with a family in Macaya or Julo.

Listing Parque Nacional Sajama

Where to stay

$$ Tomarapi Ecolodge
north of Sajama in Tomarapi community, near Caripe, ecotomarapi@yahoo.es (see tomarapi on Facebook), represented by Millenarian Tourism & Travel, Av Sánchez Lima 2193, La Paz, T02-241 4753, www. boliviamilenaria.com.
Including full board (good food) and guiding service with climbing shelter at 4900 m, helpful staff, simple but comfortable, with hot water, heating.

Transport

Bus
To get to the park, take a La Paz–Oruro bus and change at Patacamaya. Minivans from Patacamaya to Sajama Sun-Fri 1200, 3 hrs, US$2.75. Sajama to **Patacamaya** Mon-Fri 0600, some days via **Tambo Quemado**, confirm details and weekend schedule locally. From Tambo Quemado to Sajama about 1530 daily, 1 hr, US$0.75. Or take a La Paz–Arica bus, ask for Sajama, try to pay half the fare, but you may be charged full fare.

By road to Chile

the journey is worthwhile for the breathtaking views

The shortest and most widely used route from La Paz to Chile is the road to **Arica** via the border at **Tambo Quemado** (Bolivia) and **Chungará** (Chile). From La Paz take the highway south towards Oruro. Immediately before Patacamaya (see above), turn right at a green road sign to Puerto Japonés on the Río Desaguadero, then on to Tambo Quemado.

Bolivian customs and immigration are at Tambo Quemado, where there are a couple of very basic places to stay and eat. Border control is open daily 0800-2000. Shops change bolivianos, pesos chilenos and dollars. From Tambo Quemado there is a stretch of about 7 km of 'no-man's land' before you reach the Chilean frontier at Chungará. Here the border crossing, which is set against the most spectacular scenic backdrop of Lago Chungará and Volcán Parinacota, is thorough but efficient; open 0800-2000. Expect a long wait at weekends and any day behind lines of lorries. Drivers must fill in 'Relaciones de Pasajeros', US$0.25 from a kiosk at border, giving details of driver, vehicle and passengers. Do not take any livestock, plants, fruit, vegetables, coca or dairy products into Chile.

Tip...
Take extra petrol (none available after Chilean border until Arica), food and water.

An alternative crossing from Oruro: several bus companies travel southwest to Iquique, via the border posts of **Pisiga** (Bolivia) and **Colchane** (Chile). The road is paved from Oruro to Toledo (32 km) and from Opoquari to Pisiga via Huachachalla (about 100 km). The rest of the 170-km road in Bolivia is due to be paved by the end of 2015; on the Chilean side it's paved all the way to Iquique, 250 km. There is also service from Oruro to Arica via Patacamaya and Tambo Quemado.

South of Oruro

the green saline water is a sanctuary for birds

★Lago Poopó and around

From Oruro, a paved road and the railway run between Lago Poopó and the Cordillera Azanaque, south to Challapata, a very scenic ride. At **Challapata**, the road divides, one branch, fully paved, climbs southeast to Potosí, while the second branch continues south, paved to Huari and gravel and dirt beyond, to Uyuni. **Machacamarca**, about 30 minutes south of Oruro, has a good **railway museum** ① *Wed and Fri 0900-1200, 1500-1700*. There are thermal baths at **Pazña**, 91 km from Oruro (take a bus from the terminal to Challapata, 1¼ hours); there is a large swimming pool and family pools.

About 65 km south is the **Santuario de Aves Lago Poopó** (a Ramsar site), an excellent bird reserve on the lake of the same name. The lake dries up completely in winter.

The closest place to Oruro to see flamingos and other birds is **Lago Uru Uru** (the northern section of the Poopó lake system). Take a bus in the direction of Toledo (on the road to Pisiga), get off at the Puente Español, named after a colonial causeway, and walk 20 minutes from there to a peninsula to the east, or go a bit further to Villa Challacollo (minibuses 102, 10, 5 or blue micros) and walk from there. Birds start arriving with the first rains in October or November. Further along, at Km 10 is **Chusakeri**, where *chullpas* can be seen on the hillside.

Access to Lago Poopó is a little closer from Huari, 15 minutes south of **Challapata** (fiesta 15-17 July; several places to stay, eg **Residencial Virgen del Carmen**, by main plaza, and a gas station). **Huari** (124 km south of Oruro, paved) is a pleasant little town with a large brewery; there is a small museum and **Mirador Tatacuchunita**, a lookout on nearby Cerro Sullka. Sunsets over the lake are superb. There are a couple of basic *alojamientos*, eg **25 de Mayo**, two blocks from the plaza towards Challapata, shared bath, cold water in morning only. It is about an 8-km walk from Huari to the lake, depending on the water level. Near the lake is the Uru-Muratos community of **Llapallapani** with circular adobe homes, those with straw roofs are known as *chillas* and those with conical adobe roofs are *putukus*. Cabins in *putuku* style form part of a community tourism programme. Boats can be hired when the water level is high; at other times Poopó is an unattainable mirage.

Tip...
There is good walking in the Cordillera Azanaque behind Huari; take food, water, warm clothing and all gear.

Atlantis in the Andes Jim Allen's theory of Atlantis (www.atlantisbolivia.org), is well known around Oruro. **Pampa Aullagas**, the alleged Atlantis site, is 196 km from Oruro, southwest of Lago Poopó. Access is from the town of **Quillacas** along a road that branches southwest from the road to Uyuni 20 km south of Huari, or from the north through Toledo and Andamarca.

Salar de Coipasa and around

Southwest of Lago Poopó, off the Oruro–Pisiga–Iquique road (turn off at **Sabaya**), is the Salar de Coipasa, 225 km from Oruro. It is smaller and less visited than the Salar de Uyuni, and has a turquoise lake in the middle of the salt pan surrounded by mountains with gorgeous views and large cacti. Towards the northwest of the *salar* is a large island with **Cerro Villa Pucarani**, a 4910-m mountain in the centre.

> **Tip...**
> A visit to Pampa Aullagas can be combined with a trip to the Salar de Coipasa.

Coipasa, the main village lies in the northeast of the island; there are other hamlets along the south shore. People on the island grow potatoes, herd llamas and mine salt. There are no services whatsoever for visitors in Coipasa. To the south of the main island are a couple of smaller ones.

Northeast of the Salar de Coipasa, reached from Huallacalla (on the Oruro–Pisiga road) is **Escara**, a friendlly village with a beautiful plaza and further south, along a tributary of the Río Lauca, is **Chipaya**, 186 km from Oruro. The Chipaya people are considered one of the oldest surviving nations of the Andes, an Uru group, descendants of the Chulpas believed to have inhabited the area around 2500 BC. They lead a traditional life, wear distinctive dress and speak Puki, their own language. Chipaya homes are round, like those in Llapallapani, see above. Survival of the Chipaya is at risk due to the migration of young people. The Chipaya have been the focus of studies for many years and are now reluctant to receive outsiders. Rather than impose yourself on them, see the display at the anthropology museum in Oruro.

Coipasa is northwest of the Salar de Uyuni and travel from one to the other is possible with a private vehicle along the impressive Ruta Intersalar. Along the way are tombs, terracing and ancient irrigation canals at the archaeological site of **Alcaya** ① *US$1.25*, gradually being developed by the local community. It is near **Salinas de Garci Mendoza**, locally known as Salinas (SalinasDeGarciMendoza on Facebook), a pleasant colonial town with basic services and places to stay and eat and a petrol station.

Volcán Tunupa and the Ruta Intersalar

Southwest of Salinas, near the northwestern shore of the Salar de Uyuni, is **Llica**, another town with basic services, including bus transport across the *salar* from Uyuni, and road access from Oruro via Quillacas and Salinas. Here too are archaeological sites. Llama and other wool handicrafts are produced here. On a peninsula that juts into the Salar de Uyuni is the lovely snow-capped **Volcán Tunupa** (or Thunupa, 5432 m), important in the local mythology about the creation of the *salar* and a landmark that can be seen in the distance from most of the Salar de Uyuni. Tunupa can be climbed from several of the villages at its base, the views of the *salares* are beautiful but note that the climb to the summit is demanding. There are some ancient ruins on its flanks. With a private vehicle it is possible to circumnavigate the volcano, passing several villages. Allow a full day if you plan to stop at the multiple photo opportunities.

The **Ruta Intersalar** goes south from Salinas to a fork, where you can go left (clockwise) or right (counterclockwise) around the volcano. The former leads more directly to the Salar de Uyuni and to villages with accommodation. **Jirira**, a tiny village 55 km from Salinas along the left fork, has a ramp to enter the Salar de Uyuni and a salt hotel (see Where to stay) and airstream camper vans run by **Crillon Tours** (www.uyuni.travel). You can climb in four hours to a mirador (4650 m), with stunning views over the *salar* and Tunupa's crater; the trail is rocky and marked by cairns. Local guides charge US$10 to the mirador and US$20 to the summit. From Jirira, a particularly scenic 7-km stretch of road follows the northern shore of the *salar*, past the hamlet of **Ayque** with a 5-ha archaeological site nearby, to **Coquesa**, a somewhat bigger place with several lodgings (working mostly with groups and closed in the rainy season). This is another good base for climbing Tunupa, here too is a mirador at 4120 m and a cave with mummies, thought to belong to the Aymara kingdoms period, around 1250. Just ahead, at **Chantani** is an access ramp to the *salar* and a small museum with regional ceramics and petrified algae. **Tahua**, 5 km beyond, is a town with a lovely church just at the edge of the *salar*, ramp access to the salt flat, places to sleep and eat, a telephone and possibly petrol. At Tahua, the road leaves the shore of the *salar* and goes north through desolate countryside to the village of **Alianza** before closing the loop.

Listings South of Oruro

Where to stay

$ Alojamiento Paraíso
Sabaya.
Take a sleeping bag, shared bath, cold water, meals on request or take own food. Sells petrol.

$ Doña Wadi
Salinas de Garci Mendoza, C Germán Busch, near main plaza, T02-513 8015.
Shared bath, hot water, basic but clean, meals available.

$ Posada Doña Lupe
Jirira.
Partly made of salt , hot water, cheaper without bath, use of kitchen but bring your own food, no meals available, caters to tour groups, pleasant, comfortable.

$ Zuk'arani
on a hillside overlooking Salinas de Garci Mendoza and the salar, T02-513 7086, zukarani@hotmail.com.
2 cabins for 4, with bath, hot water, cheaper in rooms with shared bath, hot water, meals on request.

Transport

Bus

To **Coipasa** ask if **Trans Pisiga** (see page 134 is running a fortnightly service. If not, you can take one of the buses for Iquique and get off at the turn-off, but it's difficult to hire a private vehicle for onward transportation in this sparsely populated area. Salinas de Garci Mendoza from **Oruro**, **Trans Cabrera**, C Tejerina y Caro, daily except Sat (Mon, Wed Fri, Sun 1900, Tue, Thu 0830, Sun also at 0730). Return to Oruro same days, US$3.40, 7 hrs. Also **Trans Thunupa**, daily 1800, 1900, office at Tarapacá 1144 entre Caro y Montesinos, T7231 6471.

Salar de Uyuni & around

The Salar de Uyuni is the highest and largest salt lake in the world at an altitude of 3653 m and covering about 12,000 sq km, twice the size of the Great Salt Lake in the United States. For neighbours it has the Salares de Coipasa to the north (see above), Empexa to the west and Chiguana and Chalviri to the south. Driving across a *salar* is one of the most fantastic experiences anywhere on the continent. When it is dry, the surface is covered in pentagonal and hexagonal shapes; bright blue skies contrast with the blinding-white salt crust. To stand on the salt when it is covered by water feels a bit like being an ant on a giant mirror. If there is too much water, it is not possible to drive on the *salares*, but the views of the mountains reflected in the lake make the trip along the edge just as rewarding.

The remarkable landscapes continue to the south in the Lípez region and the Reserva de Fauna Andina Eduardo Avaroa (REA), with magnificent coloured lakes of which the bright red Laguna Colorada and jade-green Laguna Verde are best known. These spectacular soda lakes, rich in birdlife, lie 350 km southwest of Uyuni, across a surreal desert landscape and over unmarked, rugged truck tracks.

Uyuni (population 18,000, altitude 3670 m) lies near the eastern edge of the Salar de Uyuni and is one of the jumping-off points for trips to the salt flats, volcanoes and lakes of southwest Bolivia. With the arrival of regular flights to Uyuni and the paving of the Uyuni–Potosí road, tourism in the area is changing fast, with new hotels and new packages being offered. Still a commercial and communication centre, Uyuni was, for much of the 20th century, important as a major railway junction.

Two monuments dominate Avenida Ferroviaria: one of a railway worker, erected after the 1952 Revolution, and the other commemorating those who died in the Chaco War. Most services are near the station. **Museo Arqueológico y Antropológico de los Andes Meridionales** ① *Arce y Potosí, Mon-Fri 0830-1200, 1400-1800, Sat-Sun 0900-1300, US$0.35*, is small museum with local artefacts. The market is at Potosí y Bolívar and the town's fiesta is 11 July. There is a Railway Cemetery of sorts outside town with engines from 1907 to the 1950s, now rusting hulks. **Pulacayo**, 25 km from Uyuni on the road to Potosí, is a town at the site of a 19th-century silver mine. The

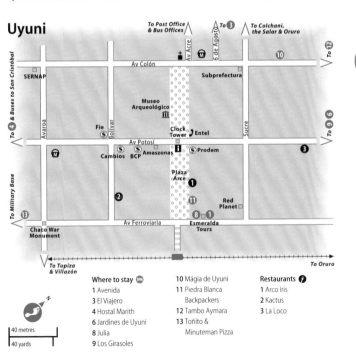

Uyuni

Where to stay
1 Avenida
3 El Viajero
4 Hostal Marith
6 Jardines de Uyuni
8 Julia
9 Los Girasoles
10 Mágia de Uyuni
11 Piedra Blanca Backpackers
12 Tambo Aymara
13 Toñito & Minuteman Pizza

Restaurants
1 Arco Iris
2 Kactus
3 La Loco

train cemetery here is more interesting and contains the first locomotive in Bolivia and the train robbed by Butch Cassidy and the Sundance Kid.

There are ATMs of **Banco FIE** and **BNB**, but they may not always have funds. To be sure, take some cash.

Listings Uyuni *map p145*

Tourist information

Dirección de Turismo Uyuni
At the clock tower, T02-693 2060, or 6794 5797, Mon-Sat 0800-1200, 1430-1830, Sun 0900-1200.
There is another office at the airport.

Subprefectura de Potosí
Colón y Sucre, Mon-Fri 0800-1200, 1430-1830, Sat 0800-1200.
Departmental information office, the place to file complaints in writing.

Immigration office
Calle Potosí, casi Sucre, T7307 9328, Mon-Fri 0830-1230, 1430-1830, Sat-Sun 0900-1100.
For visa extensions.

Safety on the altiplano
Getting stranded out on the altiplano or, worse yet on the *salar* itself, is dangerous because of extreme temperatures and total lack of drinking water. It is best to visit this area with a tour operator that can take you, for example, from Oruro through the *salares* to Uyuni. Travellers with their own vehicles should only attempt this route following extensive local inquiry or after taking on a guide to avoid becoming lost or bogged. The edges of the *salares* are soft and only established entry points or ramps (*terraplenes*) should be used to cross onto or off the salt.

Where to stay

Many hotels fill early, reservations are advised in high season, but new hotels are opening as air and road connections improve. Be conservative with water use, this is a very dry area, water is scarce and supplied at limited hours (better hotels have reserve tanks).

$$$ Jardines de Uyuni
Potosí 113, T02-693 2989, www.hotelesrusticosjardines.com.
Tastefully decorated, comfortable, heating, open fire in the lounge, small pool, parking.

$$$ Mágia de Uyuni
Av Colón 432, T02-693 2541, www.hostalmagiauyuni.com.
Nice ample rooms and suites upstairs with heating, cheaper in older colder rooms downstairs (ask for a heater), parking.

$$$-$$ Los Girasoles
Santa Cruz 155, T693 3323, www.girasoleshotel.hostel.com.
Buffet breakfast, bright and warm (especially 2nd floor), comfortable, nice decor, heaters, cheaper in old section, internet extra.

$$$-$$ Tambo Aymara
Camacho s/n y Colón, T02-693 2227, tamboaymara@gmail.com.
Lovely colonial-style modern hotel, large comfortable rooms, heating, Belgian/Bolivian-owned, operate their own tours.

$$-$ Toñito
Av Ferroviaria 60, T02-693 3186,
www.bolivianexpeditions.com.
Spacious rooms with good beds, solar-
powered showers and heating in new
wing, cheaper in old section with electric
showers, parking, book exchange, tours.

$ Avenida
Av Ferroviaria 11, near train station,
T02-693 2078.
Simple but well maintained, cheaper
with shared bath, hot water (shared
showers 0700-2100), long patio with
laundry facilities, family-run, helpful,
good value, popular and often full.

$ El Viajero
Cabrera 334 y 6 de Agosto, near bus
terminals, T02-693 3549.
Basic rooms, cheaper with shared bath,
electric shower, parking.

$ Hostal Marith
Av Potosí 61, T02-693 2174.
Basic, cheaper with shared bath and in
dorm, electric showers from 0830, patio
with laundry facilities, tours (have salt
hotel at Atulcha near the *salar*).

$ Julia
Ferroviaria 314 y Arce, T02-693 2134,
www.juliahoteluyuni.com.
Spacious rooms, cheaper with shared
bath, electric showers, internet extra.

$ Piedra Blanca Backpackers
Av Arce 27, T7643 7643, www.
piedrablancabackpackers.hostel.com.
Warm, comfortable, private rooms,
some with bath, and dorms, luggage
store extra, has Wi-Fi in common areas,
simple breakfast.

Restaurants

Plaza Arce has various tourist restaurants
serving mostly mediocre pizza.

$$-$ Kactus
Bolívar y Ferroviaria. Daily 0830-2200.
Set lunches and international food à la
carte, also sells pastries and whole-
wheat bread, slow service.

$$-$ La Loco
Av Potosí y Camacho, T693 3105. Mon-Sat
1600-0200 (food until about 2130), closed
Jan-Feb.
International food with a Bolivian and
French touch, music and drinks till late,
open fire, popular, reserve in Jul-Aug.
Also run a small exclusive guesthouse:
La Petite Porte ($$$ www.hotel-
lapetiteporte-uyuni.com), which has a
good reputation.

$ Arco Iris
Plaza Arce. Daily 1600-2230.
Good Italian food, pizza, and
atmosphere, occasional live music.

$ Extreme Fun Pub
Potosí 9.
Restaurant/ pub, pleasant atmosphere,
good service, videos, friendly owner is
very knowledgeable about Bolivia.

$ Minuteman
Attached to Toñito Hotel (see above).
Good pizzas and soups, also serves
breakfast.

What to do

There are over 70 agencies in Uyuni
offering Salar tours and quality varies
greatly. You generally get what you
pay for but your experience will
depend more on your particular
driver, cook and companions than
the agency that sells you the tour.

Tour operators

Andes Travel Office (ATO), *in Hotel Tambo Aymara (see above), T02-693 2227, tamboaymara@gmail.com.* Upmarket private tours, Belgian/Bolivian-owned, English and French spoken, reliable.
Atacama Mística, *www.atacamamistica. cl.* Chilean-Bolivian company, daily tours with transfer to San Pedro de Atacama where the company is based.
Creative Tours, *Sucre 362, T02-693 3543, www.creativetours.com.bo.* Long-established company, partners in the **Tayka** chain of hotels, see above. Premium tours in the region and throughout the country, with another office in Cochabamba and representatives in the main cities.
Esmeralda, *Av Ferroviaria y Arce, T02-693 2130, www.esmeraldatoursuyuni.com.* At the more economical end of market, tours from 1 to 4 days.
Hidalgo Tours, *Av Potosí 113 at Hotel Jardines de Uyuni, www.salardeuyuni.net.* Well-established operator for tours to salt flats and Reserva Eduardo Avaroa, also runs the world's first salt hotel, **Palacio de Sal** and **Mallku Cueva** hotels; also in Potosí.
Mammut, *Peú y Sucre, T7240 4720, www. expedicionesmammut.com.* 1, 2 and 3-day tours to the salt flats and Reserva Eduardo Avaroa, transfers to San Pedro de Atacama and express service to La Paz, Tupiza and other cities. Spanish-speaking guides only.
Red Planet, *Sucre entre Potosí y Av Ferroviaria, T7240 3896, http://redplanet expedition.com.* Tours to the *salar*, 1, 2 and 3 days, also from Potosí, transport from La Paz for groups. English-speaking guides.

Transport

Air
To/from **La Paz**, **Amaszonas**, Potosí y Arce, T02-693 3333, 1 or 2 daily, US$165, also **TAM** 3 times a week.

Bus
Most offices are on Av Arce and Cabrera. A bus terminal is due to be built. To **La Paz**, US$13.75-19.50, 11 hrs, daily at 2000 (La Paz-Uyuni at 1900) with **Panasur**, www.uyunipanasur.com, **Cruz del Norte**, and **Trans Omar**, www.transomar.com; or transfer in Oruro. Tourist buses with **Todo Turismo**, Cabrera 158, T02-693 3337, www.todoturismo.bo, daily at 2000, US$34 (La Paz office, Av Uruguay 102, Edif Paola, p1 of 6, opposite the bus terminal, T02-211 9418, daily to Uyuni at 2100), note this service does not run if the road is poor during the rainy season. **Oruro**, several companies 2000-2130, US$7-10.75, 7 hrs; **Todo Turismo** (see above), US$20. To **Potosí** several companies around 1000 and 1900, US$6, 3-4 hrs, spectacular scenery. To **Sucre**, **6 de Octubre** and **Emperador** at 1000, US$8.35-11.75, 7 hrs; or transfer in Potosí. To **Tupiza** US$8, 8 hrs, via **Atocha**, several companies daily at 0600 and 2030 (from Tupiza at 1000 and 1800), continuing to **Villazón** on the Argentine border, US$11, 11 hrs. For **Tarija** change in Potosí or Tupiza. Regional services to villages in **Nor- and Sud-Lípez** operate about 3 times a week, confirm details locally. To **Pulacayo** take any bus for Potosí.

Car and train
A road and rail line run south from Oruro, through Río Mulato, to Uyuni (323 km, each 7 hrs). The road is sandy (very bad after rain, especially south of Río Mulato). The train journey is more comfortable.

Expreso del Sur leaves for **Oruro** on Thu and Sun at 0005, arriving 0700. **Wara Wara del Sur** leaves on Tue and Fri at 0145, arriving 0910 (prices for both under Oruro, page 134). To **Atocha**, **Tupiza** and **Villazón Expreso del Sur** leaves Uyuni on Tue and Fri at 2240, arriving, respectively, at 0450, 0400 and 0705. **Wara Wara** leaves on Mon and Thu at 0250, arriving 0500, 0835 and 1205. The ticket office (T02-693 2153) opens Mon-Fri 0900-1200, 1430-1800, Sat-Sun 1000-1100, and 1 hr before the trains leave. It closes once tickets are sold – get there early or buy through a tour agent (more expensive).

Advance preparations are required to drive across the *salar* and REA. Fuel is not easily available in the Lípez region, so you must take jerrycans. A permit from the Dirección General de Substancias Controladas in La Paz is needed to fill jerrycans (only two 60 l cans). Fuel for vehicles with foreign plates may be considerably more expensive than for those with local plates.

Salar de Uyuni *Colour map 3, B1/2.*

magical, blinding-white salt flats

★With the uplifting of the Andes 25 million years ago, the altiplano, formerly at sea level, became an immense depression between two mountain ranges. Salt deposits scattered about the surface were dissolved and transported by water courses to the lower lying areas to the south. A series of flooding and drying cycles followed, the most recent of which were Lake Minchín, which flooded the southern altiplano 40,000 to 25,000 years ago, followed by Lake Tauca about 15,000 years ago. The latter filled today's Uyuni and Coipasa salt lakes as well as Lago Poopó for some 3000 years, before drying and leaving the landscape we know today. Drilling in the Salar de Uyuni has revealed successive layers of salt and clay 120 m deep and geophysical studies suggest salt accumulation 500 m below the surface.

Within the salt lakes are islands of volcanic origin, home to a fragile ecosystem. Most evident and striking are a few species of slow-growing columnar cacti, some reaching over 10 m in height. *Vizcachas* (long-tailed rodents) might be seen on the islands as well as a variety of birds. During the warmer rainy season, flamingos nest on shallow parts of the *salar*. On the sides of the islands, terraces mark the level of ancient lakes and in some places, fossilized algae can be seen covering the rock.

The shores of the *salares* have been inhabited for thousands of years; several archaeological sites are found in the region between the salt lakes of Uyuni and Coipasa. People here continue to live a traditional life, growing quinua and potatoes, herding llamas and harvesting salt for trade. The Salar de Uyuni is also rich in minerals and holds the largest deposits of lithium in the world. President Evo Morales declared the deposits a permanent reserve of the state and plans exist to develop the complete production process in Bolivia, from mining to batteries (lithium's prime end-use). A pilot project (away from usual tourist routes) has commenced. The north and west shores of the Salar de Uyuni are populated

Essential Salar de Uyuni

Getting around

Travel is in 4WD Land Cruisers, cramped for those on the back seat, but the staggering scenery makes up for any discomfort.

Booking a tour

Always check the itinerary, the vehicle, the menu (especially vegetarians), what is included in the price and what is not. The most popular trips are three to four days: Salar de Uyuni, Reserva Eduardo Avaroa, and back to Uyuni or on to San Pedro de Atacama (Chile); or Tupiza to Uyuni, San Pedro de Atacama or back to Tupiza. There are also one-to two-day tours. Prices range from US$50-350 pp plus park fee of Bs 150 (US$20) The cheapest tours are not recommended and usually involve crowding, insufficient staff and food, poor vehicles (fatal accidents have taken place) and accommodation. The best value is at the mid- to high-end, where you can assemble your own tour for a total of four or five passengers, with driver, cook, good equipment and services.

Three factors often lead to misunderstandings between what is offered and what is actually delivered by the tour operator:

1 Agencies pool clients when there are not enough passengers to fill a vehicle.
2 Agencies all over Bolivia sell Salar tours, but booking from far away may not give full information on the local operator.

3 Many drivers work for multiple agencies and will cut tours short.

If the tour seriously fails to match the contract and the operator refuses any redress, complaints can be taken to the **Subprefectura de Potosí** in Uyuni (see above) but don't expect a quick refund or apology. Try to speak to travellers who have just returned from a tour before booking your own, and ignore touts on the street and at the rail or bus stations. For tour operators, see Tupiza, page 164.

When to go

The temperature in the salares fluctuates greatly. In direct sun it can reach 30°C in the summer (December to April), it is much cooler in the shade and can fall well below freezing at night, with record low temperatures of -30°C registered in the winter (June to September). The average temperature is 6°C.

During the rainy season (December to April), water can cover part or all of the salar. After the rains, the intense solar radiation and the wind dry the surface and a pure white crust is formed. Beneath this layer, the salt is still wet. As the surface crust cracks, the brine moves up by capillary action, the salt crystalizes as it dries up, forming polygons on the surface. Ojos de agua are round holes that allow you to see water welling up from under the salt crust.

by Aymara people, while Quechuas live near the southern and eastern shores. For information on the north shore of the *salar*, see South of Oruro, page 140.

Trips to the Salar de Uyuni originating in Uyuni enter via the *terraplén* (ramp) at **Colchani,** a small, salt-mining town which has a Museo de la Llama y de la Sal selling souvenirs. Once the salt piles mined in the *salar* have dried, these are trucked to town, where iodine is added to table salt before it is bagged. Every year, some 20,000 tons of salt are extracted here. Tours include stops to see traditional salt mining techniques and the Ojos del Agua, perhaps a call at a salt hotel (see Where to stay, below) and a visit to the **Isla Incahuasi** ⓘ *entry US$4* (also called Isla del Pescado). This is a coral island, raised up from the ocean bed, covered in tall cactii. There is a walking trail with superb views, a café, basic lodging and toilets. If on an extended tour (see below), you may leave the *salar* by another *terraplén*, eg Puerto Chuvica in the southwest. Some tours also include **Gruta de la Galaxia**, an interesting cave at the edge of the *salar*.

San Cristóbal

The original village of San Cristóbal, southwest of Uyuni, was relocated in 2002 to make way for a huge open-pit mine, said to be one of the largest silver deposits in South America. The original church (1650) had been declared a national monument and was therefore rebuilt in its entirety. Ask at the Fundación San Cristóbal Office for the church to be opened as the interior artwork, restored by Italian techniques, is worth seeing. The fiesta is 27-28 July. San Cristóbal and other towns in the area, eg Alota (see below) and Culpina K, were offered tourism projects by the company in exchange for permission to allow the mine to proceed. Dubbed *pueblos auténticos* (authentic towns), they have yet to escape the look of the new money spent on them. The road San Cristóbal–Uyuni is partly paved.

Listings Salar de Uyuni

Where to stay

These *hoteles de sal* are generally visited on tours, seldom independently.

$$$$-$$$ Luna Salada
5 km north of Colchani near the edge of the salar, T7121 2007, La Paz T02-277 0885, www.lunasaladahotel.com.bo.
Lovely salt hotel, comfortable rooms, hot water, ample common areas with lovely views of the *salar*, salt floors, skylights make it warm and cosy, reserve ahead.

$$$$-$$$ Palacio de Sal
on the edge of the salar, near the ramp outside Colchani, T6482 0888, www.palaciodesal.com.bo.
Book through **Hidalgo Tours**, Potosí, T02-622 9512. Spacious, luxury salt hotel, decorated with large salt sculptures, heating, sauna, lookout on 2nd storey with views of the *salar*.

$$$ Mallku Cueva
outside Villa Mar, along the route from Tupiza to the reserve, T02-693 2989, www.hotelesrusticosjardines.com.

Nicely decorated upmarket hotel with all services, including Wi-Fi.

$$$ Tayka
Uyuni office: Sucre 7715 entre Uruguay y México, T02-693 2987, La Paz T02-241 3065, www.taykahoteles.com.
A chain of 4 upmarket hotels in Salar de Uyuni-REA area, operating in conjunction with local communities. The hotels have comfortable rooms with bath, hot water, heating, restaurant, price includes breakfast, discounts in low season. The **Hotel de Sal** (salt hotel) is in Tahua, on the north shore of the Salar; the **Hotel de Piedra** (stone hotel) is in San Pedro de Quemes, on the south shore of the Salar; the **Hotel del Desierto** (desert hotel) is in Ojo de Perdiz in the Siloli Desert, north of Laguna Colorada; the **Hotel de los Volcanes** (volcanoes hotel) is in San Pablo de Lípez, between Uturunco Volcano and Tupiza.

San Cristóbal

$$ Hotel San Cristóbal
In centre, T7264 2117.
Purpose-built and owned by the community. The bar is inside a huge oil drum, all metal furnishings. The rest is comfortable if simple, hot water, good breakfast, evening meal extra.
There are also a couple of inexpensive *alojamientos* in town.

What to do

San Cristóbal
Llama Mama, *T7240 0309.* 60 km of exclusive bicycle trails descending 2-3 or 4 hrs, depending on skill, 3 grades, all inclusive, taken up by car, with guide and communication.

Reserva Nacional de Fauna Andina Eduardo Avaroa   *Colour map 3, C2.*
some of Bolivia's most extraordinary landscapes

In the far southwest of Bolivia, in the Lípez region, is the 714,745-ha Reserva Nacional Eduardo Avaroa (REA). The park protects several endemic species including the vicuña and the nesting grounds of flamingos and other birds. This semi-desert region boasts some of the most beautiful and unusual landscapes in Bolivia.

Ninety-six species of fauna have been recorded in the reserve, including 69 species of bird. Most notable are three species of flamingo, a couple of species of coot and the *suri* (rhea). The birdlife is best seen during the southern summer, November to January. An illustrated guide (in Spanish) is **Aves de la Reserva Nacional de Fauna Andina Eduardo Avaroa** by Omar Rocha and Carmen Quiroga (Museo Nacional de Historia Natural, La Paz 1996, available in La Paz, at the museum). Among the mammals are the vicuña and the *titi* (Andean cat). The flora includes a few stands of *queñua* (polylepis) trees, *yareta* cushion plants and *tholar*, an aromatic shrub which covers the puna.
There are a number of roads and dirt tracks traversing the area between the *salar* and the REA. From Uyuni, there are several approaches, one across the *salar* then via Colcha K, San Juan and Chiguana; an alternative after crossing the *salar*, via Colcha K, San Agustín and Alota. Routes that do not involve crossing the *salar*

are Uyuni via Ramaditas and Alota, or Uyuni, Ramaditas, Culpina, Soniquera, Quetena. These routes may be impassable in the wet season. From Tupiza, access is via San Pablo de Lípez and Quetena Chico, this route involves crossing a river and may also be difficult in the rainy season. From San Pedro de Atacama, Chile, access is via the border post at Hito Cajones.

★Laguna Colorada

There are two access routes from Uyuni (one via the *salar*) and one from Tupiza. This is one of Bolivia's prime attractions and tour vehicles criss-cross the puna every day, many on the route from Uyuni to San Pedro de Atacama (Chile). Roads are still unmarked rugged tracks, however, and may be impassable in the wet season. Laguna Colorada at 4278 m, 346 km southwest of Uyuni, is just one of the highlights of the reserve, its shores and shallows encrusted with borax and salt, an arctic white counterpoint to the flaming red, algae-coloured waters in which the rare James flamingos, along with the more common Chilean and Andean flamingos, breed and live. **Laguna Verde** (lifeless because it is laden with

Essential
Reserva Nacional de Fauna Andina Eduardo Avaroa

Getting there from Tupiza

Tour operators in Tupiza run trips to the REA and Salar de Uyuni and go to places not included on tours from Uyuni (see above). These include the beautiful **Lagunas Celeste** and **Negra** below Cerro Uturunco, which is near Quetena Chico; the **Valle de las Rocas**, 4260 m, between the villages of **Alota** and **Villa Mar** (a vast extension of rocks eroded into fantastic configurations, with polylepis trees in sheltered corners); and isolated communities in the puna. The high altitude scenery is out of this world. With the exception of Quetena Chico, *alojamientos* in the villages on the tour routes cannot be booked. You turn up and search for a room. All provide kitchen space for the tour's cook or independent traveller to prepare meals, take your own stove, though. See also **Tayka** in Salar de Uyuni, Where to stay, above.

Getting around

Motorists should be aware that there are many unmarked rugged tracks that may become impassable in the wet season, it is easy to get lost, especially away from the most visited attractions. The easiest way to visit the park is with an organized tour, as there is only minimal transport to a few communities and no way to get around from one place to another.

Park information

SERNAP office at Colón y Avaroa, Uyuni, T02-693 2225, www.boliviarea. com or www.biobol.org, Monday-Friday 0830-1230, 1430-1800; entry to reserve US$20 (not included in tour prices; pay in bolivianos). Park ranger/entry points are near Laguna Colorada, Lagunas Verde and Blanca, close to the Chilean border, and at Sol de Mañana, near Quetena Chico.

arsenic) and its neighbour **Laguna Blanca**, near the Chilean border, are at the foot of Volcán Licancábur, 5868 m. Between Lagunas Colorada and Verde there are thermal pools at Laguna Blanca (blissful water, a challenge to get out into the bitter wind – no facilities) and at **Polques**, on the shores of Río Amargo/Laguna Salada by the Salar de Chalviri. A *centro comunal* at Polques has dining room, changing room and toilets. All these places are on the 'classic' tour route, across the Salar de Uyuni to **San Juan**, which has a museum of local *chullpas*, and is where most tour companies stop: plenty of lodgings. Other tours stop at **Culpina K**. Then you go to the Salar de Chiguana, Mirador del Volcán de Ollagüe, Cinco Lagunas, a chain of small, flamingo-specked lagoons, the much-photographed Arbol de Piedra in the Siloli desert, then Laguna Colorada (spend the second night here: **Hospedaje Laguna Colorada**, the newer and better $ **Don Humberto** in Huayllajara, and **Campamento Ende**). From Colorada you go over the Cuesta del Pabellón, 4850 m, to the Sol de Mañana geysers (under threat from a geothermal electricity project in 2015; not to be confused with the Sol de Mañana entry point), the Desierto de Dalí, a pure sandy desert as much Daliesque for the spacing of the rocks, with snow-covered peaks behind, as for the shape of the rocks themselves, and Laguna Verde (4400 m).

Jurisdiction of the reserve belongs to the villages of **Quetena Chico** and **Quetena Grande**, to the east of Laguna Colorada. The villagers run lodging in the reserve: Quetena Chico runs *hospedajes* at Laguna Colorada. Quetena Grande runs La Cabaña at Hito Cajones (see below). In Quetena Chico is the reserve's visitors information centre, **Centro Ecológico Ch'aska** ⓘ *daily 0730-1800*, informative displays about the region's geology, vulcanology, fauna, flora and human history; a worthwhile stop. The village has two cheap *hospedajes* (**Piedra Preciosa** and **Hostal Quetena**, hot water extra), and places to eat.

Sadly, lakes in the reserve are gradually drying up, most noticeably Laguna Verde. This has been attributed to global climate change but the real reason may be massive underground water consumption by Bolivian, Chilean and Argentine mines.

Crossing into Chile

There is a REA ranger station near Lagunas Blanca and Verde: if going from Bolivia, have your park entry receipt at hand, if crossing from Chile pay the entry fee here. Alongside is a refugio, **La Cabaña** (US$5 per person in comfortable but very cold dorms, solar-powered lighting, hot water seldom works, cooking facilities but take your own food; in high season book in advance – tour agencies can do this by radio).

There is good climbing and hiking in the area with outstanding views. You must register at the ranger station before heading out and they may insist that you take a guide (eg to climb Licancábur, US$30 for guide plus US$40 for transport).

Tip...
Mind the altitude, intense solar radiation and lack of drinking water.

From the ranger station it's 5 km to the border at **Hito Cajones** (on the Chilean side called Hito Cajón), 4500 m. Bolivian immigration open 0800-2100, charges US$2 in any currency. If you plan to cross to Chile here, you should first go to the immigration office in Uyuni (see above). There are no services or facilities at the border. A further 6 km along a good dirt road into Chile is the intersection with the fully paved road from San Pedro de Atacama to Paso de Jama, the border between Chile and Argentina. From here it's 40 km (2000 m downhill) to San Pedro. Chilean customs and immigration are just outside San Pedro and can take 45 minutes at busy times. See Transport, below.

Listings Reserva Nacional de Fauna Andina Eduardo Avaroa

Where to stay

For the Takya hotels in the REA area, see Salar de Uyuni, above.

$$$ Mallku Cueva
Outside Villa Mar, along the route from Tupiza to the reserve, T02-693 2989, www.hotelesrusticosjardines.com.
Nicely decorated upmarket hotel with all services, including Wi-Fi.

San Cristóbal

$$ Hotel San Cristóbal
In centre, T7264 2117.
Purpose-built and owned by the community. The bar is inside a huge oil drum, all metal furnishings. The rest is comfortable if simple, hot water, good breakfast, evening meal extra.

There are also a couple of inexpensive *alojamientos* in town.

What to do

San Cristóbal
Llama Mama, *T7240 0309.* 60 km of exclusive bicycle trails descending 2-3 or 4 hrs, depending on skill, 3 grades, all inclusive, taken up by car, with guide and communication.

Transport

Crossing into Chile
The easiest way is to go to San Pedro de Atacama as part of your tour to the *salar* and REA (see above). **Colque Tours** (www.colquetours.com) runs 2 minibuses daily from near the ranger station at Hito Cajones to San Pedro de Atacama, departing 1000 and 1700, US$6.50, 1 hr including stop at immigration. At other times onward transport to San Pedro must be arranged by your agency, this can cost up to US$60 if it is an add-on to your tour. The ranger station may be able to assist in an emergency. From Uyuni to **Avaroa** and on to **Calama, Centenario,** *Cabrera y Arce, Sun, Mon, Wed, Thu at 0330*, transfer at the border to **Frontera (daily** from Calama to Ollagüe) or Atacama, Thu, Mon 2000. To Avaroa, 4½ hrs; to Calama, another 4 hrs, US$21 in total; allow 2 hrs at the border (all times minimum).

If driving your own vehicle, from **Colchani** it is about 60 km across to the southern shore of the *salar.* Follow

Tip...
Chile is one hour ahead of Bolivia from mid-October to March. Chile does not allow coca, dairy produce, tea bags, fruit or vegetables to be brought in.

the tracks made by other vehicles in the dry season. The salt is soft and wet for about 2 km around the edges so only use established ramps. It is 20 km from the southern shore to Colcha K military checkpoint. From there, a poor gravel road leads 28 km to San Juan then the road enters the Salar de Chiguana, a mix of salt and mud which is often wet and soft with deep tracks which are easy to follow; 35 km away is Chiguana, another military post, then 45 km to the end of this *salar*, a few kilometres before border at Ollagüe. This latter part is the most dangerous; very slippery with little traffic. Or take the route that tours use to Laguna Colorada and continue to Hito Cajones. **Atacama Mística** of Uyuni will let you follow one of their groups if you arrange in advance. There is no fuel between Uyuni and Calama (Chile) if going via Ollagüe, but expensive fuel is sold in San Pedro de Atacama. Keep to the road at all times; the road is impassable after rain.

Tupiza *Colour map 3, C3.*

last hideout of Butch Cassidy and the Sundance Kid

Set in a landscape of colourful, eroded mountains and stands of huge cactii (usually flowering December-February), Tupiza, 200 km south of Uyuni, is a pleasant town (population 25,709) with a lower altitude (2975 m) and milder climate, making it a good alternative for visits to the Reserva Eduardo Avaroa and the *salar*.

Several Tupiza operators offer Salar, REA and local tours. The town lies in the narrow, fertile valley of the Río Tupiza with a microclimate, much warmer than other towns at an equivalent altitude. Capital of the Sud Chichas province of the department of the Potosí, Tupiza was a centre of the silver, tin, lead and bismuth mining industries. The simple **Museo Municipal** ⓘ *Calle Sucre by Plaza Independencia, 2nd floor, T02-694 2304, Mon-Fri 1800-1900 (on request at other times) free*, has photographs, mining equipment and military artefacts. Beautiful sunsets over the fertile Tupiza valley can be seen from the foot of a statue of Christ on a hill behind the plaza, **Cerro Corazón de Jesús**. For a more spectacular view, climb to the cross at **Cerro de la Cruz**, on the opposite side of the river. In the hills behind the cross is **Cerro Elefante**, with a remarkable likeness to an elephant. The climb makes pleasant half day trip with great views. Note that access is from the same side as the elephant's trunk, not the blue sign.

> **Tip...**
> Don't rely on the ATMs in Tupiza; take cash.

Around Tupiza

Circuitos Bioculturales There is good hiking around Tupiza but be prepared for sudden changes of climate, including hailstorms, and note that dry gullies are prone to flash flooding. The routes are very scenic and the villages are tranquil. You can arrange to spend a couple of days relaxing there. A worthwhile excursion is to **Quebrada Palala**, a good place to admire the local vegetation, particularly four species of the giant *Trichocereus* cacti and spectacular red stone formations.

You can take a minibus marked Palala (No 2) on Avenida Chichas, opposite the Mercado Negro, to the village of Palala at the end of the line, where the road meets the *quebrada* (dry river bed), follow it to the west (left), there is much to explore in the main and side valleys. Vehicles go along the river bed, follow their tracks. In about 3 km the gully splits, Quebrada Palala continues along the right branch, while straight on, along the left branch in 6.5 km you reach the 'Stone Forest', **Bosque e Piedra**, a breathtaking area of eroded stone pinnacles. Here is the hamlet of **Torre Huayco**, part of a community tourism project, Circuitos Bioculturales. **Oploca**, a small town 17 km northwest of Tupiza with a lovely colonial church, is also part of the project, as is **Chuquiago**, 30 km south of Tupiza, along the rail line. Each has a small *eco-albergue* ($ per person, with breakfast, simple comfortable rooms, kitchen) and guides. A circuit can be done in one to three days by bicycle, horse, trekking, jeep, or a combination of these (US$35-50 per day, ask tour operators in Tupiza).

★**El Cañon** In about two hours you can walk from Tupiza to El Cañon. Follow the road to the left of the cathedral out of town between the cemetery and the barracks. Continue as the road curves right until you reach a dry river bed. Follow this to the left towards the hills. Here are some superb rock formations – huge pinnacles of rock and soil, only a few inches thick, which seem to defy gravity. The valley narrows rapidly but the path follows a stream bed for several hundred metres to a series of picturesque waterfalls (dry most of the year).

★**Valle de los Machos and El Cañon del Inca** From the Plazuela El Castillín, walk up 26 de Agosto, turn left and then between two hills. Follow the road 1.5 km until it crosses the large dry river bed of Quebrada Palmira. From here you will see the **Puerta del Diablo** (Devil's Doorway) on your right-hand side, which resembles huge plates from the spine of a stegosaurus. Pass through these, follow the riverbed, where this forks, stay right. About 500 m later you arrive at a collection of phallic pinnacles, aptly named Valle de los Machos. Continue ahead to the start of El Cañon del Inca. Be prepared to climb what would be, in the rainy season, small waterfalls; when in doubt, always take the right fork. You don't have to continue to the end of the canyon, but if you do, you can climb to the saddle which divides El Cañon del Inca from El Cañon, see above. The round trip from Tupiza, returning via El Cañon takes about six hours.

★**South of Tupiza** To the south of town are five sights; you can walk to them or visit them with a tour. **Quebrada Seca**, is a riverbed with dry vegetation where water seldom runs. You are supposed to see nine contrasting colours in the hills, from purples to greens. To get there take a Villa Florida bus to the end of the line and walk about 500 m; before the YPFB plant turn right. You can continue for 10 km to **Toroyoj** on the Río San Juan de Oro, which is a good place to picnic on a sandy shore beneath weeping willows. **La Torre**, a 40-m-high eroded pinnacle, also on the Río San Juan de Oro, is 14 km from Tupiza. The stretch along the river between Toroyoj and La Torre is beautiful and good for horse riding or walking (cross at the bridge in Toroyoj and follow the south shore downriver). From La Torre you can continue downriver 2 km to **Entre Ríos**, the confluence of the Río San Juan de Oro (red) and Río Tupiza (green); here you meet the road to Villazón. Along the road going back to Tupiza is **El Angosto**, where the road and train track head through two tunnels.

Butch Cassidy and the Sundance Kid tours The statue in the main plaza in Tupiza is to **Víctor Carlos Aramayo** (1802-1882), of the 19th-century mining dynasty. Butch and Sundance's last holdup was of an Aramayo company payroll at Huaca Huañusca on 4 November 1908. The payroll set out from Chajra Huasi, the Aramayo's palazzo-style home, just out of town across the Río Tupiza (the house is in disrepair). They are believed by some (see *Digging Up Butch and Sundance*, by Anne Meadows, Bison Books, 2003) to have died soon afterwards at the hands of a police patrol in **San Vicente**, a tiny mining camp at 4500 m, but no grave in the San Vicente cemetery has yet to be positively identified as theirs. There is a small museum with local artifacts but no lodging or other services. Visits can be arranged by Tupiza agencies (see below).

Tupiza

| 100 metres |
| 100 yards |

Where to stay 🛏
1 Hostales Alvarez & Pedro Arraya
2 Hostal Valle Hermoso

3 Hostal Valle Hermoso II
4 La Torre
5 Los Salares
6 Mitru Annex
7 Mitru & Tupiza Tours
8 Refugio del Turista

9 Res Centro

Restaurants 🍴
1 California
2 Heladería Cremalín & Muxsa

3 La Pepsi
4 Los Alamos
5 Parrillero El Sauna
6 Tu Pizza

ON THE ROAD

A tale of two outlaws

The movie *Butch Cassidy and the Sundance Kid* is based on a true story. Butch Cassidy, born Robert Leroy Parker in 1866, was the eldest of 13 children in a Mormon family in Utah. A cowboy named Cassidy and a stint as a butcher inspired his nom de crime. Sundance, born Harry Alonzo Longabaugh in 1867, was the youngest of five children in a Baptist family from Pennsylvania. He got his name by serving 18 months in jail at Sundance, Wyoming, for stealing a horse. Butch and Sundance belonged to a gang dubbed the Wild Bunch. They held up trains, banks and mine payrolls in the Rocky Mountain West. With US$1000 rewards on their heads and the Pinkerton Detective Agency (later to become the FBI) on their tail, Butch and Sundance fled to South America in 1901, settling in Patagonia in Argentina, where they peacefully homesteaded a ranch, raising sheep, cattle and horses. The peaceful life didn't last, however. Their names were linked to a bank robbery in Río Gallegos and the police issued an order for their arrest. In 1906, they found work at the Concordia Tin Mine in the central Bolivian Andes, but Butch still wanted to settle down as a respectable rancher. The bandits quit their jobs in 1908, soon after turning up in the mining centre of Tupiza, where they intended to rob a bank, perhaps to finance their retirement. They soon turned their attention to the Aramayo mining company, after Butch learned that the local manager would be taking an unguarded payroll from Tupiza to Quechisla, a three-day journey to the northwest. So, on 3 November, the manager set off. As he made his way up

South to Argentine border

Villazón The Argentine border is at Villazón (population 37,133, altitude 3443 m), 81 km south of Tupiza. There is a museum about the Chicha culture at the plaza. Of traditional villages in the surroundings, those to the west, like **Berque**, are known for their pottery. Many *casas de cambio* on Avenida República de Argentina, leading to the border, change US dollars, pesos and euros, all at poor rates. There are banks and an ATM in town. The border area must not be photographed.

Border with Argentina The Bolivian immigration office is on Avenida República de Argentina just before bridge, open daily 0600-2000, taxi from Villazón bus terminal US$0.50 per person. Queuing begins at 0500 and there may be long delays. Argentine immigration (open 0700-2400 Argentine time, see below) is on the other side of the bridge, 10 blocks from La Quiaca bus terminal, taxi US$1. Entering Bolivia, boys offer to wheel your bags uphill to the bus stations, US$1, but they will ask for more. The Argentine consulate is at Plaza 6 de Agosto 121, T02-597 2011, Monday-Friday 0800-1300. **Note** Argentine time is one hour later than Bolivia, two hours when Buenos Aires adopts daylight saving.

> **Tip...**
> Change all your bolivianos in Villazón as there is nowhere to do so in La Quiaca or beyond.

Huaca Huañusca (Dead Cow Hill), near Salo, he was held up by two bandits. Once the bandits had departed, the manager alerted his bosses and the alarm went out to local authorities, as well as to Argentine and Chilean border officials. With military patrols and armed miners (whose pay had been stolen) in pursuit, the pair headed north towards Uyuni. They followed the long, rugged trail to San Vicente, a tiny mining village set in an utterly barren landscape 4000 m up in the Cordillera Occidental. At sundown on 6 November 1908, they rode into town and were given a room for the night. There they met Cleto Bellot, with whom they discussed their plans to head north to Uyuni. Bellot went straight to the home of a neighbour, where a four-man posse from Uyuni was staying. They had galloped in that afternoon and told Bellot to be on the lookout for two Yankees. Accompanied by Bellot, they went to the house. A gun battle ensued, then all went quiet. At dawn they entered the house, where they found the two bandits stretched out on the floor, dead, both with bullet holes in the head. Butch had shot his partner and then turned the gun on himself. The outlaws were buried in the local cemetery that afternoon in unmarked graves, but their deaths were not widely reported in the United States until 1930. In the meantime, wild stories of their demise circulated. Some claim that the two outlaws killed in San Vicente were not actually Butch and Sundance and sightings of them were reported after the event. An exhumation at the San Vicente cemetery in 1991 failed to settle this long-running controversy. (Adapted from *Death in the Andes: The Last Days of Butch Cassidy and The Sundance Kid*, by Daniel Buck and Anne Meadows, Washington DC.)

Listings Tupiza maps p159 and p163

Where to stay

$$-$ Mitru
Av Chichas 187, T02-694 3001,
www.hotelmitru.com.
Pleasant ample grounds with pool, nice atmosphere, a variety of rooms and prices, the more expensive rooms have king-size beds, a/c and hairdryers, cheaper in older section with private bath and even cheaper with shared bath. All include good buffet breakfast with bread made on the premises, reliable solar hot water, parking, luggage store, book exchange, Wi-Fi. Very helpful and knowledgeable, popular, reserve ahead in high season. Warmly recommended.

$ Hostal Alvarez
Av P Arraya 492, T02-694 5327.
Near the bus and train stations, Small 10-room hostel, brighter rooms on 2nd storey, cheaper with shared bath, extra charge for a/c and breakfast, new in 2013.

$ Hostal Pedro Arraya
Av P Arraya 494, T02-694 2734,
www.hostalpedroarraya.com.
Convenient to bus and train stations, small rooms, cheaper with shared bath,

hot water, breakfast available, laundry
facilities, terrace, family-run.

$ Hostal Valle Hermoso
Av Pedro Arraya 478, T02-694 3441,
www.vallehermosotours.com.
Breakfast available, cheaper with shared
bath, cheaper in dorm. TV/breakfast
room, book exchange, motorbike
parking. Second location, **Valle
Hermoso II**, Av Pedro Arraya 585, near
the bus station, 3 simple rooms with
bath, several dorms with bunk beds,
same prices as No 1.

$ La Torre
Av Chichas 220, T02-694 2633,
www.latorretours-tupiza.com.
Lovely refurbished house, newer rooms
at back, comfortable, cheaper with
shared bath and no TV, great service,
good value. Recommended.

$ Los Salares
C Ecuador s/n, Zona Chajrahuasi, behind
petrol station, T02-694 5813,
www.lossalares.hostel.com.
9 rooms, 1 without bath (cheaper),
continental breakfast and kitchen,
parking, a bit out of town.

$ Mitru Annex
Avaroa 20, T02-694 3002,
www.tupizatours.com.
Nicely refurbished older hotel, buffet
breakfast, cheaper with shared bath,
good hot showers, Wi-Fi, use of pool and
games room at **Hotel Mitru** (see above).

$ Refugio del Turista
Av Santa Cruz 240, T02-694 3155,
www.tupizatours.com.
Refurbished home with garden, shared
bath, reliable hot water, well-equipped
kitchen, laundry facilities, parking and
electric outlet for camper vans, popular
budget option, good value.

$ Residencial Centro
Av Santa Cruz 287, T02-694 2705.
Nice patio, couple of rooms with private
bath, most shared, basic but clean,
hot water, parking, helpful owner,
good value.

Villazón

$ Hostal Plaza
Plaza 6 de Agosto 138, T02-597 3535.
Adequate rooms, cheaper without
bath, electric shower, includes simple
breakfast, good restaurant, **La Perla**,
underneath hotel, also internet below.

$ Olimpo
Av República Argentina 116
y Chorolque, T02-597 2219,
www.olimpogranhotel.com.
Among the better hotels in town,
cheaper with shared bath, includes
simple breakfast.

$ Tierra Andina
25 de Mayo 52, T02-594 5133.
Another good option, with and without
bath and most economical in 4-bed
dorms, includes a very basic breakfast.

Restaurants

Several touristy pizza places on C
Florida are mediocre to terrible, also
watch your belongings here. The
best options are just outside town
(all **$$-$**), they serve grilled meat and
good regional specialities like *picante
de cabrito* (spicy goat) but open only
Sat or Sun midday – go early. These
include: **La Campiña**, in Tambillo
Alto, 45 mins' walk north along the
river; and La Estancia, 2 km north in
Villa Remedios. There are food stalls
upstairs in the market but mind
the cleanliness.

$$-$ Café Muxsa
Cochabamba 133 y Florida, on Plaza,
Tue-Sun 1700-2200.
A variety of good-quality sandwiches,
tacos and salads, nicely served, good
coffee, pastries, Wi-Fi, popular.

$ California
Cochabamba 413, 2nd floor.
Set lunches, hamburgers and snacks
in the evening when service is slow.

$ Los Alamos
Av Chichas 157. Open 0800-2400.
Local and international dishes, good

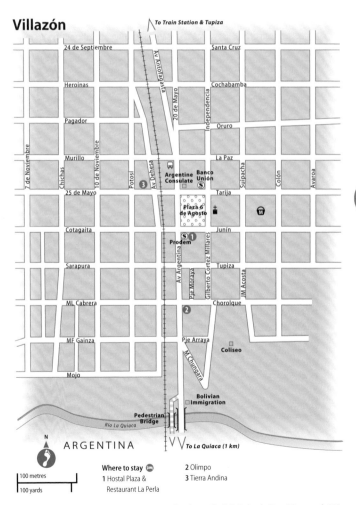

Villazón

Where to stay
1 Hostal Plaza &
  Restaurant La Perla

2 Olimpo
3 Tierra Andina

atmosphere, average food, good juices, large portions, popular with tourists.

$ Parrillero El Sauna
Av Santa Cruz entre Avaroa y Junín. Tue-Sun from 1700.
Very good *parrilladas* with Argentine meat, salad buffet.

$ Tu Pizza
Sucre y 7 de Noviembre, on Plaza. Mon-Sat 1830-2300.
Cute name, variety of pizzas, very slow service.

Heladería Cremalín
Cochabamba y Florida, on Plaza, ice cream, juices and fruit shakes.

La Pepsi
Avaroa s/n, Mon-Sat 0830-1830.
Salteñas in the morning, also very good sweet and savoury pastries, sandwiches, juices, cappuccino.

What to do

Tour operators in Tupiza run trips to the REA and Salar de Uyuni and go to places not included on tours from Uyuni.

Tours on offer include 1-day jeep tours US$35 pp for group of 5; horse riding 3-, 5- and 7-hr tours, the latter includes lunch, US$10 per hr, multi-day tours US$70 per day; 2-day San Vicente plus colonial town of Portugalete US$80 pp (plus lodging); Salar de Uyuni and REA, 4 days with Spanish-speaking guide, US$200 pp for a group of 5, plus Bs150 (US$20) park fee. Add US$23 pp for English-speaking guide.
La Torre Tours, *in Hotel La Torre (see above)*. Salar/REA tours and local trips on jeep, bicycle, walking or horse riding.
Tupiza Tours, *in Hotel Mitru (see above), www.tupizatours.com.* Highly experienced and well organized for Salar/REA and local tours. Also offer 1-day 'triathlon' of horse riding, biking and jeep, US$50 pp for group of 5, a good way to see the area if you only have 1 day; Butch Cassidy tours; Paseos Bioculturales, and extensions to the Uyuni tour. Have offices in La Paz and Tarija, and offer tours in all regions of Bolivia. Highly recommended.
Valle Hermoso Tours, *in Hostal Valle Hermoso 1 (see above), www. vallehermosotours.com.* Offers similar tours on horse or jeep, as do several other agencies and most Tupiza hotels.

Transport

Bus
There is a small, well-organized bus terminal at the south end of Av Pedro Arraya. To **Villazón** several buses daily, USUS2.75, 2 hrs; also **ATL** minibuses from opposite terminal, leave when full, US$4. To **Potosí**, several companies around 1000 and 2100, US$6, 8 hrs. To **Sucre**, **Expreso Villazón** at 1500, **Trans Illimani** at 2030 (more comfortable but known to speed), US$11.50, 12 hrs; or transfer in Potosí. To **Tarija**, several around 1930-2030, US$9.50-12.25, 6 hrs (change here for **Santa Cruz**). To **Uyuni**, several companies around 1000 and 1800, US$8, 8 hrs. To **Oruro**, **Trans Illimani** at 1300, 1800, US$13, 12 hrs; continuing to **Cochabamba**, US$19, 17 hrs. To **La Paz** several at 1200 and 1730-2030, US$19-25, 16-17 hrs. Agent for the Argentine company **Balut** at terminal sells tickets to Jujuy, Salta, Buenos Aires or Córdoba (local bus to the border at Villazón, then change to Balut), but beware overcharging or buy tickets directly from local companies once in Argentina.

Train

Train station ticket office, T02-694 2529, open Mon-Sat 0800-1100, 1530-1730, and early morning 30 minutes before trains arrive. To **Villazón**: **Expreso del Sur** Wed and Sat at 0410; **Wara Wara** Mon and Thu at 0905. To **Atocha**, **Uyuni** and **Oruro**: **Expreso del Sur** Wed and Sat at 1825; **Wara Wara** Mon and Thu at 1905. Fares are given under Oruro, page 134.

Villazón
Bus

Bus terminal is near the plaza, 5 blocks from the border. Lots of company offices. Taxi to border, US$0.50 or hire a porter, US$1, and walk. From **La Paz**, several companies, 18 hrs, US$18.75-25, *bus-cama* US$36 (even though buses are called 'direct', you may have to change in Potosí), depart La Paz 1630, depart **Villazón** 0830-1000 and 1830-1900. To **Potosí** several between 0800-0900 and 1830-1900, US$11, 10 hrs. To **Tupiza**, several daily, US$2.75. To **Tarija**, US$6.40, 7 hrs. Tickets for buses in **Argentina** are sold in Villazón but beware of scams and overcharging. Buy only from company offices, never from sellers in the street. Safer still, cross to La Quiaca and buy onward tickets there.

Car

The road north from Villazón through Tupiza, Potosí and Sucre, to Cochabamba or Santa Cruz is paved. About 30% of the scenic road to Tarija is paved. A second road from Tupiza to Tarija is mostly paved.

Train

Station about 1 km north of border on main road, T02-597 2565. To Tupiza, Atocha, Uyuni and Oruro: **Expreso del Sur** Wed and Sat at 1530; **Wara Wara** Mon and Thu at 1530. Fares are given under Oruro, page 134.

Central & southern highlands

Sucre and Potosí are the finest examples of Bolivia's colonial heritage and two of its main tourist attractions. They lie only three hours apart but couldn't be more different.

Isolation has helped Sucre preserve its courtly charm and the assured confidence befitting the country's official capital, legal centre and major university city. Surrounding this sparkling white colonial masterpiece is a hinterland of traditional weaving villages, which burst into life during market days and festivals. Dinosaur-hunters are also making tracks for Sucre, with the discovery of many prehistoric footprints.

Potosí is not only the highest city in the world, at over 4000 m, but was once the largest, wealthiest city in the Americas. All around are reminders of its silver-mining heyday, while towering over the city is the giant pink hulk of Cerro Rico – Rich Mountain – from which the silver was extracted, at an unimaginable human cost. Visitors can join miners and burrow down into its bowels and experience what life was like for those who were forced to enter the 'Mouth of Hell'.

Further south is Tarija, a pleasant city with a delightful climate, known for its fruit and wines, and for its traditions, which set it apart from the rest of the country.

Best for
Colonial history ▪ Fossils ▪ Textiles ▪ Wine

Footprint picks

★ **Dinosaur footprints around Sucre**, page 173
The world's largest palaeontological site.

★ **Textile shopping**, page 180
Traditional weaving in the Chuquisaca region.

★ **Casa Nacional de Moneda**, page 185
The National Mint is one of South America's
finest museums.

★ **Cerro Rico mines**, page 190
Fascinating but disturbing journey into a working mine.

★ **Chapaco life in Tarija**, page 202
One of the most laid-back and friendly towns in
the country.

★ **Wine tasting around Tarija**, page 210
Bolivia's only wine region has the highest vinyards in
the world.

Footprint
picks

1 **Dinosaur footprints around Sucre**, page 173
2 **Textile shopping**, page 180
3 **Casa Nacional de Moneda**, page 185
4 **Cerro Rico mines**, page 190
5 **Chapaco life in Tarija**, page 202
6 **Wine tasting around Tarija**, page 210

Sucre

Sucre is sometimes referred to as La Ciudad Blanca, owing to the tradition that all buildings in the centre are painted in their original colonial white. This works to beautiful effect and in 1991 UNESCO declared the city a World Heritage Site. There are two universities, the older dating from 1624. Founded in 1538 as La Plata, Sucre became capital of the Audiencia of Charcas in 1559. Its name was later changed to Chuquisaca before the present name was adopted in 1825 in honour of the second president of the new republic. From 1825 to 1899 Sucre was the only capital of Bolivia; nowadays, with a population of 338,281, it remains the constitutional capital as it is home to Bolivia's judicial branch although La Paz is the administrative one. *La capitalidad* remains an emotionally charged issue among *sucrenses*, who strive to see Sucre regain its status as the only capital.

Weather Sucre

Month	High	Low	Rainfall
January	21°C	11°C	114mm
February	20°C	10°C	103mm
March	20°C	10°C	66mm
April	21°C	9°C	26mm
May	21°C	7°C	5mm
June	21°C	5°C	.3mm
July	20°C	5°C	8mm
August	21°C	6°C	5mm
September	22°C	7°C	25mm
October	22°C	9°C	40mm
November	22°C	10°C	57mm
December	22°C	11°C	76mm

Plaza 25 de Mayo and around

Plaza 25 de Mayo is large, spacious, full of trees and surrounded by elegant buildings. Among these are the **Casa de la Libertad** ⓘ *T04-645 4200, Tue-Sat 0900-1230, 1430-1800, US$2.15 with tour; US$5.80 video.* Formerly the Assembly Hall of the Jesuit University, where the country's Declaration of Independence was signed, this house contains a famous portrait of Simón Bolívar by the Peruvian artist Gil de Castro, admired for its likeness. Also on the plaza are the beautiful 17th-century **cathedral** and **Museo Eclesiástico** ⓘ *Ortiz 61, T04-645 2257, Mon-Fri 1000-1200, 1500-1700, US$1.45.* Worth seeing are the famous jewel-encrusted Virgin of Guadalupe, 1601, and works by Viti, the first great painter of the New World, who studied under Raphael.

Essential Sucre

Finding your feet

Sucre's airport, 5 km northwest of town, has regular services to and from La Paz, Santa Cruz, Cochabamba and Tarija. Access by road to Potosí is straightforward and quite quick. To get elsewhere by road takes time, but there are daily bus services to all major cities. The bus terminal is on the northern outskirts of town, 3 km from the centre. See also Transport, page 178.

When to go

Sucre has a pleasant climate. In winter, May-August, days are sunny and mild, nights are cold (temperatures can drop below freezing in June to July). December-March there is rain, but also many sunny days.

Safety

Caution is advised after 2200 and in market areas.

Time required

Two or three days.

South of the plaza Visits to **San Felipe Neri** ⓘ *entrance through school, Ortiz 165 y Azurduy, T04-645 4333, Mon-Sat 1400-1800, US$1.45 (extra charge for photos),* include the neoclassical church with its courtyard, the crypt and the roof (note the penitents' benches), which offers fine views over the city. The monastery is used as a school. Diagonally opposite is the church of **La Merced** ⓘ *T04-645 1338,* which is notable for its gilded central and side altars. The **Museo Universitario Charcas** ⓘ *Bolívar 698, T04-645 3285, Mon-Fri 0800-1200, 1400-1800, Sat 0800-1200, US$0.50, photos extra,* has anthropological, archaeological and folkloric exhibits, and colonial collections and presidential and modern-art galleries.

East of the plaza **San Lázaro** (1538) ⓘ *Calvo y Padilla, Mass daily 0700, Sun also 1900,* is regarded as the first cathedral of La Plata (Sucre). On the nave walls are six paintings attributed to Zurbarán; it has fine silverwork and alabaster in the baptistery. San Miguel, San Francisco and San Lázaro are only open during Mass. The **Monasterio de Santa Clara** ⓘ *Calvo 212, Mass daily*

0730, museum open Mon-Fri 1400-1800, Sat 1400-1730, US$2, good guided tours in Spanish, displays paintings by Bitti, sculptures, books, vestments, some silver and musical instruments (including a 1664 organ). Small items made by the nuns are on sale. The excellent **Museo de Arte Indígena ASUR (Museo Téxtil Etnográfico)**

Sucre

To Mercado Campesino

To Buses to Tarabuco

To ASUR & ❸ ❹

100 metres

100 yards

Where to stay
1 Austria *B3*
2 Casa de Huéspedes Finita *D3*
3 Casa Kolping *D3*
4 El Hostal de Su Merced *D2*
5 Forastero *C1*
6 Grand *C2*
7 Hostal Charcas *C2*
8 Hostal Colón 220 *D1*
9 Hostal Los Pinos *D1*
10 Hostal San Francisco *B2*
11 Hostal Santa Teresa de Jesús *D3*
12 Hostelling International Sucre *B3*
13 Independencia *C2*
14 Kultur Berlin *D3*
15 La Posada *D2*
16 La Selenita *D3*
17 Monasterio *D3*
18 Pachamama Hostal *A3*
19 Parador Santa María La Real *D2*
20 San Marino Royal *C2*
21 Villa Antigua *D3*
22 Villa de la Plata *B3*

Restaurants
1 Amsterdam *C3*
2 Bibliocafé *D2*
3 Café Florín *D2*
4 Café Mirador *D3*
5 El Germen *C3*
6 El Patio *C2*
7 El Tapado *C1*
8 Joy Ride Café, tour agency & shop *D2*
9 Kultur Berlin *D3*
10 La Patisserie *D2*
11 La Taverne *C2*
12 Locot's Café Aventura *C3*
13 Los Balcones & Abis *C2*
14 Metro Café *C2*
15 Nouvelle Cuisine *D3*

① *Pasaje Iturricha 314, opposite Casa Kolping in La Recoleta, T04-645 6651, www. asur.org.bo, Mon-Fri 0900-1200, 1430-1830, Sat 0930-1200, 1400-1800, US$3, English and French-speaking guides*, displays regional textiles and traditional techniques, shop sells crafts. Near the main plaza is the **Museo Nacional de Etnografía y Folklore (MUSEF)** ① *España 74 y San Alberto, T04-645 5293, www.musef.org.bo, Tue-Fri 0930-1230, 1430-1830, Sat 0930-1230, free*, with an impressive display of masks and an exhibition on the Uru-Chipaya culture.

North of the plaza **San Miguel** ① *Arenales 10, T04-645 1026, Mass Mon-Sat 0800 and 1915, Sun 1100, no shorts, short skirts or short sleeves allowed*, completed in 1628, has been restored and is very beautiful with Moorish-style carved and painted ceilings, *alfarjes* (early 17th century), pure-white walls and gold and silver altar. Some early sculpture can be seen in the sacristy. Nearby **Santa Mónica** ① *Arenales y Junín*, is one of the finest gems of Spanish architecture in the Americas, but has been converted into the theatre and hall for the Colegio Sagrado Corazón. Near the Mercado Central, **San Francisco** (1581) ① *Ravelo y Arce, Mass daily 0700 and 1900, Sun also 1030 and 1700*, has altars coated in gold leaf and 17th-century ceilings; one of its bells summoned the people of Sucre to struggle for independence.

Four blocks northwest of Plaza 25 de Mayo is the **Corte Suprema de Justicia** ① *Luis Paz Arce 352, Mon-Fri 1000-1200, 1500-1800, free*, the seat of Bolivia's national judiciary and what remains of the city's official status as capital of Bolivia. To enter you must be smartly dressed and leave your passport with the guard; guides can be found in the public relations office. The nearby **Parque Bolívar** contains a monument and a miniature of the Eiffel Tower and Arc de Triomphe in honour of one of Bolivia's richest 20th-century tin barons, Francisco Argandoña, who created much of Sucre's splendour. At the downhill-end of the park is the **Fuente del Bicentenario**, where a **sound and light show** ① *Thu-Sun 1900-2100*, is displayed. The **obelisk** opposite the Teatro Gran Mariscal, in Plazuela Libertad, was erected with money raised by fining bakers who cheated on the size and weight of their bread. Also on this plaza is the Hospital Santa Bárbara (1574).

Around Sucre

South of Sucre Southeast of the city, at the top of Dalence is **La Recoleta**, a lookout with arches, offering good views over the city. Here, within the Franciscan convent of La Recoleta is the **Museo de la Recoleta** ① *Plaza Pedro de Anzúrez, T04-645 1987, Mon-Fri 0830-1200, 1430-1730, Sat 1500-1700, US$1.45 for entrance to all collections, guided tours only*, notable mainly for the beauty of its cloisters and gardens; the carved wooden choir stalls above the nave of the church are especially fine (see the martyrs transfixed by lances). In the grounds is the Cedro Milenario, a 1400-year-old cedar. Behind Recoleta monastery a road flanked by Stations of the Cross ascends an attractive hill, **Cerro Churuquella**, with large eucalyptus trees on its slopes, to a statue of Christ at the top.

About 5 km south on the Potosí road is the **Castillo de la Glorieta** ① *Tue-Sat 0900-1630, US$2.50, US$1.25 to take photos, take Micro 4 marked Liceo Militar.*

The former mansion of the Argandoña family, built in a mixture of contrasting European styles with painted ceilings, is in the military compound. Ask to see the paintings of the visit of the pope, in a locked room.

★**North of Sucre** Some 3 km north of Sucre is **Cal Orcko**, considered the world's largest palaeontological site, where tracks from eight types of dinosaur have been identified (inside the Fancesa cement works, not open to the public). Nearby is **Parque Cretácico** ⓘ *T04-645 7392, http://parquecretacicosucre.com, Mon-Fri 0900-1700, Sat 1000-2000, Sun 1000-1700, US$4.35, children US$0.75, crowded at weekends*, with fibreglass dinosaurs, recorded growls, a 30-minute guided tour and binoculars through which (for an extra US$0.30) you can look at the prints on Cal Orcko, 300 m away. The **Sauro Tours** bus leaves daily 0930, 1200, 1430 from corner of cathedral, US$1.75 return, or take Micros 4 or H from Calle Arenales y Junín.

Listings Sucre *map p171*

Tourist information

Dirección de Turismo de la Alcaldía
Argentina 65, p 2, Casa de la Cultura, T04-643 5240, www.sucreturistico.gob. bo, Mon-Fri 0800-1200, 1400-1800.
Some English spoken; also have information kiosks at the **airport**, **bus terminal**, **Plazuela Libertad**, *Destacamento 111 y Arenales* and **La Recoleta**, *Polanco e Iturrichia*.

Tourist office
Estudiantes 25, T04-644 7644, open Mon-Fri 0900-1200, 1500-1830.
Staffed by university students and is open only during term.

Where to stay

$$$ Parador Santa María La Real
Bolívar 625, T04-691 1920, www.parador.com.bo.
Tastefully restored and upgraded colonial house, bathtub, safety box, frigobar, heating. It has a shop, spa and restaurant.

$$$ Refugio Andino Bramadero
30 km from the city towards Ravelo, details from Raul y Mabel Cagigao, Avaroa 472, T04-645 5592, bramader@ yahoo.com, or Restaurant Salamandra (Avaroa 510, good food, open 24 hrs).
Cabins or rooms, well furnished, full board, drinks and transport included, excellent value, owner Raúl can advise on hikes and astronomy, book in advance. Recommended.

$$$ Sky Hacienda
in Mosoj Llacta, by Yotala, 19 km south of Sucre along the road to Potosí, T04-643 0045, www.skyhacienda.com.
Upmarket hotel in a rural setting, nice views from the rooms with heating, jacuzzi, restaurant, nice patio and garden, pool, horse riding, bicycles, minimum stay 2 nights, no children under 12. Transfers to airport and bus station are extra.

$$$ Villa Antigua
Calvo 237, T04-644 3437, www.villaantiguahotel.com.
Tastefully restored colonial house with garden, internet room, gym, large

rooftop terrace has great views, some suites with kitchenette, airport transfers.

$$$ La Posada
Audiencia 92, T04-646 0101,
www.hotellaposada.com.bo.
Smart, colonial-style, good restaurant. Recommended.

$$$-$$ Monasterio
Calvo 140, T04-641 5222,
www.hotelmonasteriosucre.com.
Beautiful 16th-century house with colonial and neoclassic architecture. Elegant common areas, heated rooms and suites, restaurant serves international dishes, quiet terrace, airport transfers.

$$ Casa Kolping
Pasaje Iturricha 265, La Recoleta,
T04642 3812, sucre.bo@kolping.net.
Pleasant, lovely location with nice views, good **Munay Pata** restaurant ($$-$),internet lounge, wheelchair access, parking. Part of the Kolping International network, www.kolping.net.

$$ El Hostal de Su Merced
Azurduy 16, T04-644 2706,
www.desumerced.com.
Beautifully restored colonial building, lots of character, owner and staff speak French and English, good breakfast buffet, sun terrace, restaurant. Airport transfer US$7.50. Recommended.

$$ Hostal Santa Teresa de Jesús
San Alberto 431, T04-645 4189,
www.santateresahostal.com.
Refurbished colonial house, restaurant, comfortable, garage. Recommended.

$$ Independencia
Calvo 31, T04-644 2256,
www.independenciahotel.com.
Historic colonial house, opulent salon, spiral stairs, lovely garden, comfortable,

some rooms with bathtub, café, attentive service.

$ La Selenita
J Mostajo 145, T7285 9993,
www.laselenita.com.
Pleasant guesthouse with 4 cabins for 2-3 persons, 2 types of breakfast with home-made bread and jam available, nice gardens, quiet, panoramic views of the colonial city, French/Belgian-run.

$$ San Marino Royal
Arenales 13, T04-645 1646,
www.sanmarinoroyalhotel.com.bo.
Nicely converted colonial house, frigobar, cafeteria, **$$$** for suite.

$$-$ Austria
Av Ostria Gutiérrez 506, by bus station,
T04-645 4202, www.hostalaustria.com.bo.
Hot showers, good beds and carpeted rooms, cafeteria, parking, cheaper with shared bath and no breakfast, parking extra.

$$-$ Hostelling International Sucre
G Loayza 119 y Ostria
Gutiérrez, T04-644 0471,
www.hosteltrail.com/hostels/hisucre.
Functional hostel 1½ blocks from bus terminal, cheaper without bath and in dorms, breakfast available, garden, internet extra, parking, Spanish language classes, discount for HI members.

$$-$ Kultur Berlin "Sleep"
Avaroa 326, T646 6854,
http://kulturberlin.com.
Associated with the Kultur Berlin café and the Insituto Cultural Boliviano-Alemán, imaginatively designed, spotless rooms with solar hot water, some with kitchenette. Recommended.

$ Casa de Huéspedes Finita
Padilla 233 (no sign), T04-645 3220,
delfi_eguez@hotmail.com.

Some rooms with bath, good breakfast, hot water, heaters, garden, tasty lunch available on request also apartments with fully equipped kitchens for longer stays. Good value and recommended.

$ Forastero
Destacamento 111 No 394, T7181-3654, pichicamichel@hotmail.com.
2 adjacent houses, 1 with comfortable rooms with and without bath, the 2nd with economical dorms with 3 to 7 beds, bath and individual safety boxes, good hot showers, kitchen facilities, common areas, restaurant (quinoa specialities) in nice garden, tours, discounts for groups and long stays, helpful, enthusiastic owner, English spoken. Recommended.

$ Grand
Arce 61, T04-645 2461, grandhotel_sucre@hotmail.com.
Older hotel but well maintained, comfortable (ask for room 18), ground floor at the back is noisy, some rooms dark, electric showers, good-value lunch in **Arcos** restaurant, Wi-Fi in patio, motorcycle parking.

$ Hostal Charcas
Ravelo 62, T04-645 3972, hostalcharcas@yahoo.com.
Cheaper without bath or TV, good value, huge breakfast extra, hot showers, at times runs bus to Tarabuco on Sun.

$ Hostal Colón 220
Colón 220, T04-645 5823, colon220@bolivia.com.
Very nice guesthouse, cheaper with shared bath, laundry, helpful owner speaks English and German and has tourist information, coffee room.

$ Hostal los Pinos
Colón 502, T04-645 5639.
Comfortable, hot showers, garden, quiet, peaceful, parking.

$ Hostal San Francisco
Av Arce 191 y Camargo, T04-645 2117.
Colonial building, electric showers, breakfast available, quiet, patio, good value.

$ Pachamama Hostal
Arce 450, T04-645 3673, hostal_ pachamama@hotmail.com.
Simple rooms with bath, electric shower, pleasant patio, parking, good value.

$ Villa de la Plata
Arce 369, T04-645 6849, villadelaplata888@gmail.com.
Good-value apartments with kitchenette, discounts for long stays, popular.

Restaurants

Sausages and chocolates are among the locally produced specialities.

$$ El Huerto
Ladislao Cabrera 86, San Matías, T04-645 1538. Daily 1130-1600 and Thu-Sun 1830-2100.
International food with salad bar, good *almuerzo*, in a beautiful garden. Take a taxi there at night.

$$ El Tapado
Olañeta 165 y Loa, T04-643 8778. Opendaily, all day.
Extensive breakfast and dinner menu, llama dishes, sandwiches, a choice of drinks including microbrews, parties in the patio on Fri and Sat night.

$$ La Taverne
Arce 35, in the Alliance Française. Mon-Sat 1200-1500, 1800-2230, Sun 1900-2200.
Lovely terrace seating, weekly lunch specials, international food, also regular cultural events.

$$-$ El Germen
San Alberto 231. Mon-Sat 0800-2200.
Mostly vegetarian, set lunches, excellent breakfast, German pastries, book exchange, German magazines. Recommended.

$$-$ Los Balcones
Plaza 25 de Mayo 34, upstairs. Open 1200-2400.
Good food, popular with locals, set lunch with salad bar, views over plaza.

$$-$ Nouvelle Cuisine
Avaroa 537. Daily 1100-2300.
Excellent *churrasquería* (grill), good value.

Cafés

Abis
Plaza 25 de Mayo 32.
Belgian-owned café and *heladería*, with coffees, breakfasts, sandwiches, light meals, ice cream.

Amsterdam
Bolívar 426. Mon-Fri from 1200, Sun from 1530.
Drinks, snacks and meals, book exchange, Wi-Fi, live music Wed-Thu. Dutch-run, works with a programme for migrant children from the countryside.

Bibliocafé
N Ortiz 50, near plaza.
Pasta and light meals. *Almuerzo* 1200-1500, 1800-0200, Sun 1900-2400. Music and drinks, Wi-Fi.

Café Florín
Bolívar 567. Daily 0730-0200, weekends to 0300.
Breakfast, sandwiches, snacks and international meals (**$$**), large portions, microbrews. Sunny patio, Wi-Fi, tour bookings, cosy atmosphere, Dutch-run.

Café Mirador
Pasaje Iturricha 297, La Recoleta. Open 0930-2000.
Very good garden café, fine views, good juices, snacks and music, popular.

El Patio
San Alberto 18.
Small place for delicious *salteñas/empanadas*.

Joy Ride Café
N Ortiz 14, www.joyridebol.com. Daily 0730-2300.
Great international food and drink, music, Wi-Fi, very popular, upstairs lounge shows films, also cultural events. Joy Ride has a new hostel (**$**) at Avaroa 431, T04-645 0035.

Kultur Berlin "Eat & Drink"
Avaroa 326, T646 6854, http://kulturberlin.com.
German, Bolivian and international dishes andd themed evenings.

La Patisserie
Audiencia 17.
0830-1230, 1530-2030. French-owned, popular for crêpes, salads and puddings.

Locot's Café Aventura
Bolívar 465, T04-691 5958. Mon-Sat 0800-2400, Sun 1100-2300.
Bar serving international and Mexican food, live music and theatre, Wi-Fi, also offer many types of adventure sports: mountain biking, hiking, riding, paragliding.

Metro Café
Calvo y España on Plaza 25 de Mayo.
A variety of coffees, sandwiches,
breakfasts, pastries, desserts, juices;
delicious and good service.

Bars and clubs

Mitos
*F Cerro 60, near Junín, Disco-Mitos
on Facebook. Thu-Sat 2100-0300.*
Disco, popular with travellers.

Stigma
*Bolívar 128 y Camargo,
www.stigmasucre.com.*
Varied music, young crowd.

Festivals

24-26 May **Independence** celebrations,
most services, museums and restaurants
closed on 25.
8 Sep **Virgen de Guadalupe**, 2-day
fiesta.
21 Sep **Día del Estudiante**, music
around main plaza.
Oct/Nov **Festival Internacional de la
Cultura**, 2nd week, shared with Potosí.

Shopping

Handicrafts
ASUR, *opposite Casa Kolping in La
Recoleta.* Sells weavings from around
Tarabuco and from the Jalq'a. Weavings
are more expensive, but of higher quality
than elsewhere.
Artesanías Calcha, *Arce 103, opposite
San Francisco church.* Recommended and
has a knowledgeable proprietor. There
are several others nearby.
Bolsa Boliviana, *Calvo 64.* Non-profit,
has many nice items, especially bags.

Casa de Turismo, *Bustillos 131.* Groups
several craft shops and tour operators
under one roof.
Centro Cultural Masis, *Bolívar 591, T04-
645 3403, www.losmasis.com.* Teaches
local youth traditional music and culture
and has items for sale; visitors are
welcome at events and exhibitions.
Incapallay, *Audiencia 97 y Bolívar, T04-
646 1936, www.incapallay.org.* A Fairtrade
shop, sells textiles by Tarabuco and
Jalq'a weavers; also in Tarabuco and La
Paz. Artisans sell their wares at the **La
Recoleta** lookout.
Chocolates Para Tí, *Arenales 7, Audiencia
68, at the airport and bus terminal.* One of
the best chocolate shops in Sucre.
Taboada, *Arce y Arenales, Daniel Campos 82,
at airport and bus terminal, www.taboada.
com.bo.* Also very good for chocolates.

Markets
The central market is colourful with
some stalls selling *artesanía*, but beware
of theft and crafty vendors.

What to do

Language classes
**Academia Latinoamericana de
Español**, *Dalence 109, T04-643 9613,
www.latinoschool.com.* Professional,
good extracurricular activities, US$180
for 20 hrs per week, US$350 with home
stay (US$300 for private teacher).
Alianza Francesa, *Aniceto Arce 35, T04-
645 3599, www.sucre.alianzafrancesa.org.
bo.* Spanish and French classes.
Bolivian Spanish School, *Kilómetro
7 No 250, T04-644 3841, www.
bolivianspanishschool.com.* Near Parque
Bolívar, pleasant school, good value,
excellent teachers.
Centro Boliviano Americano, *Calvo
301, T04-644 1608, www.cbasucre.org.*

Recommended for language courses. These centres run cultural events, have libraries and branches in La Paz.

Continental Spanish School, *Olañeta 224, T04-643 8093, www. schoolcontinental.com*. Good teachers and fun activities.

Fox Academy, *Av Destacamento Chuquisaca 134, T04-644 0688, www. foxacademysucre.com*. Spanish and Quechua classes, US$5 per hr, non-profit, proceeds go to teaching English to children, volunteering arranged.

Instituto Cultural Boliviano-Alemán (ICBA, Goethe Institute), *Bolívar 609, T04-645 2091, www.icba-sucre.edu. bo*. Spanish, German, Portuguese and Quechua courses, US$7.50 pp per lesson; also has an Ecomuseum.

Sucre Spanish School, *Calvo 350, T04-643 6727, www.sucrespanishschool. com*. US$6.50 per hr, friendly and flexible, home stays or lodging at **Kultur Berlin**, can arrange tours and volunteering.

Tour operators

Bolivia Specialist, *N Ortiz 30, T04-643 7389, www.boliviaspecialist.com*. Dutchman Dirk Dekker's agency for local hikes, horse riding and 4WD trips, all sorts of tours throughout Bolivia and Peru; also bus and plane tickets, loads of information and connections.

Candelaria Tours, *JJ Pérez 301 y Colón, T04-644 0340, www.candelariatours.com*. Hikes around Sucre, tours to weaving communities, English spoken.

Cóndor Trekkers, *Calvo 102 y Bolívar, T7289 1740, www.condortrekkers.org*. Not-for-profit trekking company using local guides supported by volunteers, city walks and treks around Sucre, proceeds go to social projects, first-aid carried.

Joy Ride Tourism, *N Ortiz 26, at corner of Plaza, T04-645 7603, www.joyridebol.*

com. Mountain- and motorbiking, hiking, climbing, horse riding, paragliding, tours to Potosí and Salar de Uyuni.

L y D, *final Panamá 127 y Comarapa, Barrio Petrolero, T04-642 0752, turismo_ lyd@hotmail.com*. Lucho and Dely Loredo and son Carlos (who speaks English) offer custom-made tours using private or public transport, to regional communities and attractions, and further afield.

Oasis Tours, *Arce 95, of 2, T04-643 2438, www.oasistours-bo.com*. City walking tour, indigenous communities, Chataquila, Inca trail. Also sell bus tickets and have their own office in Uyuni for Salar trips. Very helpful owner.

Seatur, *Plaza 25 de Mayo 25, T04-646 2425*. Local tours, hiking trips, English, German, French spoken.

Transport

Air

Juana Azurduy de Padilla airport is 5 km northwest of town (T04-645 4445). **BoA** (Audiencia 21, T04-691 2360) direct flights to Santa Cruz and to Cochabamba for connections. **TAM** (Arenales 217, T04-646 0944, or 02-268 1111) daily to **La Paz**, **Santa Cruz** and **Cochabamba**, less frequently to **Tarija** and **Yacuiba**. Ecojet (T901-105055), direct to **Cochabamba**, **Santa Cruz** and **Tarija**. Airport tax US$1.60. Micros 1, 3, 7, A and F go from entrance to Av Hernando Siles, a couple of blocks from main plaza, US$0.20, 25 mins. Taxi US$3.50.

Bus

Bus terminal is on north outskirts of town, 3 km from centre on Ostria Gutiérrez, T04-644 1292; taxi US$1.15; Micro A or 3. Daily to/from **La Paz** several companies at 1700-2000, 12 hrs, regular

US$12.75, *semi-cama* US$17.75, *cama* US$25.50. To **Cochabamba**: several companies daily at 1830-1930, 9 hrs via Aiquile; at 2100 via Oruro, 12 hrs, US$9.65, *semi-cama* US$12.50, *cama* US$19.50. To **Potosí**: frequent departures between 0630 and 1800, US$3-6, 3 hrs. Shared taxis with pick-up service: **Cielito Lindo**, at Casa de Turismo, Bustillos 131, T04-643 2309, **Cielito Express**, T04-643 1000 and **Expreso Dinos**, T04-643 7444, both outside the bus terminal, 2½ hrs, US$7 pp. To **Oruro**: 2000-2200, 4 companies via Potosí, 8 hrs, US$9-12, *cama* US$17.75. To **Tarija**: 4 companies, at 1500-1600, 14 hrs, US$14 via Potosí. To **Uyuni**: direct at 0830, **6 de Octubre**, 7 hrs, **Emperador** 0700, 1230, with change and long wait in Potosí, US$8.35-11.75. Or catch a bus to Potosí and change; try to book the connecting bus in advance. To **Villazón**

via Potosí and Tupiza: at 1330, 1730, **6 de Octubre**, 12 hrs, US$14; to **Tupiza**, 9 hrs, US$11.50. To **Santa Cruz**: many companies 1600-1730, 15 hrs, US$13.75; *semi-cama* US$18, *cama* US$24.

To Tarabuco Minivans leave when full from C Túpac Yupanqui (Parada de Tarabuco), daily starting 0630, US$1, 1¼ hrs on a good paved road. To get to the Parada take a micro "C" or "7" from the Mercado Central. Also buses to Tarabuco from Av de las Américas y Jaime Mendoza, same fare and times. Tourist bus from the cathedral on Sun at 0830, US$5 round-trip, reserve at **Oasis Tours** (address above); also **Real Audiencia**, depart San Alberto 181 y España, T04-644 3119, at 0830, return 1330; you must use the same bus you went on. Shared taxi with **Cielito Lindo** (see Transport to Potosí above), Sun at 0900, US$5 return.

Tarabuco and around   *Colour map 3, B4.*

hand-woven textiles, indigenous markets and wild, mountainous landscapes

Tarabuco, 64 km southeast of Sucre, is best known for its colourful indigenous market on Sunday. The local people wear their traditional dress of conquistador-style helmets, multicoloured ponchos, *chuspas* (bags for carrying coca leaves) and the elaborate *axsu*, an overskirt worn by women.

The market starts around 0930-1000 and is very popular with tourists. Textiles are sold in a purpose-built market on Calle Murillo. Next to the market is a small museum, **Incapallay** ⓘ *Murillo 52, T04-646 1936, www.incapallay.org, Sun 0930-1400*, run by a weavers' association. The market is not held at Carnaval (when all Tarabuco is dancing in Sucre), Pujllay, Easter Sunday or All Saints' Day. The *Pujllay* independence celebration on the third Sunday in March is very vibrant. It celebrates the independence Battle of Jumbate, where the Spaniards were defeated on 12 March 1816. Thousands of people from 30 communities, dressed in elaborate costumes, participate in a colourful traditional event, which involves music with native instruments and vigorous dancing in order to invoke the souls of the fallen indigenous soldiers and plenty of local food and *chicha*. No one sleeps during this fiesta but basic accommodation is available if arranged in advance.

Other villages east of Sucre that carry on the weaving tradition include: **Yamparáez**, halfway between Sucre and Tarabuco (it is possible to see condors at **Condor Kaka** nearby); **Candelaria**, 24 km southeast of Tarabuco, with a colonial

ON THE ROAD

Reviving the past

⭐ The textile traditions of the Chuquisaca area might have vanished into obscurity had it not been for the dedication and hard work of two anthropologists, Spanish-born Gabriel Martínez and his Chilean wife Verónica Cereceda. They set out to trace the origins of a number of weavings that, years before, had been passed off as antiques in tourist shops in La Paz and other Bolivian cities. Little was known about the creators of these textiles. Collectors and merchants referred to them as 'Potolo pieces', after the largest town (of some 600 families) in the area of their origin, 50 km northeast of Sucre. This area was inhabited by an impoverished group of nearly 25,000 people who called themselves Jalq'a. Martínez and Cereceda, along with Bolivian ethnologist Ramiro Molina, were pleased to see most villagers still wearing traditional dress, but the women's *axsus*, or overskirts, were a pale reflection of the weavings that had inspired their search. Gone were the subtle colours and exotic animal motifs, replaced by repetitive rows of geometric designs. The reason for this was economic necessity. In the 1960s and 70s a ready source of much-needed income became available. A growing market for Andean textiles among tourists and overseas dealers spawned many traders who scoured the countryside for ponchos, shawls, axsus, belts and bags to sell on. The Jalq'a motifs were particularly sought after, but the people never learned the true market value of their finest textiles. When the boom was over the Jalq'a found the core of their weaving inheritance – their ritual costumes, wedding garments and family heirlooms

hacienda that offers lodging; and **Zudáñez**, 50 km from Tarabuco on the road to Monteagudo. **Presto**, 37 km north of Tarabuco, is the access to the **Reserva El Palmar**, one of the national protected areas, three hours beyond. The reserve lies on the flanks of the Cordillera Oriental between 1000 and 3200 m and protects temperate dry valleys, cloudforest and semi-dry valleys.

Beyond Tarabuco the main road southeast continues towards ever greener valleys and mountains that signal the proximity of the tropical eastern lowlands and El Chaco. It winds through the colonial towns of **Zudáñez** (Km 110), **Tomina** (Km 153) and **Padilla** (Km 187); from the latter two, roads go north to Villa Serrano (see below). Next is **Monteagudo** (Km 314, population 27,500, altitude 1130 m), Chuquisaca's second city after Sucre; the centre of a cattle ranching and agricultural area, it has all services. This is the access to **Parque Nacional Serranía del Iñao**, created in 2004 to protect Tucumano–Boliviano and highland Chaco habitats between 600 and 2800 m. Further southeast is **Muyupampa** or Villa Vaca Guzmán (Km 367), along the southern section of the Che Guevara trail and another access to Iñao, before joining the paved Santa Cruz–Yacuiba road at **Ipati**, 33 km north of **Camiri** (see page 263).

– gone. With no models to inspire the next generation of weavers, the tradition seemed to have vanished for ever. But Martínez and Cereceda were determined to revive the ancient weaving traditions in this area. They started an organization called Antropólogos del Sur Andino (ASUR), whose centre can be visited in Sucre. ASUR encouraged the ritual life among the Jalq'a communities. They also want to recover traditional songs and dances that had been fading from community life and encourage wearing traditional costumes at festivals. The main problem was that women still knew how to weave, but they could not recall the many strange animals, called khurus, which had been the hallmark of the Jalq'a designs. The solution was to contact the dealers and collectors in Bolivia and overseas and get them to send photographs of their weavings. Eventually enough photographs were assembled to be circulated throughout the local communities, inspiring renewed enthusiasm in their tradition and provoking a textile revival. But that was not enough. Martínez and Cereceda wanted to let the outside world know what was going on. They collected the best of the new textiles and showcased them throughout Bolivia. This created a new respect among city dwellers not only for the neglected Jalq'a but also for other ethnic groups in the region. The effects of this were great. The price of the textiles began to rise along with the quality of weaving and women began to create their own designs, proving that the Jalq'a were at last back in touch with the same cultural sources that inspired their ancestors. This time the Jalq'a understood the value of what they were producing and could meet outside demand without selling off their inheritance. (Adapted from an article by Kevin Healy in Grassroots Development, 1992.)

At **Padilla**, centre of an agricultural area producing many varieties of hot peppers and another access point to Parque Nacional Iñao, a road heads north 20 km to **Villa Serrano**, where the musician, charango designer and sculptor Mauro Núñez lived. There is a museum, and a music festival is held on 28-29 December. It is a beautiful journey through wild mountains. This road continues towards the tiny settlement of **La Higuera**, famous as the scene of Ché Guevara's fatal last battle (see page 257) and **Vallegrande**.

West of Sucre: Jalq'a communities

weaving communities, Inca trail and ancient cave paintings

To the west of the city are communities of the Jalq'a ethnic group, best known for their distinctive textiles, see Reviving the past, page 180. The area also has natural attractions, operators offer tours to many of them. An important unpaved road goes northwest to Ravelo on the border with Potosí. Several secondary roads branch off the main one and lead to the many communities.

About 24 km northwest of Sucre, at a pass at 3450 m, on the road that branches off at **Punilla** and leads to Potolo, is **Chataquila**, a stone sanctuary to the Virgen de la Exaltación (pilgrimage 16 September). Just past the sanctuary, to the left of the road, starts a 4-km fragment of an **Inca road**. It is an easy two-hour walk downhill to the village of **Chaunaca** at the confluence of the Potolo and Ravelo rivers, 37 km from Sucre. The community charges US$1.50 for the use of the trail. In Chaunaca is **Hacienda Samay Huasi ($$$**, T04-645 2935, 7116 1578), which offers transport and accommodation (arrange in advance; more economical options are available in Potolo and Maragua). You can reach the trailhead by bus, but it is difficult to get transport back to Sucre the same day, see Transport, page 178. From Chataquila you can also walk over the summit of **Cerro Chataquila** to the cave paintings of **Incamachay** and **Pumamachay**, 12 km to the north; these can also be reached from Chaunaca, Punilla, or from **Bramadero**, an area with planted pine and eucalyptus stands on the northern slopes of the Chataquila range. Here **Refugio Bramadero** offers transport and (see Where to stay, below). Some 15 km beyond Chaunaca is the weaver community of **Potolo** (52 km from Sucre), whose characteristic textiles are of red zoomorphic and geometric figures on a black or brown background, see page 180. People weave and sell their wares in their homes, there is a community museum (US$1.40). Further south, more remote and often inaccessible in the wet, is **Maragua**, an 8-sq-km crater-like formation with colourful cliffs on the rim. Here are the communities of Maragua, Irupampa and to the southwest Humaca and Niñu Mayu. The area has walking opportunities, waterfalls, textiles, dinosaur tracks and fossil deposits. It can be reached from Chaunaca (two to three hours' walking), Quila Quila (see below) or walking from Potolo. Ask at **ASUR** in Sucre (see above) for accommodation and transport details to this region.

Along a different road leading southwest is the colonial town of **Quila Quila**, 32 km from Sucre, with a nice church and adobe houses. One kilometre away are the **Marca Rumi** petroglyphs on large boulders. Nearby is **Cerro Obispo** (3642 m), among the highest peaks around Sucre. There is no accommodation; an early start is needed to do it in one day and food and drink should be taken. A guide can be found in the village.

Listings West of Sucre: Jalq'a communities

Bus and truck

Transport departs from the 'Parada Yurac Yurac' by the Rotonda de Yurac Yurac, camino al aeropuerto, a large lot where buses and trucks stop. Take Micro D from the Mercado Central, 20-30 mins. For **Chataquila**, **Chaunaca** and **Potolo**, a bus leaves 0900-1000 (in the dry season there may be 2 or 3 buses, all around the same time), US$1.40, it gets crowded so get there early and purchase your ticket from the tin kiosk. The buses return from Potolo early in the morning. If you are walking the Inca trail, you will not reach Chaunaca in time to catch the returning bus to Sucre; you might be able to get a truck back, but you might also be stuck. Better plan to stay overnight, which requires advanced arrangements.

To **Maragua**, direct service from Yurac Yurac on Sun only, other days get off at Chaunaca and walk from there. Note that in the rainy season it may not be possible to reach Maragua from Chaunaca. There is also access from Quila Quila.

To **Bramadero**, transport is offered by **Refugio Andino Bramadero**. Otherwise take bus to Potolo, get off at Punilla, it is 5 km to Silvico where the road branches and 2 km from there.

To **Quila Quila**, a bus and trucks go from Salida a ENDE, C Osvaldo Molina, by Plaza Moto Méndez northwest of the cemetery, at 0600 or earlier. They return after midday.

Car

164 km from **Potosí** (fully paved), 366 km to **Cochabamba** (mostly paved except for some segments in the Puente Arce–Aiquile–Epizana segment, which are being paved in 2015).

Taxi

US$0.60 per person within city limits.

Train

Station at El Tejar, 1 km south on Potosí road, take Micro 4, T04-644 0751, www.fca.com.bo. A 25-passenger railcar to **Potosí**, Mon, Wed, Fri at 0800, US$3.60, 6 hrs; tickets go on sale at 0600.

Sucre to Potosí

Sucre's main connection with the rest of the country

A scenic paved road leads from Sucre to Potosí, 164 km to the southwest. The pleasant town of **Yotala**, 15 km from Sucre, has several restaurants with pools offering *parrilladas* and regional specialities at weekends. Carnival is celebrated here a week later than everywhere else. There is good walking in the surrounding hills (good footwear is necessary for the rocky paths and many spiny bushes and cacti).

A good two- to three-hour hike with great views goes to the village of **Cachimayu**. Cross the pedestrian bridge, at the train tracks turn right, just before the train station follow the path uphill. The second time you meet the car road, follow it until just after the pass, where a trail goes to the right. If you prefer not to be covered in dust by passing trucks, continue on the trail to the top of the ridge, from where you go down towards the left to meet the road at the pass. This takes longer, but the views back to the Yotala Valley and the rock face of Cerro El Obispo in the opposite direction make it worthwhile. Go down the trail that starts after the pass, it is a lovely stretch with native vegetation. You will meet the road again before Cachimayu, follow it to the right. The Río Cachimayu is lovely, note the large hacienda on the shore.

After Yotala, the road crosses to the department of Potosí at Puente Méndez, a bridge over the Río Pilcomayo; next to the modern bridge is a 16th-century suspension bridge. The road goes through Betanzos, where there are a few places to stay ($). The town holds its **Feria de la Papa** within the first two weeks of May with folk dances, music and costumes. There is also a good market and 6 km away there are well-preserved rock paintings at Incahuasi. The road also passes **Don Diego** and **Chaquí**. There is also a rail service between Sucre and Potosí (see Transport, page 194).

Potosí

At an altitude of 3977 m and with a population of 175,562, Potosí is the highest city of its size in the world. Towering over the city like a giant pink headstone is the 4824-m Cerro Rico (Rich Mountain), originally Sumaj Orcko (Great Mountain). Silver from this mountain made Potosí the biggest city in the Americas and one of the richest in the world, rivalled only by Paris, London and Seville. But Cerro Rico also claimed the lives of countless thousands of indigenous slaves. This painful history still haunts the city and is as much a part of its colonial legacy as the many magnificent old buildings that led it to be declared *Patrimonio de la Humanidad* (World Cultural Heritage Site) by UNESCO in 1987. The Spanish still have a saying 'vale un Potosí' (it's worth a Potosí) for anything incredibly valuable, even though Potosi's wealth is now only a distant memory; still, it remains one of Bolivia's greatest attractions and is certainly well worth a visit.

Sights *Colour map 3, B3.*

one of the most beautiful, saddest and fascinating places you'll ever experience

Plaza 10 de Noviembre and around

Large parts of Potosí are colonial, with twisting streets and an occasional great mansion with its coat of arms over the doorway. The city, which has a population of 175,562, is a UNESCO World Heritage Site. Some of the best buildings are grouped round the Plaza 10 de Noviembre. The old Cabildo and the Royal Treasury – Las Cajas Reales – are both here, converted to other uses. The massive cathedral faces Plaza 10 de Noviembre.

> **Tip...**
> Take it easy on arrival; remember Potosí is higher than La Paz.

West of the plaza

The ★**Casa Nacional de Moneda (Mint)** ⓘ *C Ayacucho, T02-622 2777, www. bolivian.com/cnm, Tue-Sat 0900-1230, 1430-1830, Sun 0900-1230, entry US$3, plus US$3 to take photos, US$6 for video, entry by regular, 2-hr guided tour only (in English or French if there are 10 or more people, at 0900, 1030, 1430 and 1630),* is near the plaza. Founded in 1572, rebuilt 1759-1773, it is one of the chief monuments of civil building in Hispanic America. Thirty of its 160 rooms are a museum with sections on mineralogy, silverware and an art gallery in a splendid salon on the first floor. One section is dedicated to the works of the acclaimed 17th- to 18th-century religious painter Melchor Pérez de Holguín. Elsewhere are coin dies and huge wooden presses which made the silver strips from which coins were cut. The smelting houses have carved altar pieces from Potosí's ruined churches. You can't fail to notice the huge, grinning mask of Bacchus over an archway between two principal courtyards. Erected in 1865, its smile is said to be ironic and aimed at the departing Spanish. Wear warm clothes; it's cold inside.

Potosí has many outstanding colonial churches. Among its baroque churches, typical of 18th-century Andean or 'mestizo' architecture, are the Jesuit **Compañia de Jesús church and bell-gable** ⓘ *Ayacucho entre Bustillos y Oruro,* whose beautiful façade hides the modern tourist office building, and whose tower has a **mirador** ⓘ *0800-1200, 1400-1800, 30 mins later Sat-Sun, US$1.40.*

Further west, the **Convento y Museo de Santa Teresa** ⓘ *Santa Teresa y Ayacucho, T02-622 3847, http:// museosantateresa.blogspot.co.uk, only by guided tour in Spanish or English, Mon-Sat 0900-1230, 1500-1800; Sun 0900-1200, 1500-1800, museum is closed Tue and Sun morning; US$3, US$1.50 to take photos, US$25 for video,* has an impressive amount of giltwork inside and an interesting collection of colonial and religious art.

South of the plaza

Another interesting church, **San Francisco** ⓘ *Tarija y Nogales, T02-622 2539, Mon-Fri 0900-1100, 1430-1700, Sat 0900-1100, US$2.15,* has a fine organ and is worthwhile for the views from the tower and roof, the museum of ecclesiastical art and an underground tunnel system.

Three blocks east, the **Museo del Ingenio de San Marcos** ⓘ *La Paz 1565 y Betanzos, T02-622 6717, 1000-1500,*

US$1.40; textiles museum and shop Mon-Sat 1430-2200; restaurant 1000-1530, 1830-2200, is a well-preserved example of the city's industrial past, with machinery used in grinding down the silver ore. It also has cultural activities and an exhibition of Calcha textiles.

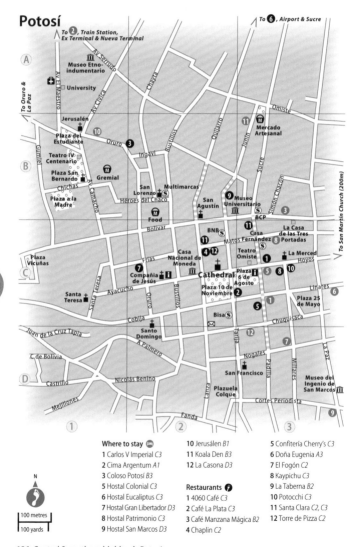

Potosí

Where to stay 🛏
1 Carlos V Imperial *C3*
2 Cima Argentum *A1*
3 Coloso Potosí *B3*
5 Hostal Colonial *C3*
6 Hostal Eucaliptus *C3*
7 Hostal Gran Libertador *D3*
8 Hostal Patrimonio *C3*
9 Hostal San Marcos *D3*
10 Jerusalén *B1*
11 Koala Den *B3*
12 La Casona *D3*

Restaurants 🍴
1 4060 Café *C3*
2 Café La Plata *C3*
3 Café Manzana Mágica *B2*
4 Chaplin *C2*
5 Confitería Cherry's *C3*
6 Doña Eugenia *A3*
7 El Fogón *C2*
8 Kaypichu *C3*
9 La Taberna *B2*
10 Potocchi *C3*
11 Santa Clara *C2, C3*
12 Torre de Pizza *C2*

ON THE ROAD
A man's gotta chew

Apart from the dream of striking it rich, it is coca that keeps the miners going. The only real break they get down in the bowels of the earth is el acullicu, when they chew coca. The sacred leaves are masticated with lejía, a paste moulded from plant ashes, which activates with saliva to produce the desired effect from the coca. This numbs the senses and staves off hunger pangs and exhaustion. It is only by chewing coca that the miners can work at all. "No coca, no work", as one miner put it. In the morning, before entering the mine, they spend about one hour pijcheando, preparing the bolo, the ball of masticated coca, which they keep in their mouth for the next four hours until it loses its potency. Not only does coca give the miners the energy to carry on working without food, they also believe that it acts as a filter of dust and toxic gases. The centuries-old Andean tradition of chewing coca is not only an essential part of a miner's daily routine, it is a common practice among bus and truck drivers, campesinos, and a number of urban dwellers. It is very much part of the essence of things Bolivian.

North of the plaza
On the north side of the Plaza 6 de Agosto, the **Teatro Omiste** has an imposing façade. Finished in 1753 as the Belén Church, it has since been a hospital, royalist headquarters in 1823 during the wars of independence (the royalists knocked down the twin towers of the church in order to improve their cannon emplacements), a theatre from 1862 and then a cinema in the 20th century, before returning to life as a theatre and a café-restaurant with a lookout.

To the east are the churches of **La Merced** ① *Hoyos y Millares, US$1.40 for museo sacro and mirador, US$0.70 for mirador only (with café)*, with great views of Cerro Rico and the city, and **San Martín** ① *on Hoyos, T02-622 3682, Mon-Sat 1000-1200, 1500-1830, free*, which has an uninviting exterior, but is beautiful inside. It is normally closed for fear of theft so ask the German Redemptorist Fathers to show you around; their office is just to the left of the church.

Directly north of the plaza, the **Museo Universitario** ① *C Bolívar 54 y Sucre, T02-622 7310, Mon-Fri 0800-1200, 1400-1800, US$0.70*, displays archaeology, fossils, costumes, musical instruments and some good modern Bolivian painting. Guided tour to the *mirador* (tower) offers great views, US$0.70. Nearby is the church of **San Agustín** ① *Bolívar y Quijarro, open only for Mass*, which has crypts and catacombs (much of the city was interconnected by tunnels in colonial times), and **San Lorenzo** ① *Héroes del Chaco y Bustillos, Mass 0700-1000*, (1728-1744) with a rich portal and fine views from the tower.

Further north, the fascinating **Museo Etno-indumentario** ① *Av Serrudo 152, T02-622 3258, Mon-Fri 0930-1200, 1430-1800, Sat 0930-1200, US$1.40, includes tour*, displays in detail the dress, customs and histories of Potosí department's 16 provinces.

BACKGROUND

Potosí

According to legend, the Inca Huayna Capac was on the point of mining silver in 1462 when a voice from above told him that he should leave it where it was because it was for someone else. The Inca then referred to the area as *Ppotojsi*, Quechua for ruin or spoil. According to another version, Huayna Capac described the voice as *photoj nin* (a great din). Another story says the name comes from the Aymara-Quechua word *Ppotoj*, meaning spring, from the numerous springs in and around the city. Yet another that it is from *Potocchi* (source of silver).

Further legend says the silver was discovered in 1544 by Diego Huallpa who had lost some llamas and climbed Sumaj Orcko, as Cerro Rico was then called. It got late, he got cold and so made a fire, which by morning had smelted a vein of silver. Huallpa told his mate Chalco (or Guanca) about the silver and they started mining. Chalco unwisely told the Spanish, who promptly took possession of the mountain and founded the city in 1545 as the 'Villa Imperial de Carlos V'. The official shield of the city carries the words "Soy el rico Potosí, del mundo soy el tesoro; soy el rey de los montes, envidia soy de los reyes" (I am rich Potosí, the treasure of the world; the king of mountains, the envy of kings). Within 18 months of the Spanish learning about the silver, the city had grown to 14,000. Twenty-five years later the population numbered 120,000 making it the biggest city in the Americas and so it remained until well into the 17th century. Over the next two centuries Potosí's silver riches dwindled to almost nothing. A brief reprieve came from a boom in tin in the early 20th century, but the fabulous riches of Potosí's past have long gone. Now only the baroque churches remain to pay homage to the many hundreds of thousands who sacrificed their lives for the greed of their colonial rulers.

Over the course of the 16th century, Potosí became the biggest single source of silver in the world despite the fact that it was being extracted by pre-Columbian methods. Within 20 years of the Spanish appropriation the surface deposits had been used up and people started going underground. The percentage of silver in the ore fell, increasing the costs of extracting it and Potosí entered the first of many crises.

The Viceroy of Lima, Francisco de Toledo, arrived in 1572 to improve mining efficiency. He introduced the use of mercury to extract the silver (and a royal monopoly on mercury supplies), set up the Casa Real de Moneda to turn all silver mined into ingots so it could be taxed (20% went direct to the Spanish Crown) and reintroduced the *mita*, an Inca forced collective-labour scheme.

The most expensive part of mining was the manual labour needed to build and maintain a gallery – equal to the cost of a cathedral. The source of power to grind the ore was water, but this required a system of artificial lakes and aqueducts for which there was simply not the capital to pay someone to build.

Toledo dealt with this by dividing up what was then Alto Perú, from Cuzco to Potosí, into 16 provinces from which one-seventh of the adult male population had to work in Potosí for one year at a time, three weeks on, three weeks off. This provided 13,500 men (*mitayukuna*) a year, between a half and two thirds of the Potosí mining force. They were paid a nominal salary which did not cover living costs and so they were supported by their communities.

Toledo's reforms turned Potosí into a boom city again. By 1585 there were 612 registered mines in Cerro Rico and a census in 1611 found there were 150,000 people living in the city including 6000 black slaves. John Hemming, in his *Conquest of the Incas*, describes how, by the turn of the 17th century, Potosí had become one of the largest cities in Christendom. He states: "By the end of the 16th century the boom city of Potosí had all the trappings of a Klondike or Las Vegas: 14 dance halls, 36 gambling houses, seven or eight hundred professional gamblers, a theatre, 120 prostitutes and dozens of baroque churches".

Between 1570 and 1650, Potosí was the source of more than half the silver produced in the Americas. This fuelled long-term inflation and growth in Europe and paid for the import of goods from Asia. The city and its surroundings could not support such a large population itself so other areas supplied the goods they needed: wheat and maize from Cochabamba; coca from the Yungas; mules, wines and sugar from northeast Argentina; cereals and wines from Tarija; and llamas from the northern altiplano to transport the goods.

The silver was carried out to the coast by mule train. It took 25 days to cover the 885 km to Cobija on the Pacific coast, though Toledo also studied the geography and ordered the building of Arica, further north and a mere 750 km from Potosí. When what is now Bolivia was under the control of the Viceroy of La Plata (Buenos Aires) the silver had to be carried for 2500 km to reach the Atlantic, a 52-day walk.

Silver production peaked in 1650 and then went into a century-long decline – Mexico took over as the biggest source. By 1690 the *mitayukuna* were down to 2000. An outbreak of typhoid in 1719 killed an estimated 22,000 people in less than a year and by 1750 the population of Potosí was 70,000. By the 1780s it had fallen to 35,000.

From 1730 silver production picked up slowly, but it never reached earlier levels. However, at the start of the 19th century Potosí was still a prize worth fighting for during Bolivia's 16-year-long struggle for independence from the Spanish, Lima and Buenos Aries. Potosí suffered badly and when independence was won, the city was down to 8000 inhabitants and 50 working mines.

The demand for tin – a metal the Spaniards ignored – saved the city from absolute poverty in the first half of the 20th century, until the price slumped due to over-supply. Bolivia's mines where nationalized following the 1952 Revolution and the Corporación Minera Boliviana (Comibol) continued to work Cerro Rico until the 1980s when they were privatized. With its highs and lows, mining continues in the treacherous tunnels that riddle Cerro Rico – now in the hands of miner's cooperatives, which extract silver, tin, zinc, lead, antimony and wolfram. Periodic increases in world metal prices give Potosí a boost and cooperatives hire (or fire) miners who continue to work in appalling conditions.

City centre walk

Walk around and admire the architecture. **Calle Quijarro**, running north from Plaza 10 de Noviembre, is one of Potosí's best-preserved streets; in colonial times it was known as Calle de la Ollería (potmakers) and Calle de los Sombreros (hats). At Quijarro and Omiste is the **Esquina de las Cuatro Portadas** (four houses with double doors, two of which remain), or Balcón de Llamacancha. Heading south again along Junín, there is a fine stone doorway at the **Casa del Marqués de Otavi**, now BNB bank, between Matos and Bolívar. Off Junín is the twisty **Pasaje de las Siete Vueltas**. On Millares, south of the plaza between Chuquisaca and Nogales, is a doorway with two rampant lions in low relief on the lintel, and on the opposite side of the street another sculpted stone doorway. Turning left up Nogales you come to an old mansion in a little plaza. Turn left along La Paz and one block along there is another stone doorway with suns in relief. At La Paz y Bolívar is the **Casa del Balcón de la Horca** (gallows). Turn left here into Calle Bolívar and about 50 m down on the left is the highly decorated **Casa de las Tres Portadas** (which is now a *hostal*).

★Cerro Rico mine tours

For many, the main reason for being in Potosí is to visit the mines of Cerro Rico. The state mines were closed in the 1980s and are now worked as cooperatives by small groups of miners in conditions which are, if anything, more dangerous than in colonial times. An estimated 14,000 miners work in 49 cooperatives; some 800 are children. *The Devil's Miner* is a recommended documentary film about child labour in the mines, shown regularly by Potosí agencies and Sucre cafés.

A tour to the mines and ore-processing plant involves meeting miners and seeing them at work first-hand. Cerro Rico was described by one Spanish chronicler in the mid-16th century as "the mouth of hell", and visitors should be aware that descending into its bowels can be both physically and emotionally draining. The deeper you go, the warmer it gets and the narrower and lower the tunnel will be; if you go deep enough, you need to crouch and eventually even crawl.

Mine entrances are above 4000 m and temperatures inside can reach 40°C, with noxious dust and gasses. You should be acclimatized, fit and have no heart or breathing problems, such as asthma.

Guided tours are conducted by former miners; by law all guides have to work with a tour agency and carry an ID card issued by the Prefectura. Essential equipment is provided: helmet, lamp and usually protective clothing but large-size boots may not be available. Wear old clothes and take torch and a handkerchief or mask to filter the dusty air. The smaller the tour group, the better. Some are as large as 20 people, which is excessive. Tours cost about US$10.50-13 per person and include transport. Many agencies say they give part of their proceeds to miners but such claims are difficult to verify. You can also contribute directly, for example by

> **Tip...**
> If you suffer from claustrophobia, consider seriously whether you should enter the mines. The length and difficulty of tours varies, up to five hours; you can ask for a shorter, less gruelling, visit if you wish.

taking medicines to the health centre (*Posta Sanitaria*) on Cerro Rico. Saturday and Sunday are the quietest days (Sunday is the miners' day off).

The tour begins with a visit to **Mercado Calvario**, where you are expected to buy presents for the miners such as coca leaves, meths, ammonium nitrate and cigarettes. **Note**   Tourists are not allowed to buy dynamite to give to miners.

A tour might go down all the way to the fourth level, meeting and talking to working miners on the way. You will see how dynamite is used and also meet El Tío, the god of the underworld (Friday afternoon is the main day for making offerings to El Tío). A good guide will be able to explain mining practices, customs and traditions (little changed since the Spanish left) and enable you to communicate with the miners. There is no problem with women visiting the mines. Women worked the mines during the Chaco War 1932-1935; female miners are called *palliri*.

There are over 5000 mine shafts snaking their way through Cerro Rico. The Spaniards introduced the use of *socavones*, horizontal galleries to intersect workings, allowing simpler access, ventilation and drainage and much deeper mines. But at the lowest depths of the mines, ventilation is scarce. If a miner finds a vein of ore, he starts chipping away at it and follows it along. It may happen that someone else found the same vein approaching it from a different tunnel and they work it until they meet. The mountain is like a giant Swiss cheese and there are concerns of an eventual immense collapse.

When the Comibol mines where privatized in the 1980s, miners formed cooperatives and continued working for themselves. Over time, however, the *cooperativistas* started hiring *peones* (labourers) who, for a meagre salary, do the dirty dangerous work for them. Today there are far more *peones* than *cooperativistas*. Miners work alone or in pairs, the cooperative members sell what the labourers extract at the market price and the cooperative gets a percentage.

Museo Histórico Minero Diego Huallpa ⓘ *by Mina Pailaviri on Cerro Rico, city buses P, Q, 70 and others, T02-623 1143, Mon-Sat 0900-1200, 1430-1800, Sun 0900-1500, US$10*, has exhibits of minerals and mining techniques; two-hour visits include mine tunnels with mannequins instead of real miners.

Listings Potosí

Where to stay

Unless otherwise stated hotels have no heating.

$$$ Coloso Potosí
Bolívar 965, T02-622 2627,
www.potosihotel.com.
Comfortable modern rooms with frigobar, heating, bath tubs and nice views. Small indoor pool, sauna, parking.

$$$-$$ Cima Argentum
Av Villazón 239, T02-622 9538,
www.hca-potosi.com.
Modern comfortable rooms and suites, warm and bright, heating, frigobar and safe in each room.

$$$-$$ Hostal Patrimonio
Matos 62, T02-622 2659,
www.hostalpatrimonio.com.

Bright, warm, modern hotel. Heating, frigobar and safe in each room, sauna and jacuzzi (suites each have their own).

$$ Gran Libertador
Millares 58, T02-622 7877, www.hotelgranlibertador.com.
Colonial-style hotel, good buffet breakfast, cafeteria, comfortable rooms, central heating, quiet, helpful, parking.

$$ Hostal Colonial
Hoyos 8, T02-622 4809, www.hostalcolonialpotosi.com.
Older place but well located, breakfast extra, carpeted, heating, bathtubs, frigobar.

$$-$ Jerusalén
Oruro 143, T02-622 4633, http://hoteljerusalen.es.tl.
HI affiliated, private rooms and dorms, near Mercado Gremial, family-run, money exchange, book exchange, common and TV room, laundry service, café.

$ Carlos V Imperial
Linares 42, T02-623 1010, http:// mobusapp.com/comunidad/2896-hostal-carlos-v/profile.
Cheaper rooms without bath, hot water, kitchen facilities.

$ Hostal Eucalyptus
Linares 88A, T7240 1884, part of Koala Tours (see below).
Pleasant bright rooms, cheaper with shared bath, heating, good breakfast, 350 m from the main plaza.

$ Hostal San Marcos
La Paz 1626 y Periodista, T02-623 001, hostalsanmarcos@hotmail.com.
Colonial house, nice comfortable rooms, heating, cooking facilities.

$ Koala Den
Junín 56, T02-622 6467, papaimilla@ hotmail.com (Koala-Den on Facebook).
Private rooms with bath and breakfast (cheaper in dorm), heating, TV and video, use of kitchen, popular and often full.

$ La Casona
Chuquisaca 460, T02-623 0523, www.hotelpotosi.com.
Cheaper with shared bath and in dorm, courtyard, kitchen facilities.

Restaurants

$$ 4060 Café
Hoyos y Sucre. Open 1600-late, food until 2300.
Restaurant/bar serving good meals, varied menu, large portions, nice atmosphere, heating. Recommended.

$$ El Fogón
Frías 58 y Oruro. Daily 1200-2300.
Restaurant/grill, good food and atmosphere.

$$-$ Kaypichu
Millares 16. Tue-Sun 0700-1300, 1700-2300.
Breakfast, vegetarian options, *peña* in high season.

$$-$ La Taberna
Junín 12, open all day.
Bolivian and international food, set lunch and à la carte in the evening, good service.

$$-$ Potocchi
Millares 24, T622 2759. Open 0800-2230.
International and local dishes, can accommodate special diets with advance notice, *peña* in high season.

$ Doña Eugenia
Santa Cruz y Ortega. Open 0900-1300.
Typical food such as the warming

kalapurca soup with corn and meat (be careful it is hot) and *chicharrón de cerdo*, pork crackling.

$ Torre de Pizza
Matos 14. Open 0700-2200.
Pizza, pasta, vegetarian options, also breakfast, family-run, attentive service.

Cafés

Café La Plata
Tarija y Linares at Plaza 10 de Noviembre. Mon-Sat 1000-2200.
Upmarket place for coffee, sweets and drinks. Nice atmosphere, English and French spoken.

Café Manzana Mágica
Oruro 239.
Meat-free meals only, a popular, small café.

Chaplin
Matos y Quijarro. Mon-Fri 0830-1200.
Breakfasts and excellent *tucumanas* (fried *empanadas*).

Confitería Cherry's
Padilla 8. Open 0800-2230.
Small economical place, good cakes, breakfast.

Santa Clara
Quijarro 32 y Matos, also Sucre 33 y Bolívar and other locations. Mon-Sat 0700-2300.
Popular with locals for afternoon snacks.

Festivals

Potosí is sometimes called the 'Ciudad de las Costumbres', especially at Corpus Cristi, Todos Santos and Carnaval, when special sweets are prepared, families go visiting friends, etc.
Jan/Feb Carnaval Minero, 2 weeks before Carnaval in Oruro, includes **Tata Ckascho**, when miners dance down Cerro Rico and El Tío (the *Dios Minero*) is paraded.
End May/beginning Jun Fiesta de Manquiri: on 3 consecutive Sat llama sacrifices are made at the cooperative mines in honour of *Pachamama*.
Aug San Bartolomé, or **Chutillos**, is held from the middle of Aug, with the main event being processions of dancers on the weekend closest to the 24-26 Aug; Sat features Potosino, and Sun national, groups. Costumes can be hired in the *artesanía* market on C Sucre. Hotel and transport prices go up by 30% for the whole of that weekend.
10 Nov Fiesta Aniversario de Potosí.

Shopping

Mercado Artesanal, *Sucre y Omiste. Mon-Sat 0830-1230, 1430-1830.* Sells handwoven cloth and regional handicrafts. There are several craft shops on C Sucre between Omiste and Bustillos.
Mercado Central, *Bustillos y Bolívar*, sells mainly meat and some produce.
Mercado Gremial, *between Av Camacho and Oruro.* For household goods.

What to do

All agencies offer mine tours (see page 190), trips to the Salar de Uyuni and REA (see page 150) and trekking at Kari Kari lakes, the artificial water sources for the city and mines.

Claudia Tours, *Ayacucho 7, T02-622 5000, www.turismoclaudia.com.* City tours, mines and trekking; also in Uyuni, Av Ferroviaria opposite Hotel Avenida.
Hidalgo Tours, *La Paz 1133, T02-622 9512, www.salardeuyuni.net; also Av Potosí 113, Uyuni.* Specialized services in Potosí and to Salar de Uyuni. Guide Efraín Huanca

has been recommended for mine tours. Pioneering tour operator for the Uyuni salt flats and the lagoons, having the first salt hotel in the world, the **Palacio de Sal Hotel**.

Koala Tours, *Ayacucho 3, T02-622 2092, koalabolivia@hotmail.com*. Owner Eduardo Garnica speaks English and French. Their mine tours are popular and have been recommended.

Silver Tours, *Quijarro 12, T02-622 3600, www.silvertours.8m.com*. Economical mine tours.

Sin Fronteras, *Ayacucho 17 y Bustillos, T02-622 4058, frontpoi@entelnet.bo*. Owner Juan Carlos Gonzales speaks English and French and is very helpful. Also hires camping gear.

Turismo Potosí, *Lanza 12 y Chuquisaca, T02-622 8212*. Guide and owner Santos Mamani has been recommended.

Transport

Air
The airport, Capitán Nicolás Rojas, is 6 km from Potosí on the road to Sucre. **Aerocon**, Plaza del Estudiante, Edif 4º Centenario, T6960 7526, Mon-Sat from La Paz at 0940, to La Paz at 1105, 1 hr 5 mins.

Bus
Large modern bus terminal (Nueva Terminal, use fee US$0.30) with ATMs, luggage store, information office, Tourist Police and food court. **Note** it is far from the centre: taxi US$2; city buses F, I, 150,

US$0.20, but there are no city buses or taxis late at night; not safe to go out on the street, try to arrive by day or wait inside until morning. Daily services: **La Paz** several companies 1900-2230, US$9-13, 10 hrs by paved road; *bus-cama* US$18.25 (departures from La Paz 1830-2030). To travel by day, go to **Oruro, San Miguel** and others, all day, US$5.40-7.50, 5 hrs. Buses to **Uyuni** leave from either side of the railway line at Av Toledo y Av Universitaria, 1000-1200 and 1800-2000, US$6, 3-4 hrs on a new road, superb scenery; book in advance. **Cochabamba** several companies 1830-2030, US$9-13, *bus-cama* US$18.75, 10 hrs. **Sucre** frequent service 0630-1800, US$3-6, 3 hrs; also shared taxis from behind the old bus terminal, **Cielito Lindo**, T02-624 3381, 2½ hrs, US$7 pp, drop-off at your hotel. For **Santa Cruz** change in Sucre or Cochabamba. **Tupiza** several companies around 0730 and 2000, US$6, 8 hrs; continuing to **Villazón**, US$11, 10 hrs. **Tarija** several companies 1800-1830, US$10.35-13.60, 8 hrs, spectacular journey. To go by day take a bus to **Camargo**, 5 hrs, US$6, then change. Camargo buses leave from offices outside main terminal.

Train
Station is at Av Sevilla y Villazón, T02-622 3101, www.fca.com.bo. A 25-passenger railcar to **Sucre** leaves on Tue, Thu, Sat 0800, 6 hrs, US$3.60; confirm details in advance.

Towards Oruro

La Puerta A village 6 km from Potosí on the road to Oruro and site of the **Capilla de San Bartolomé**, La Puerta is visited by Potosinos during the Festival of **Chutillos** in August. Nearby is the **Devil's Cave**; many legends have been told about it. Chutillos is a classic blend of Catholic and indigenous traditions that have merged to the point of becoming indistinguishable. It is both the feast day of San Bartolomé and the celebration of the saint's victory over Umphurruna, an evil spirit who had kidnapped the sun and held it hostage in a dark cave.

Hacienda Cayara, which belonged to the Marqués de Otavi, is one of the best-preserved haciendas in the area, 25 km northwest of the city, with colonial paintings and furniture. It is now a **Hotel Museo** (see Where to stay, below). The hacienda is 7 km from the turning off the road to Tarapaya.

Thermal baths The **Complejo Recreacional Tarapaya**, 21 km outside the city on the road to Oruro, by the town of Tarapaya, has thermal baths worth visiting (see complejorecreacional.detarapaya on Facebook). There are public pools (US$0.50) and private baths (US$1.20 per hour). The complex also has cabins ($) and camping, US$4.25.

On the other side of the river from the baths is **Laguna de Tarapaya**, a 60-m-diameter volcanic crater lake, with 30-34°C water on the surface, much more at the source in the centre. Take sun protection. Below the crater lake are boiling

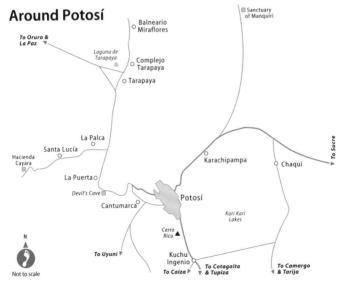

Around Potosí

Not to scale

ponds. Be very careful, several people have drowned here and agencies do not warn of the dangers. You can camp by the lake and there are also cabins to rent.

Further north, 25 km north of Potosí is **Balneario Miraflores** ⓘ *pools US$0.35, private baths US$2.80 per hr*. The water in the pools here is hotter than in Tarapaya, it is popular with locals but not as clean; there are basic *alojamientos* ($).

North of Miraflores, 30 km from Potosí, is the colonial **Hacienda Mondragón**, set in a beautiful canyon, which is visited on some tours. Just south of the hacienda is **Chullpapata**, a 100-m-high rock with archaeological remains on top.

Towards Sucre

Kari Kari Lakes Following Viceroy Toledo's reforms in the early 1570s, 32 artificial lakes were built to the southeast of the city to supply the *ingenios* with a steady supply of water to grind down the ore. About 20,000 *indígenas* built the dams over a 50-year period. On the afternoon of 15 March 1626 one dam wall broke sending a tidal wave through the city killing between 2500 and 10,000 people, depending on who you believe. It was said that the ghosts of the dead inhabited the dam until the survivors said enough prayers to placate them. Fifteen lakes remain. These proved useful in the drought of 1983, having enough water to supply domestic and industrial needs in Potosí. The series of lakes makes a pleasant trekking area, but at an average altitude of 4600 m it is for the acclimatized only. One- and two-day tours are organized by some of the tour operators in Potosí.

Thermal baths There are thermal baths at **Chaquí** ⓘ *closed Wed*, east of the city along a road that branches south off the road to Sucre. Take a truck or bus from Mercado Uyuni; it can also be reached on foot from the Kari Kari lakes. There are a few basic places to stay in Chaquí, and the baths, popular with the local people, are pleasant.

Listings Around Potosí

Where to stay

$$$ Hotel Museo Cayara
25 km northwest of Potosí (office in Potosí: Cochabamba 532, T6740 9097), www.hotelmuseocayara.com.
Hacienda with beautiful rooms, furniture and grounds, bedrooms with and without bath, and a restaurant.

Festivals

Aug Festival de Chutillos (see La Puerta, above). Participants visit the cave and thousands of parades and activities take place in the city and surroundings.

Transport

Minibuses to Tarapaya and Miraflores leave from outside the Mercado Chuquimia on Av Universitaria, near the bus terminal, about every 30 mins 0600-1800, US$0.75, 30 mins. A **taxi** is US$9 for a group. The last bus back from Miraflores leaves at 1800.

striking red cliffs, lush vineyards and dinosaur footprints

To the south of Potosí are several parallel mountain ranges running north–south. Between them run deep river valleys and the roads connecting with the south of the country. A paved road runs south of Potosí. At Ingenio Cucho (Km 38) the road splits. The paved road continues south to Cotagaita, then unpaved to Tupiza and Villazón (see page 160). A secondary dirt road goes to Caiza, with a pleasant climate and a hotel, where cooperatives produce tin and silver handicrafts. Transport leaves from Plaza El Minero in Potosí in the afternoon. A third road goes east to the next valley then south to Camargo and the Valle de Cinti to El Puente, where it climbs to the altiplano before descending eventually to Tarija. It is paved all the way.

Camargo and around *Colour map 3, B4.*

The tranquil and friendly colonial town of Camargo (population 14,200), surrounded by vineyards and fruit orchards, is 186 km south of Potosí. Straddling the Río Chico and flanked by crumbling red sandstone cliffs on one side and rolling hills on the other, the town has a very pretty setting. The church is by the main square, **Plaza 6 de Agosto**. The bus terminal and a small market are along Avenida Chuquisaca, closer to **Plazuela Avaroa**. The main market is at the opposite end of town past the main plaza. Also along Avenida Chuquisaca is the **Alcaldía**, where you can get information about the area. Many shops sell excellent fruit preserves, *singani*, wine and *palqui*, a coffee substitute ground from the pod of the *palqui* tree, an acacia abundant in the area.

This is where the Spaniards found the most suitable conditions for growing grapes for wine for Potosí. First on men's shoulders, then on donkeys and mules the wine was carried to the city. *Singani* was originally produced using wood-fired stills called *k'onchanas*, which became more sophisticated as *falcas* or *aguardienteras*. Examples of these and other historic items can be seen at the **Museo Etno Antropológico de Cinti** ⓘ *Comunidad El Chical, just south of Camargo, T04-629 2092, US$1.50*, curated by Don Benjamín Aramayo Sivila. It also contains archaeological and domestic objects and has a nice garden.

Around Camargo The countryside around Camargo is beautiful. The **Cañón Colorado del Cinti** (the cliffs by town) extends 15 km north and 35 km to the south. The contrast of the eroded red cliffs and the green vineyards in the river valley is quite striking. To the south, 14 km from town, is **Palca Grande**, which has the disused *bodega* of San Remo, which can be visited. The town is the base for a two-hour tour to Los Dólmenes, fantastic rock formations, fossils, caves and petroglyphs (contact **Cinti Tours**, see under Vineyards, below). To the west of Palca Grande a dirt road crosses a range and goes to Cotagaita. Going east, the side road goes 45 km to the fruit-growing plains of **Culpina** and on to **Incahuasi**, near where a number of important fossils have been found, as well as a variety of cacti. On the way to Culpina is **San Pedro**, where petroglyphs can be seen. Near

Tacaquina some 12 km north of Camargo is **Ciudadela de Piedra**, a prehispanic burial site.

Vineyards Vineyards that can be visited include **Ocho Estrellas** ① *El Chilcar, Don Luperio Martínez, T04-629 2192, vinosochoestrellas@gmail.com,* mainly a *singani* producer; **La Casona de Molina** ① *El Porvenir, T7294 3850, lacasonademolina@yahoo.com,* a 'boutique' bodega, more modern than some, with a restaurant; **Cepas Mendocinas** ① *Media Luna, T04-629 2556, contact through Cinti Tours, T6731 4043, cintitours_camargo@hotmail.com,* which also has a *hotel campestre* with 8 basic, but comfortable rooms; and **Cepa de Oro** ① *Vivicha, 20 km from Camargo, Jaime and Carmen Rosa Rivera, T6760 1515, cepadeoro@hotmail.com,* where you can see vines cultivated in the traditional way, growing up *molle* and *chañar* trees. You can also eat here. See page 199 for transport to the vineyards or page 208 for tour operators.

> **Tip...**
> Don't rely on the banks in Camargo; take cash.

South of Camargo
The main road runs south from Camargo, between the Río Chico and towering red cliffs, 42 km to **Villa Abecia**, a lovely small town surrounded by vineyards and fruit orchards on the banks of the Río Grande. It has several places to stay and eat and *bodegas* (eg **Don Tomás**, shop on the plaza, T7348 8622). In the area are many cave paintings and petroglyphs, as well as river-bathing beaches.

Beyond Villa Abecia is **Las Carreras**, in the far southern reaches of the department of Chuquisaca, where a small bodega, La Casa de Barro, is denominated a Museo de Sitio Vivo, with its vines clambering over *molle* and *chañar* trees. Here the road crosses the Río Grande. The region has petroglyphs and dinosaur footprints. Next is **El Puente**, where the road turns east and crosses the Río San Juan de Oro into the department of Tarija. From here it climbs steeply along cacti-covered slopes with beautiful views to the **Altiplano de Tarija**, a high plateau at about 3500 m, where the town of **Iscayachi** lies in a long cultivated valley – a ribbon of green in the high plateau. There are basic accommodations in town. Just before Iscayachi is the junction with a road going southwest to the Tupiza–Villazón road, which it reaches 34 km north of Villazón and the Argentine border (see page 160). Iscayachi is at the western edge of the **Reserva Biológica Cordillera de Sama** (see page 213). The road to Villazón, as well as the road to Tarija go through this lovely park. From Iscayachi, the road to Tarija crosses the reserve as it climbs to a pass before the **Falda la Queñua** tunnel and a vertiginous 1900-m descent to the flat valley north of Tarija, the region's capital (see page 201).

Where to stay

Camargo

$$ Hostal Plaza
Grau 13, half a block from Plaza 6 de Agosto, T04-629 2977, hostalplaza. camargo@outlook.es.
Modern hotel with comfortable rooms with electric shower, patio, family-run, parking, very hospitable.

$ Hostal Chujllas
Ballivián 5, T04-626 2151.
A good, central place to stay with its own vineyard.

$ Villa Sofía
Potosí 17 near Plazuela Avaroa, T04-629 2047, www.hostalvillasofia.com.
Rooms in an old house, cheaper in adobe rooms and cheaper still in shared rooms. Through the big garden is a new part with family rooms, shared kitchen downstairs. Parking, family-run, very nice.

$ Romay
Bolívar 26, T04-629 2644.
Clean simple rooms, those in new section have bath and are much better, cheaper in older section with basic rooms and shared bath, electric showers, courtyard, parking.

South of Camargo

$$-$ Hostal Cepas de Mi Abuelo
near the plaza in Villa Abecia, T7299 0111, www.cepasdemiabuelo.com.
Rooms for 1 to 3 people and a dorm, traditional linen, hot water, home-made bread, wine and ham, home-grown produce, crochet work for sale, delightful, can arrange walking trips.

Festivals

Camargo
Mar Feria del Vino, Singani y de la Canción Cinteña and **Feria del Durazno** are held at variable dates at the end of the summer.
25 May Feria Artesanal displays the arts and crafts of the region's rural communities, including wine casks, basketry and textiles.
25 Jul Santiago Apóstol, following the religious procession there is a folkloric parade with participation of dance and music groups from regional communities.

South of Camargo
23 Mar Feria del Durazno, the town of Villa Abecia celebrates its anniversary. Fruit and preserves are brought in from the surrounding communities, traditional dishes are served.
3 May Fiesta de la Cruz, a procession goes to the cross atop a hill, which is adorned with fruits and flowers. The Pachamama is asked for well-being and a good harvest.
7 Oct Virgen del Rosario, the image is dressed in elaborate clothing, the church is decorated with flowers, a Mass is held. After Mass, a procession carrying the image of the Virgin takes place.

Transport

Camargo
Bus
Regional For the vineyards south of town, 3 minibuses a day leave for **La Vidriera**. It passes the **Vivicha** area, ask for the vineyard you are interested

in, they are spread out, US$0.50. **23 de Marzo** and **Expreso Camargo/Villa Charcas** have afternoon departures southeast to **Culpina**, US$2, 2 hrs; **Incahuasi**, US$2.50, 2½ hrs; and **Villa Charcas**, US$2.50, 3 hrs.

Long distance To **Potosí**, 6 de Octubre at 1230 and 2000, US$6, 5 hrs (3 hrs by private car), continues to **Sucre**. Buses originating in Tarija, bound for Potosí or **La Paz** pass 2000-2200. To **Tarija**, **23 de Marzo** and **Expreso Camargo/Villa Charcas** alternate days, at 1230 and 2030, US$4.50, 2½ -3 hrs, from Tarija at 0730 and 1630. Buses originating in La Paz at 1700 pass through to Tarija 0500-0700.

Taxi

Taxis charge US$3.50 per hr, to be dropped at a vineyard will cost US$3.50, US$7 for a return trip with waiting time.

Tarija

This pleasant city on the banks of the Río Guadalquivir, with streets and plazas planted with flowering trees, is blessed with plenty of sun and a spring-like climate almost all year round. Tarija is known for the fruit and wines of the fertile Valle Central in which it sits. Tarija has a strong cultural heritage which sets it apart from the rest of the country; *tarijeños*, or *chapacos*, as they are also known, have a reputation for being easy-going and closer to Argentina than to the rest of Bolivia.

Tarija is the capital and, with a population of 234,422, is the largest city of the department of the same name. Since 2005 it has experienced an economic boom thanks to the development of natural gas in the department. Nevertheless, in the Valle Central there are several quaint colonial towns and further afield the department boasts little-explored natural areas as diverse as the altiplano (between 3500 and 4000 m), sub-Andean *yungas* (from 1000 to 2000 m) and Chaco (below 400 m). Three national parks have been created to protect sections of these ecosystems.

an easy-going city with shady parks and flower-filled plazas

★Tarija's centre is at Plaza Luis de Fuentes y Vargas with a statue of the city's founder. Around it are the the Alcaldía and Prefectura and some restaurants with pavement seating.

A block away, on Calle Campero y La Madrid, is the **cathedral** ⓘ *open for Mass evenings from 1730 and Sun 0700-1100*, first built in 1611 and the only one in Bolivia not on the main plaza. It contains a chapel holding the remains of many prominent *chapacos*.

The oldest and most interesting church in the city is the **Basílica de San Francisco** ⓘ *corner of La Madrid y Daniel Campos, 0700-1000, 1800-2000, Sun 0630-1200, 1800-2000*. It is beautifully painted inside, with praying angels depicted on the ceiling and the four evangelists at the four corners below the dome. The library is divided into old and new sections, the old containing some 15,000 volumes, the new a further 5000. To see the library, go to the door at Ingavi O-0137. Behind the church is the **Museo Fray Francisco Miguel de Mari** ⓘ *Colón 641, entre La Madrid e Ingavi, T664 4909, www.franciscanosdetarija.com, Mon-Fri 0900-1200, 1500-1700, US$2.15*, with colonial and contemporary art collections, colonial books, the oldest of which is a 1501 *Iliad*, 19th-century photograph albums and other items.

Essential Tarija

Finding your feet

Daily scheduled flights to La Paz, Cochabamba and Santa Cruz. There are paved roads to Potosí, where good connections can be made elsewhere, and Bermejo on the Argentine border. Roads west to Tupiza and east to the Chaco for the route to Santa Cruz are being improved – slowly.

Getting around

The city is easy to walk around, although the narrow streets can get congested at peak hours. There are city buses (micros) and taxis for longer journeys (starting at US$0.55 within the city centre). Note that blocks west of Calle Colón have a small O before number (oeste), and all blocks east have an E (este); blocks are numbered from Colón outwards. All streets north of Avenida Las Américas (nearly all on our map) are preceded by N (norte). Avenida Las Américas, Costanera or Víctor Paz Estenssoro is an important artery that follows the north bank of the Río Gudalquivir. It has three lanes and it is not obvious in which direction traffic runs. Three bridges span the river connecting with the suburbs to the south.

When to go

The best time to visit is from January onwards, when the fruit is in season, but September, after the spring rains begin, is also nice. The months when most rain falls are October to March.

Time required

Two to three days in the city and surroundings, but if travelling onwards overland, allow another day to get to your next destination.

BACKGROUND

Tarija

Founded 4 July 1574 by Capitán Luis de Fuentes y Vargas, the city declared itself independent of Spain in 1807, becoming the first region in all of Latin America to do so. On 15 April 1817, at the Battle of La Tablada on the outskirts of the city, a local militia under José Eustaquio Méndez defeated a superior Spanish force, securing its existence as an independent republic, until opting to join Bolivia in 1825. Although no longer independent, Tarija's remoteness forced it to remain self-sufficient, its economy based on wine, fruit and cattle ranching. As a result of the War of the Pacific (1878-1880), the city gained importance as a trade centre en route to Argentine ports. This fuelled Tarija's growth and some of the grand mansions in the city date to that era. Petroleum extraction started in 1924, but it was not until the late 1990s that attention turned to the exploitation of the country's largest natural gas fields. This prompted renewed prosperity and has led to an influx of people from other regions.

Five blocks north of the cathedral on Avenida General Bernardo Trigo and next to a pleasant, shady plaza is the **Parroquía de San Roque** ⓘ *Mon-Sat 0700-0900, 1830-2000, Sun 0730-0830, 1000-1100, 1900-2000*, built in 1880 and dedicated to the town's patron saint. The battleship-grey building is architecturally most interesting and it serves as the starting point for the San Roque processions (see Festivals, below). To the left of the church in the **Casa Parroquial** is a small museum with the robes made for the saint's image. The **Capilla San Juan de Dios** ⓘ *Mon-Sat 0830-0930, 1900-2000, Sun 0800-0900*, four blocks northwest of the cathedral, at the end of Avenida Bolívar, was built in 1632 and marks the site where the Spaniards officially surrendered after the Battle of La Tablada. It has stained glass above an ornate carved door. There are views of the city and its surroundings from the **Loma de San Juan**, a park with a statue of Christ (Sagrado Corazón de Jesús) on top, due north of the Capilla San Juan.

Casa Dorada ⓘ *Ingavi 370 entre Trigo y Sucre, http://casadelaculturatarija. com, guided tours Mon-Fri at 0900, 1000, 1100, 1500, 1600, and 1700, Sat 0900, 1000, 1100, US$0.70*. Begun in 1886 and also known as the Maison d'Or, it is now part of Casa de la Cultura. It belonged to importer/exporter Moisés Navajas and his wife Esperanza Morales and has been beautifully restored inside and out. The exterior is painted gold and silver and inside it displays the ultimate opulence from its era, including Italian murals (two Italian artists spent years on site), European furniture, Persian rugs, a Sistine Chapel-style painted ceiling in the private chapel, much gold leaf, crystal table lamps in the form of bunches of grapes in the dining room and much more. It now has an art gallery, theatre and library. Another of Navajas' houses, the **Castillo Azul** ⓘ *Bolívar E-644, entre Junín y O'Connor, near Parque Bolívar*, is painted, as the name suggests, a startling blue. It is closed to the public.

Tarija's **Museo de Arqueología y Paleontología** ⓘ *Trigo 402 y Lema, T04-663 6680, Mon-Fri 0800-1200, 1500-1800, Sat 0900-1200, 1500-1800, US$0.45*, contains a palaeontological collection (fossils, remains of several Andean elephants of the

Pleistocene), as well as smaller mineralogical, ethnographic and anthropological collections. The outskirts of the city can be a good place to look for fossils, but report any finds to the university. For example, **Morros Blancos** south of town (take a micro or taxi in the direction of the airport) before the police control (*tranca* or *garita*), where you can see lovely structures of sand looking like a small canyon. Another place to check is **Parque Los Barrancos**, an area of dramatic erosion, 4 km

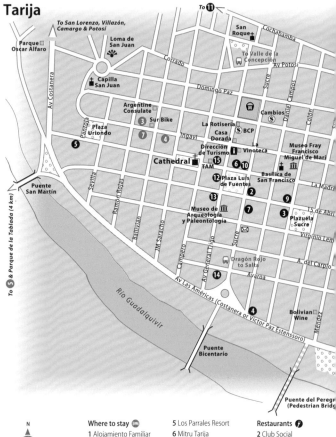

Tarija

N

200 metres
200 yards

Where to stay
1 Alojamiento Familiar
2 Altiplano
3 Hostal Carmen &
  VTB Tours
4 Hostel Casa Blanca

5 Los Parrales Resort
6 Mitru Tarija
7 Residencial Rosario
8 Terravina

Restaurants
2 Club Social
3 DeliGelato
4 Don Pepe Rodizio
5 El Fogón del Gringo
6 El Marqués

to the north (take micro A or B from Domingo Paz y Campero). **Padcaya**, 45 km south of Tarija along the road to Bermejo (transport from Parada del Chaco, every 20 minutes, US$0.60) is another area rich in fossils. Tour operators offer trips to see fossils (see What to do, below).

Tourist information

See the website www.tarija.thus side.nl for constantly updated information on the region.

Dirección de Turismo
Ingavi y Gral Trigo, T04-667 2633, Mon-Fri 0800-1200, 1500-1900, also at airport.
Helpful, and they provide a city and departmental map.

Dirección Municipal de Turismo
C 15 de Abril y Mcal Sucre, T04-663 3581, Mon-Fri 0800-1200, 1430-1830, helpful, city map, some English spoken; also has a booth at the Terminal de Buses, T04-666 7701, 0700-1100, 1430-2200.
The municipal office is in the Alcaldía, on the south side of the Plaza Luis de Fuentes, which also contains the Patio del Cabildo, where events and concerts are held.

Where to stay

Some hotels may offer low-season discounts, May-Aug.

$$$$-$$$ Los Parrales Resort
Urbanización Carmen de Aranjuez Km 3.5, T04-664 8444, www.los parraleshotel.com.
Large luxury hotel offering fine views over the city and surrounding hills. Includes buffet breakfast, pool, spa, gym, Wi-Fi in communal areas.

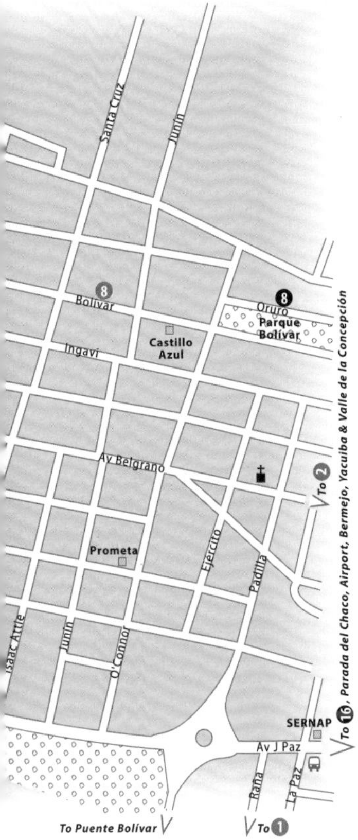

7 El Patio
8 Guadalquivir
9 Guten
10 La Taberna Gattopardo
11 Miiga Comida Coreana
12 Nobu
13 Nougat Café Bar
14 Panadería Sofía
15 Plaza Mayor
16 Sabores del Río

Non-guests can pay to use the pool and other facilities.

$$$ Altiplano
Belgrano 1640 entre Lazcano y Gral Sosa, T04-666 3550, www.altiplanohotel.com.
A high-standard B&B owned by a couple from New Zealand, a bit of a walk from the centre, cosy elegant, contemporary design with traditional fabrics, delightful rooms, very comfortable, good breakfast, thoughtful service with attention to detail. Warmly recommended.

$$$ Terravina
Bolívar E 525 entre Santa Cruz y Junín, T04-666 8673, terravinatarija@gmail.com.
Modern boutique hotel with a wine theme, rooms with fridge and heating and fully furnished 1- and 2-bedroom apartments, 2 rooms on the ground floor are equipped for disabled guests, includes buffet breakfast.

$$$-$$ Mitru Tarija
Avaroa 450, entre Isaac Attie y Delgadillo, T04-664 3930, www.hotelmitru.com.
Brand new hotel built around a central garden, convenient, large comfortable rooms with a/c, heating and safe, also family rooms, light and airy, in the same group as, and with the same high standards as the Mitru hotels in Tupiza and La Paz.

$$ Hostal Carmen
Ingavi O-0784, T04-664 3372, www.hostalcarmentarija.com.
Older place but well maintained, excellent buffet breakfast, hot water, heating, airport transfers available. Often full, advance booking advised, very helpful, good value. Recommended.

$ Alojamiento Familiar
Rana S-0231 y Navajas, T04-664 0832.
Shared bath, hot shower, cheap, helpful, close to bus terminal, traffic noise.

$ Hostel Casa Blanca
Ingavi 645 entre Juan Misael Saracho y Ballivian, T04-664 2909, luiszilvetiali@ gmail.com (see also Facebook HostelCasaBlancaTarija).
Good cheap option, popular with foreign travellers, conveniently placed 3 blocks from the main plaza, English spoken, lots of information, café.

$ Residencial Rosario
Ingavi O-0777, T04-664 2942.
Simple rooms, cheaper with shared bath, hot water, good budget option, family atmosphere, helpful.

Restaurants

Many restaurants (and much else in town) close between 1400 and 1600.

$$$-$$ Don Pepe Rodizio
D Campos N-0138, near Av Las Américas.
Stylish restaurant serving tasty daily set lunch, all-you-can-eat *rodizio* at weekends for US$10.

$$$-$$ El Fogón del Gringo
La Madrid O-1053, Plaza Uriondo. Mon-Sat 1900-2300, Fri-Sun also 1200-1430.
Upmarket *parillada* includes excellent salad bar.

$$$-$$ Plaza Mayor
La Madrid entre Trigo y Campero, ½ block from Cathedral.
Mid-sized restaurant serving good Tarijeña food and wine, pleasant atmosphere.

$$$-$$ Sabores del Río
Av Jaime Paz 2313 esq Romero,
T04-665 2686.
A very good fish restaurant not far from
the entrance to the airport.

$$ Guten
15 de Abril y Colón, Plaza Sucre,
T04-6676445.
Limited menu of meat and fish dishes
with a German touch, pasta and a snack
menu, desserts, also bar, sports TV
screens, low-key, good for a light meal.

$$ El Marqués
La Madrid entre Trigo y
Sucre, on the main plaza,
www.elmarquesrestaurant.com.
In the beautiful historic Casa El Marqués
de Tojo, specializing in international
food, seafood and fish, caters for
events, popular.

$$ La Taberna Gattopardo
La Madrid y Sucre, on main plaza. Daily
0800-2100.
Pizza, *parrillada* with Argentine beef,
local wines, deserts, snacks, excellent
salads, popular meeting place, Wi-Fi.

$ Club Social
Sucre 508 y 15 de Abril.
In a traditional setting on the main
plaza, serves good-value, local almuerzo
and meat dishes, also has a hostal,
La Estrella.

$ Guadalquivir
Oruro entre O'Connor y Carlos Paz, on
Parque Bolívar opposite the monument.
Economical restaurant offering daily
almuerzos and a salad buffet, open
every day.

$ Miiga Comida Coreana
Cochabamba 813 y Ballivian. Open every
night except Tue.

Sushi with salmon and a small but tasty
range of Korean dishes. Also has a disco.

$ El Patio
Sucre N-0458. Mon-Sat.
Good set lunch with small salad bar,
pleasant seating in patio, also great
tucumanas al horno.

Cafés

DeliGelato
Colón N-0421, Plaza Sucre. Daily until
2130.
Good ice cream.

Nobu
Gral Trigo on the main plaza.
Serving coffee, juices and cakes.

Nougat Café-Bar
Gral Trigo corner 15 de Abril. Daily
0800-2400.
Nicely decorated European-style café.
Breakfast, à la carte dishes, snacks and
sweets, Wi-Fi.

$ Panificadora Sofía
Avaroa entre Sucre y Gral Trigo.
Nice fancy bakery with Middle-Eastern
pastries, a variety of breads and a café.

Festivals

Tarija is known for its fiestas. For festivals
in the surrounding area, see page 215.
Feb/Mar Carnaval Chapaco is
lively and colourful; **Compadres and
Comadres**, celebrated on the Thu
preceding carnival, are an important
part of the tradition.
Apr Abril en Tarija, cultural events are
held throughout the month.
**15 Aug-14 Sep La Virgen de
Chaguaya**, a 45-km pilgrimage from
the city to the Santuario Chaguaya,
south of El Valle. For less devoted souls,
Línea P *trufi* from Plaza Sucre, Tarija, to

Padcaya, US$1; bus to Chaguaya and Padcaya from terminal daily, 0700, returns 1700, US$1.35.

16 Aug-1st week Sep **San Roque**, Tarija's main festival. *Chunchos*, male devotees of the saint wearing tall, brightly stripped turbans, veils, colourful shawls and calf-length robes, carry the image of San Roque and dance to the tunes of unusual instruments. These processions take place throughout the first week of Sep. A different church is visited every day and on the main day, the 1st Sun, the procession with the richly dressed saint's statue goes to all the churches and ends in the church of San Roque. No alcohol is consumed. **Dec** Christmas is the time of the **Adoraciones**, when children dance around a pole to the music of *tambores y quenas* (drums and flutes).

Shopping

Handicrafts
Artesanías Bolivia, *Sucre 952 entre D Paz y Corrado, T04-664 6947*. For local handicrafts and musical instruments.

Local produce and wine
See Valle Central, below, for shops selling local produce and wine.
La Vinoteca, *Ingavi O-0731 y Gral Trigo, Mon-Sat 0900-1200, 1500-1900*. Sells wine at bodega prices, cheese and ham.
La Rotisería, *Gral Trigo y Bolívar*. For meats, cheeses and wines.

Markets
The main **market** is in the block between Domingo Paz, Sucre, Bolívar and Trigo. In 2015 it was being rebuilt and was in a temporary location on Domingo Paz. On Sun there is a **Mercado Campesino** on La Loma de San Juan. There is also a

book market on Ingavi entre JM Saracho y Campero. The **wholesale market** is on the road heading north out of town towards San Lorenzo.

What to do

There are several tour operators in the city, offering wine tours, tours of surroundings (Campiña and Chapaca), city tours, and the Camino del Inca.

Bolivian Wine Tours, *Méndez entre Avaroa y Av Las Américas, T04-663 2975, 7022 5715, info@bolivianwinetours.com*. Speciality tours to vineyards and wine cellars (*bodegas*) in the Valle Central and Valle de Cinti, focusing not only on the production of high-altitude wines but also on local culture. Ask here also about trips to the Reserva Biológica Cordillera de Sama and the Camino del Inca and to the Valle de Cóndores, a hard, 1½-day walk from Rosillas, near Padcaya, to see condors.
Educación y Futuro, *at the Ecosol shop, Virgino Lema y Suipacha, Plazuela Sucre, T04-666 4973, www.educacionyfuturo. com*. An NGO giving information on homestays with rural families, cheese making and guided trekking in the Valle de Los Cóndores.
Sur Bike, *Ballivián 601 e Ingavi, T7619 4200*. Bike rentals US$16.50 per day.
Tupiza Tours, *at Hotel Mitru, T04-663 2974, www.tupizatours.com*. The Tarija contact of the Tupiza agency.
VTB, *Ingavi 784 entre Ballivian y R Rojas, at Hostal Carmen (see Where to stay, above), T04-664 4341, www.vtbtourtarija.com*. All tours include a free city tour; 4- to 6-hr trips including bodegas, US$23 pp; comprehensive 10-hr 'Tarija and surroundings in 1 Day', US$35; you can also try your hand at excavation with a

palaeontology specialist! Good vehicles, recommended.

Viva Tours, *Bolívar 251, entre Sucre y Daniel Campos, Edif Ex Hansa p 2, of 6, T04-663 8325, auriventur@hotmail.com.* Vineyard tours US$30 with lunch.

Transport

Air

BoA (General Trigo 327 entre V Lema y A del Carpio, T04-665 4004) flies to **Cochabamba**, **La Paz** and **Santa Cruz**, with connections to other Bolivian cities. **TAM** (La Madrid O-0470 entre Trigo y Campero, T04-664 2734), to **La Paz**, **Sucre**, **Santa Cruz** or **Yacuiba**, depending on day of week. **Aerocon** (at airport, T04-665 8595) flies to **Santa Cruz**. Amaszonas (Trigo y Lema, T04-667 6800) has daily flights to **Santa Cruz**; also to **Salta** (Argentina) Mon, Wed and Fri. **Ecojet** (La Madrid 590 esq Colón, T04-611 3427), daily to **Santa Cruz** early morning with return same day. **Bus** To **La Paz** several buses at 0700-0800 and 1700 (935 km) 13 hrs, US$18.70-25, via Potosí and **Oruro** (US$14.50); check which company operates the best buses. To **Potosí**; several additional departures 1630-1800, 8 hrs, US$10.35-13.60 To **Camargo**, from La Parada del Norte (Carretera a Tomatitas, past the wholesale market), US$7, 2½ hrs. To **Sucre** at 1630 and 1800, US$14. To Potosi *trufis* run a faster service than buses (6 hrs), US$15, likewise to Sucre.

To **Tupiza**, US$9.50, **Diamante**, 1930, and **Juárez**, 2030 and 2100 (with loo, good service, US$12.25), 6 hrs. To **Santa Cruz** via Villamontes, several companies at 1830, US$18.70-27, 17 hrs. To get to Villamontes in daylight, take a **La Guadalupana** or **La Entreriana** *trufi* from Parada del Chaco (east end of Av Las Américas) to **Entre Ríos**, US$3, 1½ hrs, some continue to Villamontes (spectacular route), mostly in daylight. Entre Ríos to Villamontes can take up to 8 hrs.

   To Argentina: to **Villazón**, several companies daily, 1930-2030, 8 hrs, US$6.40. To **Bermejo**, shared taxis (*trufis*) eg 7 de Diciembre del Sur, El Fronterizo, leave when full from opposite the bus station and go as fast as they are allowed, 3 hrs, US$7; bus US$4, 4½ hrs. To **Salta**: **Juárez**, Sun, Thu 1900, take photocopy of passport when booking, US$36, no change of bus at border, and **Dragón Rojo**, C Sucre N-0235, T04-666 5014, www.transportedragonrojo.com, US$36, daily, 2000, transfer to shared taxis or a different bus once in Argentina. Buses to **Yacuiba** US$8, up to 11 hrs via Villamontes, most depart in the evening. There is an alternative route via Carapari, further south, which also crosses the Serranía de Aguaragüe, which is shorter.

Taxis
Within the city centre, journeys start at about US$0.55.

Around Tarija
enjoy the local food and wine, hunt for fossils and trek the Inca Trail, not necessarily in that order

Valle Central
The Valle Central, which surrounds Tarija, offers many opportunities for excursions in pleasant countryside at about 1800 m. As well as the fossil deposits, there are vineyards and bodegas (wineries), riverside beaches, waterfalls and colonial

BACKGROUND
★Wineries of Tarija

Aranjuez
*T04-664 2552, gcomercial@
vinosaranjuez.com.*

Bodega
*At Avenida Dr A Baldivieso E-1976,
Barrio Aranjuez, across the river within
walking distance of town.*
One of the smallest, produces
only wine.

Campos de Solana
*15 de Abril E-0259 entre Suipacha y
Méndez (tienda), T04-664 8482, www.
camposdesolana.com.*
Increasingly recognized for their
selection of fine wines (the Malbec is
highly regarded), as well as the popular
Casa Real brand of *singani* (same
company, same shop but different
bodega, T04-664 5498, http://casa-real.
com). The Campos de Solana bodega is
in El Portillo, 6 km on road to Bermejo,
and the Casa Real bodega (T6737 0868,
visitas@casa-real.com) is in Santa Ana,
about 15 km off the road to Bermejo.

Casa Vieja
*Trigo casi Corrado (shop), T04-666 2605,
www.lacasavieja.info, Mon-Sun 1000-
1600. A traditional bodega artesanal,
small-scale winery, located in Valle de la
Concepción, 25 km from Tarija.*

Interesting and recommended. It also
has a popular restaurant overlooking
the vines, open daily for lunch (dishes
US$3-7) and, on Sunday, live music and
roast suckling pig (chancho a la cruz),
US$10.

Kohlberg
*Av Francisco Lazcano, Barrio San Jorge
No 1, T04-666 6366, http://kohlberg.
com.bo. Bodega La Caba, in Santa
Ana, 15 km from town off the road to
Bermejo.*
The first industrial winery and now the
largest. Specializes in table wines; their
Syrah is well regarded.

La Concepción
*Colón entre 15 de Abril y La Madrid
(shop), T04-664 5040, T04-666
3787 (bodega), 7870 9646, www.
laconcepcion.bo.*
Wines (try their Cabernet Sauvignon)
and Rujero *singani*, bodega in Valle
de Concepción.

Bodega Magnus
*T04-611 2462 (bodega), www.
bodegasmagnus.com.*
A relatively new winery which is open
to tourists, concentrating on reds and
rosé, in Valle de la Concepción.

towns. It is this zone which inspires the nickname Andalucía of Bolivia because of
its fruit and berry production, vegetables, ham cured Serrano-style, goat's cheese,
preserves and honey.

★**Wineries** Tarija is proud of its wine and *singani* (clear brandy) production,
the best in Bolivia. Winemaking has flourished in the region since grapes were
introduced in 1584. The old traditions of pressing grapes by foot, known as *vino
patero*, or 'foot wine', still persist and can be seen in *bodegas artesanales*. There are

also modern large-scale wineries that have made the region's wine much more widely available. Tarija's vineyards lie between 1600 and 2850 m producing *vino* and *singani de altura*, high-altitude wine and brandy. A huge variety of grapes are grown, but the most important for red wine include Syrah, Cabernet Sauvignon, Malbec, Merlot and Tannat. For white wine, varieties include Sauvignon Blanc, Riesling, Chardonnay and Moscatel de Alejandría. The last-named is the principal grape for *singani*, the best being of Moscatel alone, next best is Moscatel/Misionera mixed and the lowest quality Misionera alone. There are two distinct wine-producing regions near Tarija. The first is in the **Valle de Cinti**, which has been described above in the section South to Tarija (see page 197). This can easily be reached from Tarija. The best option is to take a tour (see What to do, page 208) that provides transport and allows you to visit several different bodegas on the same day. The same applies to the second region, south of town in the **Valle Central**. To visit independently those bodegas that receive visitors – not all do – contact the bodega directly to reserve a tour, or visit the bodega's shop in town beforehand to make arrangements. See Wineries of Tarija, page 210, for a selection of wine producers. The main centres for wine are Santa Ana and Valle de la Concepción.

Observatorio Astronómico Nacional ⓘ *about 15 km off the road to Bermejo, near Bodega Casa Real, T7186 0979, rozalles@hotmail.co, Mon, Tue, Thu, Fri from 1900.* The observatory has two Russian telescopes and is a good place to observe the stars. It also has an atomic clock, which keeps official time for Bolivia. It also puts on night-time shows. Transport from Corrado y General Trigo, every 25 minutes, US$0.75.

Valle de la Concepción This colonial town 25 km south of Tarija is surrounded by vineyards. Its plaza is filled with bitter orange and ceibo trees and has examples of the art produced during the annual Encuentro El Arte y El Vino (see Festivals, below). There are more objects outside the Municipio and many of the walls around town are covered with dramatic murals.

North of Tarija
Tomatitas and San Lorenzo About 15 km north of the centre is the charming town of **San Lorenzo**. The plaza is very pleasant, with palms, oranges and flowers, and the church, dating to 1709, is huge and unadorned. Just off the plaza is the **Museo Méndez** ⓘ *Mon-Sat 0900-1230, 1500-1830, minimum US$0.30 entry*, the house of the independence hero Eustaquio Méndez, 'El Moto'. The small museum exhibits his weapons, his bed, his 'testimonio'. At lunchtime on Sunday, many courtyards serve cheap meals. Minibuses from Domingo Paz y J M Saracho in Tarija, every five minutes, US$0.75. The road to San Lorenzo passes **Tomatitas** (5 km), now almost a suburb

Tip...
At weekends, Tomatitas is packed with people having lunch at the outdoor restaurants (Rincón Chapaco is very nice) and the narrow bridge over the river becomes a total bottle-neck, long traffic jams.

of Tarija, a popular picnic and river bathing area, from where a good day trip is to the waterfalls at **Coimata**, 14 km from Tarija in the foothills of the mountains. Here is a cold waterfall surrounded by vegetation. You can walk 3 km upriver to a second waterfall some 30 m high. Before Coimata is **Hotel La Pasarela** (see Where to stay). Transport from Calle Comercio, Mercado Campesino, every 20 minutes, US$0.75. Another branch of the same road leads to **Rincón de la Victoria**, also 14 km from Tarija, in a similar setting. Here too are cabins to rent: **Caserío La Victoria**, T7298 7100, http://caseriolavictoria.wix.com/caseriolavictoria, with restaurant, swimming pool and gardens, and **$$ Cabañas del Cadillar**, midway between Tomatitas and Rincón de la Victoria, T7296 3699, http://turismotarija. com, cabins for five people, country views.

Tarija's Altiplano Between Tomatitas and San Lorenzo, the main Tarija–Potosí road climbs steeply from the Valle Central to reach the altiplano. It continues northwest and descends from the altiplano to El Puente on the Río San Juan de Oro before passing through the Valle de Cinti (see page 197). Tarija's altiplano is a beautiful area of high mountains and dry inter-Andean plateaux between 3500 and 4000 m, bound by the Río Guadalquivir and the Río San Juan de Oro. This is also where most of Tarija's native Quechua-speaking people live. Just west of the town of Iscayachi (see page 198) a road branches south and crosses the high plateau on its way to Villazón. This road provides access to the main attractions in the Reserva Cordillera de Sama.

East from Tarija

A road runs east from Tarija to Entre Ríos and Villamontes where it meets the paved Santa Cruz–Yacuiba road. The first 30 km out of Tarija are paved, then it is all-weather, with dangerous curves, fog and poor maintenance. There are long-term plans to pave this route. It is, nevertheless, a very scenic road, crossing several mountain ranges until it meets the plains of the Chaco. The section between Entre Ríos and Villamontes is truly spectacular. The road is carved into the rock-face high above the El Angosto gorge of the Río Pilcomayo as it snakes its way down through densely forested slopes of the Serranía de Aguaragüe. At this point traffic is controlled to one way at a time to prevent accidents and delays.

Entre Ríos *Colour map 3, C5.*

This charming, subtropical little town, with a pretty plaza full of roses, lies halfway in terms of kilometres between Tarija and Villamontes. A statue of Christ looks over the town from a hill on the outskirts. There are great views from the top of the steps leading up to it. Two rivers pass the town, the Santa Ana and the Pajonal, where you can swim when there is enough water; ask directions. You can also hike in the surrounding hills as well as hire horses. In town there are cabañas for rent and places to eat.

Serranía de Aguaragüe This is the last mountain range before the plains of El Chaco to the east. It is a national park, just 10 km wide but 111 km long, of great biological importance since it contains two ecosystems, Bosque Tucumano-Boliviano (Yungas) and Bosque Serrano Chaqueño. The Camiri–Villamontes–Yacuiba road goes parallel and to the east of it. In 2015 **SERNAP** (T04-683 1671, www.sernap.gob.bo) had no facilities for visitors in the park.

The road across the Serranía de Aguaragüe is the first stage of one of the routes from Tarija to Argentina via the Yacuiba-Pocitos border (see page 263). From Villamontes the road is paved north and south.

South of Tarija

Reserva Biológica Cordillera de Sama To the southwest of Tarija lies the Reserva Biológica Cordillera de Sama, a 108,500-ha wildlife sanctuary between 1800 and 4700 m. In the altiplano section of the park to the southwest are the Sama wetlands, four large lakes, the **Lagunas de Tajzara**, which are a Ramsar site and home to 34 species of waterbird, including flamingo, coot, duck and many migratory birds. This area also has Bolivia's highest sand dunes. In the south of the park are the **Lagunas Bravas**, small lakes nestled among high rocky peaks. The eastern edge of the park, where the land drops abruptly towards the Valle Central has progressively more lush forests and waterfalls. The park boasts 207 species of bird, including condors, and 57 mammals, including vicuña, deer and puma, as well as several types of forests: *qewiña* (*Polylepis tomentella*) in the higher areas, *pino de cerro* (*Podocarpus parlatorei*) and alder in the lower elevations and *cardonales* (*Trichocereus tarijensis*), large cacti just below the altiplano. It is one of the main water sources for Tarija and the surrounding valleys. Within the park are 80 archaeological sites including petroglyphs, cave paintings, burial sites, fortresses and prehispanic roads. One of these roads, **La Patanka**, was a trade route used by the Chichas people and later the Incas between Tupiza and Tarija. It is a side branch of the main Inca road from Cuzco to Argentina. A 20-km part of this route between Pujzara and Pinos Sud is now used as a one- or two-day trekking route called **Camino del Inca** (Inca Trail). It is a demanding walk, the pass at Abra Calderilla is at 3823 m, from where you descend to 2212 m.

The reserve is administered jointly by **SERNAP** ① *Av Jaime Paz Zamora 1171, Tarija, T04-665 0850, www.sernap.gob.bo, Mon-Fri 0830-1230, 1500-1900*, and an association of the local communities within the park, which has the assistance of an environmental NGO: **PROMETA** ① *Alejandro del Carpio E-0659, T04-663 3873, www.prometa.org.bo, Mon-Fri 0830-1230, 1500-1900*. Additional information is available at www.camelidostarija.org.

In the reserve, at the village of **Pujzara** (6 km from the road to Villazón), near the lake area, is an *albergue* (\$ per person, rooms for two to five, shared bath, hot water, meals available with two days' notice, bikes for rent, guides for Inca Trail Pujzara–Pinos Sur). First visit SERNAP to get a permit and arrange lodging in Pujzara, then contact a local guide to meet you in Pujzara. From Pujzara you can visit the Lagunas de Tajzara, the dunes and handicraft centres. There is another *albergue* in **Calderillas**, east of Pujzara along the Inca Trail, below the pass. This is where people who do the walk in two days spend the night. From Pinos Sud, at the end of the Inca Trail, *autos* run to Tarija.

Reserva Nacional Tariquía To the southeast of Tarija, the Reserva Nacional Tariquía was created to protect 246,870 ha mainly of subtropical Yungas and of cloudforest, between 900 and 3400 m. The reserve is rich in fauna and flora and has a number of endangered species such as the jaguar, lowland tapir, spectacled bear, military macaw, cedar and podocarpus. Further information is available from **SERNAP** ① *Av Jaime Paz Zamora 1171, Tarija, T04-665 0850, www.sernap.gob. bo, Mon-Fri 0830-1230, 1500-1900.*

The reserve can be reached from the Tarija–Bermejo road (see below), either from Emborozú, where you turn off to the community of Sidras, or from Bermejo, from where you have to go to the area known as El Cajón, 65 km from Bermejo; there is a daily bus from Bermejo. From El Cajón it is 4 km to the San Antonio park rangers' camp.

There is no public transport and there is no vehicular access within the park. From Entre Ríos, a dirt road (subject to landslides after rain) goes south through the scenic Valle del Medio to the community of **Salinas**, a spread-out ranching area, rather than a village per-se. Salinas or nearby Chiquiacá are also access points.

To Argentina
The quickest route is via Bermejo, which is easily reached from Tarija; 210 km all paved, the views are also spectacular (sit on right). **Bermejo** (population 21,500, altitude 415 m) is well supplied with places to sleep and eat and there are many *casas de cambio* (including in the bus terminal); it's very hot. Immigration here normally takes about 30 minutes. An international bridge crosses the river from Bermejo to **Aguas Blancas**, Argentina. Bolivian immigration and customs are by the bridge, which is used by through buses and private vehicles. You can also cross the river by launch (US$0.65), which takes you directly to the Argentine immigration post, by the Aguas Blancas bus stop. Bermejo's bus terminal is the opposite end of town from the international bridge (taxi immigration-terminal US$3). Another option is the road to **Villazón** (see page 160), which is the shortest route to Argentina, 189 km, but it's a tiring trip along a winding, scenic mountain road. A third option, from Tarija to the Yacuiba/Pocitos border (see page 263), is 290 km away.

> **Tip...**
> Remember, Bolivia is one or two hours behind Argentina, depending on the time of year.

Listings Around Tarija

Tourist information

Valle Central
Información Turística
Plaza Principal, Valle de la Concepción, T04-667 2854, Mon-Sat 0800-1600.
Offer maps and pamphlets.

Where to stay

Valle Central

$ Hostería Valle d'Vino
Verdiguera y 6 de Julio, Valle de la Concepción, T04-665 1056, www.valledivinotarija.com.

Hostel with private rooms with bath and dorms, breakfast extra, idiosyncratic place with the small Infiernillo bodega with wine for sale and weekend fiestas, a museum with a mish-mash of items from flat irons and stoves to fossils and animal skins, a 'tunnel of love' and other oddities (tour of the property US$1.50).

North of Tarija

$$ La Pasarela
10 km north of Tarija near the village of Coimata, T04-666 1333, www.lapasarelahotel.com.
Belgian/Bolivian-owned hotel with good restaurant/bar, country views, tranquil, family atmosphere, jacuzzi, swimming pool, walking trails, mountain bikes and other activities, laundry and camping, very good.

To Argentina

$ París
La Paz y Tarija, Bermejo, T04-696 1022.
Central hotel with bath and a/c, cheaper with fan, electric shower, includes breakfast, parking.

$ Querubines
Tarija 209, Bermejo, T04-696 1882, www.querubineshotel.com.
Also central, plain rooms with bath and a/c breakfast included, parking.

Festivals

Feb/Mar Fiesta de la Vendimia, Valle de la Concepción, 25 km from Tarija, is a week-long wine vintage festival. 10 days before La Vendimia is the **Encuentro El Arte y El Vino**, with music, theatre, painting, sculpture, workshops for children. The artworks remain with the Municipio.
Mar/Apr Easter week, communities such as San Lorenzo and Padcaya welcome visitors with colourful arches and flowers to **La Pascua Florida** processions.
2nd Sun in Oct The flower festival commemorates the **Virgen del Rosario** (celebrations in the surrounding towns are recommended, eg San Lorenzo and Padcaya).

Shopping

Las Duelas Calamuchita, *opposite the sports field in village of Calamuchita near Valle de la Concepción, T04-666 8943. Open daily 0900-1700.* A shop and small winery, selling local produce, mostly *vinos artesanales* and *singani* from 9 producers, with wine tasting, and also regional preserves, ham and other items.

Transport

Valle Central
From Tarija to Valle de la Concepción, micros run from Corrado entre Trigo y Campero, all day to 1800, US$0.85 pp. Taxis leave from Corrado y JM Saracho.

North of Tarija
From Tarija to **San Lorenzo**, from Domingo Paz y JM Saracho, US$0.85, all day.

Cochabamba
& beyond

the breadbasket of Bolivia

Set in a bowl of rolling hills at a comfortable altitude, Cochabamba enjoys a wonderfully warm, dry and sunny climate. Its parks and plazas are a riot of colour, from the striking purple of the bougainvillea to the subtler tones of jasmine, magnolia and jacaranda. Many visitors particularly enjoy La Cancha market, one of the largest in Bolivia, as well as Cochabamba's very good dining and nightlife.

Economically, this region is of vital importance to Bolivia. The Cochabamba Valley is the agricultural heartland of the country and the tropical lowlands of Chapare, to the east, produce large quantities of coca leaf – both for traditional consumption and the drug trade. Markets, colonial towns and archaeological sites are all close by. Conquering Cerro Tunari is a challenge for all adventurers. Further afield, the dinosaur tracks and great scenery at Torotoro National Park are worth the trip. The paved lowland route to Santa Cruz de la Sierra has much more transport than the rough old road over the mountains via Comarapa and Samaipata. Both offer access to Carrasco and Amboró national parks.

Best for
Dinosaurs ▪ Inca ruins ▪ Markets ▪ Nightlife

Footprint
picks

★ **Cochabamba**, page 220
Plentiful fine dining with noble buildings and
cobbled streets.

★ **Tarata**, page 229
Charming colonial village and the site of the first
Franciscan convent in Bolivia.

★ **Ride the rails from Cochabamba to Aiquile**, page 229
A picturesque and authentic Bolivian experience.

★ **Torotoro National Park**, page 231
Labyrinthine caves and a landscape littered with fossils
and dinosaur footprints.

★ **Carrasco National Park**, page 232
Easily accessible park with a range of ecosystems, great for
birdwatching.

★ **Inkallajita Inca ruins**, page 233
One of the least know but most significant of Bolivia's
Inca sites.

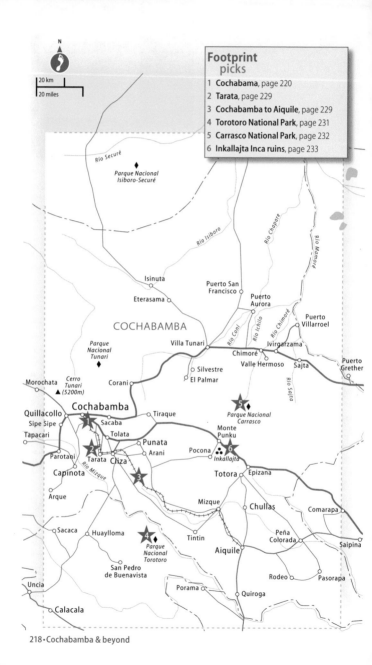

N

20 km
20 miles

Rio Securé

*Parque Nacional
Isiboro-Securé*

Rio Isiboro

Rio Chapare

Rio Mamoré

Isinuta

Puerto San
Francisco

Puerto
Aurora

Puerto
Villarroel

Eterasama

COCHABAMBA

*Parque
Nacional
Tunari*

Villa Tunari

Rio Cont.

Rio Ichilo

Rio Chimoré

Ivirgarzama

Puerto
Grether

Morochata

*Cerro
Tunari*
▲ (5200m)

Corani

Silvestre
El Palmar

Chimoré

Valle Hermoso

Sajta

Rio Sajta

Quillacollo

Cochabamba

Tiraque

*Parque
Nacional
Carrasco*

Sipe Sipe

Sacaba

Tapacari

Tolata

Monte
Punku

Parotani

Tarata

Punata

Arani

Pocona

Inkallajta

Capinota

Rio Mizque

Cliza

Totora

Epizana

Arque

Mizque

Chullas

Comarapa

Sacaca

Huaylloma

*Parque
Nacional
Torotoro*

Tintin

Aiquile

Peña
Colorada

Saipina

Uncia

San Pedro
de Buenavista

Rodeo

Pasorapa

Calacala

Porama

Quiroga

Essential Cochabamba and beyond

Finding your feet

The city is served by paved roads from La Paz and Santa Cruz. Neither airport, nor bus station are far from the centre. Buses and taxis serve both.

Getting around

The city is divided into four quadrants based on the intersection of Avenida Las Heroínas running west to east, and Avenida Ayacucho running north to south. In all longitudinal streets north of Heroínas the letter N (Norte) precedes the four numbers. South of Heroínas the numbers are preceded by S (Sur). In all transversal streets west of Ayacucho the letter O (Oeste) precedes the numbers and all streets running east are preceded by E (Este). The first two numbers refer to the block, 01 being closest to Ayacucho or Heroínas; the last two refer to the building's number. See also Transport, page 227.

Safety

Do not venture into any of the hills around town on foot (including San Sebastián, La Coronilla and San Pedro with the Cristo de la Concordia, although at the Cristo itself there are usually plenty of people about). At night take only radio taxis (marked with stickers on the back doors). Take usual precautions with your belongings in markets, on public transport and other crowded places. In the main towns in the coca-growing region of Chapare tourists are reasonably safe, but don't go off the beaten track alone. See also Safety, page 372.

When to go

Cochabamba city can be visited at any time of year, rainy season December-March. At this time roads to outlying areas can become very difficult.

Time required

Three or four days for the city and a day excursion, of which there are a few. There are other two-day trips and Torotoro requires three to four days. Stopping on the overland route to Santa Cruz can add a couple more days to a visit to this region.

Weather Cochabamba

January	February	March	April	May	June
27°C 13°C 96mm	27°C 13°C 69mm	27°C 12°C 56mm	28°C 9°C 15mm	27°C 5°C 2mm	26°C 3°C 3mm

July	August	September	October	November	December
26°C 3°C 7mm	27°C 5°C 5mm	28°C 8°C 6mm	29°C 11°C 35mm	29°C 12°C 42mm	29°C 13°C 62mm

★Old town

At the heart of the old town is the arcaded **Plaza 14 de Septiembre** with the **cathedral** ⓘ *Mon-Fri 0800-1200, 1700-1900, Sat-Sun 0800-1200*, dating from 1571, but much added to. Of the colonial churches nearby, the **Convent and Museum of Santa Teresa** ⓘ *Baptista y Ecuador, T04-422 1252, guided tours only Mon-Fri 0900, 1000, 1100, 1430, 1330, 1630 (Sat), US$2.50, camera US$ 3 extra*, original construction 1760-1790, has a lovely courtyard, a Sala Capitular with painted walls, many other paintings and a beautiful Coro (being restored in 2015).

Museo Arqueológico ⓘ *Jordán E-199 y Aguirre, T04-425 0010, www.museo. umss.edu.bo, Mon-Fri 0830-1800, guided tours in English Mon-Fri 1330-1600, US$3*, is part of the Universidad de San Simón. The museum displays artefacts including Amerindian hieroglyphic scripts, mummies, and pre-Inca textiles, through to the colonial era. There is a lot to appreciate, but descriptions are in Spanish and the presentation is a bit dated. **Casona Santiváñez** ⓘ *Santiváñez O-0156, Mon-Fri 0800-1200, 1430-1800, free*, has a nice colonial patio, and exhibition of paintings and historic photographs.

North of the old town

From Plaza Colón, at the north end of the old town, the wide **Avenida Ballivián** (known as **El Prado**) runs northwest to the wealthy modern residential areas; along it you can find restaurants and bars. Also in the north is the Patiño family's **Palacio Portales** ⓘ *Av Potosí 1450, T04-448 6414, guided tours in Spanish Tue-Fri 1530, 1630, 1730, 1800, in English 1600, 1700, in French 1600, Sat in Spanish at 0930, 1000, 1100, English 1030, 1130, French 1030, Sun Spanish 1100, English and French 1130, US$1.50. The gardens are open Tue-Fri 1500-1830, Sat-Sun 0900-1200*. Built in French Renaissance style, furnished from Europe and set in 10 ha of gardens inspired by Versailles, the Patiño mansion was finished in 1927 but never occupied. The architectural style is predominantly French Renaissance. The great halls are filled with Napoleonic and Louis XV furniture. On the upper floor are chambers containing reproductions of the Sistine Chapel; the walls are covered in brocaded silk and it is decorated throughout in Carrara marble and paintings by Velásquez. There's even a copy of the Alhambra in Granada. Everything imported and no expense spared, the Palacio Portales bears testament to inconceivable opulence. It is now the **Centro Cultural Simón I Patiño** ⓘ *http://portal.fundacionpatino.org*, with an excellent art gallery in the basement. Take a taxi (five minutes from the centre) or micro G from Avenida San Martín. Next to Palacio Portales is the very nice **Museo de Historia Natural Alcide d'Orbigny** ⓘ *Av Potosí 1458 y Buenos Aires, T04-448 6969, Mon-Fri 0830-1230, 1430-1830, US$0.65*, named after the famous 19th-century French naturalist. It houses natural history collections of international importance.

Cochabamba

Where to stay 🛏
1 Aranjuez A3
2 Chasqui Hostel A2
3 Gina's A2
4 Gran Hotel
  Cochabamba A3
5 Hostal Florida C2
6 Hostal Maya B1
7 Hostal Ñawpa House B2
8 Monserrat A2
9 Regina A2
10 Res Familiar C2
11 Res Familiar Annex B2

Restaurants 🍴
1 Café París B2
2 Casa de Campo A3
3 Casablanca A2
4 Churrasquería Tunari A3
5 Espresso Café Bar A2
6 Gopal B2
7 La Cantonata A2
8 La Estancia A3
9 Los Castores A2
10 Mocafé B2
11 Paprika A3
12 Sole Mio A3
13 Tunari A2

Bars & clubs 🍸
14 Cocafé B3
15 El Caracol A2
16 La Muela del Diablo A3
17 Na Cunna A3

BACKGROUND
Cochabamba

The name Cochabamba is derived from joining the Quechua words 'cocha' and 'pampa', which together mean swampy plain. This once swampy plain has likely been inhabited for a very long time, to judge by the wealth of pre-Columbian artefacts unearthed in 2008 at Cundisa, just one block from the main plaza. The Spanish city was founded in 1574 by Sebastián Barba de Padilla and named Villa de Oropeza in honour of the Count and Countess of Oropeza, parents of the Viceroy Francisco de Toledo, who chartered and promoted the settlement of the place. During the heyday of Potosí's silver boom, the Cochabamba Valley developed into the primary source of food for the population of that agriculturally unproductive area. Cochabamba came to be known as the 'breadbasket of Bolivia' because of its high volume of maize and wheat production. Today, the valley is still an important agricultural centre, producing not only abundant cereal crops but also orchard and citrus fruits, as well as accounting for the bulk of the country's dairy products. This high level of economic activity has seen Cochabamba grow to become Bolivia's fourth largest city, wilth a population of 650,038.

East of the old town
East of the centre is **Cerro de San Pedro**, at the top of which stands an enormous statue of **Cristo de la Concordia**. A modern **cable car** ⓘ *Tue-Sat 1000-1800, Sun 0900- 1900, US$1.50 return*, will whizz you to the top from the east end of Heroínas. Steps up to the statue are not safe, but there is a road for taxis, US$1.50. The 40.4-m, 2200-ton statue, finished in 1994, is claimed to be the biggest depiction of Christ in the world. It gives a 360º view over the city and its bowl-like setting. North of Cerro de San Pedro is the **Jardín Botánico Martín Cárdenas** ⓘ *Av Gral Galindo y R Rivera, daily 1030-1800,* with pleasant avenues of palms and jacarandas.

South of the old town
To the south of the old town lie the bus and train stations and one of the best markets in Bolivia. The huge and fascinating **La Cancha market** ⓘ *between Aguirre, Punata, República and Pulacayo*, is open all week but best on Wednesday and Saturday when it is packed with campesinos and trading spills over into surrounding streets. It has four main sections and various offshoots, with a vast array of foodstuffs and local goods. Souvenirs can be found mainly in the San Antonio section, Avenida Esteban Arze y Punata, but you can find things of interest everywhere inside.

Tourist information

Centro de Información Turística Virtual (CITV)
Plaza Colón 448, T04-466 2277, www. cochabamba.gob.bo/Turismo/index, Mon-Fri 0800-1200, 1430-1830.
This is the municipal office and the best option. Every Sun a free *Bus Turístico* leaves here at 1000 and 1500 for a 2¼-hr city tour. Other offices at the bus station (Mon-Fri 0730-1130, 1730-2230) and Jorge Wilstermann airport (Mon-Fri 0730-1130, 1700-2100). There is a kiosk behind the cathedral (Pasaje Catedral, Esteban Arze y Sucre, Mon-Fri 0900-1200, 1430-1830) but it's not always open, and another at the Cristo de la Concordia.

Tourist police
Plaza 14 de Septiembre, north side, T04-450 3880.

Where to stay

However attractive their prices, places to stay south of Av Aroma and near the bus station are unsafe at all times.

$$$ Aranjuez
Av Buenos Aires E-0563, T428 0076, www.aranjuezhotel.com.
The most beautiful of the luxury hotels with a nice garden and lots of style, 4-star, small, good restaurant, jazz in the bar Fri and Sat night, small swimming pool open to public (US$1). Recommended.

$$$ Gran Hotel Cochabamba
Plaza de la Recoleta E-0415, T448 9520, www.granhotelcochabamba.com.

One of the best hotels in Cochabamba, pool, tennis courts, business centre, airport transfers, parking.

$$ Ginas
México 346 entre España y 25 de Mayo, T422 2925, www.ginashostal.web.bo.
Has a variery of rooms for 1-5 persons, includes breakfast, safe box in rooms, convenient location in the heart of the city, monthly rates available.

$$ Monserrat
España 0342, T04-452 1011, http://hotelmonserrat.com.
Older-style hotel near many bars and restaurants, helpful, good service, convenient, cafetería, buffet breakfast.

$$ Regina
Reza 0359, T425 4629, www.hotelreginabolivia.com/regina.
Spacious, efficient, with breakfast, restaurant.

$$-$ Running Chasqui Hostel
España 449 casi México, T04-425 0559, www.runningchaski.com.bo.
Good new hostel in the nightlife zone, private rooms with bath, and dorms for girls only and mixed, US$11-13 pp, each dorm has bathroom, lockers with electric sockets, lots of information and full hostel services.

$ Hostal Florida
25 de Mayo S-0583, T425 7911.
Cheaper with shared bath, hot water, noisy, popular, safe deposit box, breakfast.

$ Hostal Maya
Colombia 710 y Suipacha, T425 9701.
Includes breakfast, private bath, hot water, central.

$ Hostal Ñawpa House
España 250, T452 7723.
Simple rooms with electric shower, large courtyard, laundry facilities, book exchange.

$ Residencial Familiar
Sucre E-0554, T422 7988.
Secure, cheaper without bath, electric showers, sunny courtyard. Its annex at 25 de Mayo N-0234 (entre Colombia y Ecuador), T422 7986, has a big courtyard, shared bath, hot water, comfortable.

Camping
13 km west of the centre in Callajchullpa district, Av Costanera y Yanparticuy, T04-431 9533, or 7140 3565, campingcochabamba@gmail.com.
US$10 pp, shared toilet/bath facilities, breakfast extra, organic produce, barbecue and campfire facilities, internet and mobile reception, laundry extra, games. Taxi service, 40 mins from airport, 35 mins bus terminal, 20 mins to supermarket; 10-min walk to public transport, 15-min walk to organic farm. New in 2015.

Restaurants
North of the Río Rocha on the Pasaje Boulevard de la Recoleta and Av Pando is a group of restaurants and bars.

$$$-$$ Casa de Campo
Pasaje Boulevard de la Recoleta 618, T04-424 3937.
Large menu of mostly local dishes, all-in-one price, very popular, open from 1200 daily, also has peña, book at weekend evenings.

$$$-$$ Churrasquería Tunari
Pasaje Boulevard de la Recoleta, T04-448 8153.

The most delicious meat you can find in Cochabamba.

$$$-$$ La Estancia
Pasaje Boulevard de la Recoleta 786, T04-424 9262.
Best steak in town, salads and international food in this traditional restaurant.

$$$-$$ Tunari 2
Av Ballivián 676 y La Paz, T04-452 8588.
Family-run restaurant specializing in local meat dishes (half-portions available), good filling food, also sandwiches.

$$ La Cantonata
España y Mayor Rocha, T04-425 9222.
Pleasant Italian restaurant with good food and service, no smoking. Recommended.

$$ Sole Mio
Av América 826 y Pando, T04-428 3379.
A smart Neapolitan pizza restaurant, delicious, also good for desserts. Attentive service.

$$-$ Paprika
Chuquisaca 688 y Antezana, www. paprika.com.bo. Opens in the evening.
Nice atmosphere, international food, good cocktails and desserts.

$ Gopal
España 250, in same precinct as Ñawpa House. Open 1130-1400, closed Sun.
Bolivian Hare-Krishna, vegetarian buffet lunch. In the same garden is Mocafé, open daily 0800-2400 (Sun 0900-2100) for juices, coffee, teas, breakfasts and light meals, cocktails and wines.

Cafés
There are several cafés at the junction of the Pasaje Catedral and Esteban Arze.

Café París
Bolívar, corner of Plaza 14 de Septiembre.
Serves good coffee and crêpes,
traditional atmosphere.

Casablanca
25 de Mayo entre Venezuela y Ecuador.
Attractive, buzzing, good food, mostly
pastas, pizzas and Mexican, and a wide
selection of coffee, popular for wine and
cocktails in the evening, indoor games
and music.

Espresso Café Bar
Av Ballivián 537 just off Plaza Colón.
Open 0830-2230.
Coffees, including Bolivian and specials,
juices, beers and other drinks, cakes and
snacks. Another branch on the Pasaje
Catedral y Arze.

Los Castores
Ballivián 790 y Oruro. Open 0800-1415.
Popular, good for *salteñas*. 2 other
branches.

Bars and clubs

The main nightlife district is on España,
Ecuador, Mayor Rocha and Av Ballivian
(El Prado) with lots of bars and a few
restaurants.

Wander around and see what takes your
fancy, eg **La Rambla** (*España y Mayor
Rocha*), a small, cheerful place for a drink;
Ruta 105 (*Mayor Rocha 311*), cocktails
and soft drinks, light bites, DJ.

Cocafé Arte
Ecuador y Antezana 279.
Friendly, family atmosphere, good place
for foreigners to meet. Street musicians
always pass by to show off their skills.

El Caracol
Mayor Rocha entre Baptista y España.
High ceilings, Mediterranean-themed

dishes, desserts, lots of drinks
and coffees.

La Muela del Diablo
*Potosí 1392 y Portales, next to Palacio
Portales.*
Bolivian rock music, theatre groups,
German beer.

Na Cúnna
Av Salamanca 577, T04-423 0729.
Thu-Sat from 1900.
Irish pub and restaurant, live music.
They also serve Guinness.

Entertainment

Art galleries and cultural centre
There are several art galleries in the
centre, such as **Salón Municipal de
Verano** (*Plaza 14 de Septiembre*); **Galería
Walter Terrazas** (*Av Heroínas y España,
T04-422 7561*).
Casa de la Cultura, *Av Heroínas 399
y 25 de Mayo, T04-425 2090, https://
casadelaculturacochabamba.wordpress.
com*. Many regular cultural activities.

Theatre and cinema
For cinema, see www.cinecenter.
com.bo.
mARTadero, *Av 27 de Agosto entre
Ollantay y Ladislao Cabrera, T04-458 8778,
www.martadero.org*. Cultural and artistic
centre for local and international artists,
exhibitions, and events, in a refurbished
slaughterhouse. Daily 1500-1800.
Micros/trufis P, Q, and 212 to Plaza de
los Arrieros.
Teatro Achá, *España 280 entre Heroínas
y Bolívar, T04-425 8054*. The city's
oldest cultural centre, with monthly
presentations.
Teatro Hecho a Mano, *Av Uyuni 635
entre Puente Recoleta y Potosí, T04-448*

5528, Hecho-a-Mano on Facebook.
Theatre school.

Festivals

Feb Carnaval is celebrated 15 days
before **Lent**. Rival groups (*comparsas*)
compete in music, dancing, and fancy
dress, culminating in El Corso on the last
Sat of the Carnaval. **Mascaritas** balls also
take place in the carnival season, when
the young women wear long hooded
satin masks.
14 Sep Día de Cochabamba.

Shopping

Camping gear, maps, etc
IGM, *16 de Julio S-237, T04-425 5503, Mon-
Thu 0800-1200, 1430-1800, Fri 0800-1200*.
Sells topographic maps of Cochabamba
department.
The Spitting Llama, *España N-615,
T04-466 2084, www.thespittingllama.com*.
Travel shop.

Handicrafts
Artesanos Andinos, *Pasaje Catedral,
T04-450 8367*. An artisans' association
selling textiles.
Fotrama, *Bolívar 0349, entre San Martín
y 25 de Mayo, www.fotrama.com*. High-
quality alpaca clothing.

What to do

Adventure sports and tours
Cochabamba is growing in popularity for
parapenting, with several outfits offering
tamdem jumps and courses more
cheaply than other places, starting at
US\$30-35 and US\$200-250 respectively.
AndesXtremo, *La Paz 138 entre Ayacucho
y Junín, T04-452 3392, www.andesxtremo.
com*. Adventure sports company offering
parapenting, climbing, rafting and

trekking, good value, professional staff.
Recommended.
Bolivia Cultura, *Ecuador 342 entre 25
de Mayo y España, T04-452 7272, www.
boliviacultura.com*. Tours to Torotoro.
They run year-round tours for 3 and
4 days to all the major sites and can
arrange longer trips. Tours also to other
local destinations.
Creative Tours, *Av Pedro Sarmieto 1820,
T04-441 7330, www.creativetours.com.bo*.
Offer Uyuni Expeditions, tours based at
the hotels of the Ruta Tayka (see page
153), river cruises on the *Reina de Enín*,
Hotel El Puente in Parque Nacional
Carrasco and **Berghotel Carolina** (see
page 230). Also tours to neighbouring
countries.
D'Orbigny Travel, *Pasaje de la Promotora
344 entre España y Heroínas, T04-451 1367*.
Run by an enthusiastic Bolivian couple,
excursions in Cochabamba department
and throughout Bolivia. Recommended.
El Mundo Verde Travel, *no storefront,
T6534 4272, www.elmundoverdetravel.
com*. Great for local information,
regional experts offer tours to Torotoro,
Pico Tunari, Inkallajta and Chimboata
village, and Chapare and throughout
Bolivia; day trips and adventure tours.
Dutch/Bolivian-run, very enthusiastic
and informative. Also 4WD tours to
Samaipata. English, Dutch and Spanish
spoken. Warmly recommended.
Salar Amazon Tours, *Condominio
Los Faros 4 en Pasaje la Sevillana (Zona
Templo Mormón), T04-458 0085, www.
salaramazon.com*. Offer Salar and jungle
tours and *Reina de Enín* cruises.

Language classes
There are many qualified language
teachers in the city.
Beyond Bolivia, *www.
beyondsouthamerica.com*. Dutch

organization which offers Spanish/Portuguese language classes, homestays and recommended volunteer programmes and internships.

Bolivia Sostenible, *Julio Arauco Prado 230, Zona Las Cuadras, T04-423 3786, www.boliviasostenible.org.* Offers homestays and paid placements for volunteers.

Centro de Idiomas Kori Simi, *Lanza 727, entre La Paz y Chuquisaca, T04-425 7248, www.korisimi.com.* Spanish and Quechua school run by staff from Switzerland, Germany and Bolivia, also offers activity programme, homestays and volunteer placements.

Runawasi, *Maurice Lefebvre 0470, Villa Juan XXIII, Av Blanco Galindo Km 4.5, T04-424 8923, www.runawasi.org.* Spanish, Quechua and Aymara, also has accommodation.

Volunteer Bolivia, *Ecuador E-0342, T04-452 6028, www.volunteerbolivia.*org. Bolivian/US-run organization which offers language classes, homestays and a recommended volunteer programme.

Transport

Air
Jorge Wilstermann airport, T04-412 0400; modern, with places to eat, *casas de cambio* and ATMs. Airport bus is Micro B from Heroínas y Ayacucho, US$0.40; taxis from airport to centre US$4. Arrive 2 hrs ahead for international flights. Cochabamba is an air transport hub with several daily flights to/from **La Paz** (35 mins) and **Santa Cruz** (40 mins) with **Amazonas**, Av Libertador Bolívar 1509, Edif El Solar, PB, T04-479 4200, **Boliviana de Aviación**, Jordán 202 y Nataniel Aguirre, T04-414 0873 or 901-105010 and **TAM** Militar, Buenos Aires entre Av

Santa Cruz y América, T04-441 1545). **Ecojet**, Plazuela Constitución 0879 entre 16 de Julio y Chuquisaca, T04-412 3700, to Sucre, Tarija, Trinidad and other northern cities. **TAM** has flights to **Trinidad**, with connections to other northern cities.

Bus
Micros and *colectivos*, US$0.25; *trufis*, US$0.30. Anything marked 'San Antonio' goes to the market. *Trufis* C and 10 go from bus terminal to the city centre.

Regional Local buses leave from Av Barrientos y Magdalena, south of La Cancha, for **Tarata**, US$0.75. From Av Barrientos y Av 6 de Agosto, for **Cliza**, US$0.75. From Av 6 de Agosto y Av República to **Punata**, US$0.75, and **Totora**, US$2.50-4.50 (minibus). Av Oquendo y Av República (be careful in this area), to **Villa Tunari**, US$4.50, 4-5 hrs, from 0400 to 2000; **Puerto Villarroel**, US$7.75, 6 hrs (from 0800 when full, daily).

Long distance The main bus terminal is on Av Aroma y Ayacucho, 600-700 m south of Plaza 14 de Septiembre (T04-422 0550). To **Santa Cruz**, almost hourly 0600-2130, 12 hrs, US$9-12.75; **Trans Copacabana** *semi-cama*, 2130; **Bolívar** *bus-cama*, US$18.55; all via the paved lowland road through Villa Tunari. See page 232. To **Mairana**, **Samaipata** and **Santa Cruz**, along the old mountain road via Epizana and Comarapa, a beautiful ride, **Trans Carrasco**, 6 de Agosto y República, T04-456 9348, daily at 0730 to Santa Cruz (14 hrs), 1200 to Mairana (11 hrs), US$8. To/from **La Paz** almost hourly 0530-2300, 7 hrs, US$7.35 (**Trans Copacabana** *semi-cama*, 2230, US$10.35, **Bolívar** *bus-cama*, 2230, 2300, US$15). To **Oruro**, 0600-1730 (Sun last bus at 2100), 4 hrs, US$4.50-5.65. To **Potosí**, departures at 2000 (US$9), 2100 (*semi-cama*, US$13) with **Bolívar** and **Trans Copacabana**, 10 hrs. Daily to **Sucre**, 8 hrs, several companies (**Bolívar** and **Trans Copacabana** at 1930, 2000 US$9.65, 2030 *semi-cama*, US$12.50). To **Sucre** by day; go to Aiquile by bus (several from Av 6 de Agosto entre

Av República y Av Barrientos, none before 1200) or **ferrobus** (see page 229), then a bus at 0200-0300 passing en route to Sucre, or Fri and Sun, 2000.

Taxi
About US$1 from anywhere to the plaza, more expensive to cross the river; double after dark.

Around Cochabamba
agricultural region with friendly market towns and a picturesque rail journey

Parque Nacional Tunari *Colour map 2, B4.*
SERNAP office, Av Atahuallpa 2367, T04-445 2534, www.sernap.gob.bo, see also www. biobol.org.

This 300,000-ha national park is just outside the city. Despite its proximity, it remains a beautiful unspoilt natural area and a good place for acclimatization to altitude. There are llamas and alpacas above 4000 m and even the occasional condor. The highest point in the park, Cerro Tunari (5035 m), offers magnificent views, even as far as Illimani. It can be climbed in a day trip; going with a local operator is recommended. **Note** Armed attacks of visitors have taken place along the marked trail from the park entrance in the north of the city. Safer alternatives, although not signposted, are along the south flank of the mountain, either reached from above **Hacienda Pairumani** (see below) or from **Berghotel Carolina**, which arranges tours with pack animals (see page 230).

Quillacollo *Colour map 2, B3.*
Quillacollo, 13 km west of the city, has a produce market on Sundays and a famous festival (see page 230). Take any *micro* or *trufi* marked "Quillacollo" along Avenida Heroínas. Some 8 km beyond town is the turn-off to the beautiful **Hacienda Pairumani** ⓘ *Sat 0830-1130, T04-426 0082 to check if it is open at other times, http://portal.fundacionpatino.org*, centre of the Patiño agricultural foundation. Also known as **Villa Albina**, it was built in 1925-1932, furnished from Europe and inhabited by Patiño's wife, Albina. Pairumani can be reached from Avenida Aroma in Cochabamba or by *trufi* 211 from Plaza Bolívar in Quillacollo.

Inka-Rakay
Some 33 km west of Cochabamba are Inka-Rakay ruins, with fine views of the Cochabamba valley and the mountains around the ruins. A day trip to the ruins can end at the plaza in nearby **Sipe Sipe** or one of its local restaurants with a bowl of *guarapo* (wine-based drink) and a plate of *charque* (sun-dried beef), served with potatoes, eggs and corn; best at weekends. Or take *trufi* "Sipe Sipe" from

Plaza Bolívar in Quillacollo and get off at the church on the main square, then ask for the way up to the ruins.

Valle Alto

The area southeast of Cochabamba, known as Valle Alto, has some interesting little towns, all easily reached from the city. The main road passes the artificial La Angostura lake, beside which fish restaurants serve lunch at weekends.

★**Tarata** Thirty-three kilometres southeast of Cochabamba, this colonial town has a traditional arcaded plaza on which stand the church of San Pedro (daily 0800-1300), with a historic organ, and the Casa Consistorial (now a museum). In the plaza, the **clock tower** ⓘ *Mon-Fri 0800-1200, 1330-1700, Sat-Sun 0800-1200*, houses a German timepiece with chimes. The **Franciscan Convent of San José** ⓘ *Mon-Sat 0930-1130, 1430-1800, US$0.30, guided visits from Casa de Cultura y Turismo, main square, T04-457 8727*, the first Franciscan convent in Bolivia, overlooks the town. Inside are the remains of the martyr, San Severino, patron saint of the town, more commonly known as the 'Saint of Rain'; the festival, on the last Sunday of November, attracts thousands of people. A large procession takes place on 3 May, day of La Santa Cruz, with fireworks and brass band. Market days are Thursday and Sunday. For fine alpaca products, visit **Doña Prima Fernández Prado** ⓘ *Arce E-0115, opposite the convent*, who sells sweaters, bags and textiles from two rooms off a beautiful colonial patio.

> **Tip...**
> Try the local sausages, they are nationally famous.

Independence hero Esteban Arze and three presidents of Bolivia were born in Tarata, including the infamous Mariano Melgarejo (1820-1871, president from 1864 till his death). His head is preserved in San Pedro church, but is so grizzly a relic that it is not on public display (Google it to see what it looks like). Several buildings have associations with Melgarejo, including his house, the Palacio de Gobierno, whose balcony overlooks the Plaza, and the Puente de Melgarejo. On the new road into town, near the military barracks, is a huge equestrian statue of Melgarejo. The old road, which branches off the new, is a much more interesting way to reach the centre. Much new building is going on, including a new market. Plaza 27 de Mayo has an outdoor market and a famous tree, known as the tree of youth or the lovers' tree.

★**Scenic rail line** Beyond Tarata are Cliza, Mizque and Aiquile, along a scenic rail line. A *ferrobús*, a bus running on train tracks, has a service on this route; in theory Tuesday, Thursday, Saturday 0800, returning from Aiquile at 0800 on Wednesday, Friday and Sunday (station at Tarata 0442, by La Cancha, T04-455 8245/6208, www.fca.com.bo).

Cliza and around Six kilometres southeast from Tarata, Cliza has a large, colourful Sunday market. From Calle Francisco del Rivero there are trucks to **Toco**, to see its large church and Byzantine cupola, a favourite subject of many artists.

About 1 km from Cliza is **Huayculi** (take a taxi or walk), known for its ceramics, and you can watch the artisans at work.

Punata and around Forty-eight kilometres southeast of Cochabamba, just off the lowland road to Santa Cruz, Punata is an important agricultural centre, famous for its festival of the Señor de los Milagros on 24 September, as well as its many baroque/mestizo works of art in the church. Behind the church, villagers line up their new vehicles for the priest to bless. The town also has a reputation for the production of the region's *chicha*. It also has a very lively and colourful market on Tuesday.

Tip...
Try the local speciality, *garapiña*, a mixture of *chicha* and ice cream.

Change bus at Punata for **Villa Rivera**, a major centre for preparing wool, dyeing and weaving. The village is famous for its woven wall hangings. At **Arani**, 7 km east of Punata, there is a good *artesanía* market on Thursday. The town's speciality is bread. About 5 km beyond is **Collpa Ciaca**, where there's another attractive church and hills to walk in.

Listings Around Cochabamba

Where to stay

Parque Nacional Tunari

$$$-$$ Berghotel Carolina
Pairumani, at the foot of the Cerro Tunari, T7213 0003, www.berghotelcarolina.com.
Arranges private transport, 45 mins from Cochabamba, 25 mins from Plaza Bolívar in Quillacollo. Mountain lodge with 5 comfortable rooms with private bath and 2 with shared bath, restaurant, bar, living room with fireplace, sauna and large terrace. Organizes guided 2-day walking tours with tent to the Laguna Cajón (4100 m), Cerro Tunari and other peaks in Parque Tunari. Walking trails start right from the lodge.

Quillacollo

$$ El Poncho Eco Center
Marquina, T04-439 2283, T7648 6666, www.elponcho.org.
Ecological cabins, camping, restaurant, pool and various outdoor activities.

Festivals

Quillacollo
14-15 Aug Fiesta de la Virgen de Urkupiña (www.urcupina.com), in Quillacollo. There's plenty of transport from Cochabamba, hotels are all full. Be there before 0900 to be sure of a seat, as you are not allowed to stand in the street. The 1st day is the most colourful with all the groups in costumes and masks, parading and dancing in the streets till late at night. Many groups have left by the 2nd day and dancing stops earlier. The 3rd day is dedicated to the pilgrimage.

caves, canyons, waterfalls, wildlife and stunning scenery

★ Parque Nacional Torotoro

Entry US$12.50 for foreigners, payable at the Dirección de Turismo, Calle Cochabamba, Main Plaza, T7227 0968, T04-413 5736, open 0700-1200, 1400-1700, all visitors must register here. SERNAP office on Calle del Olvido, 3 blocks southwest of the plaza, next to Rosas T'ika (see Shopping, below), director Edwin Villagómez Villarroel, T6822 6393 (or in Cochabamba, Av Atahuallpa 2367, T04-445 6633, www.sernap.gob.bo).

In the department of Potosí, but best reached from Cochabamba (136 km), is **Torotoro**, a small village, set amid dramatic rocky landscape in the centre of the Parque Nacional Torotoro, covering an area of 21,693 ha. The road to Torotoro is best done in daylight, which may mean taking a tour since buses run mostly at night. After Cliza (see above), the next community of any size is Anzaldo. Thereafter the landscape changes frequently with beautiful views of mountains in all shapes and colours, ravines, the broad valley of the Río Caine and several small villages. Long sections of the road are cobbled in good condition, others are unmade. In the dry season, it presents no difficulties, which is not the case in the wet, when the cobbles become slippery and river crossings may be impassable. Torotoro can also be reached along a dusty road from Sucre.

Attractions include caves, canyons, waterfalls, ruins, rock paintings, fossils and thousands of incredible fossilized dinosaur tracks, some of which can be seen by the Río Torotoro just outside the village. It's a geologist's paradise, but for non-specialists it is an intriguing place to spend a few days. Near the community of **Wayra K'asa**, about 8 km northwest of Torotoro, **Umajalanta cave**, the largest in Bolivia, has many stalactites, stalagmites and a lake with endemic blind fish; 7 km have been explored and are open to caving. Head torch and helmet are required and for hire at the entrance (US$1); it's not recommended for claustrophobics. Beyond the cave, 21 km from Torotoro village, is **Ciudad de Itas**, in the community of Ovejerías, a circular walk on top of and within an unusual rock formation with caves (some resemble gothic cathedrals) and rock paintings. Most of it is an easy walk, despite being at about 4000 m, but there is one tricky ascent. The views of the surrounding ridges and canyons are lovely and, with luck, you'll see condors. In the **Cañón de Torotoro**, 4 km from the village, are the fantastic **El Vergel** waterfalls. On the way there are huge dinosaur prints. The walk leads to an observation lookout with amazing views; if you go early enough you may see a number of endemic birds, including the endangered red-fronted macaw. A set of hundreds of steps descends to the riverbed and the foot of the falls, where you can bathe in natural pools. Depending on the time of year the creeks and falls on the way to the lookout may not have water, but the main falls run all year round and are surrounded by rich vegetation. You return via the staircase or scramble along the riverbed back to Torotoro. Fossils from the sea bed can be seen at **Siete Vueltas**, 5 km from the village. Here you can clearly appreciate how the ocean floor has been lifted up in the formation of the Andes, with stratification and plate structures easy to identify.

The **Cementerio de Tortugas** (turtle cemetery) is 3.5 km southeast of the town, with fossilized remains of sea turtles (*Cheloniidae* family).

Tours or day trips must be organized by the **Asociación de Guías (Guiaventura)** ① *Main Plaza across from the Oficina de Turismo, T7435 9152, office closed 1130-1330.* You can reserve a guide in advance, otherwise the person at the desk will phone for one; if none is available you will have to wait. Guides charge US$12.50 per route for one to six people (a little more to Itas). Every visitor gets a map. The nearer sites can be reached on foot (El Vergel, Siete Vueltas, Cementerio de Tortugas), but transport is available at US$6.25, except to Umajalanta, US$18.50 and US$35 to the cave and Itas. Four-wheel drive tours are also offered by **El Mundo Verde Travel** (www.elmundoverdetravel.com), which can also provide transport from Sucre, and other Cochabamba agencies (see page 226).

Cochabamba to Santa Cruz: the lowland road

Villa Tunari The lowland road from Cochabamba through Villa Tunari to Santa Cruz is fully paved but prone to landslides after heavy rain. Villa Tunari is a relaxing place and holds an annual Fish Fair the first weekend of August, with music, dancing and food. The Facebook page, villatunarituristica, has a lot of information. There are two options for wildlife visiting nearby: **La Hormiga** ① *www.facebook.com/lahormiga.villatunari, contact through El Mundo Verde, see page 226, What to do, Cochabamba,* where Rolanddo Mamani leads jungle walks, with good chance of seeing monkeys, birds, insects and snakes, about which he educates local farmers.

Parque Ecoturístico Machía Just outside Villa Tunari, Parque Ecoturístico Machía is managed by **Inti Wara Yassi** ① *T04-413 6572, www.intiwarayassi.org, entrance of US$0.90 payable to the municipality, donations welcome, open Tue-Sun 0900-1600 (not open when raining).* This 36-ha park includes a well-signposted 3-km interpretive trail and other trails through semi-tropical forest. The park is run by an animal rescue organization that operates two other parks, one about halfway between Santa Cruz and Trinidad and another near Rurrenabaque. Contact them for volunteer opportunities. The Río Espíritu Santa is a popular place for white-water rafting. One-day trips are organized by **Bolivia Rafting** ① *Av Integración entre Potosí y La Paz, Villa Tunari, T7076 7937, boliviarafting on Facebook.* US$30 for two people, cheaper for more people.

Puerto Villarroel At Ivirgazama, east of Villa Tunari, the road passes the turn-off to Puerto Villarroel, 27 km further north, from where cargo boats ply irregularly to Trinidad (see page 298) in about four to 10 days. You can get information from the Capitanía del Puerto noticeboard, or ask at the docks. There are only a few basic places to sleep in Villarroel and very few stores.

★**Parque Nacional Carrasco** ① *information from SERNAP, Av Atahuallpa 2367, T04-445 6633, www.sernap.gob.bo.* Southeast of Villa Tunari, this park covers 622,600 ha between 300 and 4500 m. It has 11 ecological life zones, superb birdwatching and many rivers, waterfalls, canyons and pools. Situated at the eastern foothills of the Cordillera Real, the terrain moves from mountainous in the west to flat in the east. The scenery, while not as lush as that of the Amazonian parks, is stunning nonetheless. Rainfall is heavy – rare for the otherwise dry Cochabamba department – especially in the north. Sitting at a higher altitude than most of the surrounding region, Carrasco is cool, making it a refreshing respite for the trekker.

Access is from Villa Tunari, Totora and Monte Punku – Sehuencas. From the park entrance closest to Villa Tunari, a cable car takes you across the river for a 2½-hour walking circuit to the **Cavernas de Repechón** (oilbird caves). This wildlife sanctuary consists of several caves inhabited by the *guácharo*, or oilbird. These are nocturnal, fruit-eating birds that venture out of their cave only at night, emitting a clicking sound that they use for navigation.

Guides may be hired from the **Kawsay Wasi community** ⓘ *T7939 0894, www. tusoco.com*. Julián (T7480 9714) has been recommended.

Cochabamba to Santa Cruz: the highland road

The 500-km highland road from Cochabamba to Santa Cruz is very scenic. Some sections are unpaved and the newer lowland route is preferred by most transport. Between Monte Punku (Km 119) and Epizana is the turn-off to Pocona and Inkallajta. To reach the ruins follow the road for 13 km as far as the village of Collpa, then take the left fork for a further 10 km.

★**Inkallajta** The Inca ruins of Inkallajta (1463-1472, rebuilt 1525), on a flat spur of land at the mouth of a steep valley, are extensive and the main building of the fortress is said to have been the largest roofed Inca building. There's also an area called **Inkarrakana**, which was an astronomical observatory. A few decades before the Spanish conquest, the Inca Empire had expanded to cover most of the Cochabamba Valley, in an attempt to benefit from its enormous agricultural potential. To this end, the Incas built an extensive system of roads, market centres and forts. The Inca Tupac Yupanqui ordered the construction of Inkallajta to protect the advancing Imperial Army from the attacks of the fearsome local Chirihuano tribes, but after the fort was attacked it was badly damaged and abandoned. Such was the strategic importance of the site that it was rebuilt in 1525. It was abandoned again in the aftermath of the internal strife that marked the beginning of the end of the Inca Empire. There are several good camping sites near the river and some basic facilities and services.

Aiquile The mountain road continues to **Epizana**, junction for the road to Sucre (being paved in 2015) via the beautiful colonial village of **Totora** (14 km) and the more modern town of Aiquile (population 30,900), 149 km from Sucre and 217 km from Cochabamba. Aiquile is famous for its fine hand-made *charangos* and an annual **Feria del Charango** is held at the end of October or in early November. The **Museo del Charango**, two blocks east of the post office, in the shape of the musical instrument, has archaeological as well as musical items. It is possible to visit some of the *charango* workshops. The town's other main festival

ON THE ROAD

La hoja sagrada or the Devil's leaf?

Chapare and the Yungas are Bolivia's most important coca-growing regions. The former has often been the scene of tension between coca producers and Bolivian authorities mandated by foreign interests to curb the trade. Both sides in the conflict profess moral superiority but, on closer examination, the respective black and white hats turn out to have many shades of grey.

Coca Coca has played an important role in Andean society since time immemorial. As casual as a coffee-break and as sacred as Communion, *pijcheo* or *acullicu*, as coca chewing is known, is important throughout Bolivia.

Coca leaves can be bought legally anywhere in the country and many men and women use them regularly, from *campesinos* in the highlands to non-indigenous urban middle classes.

People traditionally carried their dried coca leaves in a special woven pouch called a *chuspa*, but this has largely been replaced by ubiquitous green plastic bags. The central vein of each leaf is patiently removed and the remainder chewed into a quid held in a conspicuously bulging cheek. To this is added a bit of *cal* (mineral lime) or *lejía* (vegetable ash), the alkalinity of which facilitates the absorption of active ingredients. They slightly numb the mouth and the senses, help stave off hunger and exhaustion, and mitigate the effects of high altitude.

As well as being a prerequisite for manual labourers, such as miners, coca is also taken in a social context. The native population used to deny this because, in the eyes of the bosses and clergy, an increase in productivity was the only reason for tolerating consumption of 'the Devil's leaf'. The only places where coca is not chewed is in church and in the marital bed. The spent leaves are spat out at the bedside as well as all over the country's streets and sidewalks.

La hoja sagrada, 'the sacred leaf' as coca is sometimes called, is also used in various rituals, such as offerings to *Pachamama*, or Mother Earth, and to *El Tío*, lord of the mines and underworld. Aymara priests called *yatiris* use coca leaves to predict one's fortune much as a tarot- or palm-reader does.

Coca leaves contain no more than 2% cocaine, and they also contain various proteins, minerals and vitamins to which numerous medicinal qualities have been ascribed. Their effects are both physiological and psychological. You can, for example, see people pasting a leaf or two on their foreheads with a bit of saliva, to help get them over a headache or through a particularly rough bus ride. Mate de coca, an infusion of the leaves, is recommended to visitors as a way of diminishing the symptoms of mild altitude sickness.

Cocaine

The world's involvement with coca dates to 1862 when German chemists isolated an alkaloid from the leaves, which they labelled *cocain*. It was tried, among other things, as a cure for opium addiction and alcoholism. The young Dr Sigmund Freud, reading of its effect on tired soldiers, took some himself and pronounced it a "magical substance" that was "wonderfully stimulating". Over the years it was used in various medicines and as an ingredient in early formulas of the world's most famous soft drink. Maligned as it is today, cocaine retains important medical uses as a local anaesthetic and to stop some types of bleeding that cannot be controlled in any other way.

Yet cocaine also accounts for a great deal of human misery. There is a huge demand for this addictive drug from millions of North Americans and Europeans who pay between US$65-180 a gram for it. Supplying this demand moves billions of dollars in one of the world's largest illegal industries, which has proven adept at corrupting institutions and politicians everywhere. Not much of this immense illicit wealth filters down to the *campesinos* of Chapare, where black-market coca leaves sell for about US$4 a kilo. *Pisadores* are paid about US$10 a night to crush the leaves mixed with various toxic solvents, often barefoot, in a plastic-lined hole in the ground. From this mash is extracted *pasta básica de coca*, a coca paste, which is then further refined in clandestine labs into cocaine.

International attempts to curb the cocaine trade have to date focused on destruction of coca plantations and interception of drug shipments, with limited efforts to reduce demand in consuming countries. The burning of coca fields in Chapare by the Bolivian military under the guidance of the US Drug Enforcement Agency was a perennial source of violent conflict, until it came to an abrupt halt in 2006 following the election of President Evo Morales, himself a leader of the *cocaleros*. His government has since fostered traditional and medicinal uses of coca leaf while following a policy of 'zero cocaine, zero trafficking'.

The United Nations Office on Drugs and Crime **World Drug Report** (www. unodc.org) indicates that Bolivian coca production fell from a high point of 28,900 ha in 2007 to 25,300 in 2012. This is still significantly more than the 14,700 ha claimed as necessary for the production of coca for legitimate national use, an area the government wants to reduce to 12,000 ha. Having expelled the US Drug Enforcement Administration in 2009 after a disagreement over policy, Bolivia is attempting to cut the acreage under coca through dialogue and eradication.

While the US and European countries have been the major markets for cocaine, patterns of use have shifted in recent years. Increased consumption of various forms of crack cocaine and, to a lesser extent, powder in Brazil and other South American countries has led to changes in trafficking routes and associated criminal activities, with more of those activities, such as processing, taking place in Bolivia.

Whether coca is sacred or diabolical depends on the context in which it is used. Having removed coca from its ancestral context, we are – some 150 years later – still fumbling to stuff the genie back into its bottle.

is on 2 February in honour of **La Virgen de la Candelaria** and involves seven days of bull-running through the streets. There's also a busy Sunday market, which brings many *campesinos* from neighbouring villages.

Past Epizana the road from Cochabamba goes on, unpaved, to **Pojo**, Comarapa and Samaipata (see page 250).

Listings Around Cochabamba

Where to stay

Parque Nacional Torotoro
An upmarket community-run hotel was officially opened in Wayra K'asa, near the cave, in mid-2015. The following are in the village of Torotoro:

$$ Hostal Asteria
Guadalupe y El Olvido, T04-440 3368.
Colonial-style hotel, restaurant serving all meals, living room with books and DVDs, beautiful patio, parking.

$$ Villa Etelvina
C Lauro Hidalgo, 15-min walk from plaza, T7073 7807, www.villaetelvina.com.
Bungalow for 4 with private bath, cheaper in rooms with shared bath, includes breakfast, beautiful garden, parking, can arrange tours and activities.

$ El Molino
1.5 km from the village, T7647 5999, Cochabamba office T04-402 6172, www.elmolinotorotoro.com.
Beautiful Spanish-style country house surrounded by mountains and a river, comfortable rooms with private bath, nice common areas, fireplace, bar, pool table, indoor patio. All-inclusive 2- to 4-day tours from Cochabamba arranged.

$ El Vergel
Arteche y Charcas, T6817 2374, Sr Eduardo Santiváñez.

Rooms with and without bath, with breakfast and Wi-Fi. Same owner as Como en Casa bar, Montes y Charcas.

$ Hostal Las Hermanas
On main road from Cochabamba, 1 block before plaza on the left, T7221 1257.
Basic rooms, cheaper with shared bath, Doña Lily serves delicious food and is very attentive.

$ Hostal Urkupiña
Charcas y Cochabamba, near plaza, T6756 6790.
Single, double and family rooms with hot water, parking. Breakfast extra in restaurant which also serves coffee and cocktails.

Villa Tunari

$$$-$$ Victoria Resort
Km 156 on the road to Santa Cruz, 4 km before Villa Tunari on the right, T04-413 6538, www.victoria-resort.com.
Modern, cabaña style, 500 m from the main road in the middle of the forest, quiet, large pool, breakfast buffet.

$$ El Puente Jungle Hotel
Av de la Integración, 4 km from town, T04-458 0085, www.hotelelpuente.com. bo (or book in advance through Creative Tours, see page 148).
Cabins from 2 persons to family-size surrounded by tropical vegetation, with breakfast and bath, pool, zipline, stream and natural pools, nature treks.

Totora

$$-$ Casa de Huéspedes Villa Eva
on main road, Totora, T7437 1530.
Well-furnished country house with large
living room, fully equipped kitchen, and
comfortable rooms with private bath.

Restaurants

Parque Nacional Torotoro
Several small restaurants in Torotoro
village including **Pensión La Huella**;
El Comedor, at the food market 2 blocks
above the main plaza; **Doña Elena**,
opposite the market, all for good local
food; Doña Rosemary's **Encuentro
Torotoreño**, opposite Villa Etelvina,
serves meals, drinks and has a pool table.

Villa Tunari
There are several eating places in Villa
Tunari on both sides of the main road to
Santa Cruz. The more expensive ones
are on the riverside. The more popular
food stalls 1 block from the bus terminal
serve different fish dishes and have
also a cheap daily menu. Upstairs at the
market (breakfast and lunch) is a very
cheap option.

Festivals

Aiquile
2 Feb **La Virgen de la Candelaria**,
Aiquile.
Oct/Nov **Feria del Charango**, Aiquile.

Shopping

Parque Nacional Torotoro
Rosas T'ika, *Ascociación de Mujeres, Calle
del Olvido, 3 blocks southwest of Plaza
Principal, open every day.* Sells beautiful,
locally made textiles, clothing and bags,
mostly sheep's wool, some of llama wool.

Transport

Parque Nacional Torotoro
Bus Buses (Trans del Norte) and
minivans from the end of Av República
after C Vallegrande, near Av Barrientos,
daily except Thu at 1800, Thu, Sun 0600;
return to Cochabamba Mon-Sat at 0600,
except Fri at 1800; Sun at 1300 and 1500;
US$3.25, 4-5 hrs in the dry season, 7-8 hrs
in the wet season. Minibuses also run,
but no fixed schedule; T7144 2073 in
Cochabamba; ask around in Torotoro.
There is no bus service from Sucre, it
takes 14 hrs in a private vehicle.

Inkallajta
Take a *trufi* from 0500 onwards from
6 de Agosto y Manuripi (Av República)
in Cochabamba (ask for the "Parada
Pocona"). For 3 people the *trufi* will
drop you off at the entrance to the
Inca ruins (US$4 pp). Arrange with the
driver to pick you up at a specific time
to return to Cochabamba. If alone, ask
to get off after arriving in Collpa at a big
green sign, where the road to the ruins
turns off to the right. Walk along the
cobbled road for approximately 10 km
to the ruins. *Trufis* return from Pocona
to Cochabamba when full till 1600. Taxis
from Pocona charge around US$15 one
way to the ruins.

Santa Cruz &
eastern lowlands

Jesuit churches and vast national parks

Eastern Bolivia is made up of vast plains stretching to the Chaco of Paraguay and Pantanal of Brazil. They are mainly in the department of Santa Cruz, which accounts for almost 34% of Bolivia's territory. It is the most productive and progressive corner of the country and one of the richest in natural resources.

The capital of the department, Santa Cruz de la Sierra, is a booming modern city a world away from most people's image of Bolivia and therefore often ignored by travellers. That's their loss, for it stands on the threshold of one of the most fascinating parts of the country.

To the northeast are the Jesuit missions, a string of six dusty little towns, each boasting a beautiful colonial church. Only three hours from Santa Cruz are the natural wonders of Parque Nacional Amboró. Also in this directions are the trails and villages where Che Guevara made his final attempt to bring revolution to Bolivia.

In the far north of the department is the remote Parque Nacional Noel Kempff Mercado; to the east along the Brazilian border lies the largely undeveloped Pantanal Boliviano; and to the southwest, en route to Paraguay, is the Gran Chaco – one of South America's last and greatest hinterlands.

Best for
Archaeology ▪ Religious architecture ▪ Wildlife

Footprint
picks

★ **Samaipata**, page 250
Sleepy village with a cool climate, a popular
gringo hangout.

★ **El Fuerte**, page 251
The easternmost outpost of the Inca Empire.

★ **The Che Guevara Trail**, page 257
Follow in the final footsteps of the revolutionary hero.

★ **Amboró National Park**, page 259
Home to giant ferns and delicate orchids.

★ **Jesuit missions**, page 265
Remarkable colonial churches in a sparsely
populated plain.

★ **Noel Kempff Mercado National Park**, page 277
Remote and spectacular region with a staggering
array of wildlife.

N

50 km
50 miles

La Horquilla
Versalles
San
Ramón
Magdalena
Bella Vista
Matequa
Puerto
Villazón
Guacare
Baures
Puerto
Saucedo
Saucedo
Piso Firme
BENI
Puerto
El Carmen
El Carmen
San Pedro
Parque Nacional Noel
Kempff Mercado
Casarabe
Reserva de Vida Silvestre
Ríos Blanco y Negra
San
Ramón
El Pensamiento
La Florida
Perseverencia
Los Fierros
Villa
Banzer
Montecristo
Ingavi
Río Taibo
BRAZIL
Santa María
Yaguayu
La Junta
La Union
El Marfil
Laguna
Marfil
Ascención
San Simon
San Miguelito
Jesús
Cuyo
Rio Negro
Rio Blanco
El Paraiso
Yotau
San
Javier
Concepción
Los
Cusis
San Ignacio
de Velasco
San Diego
El Puente
San Rámon
Pavivi
San Miguel
Ascención
San Matía
Palometas
San Julian
Santa Rosa
SANTA CRUZ
Santa Ana
San Rafael
Las Petas
Melgar
Virtudes
Rio Grande (Guapay)
Los Troncos
Okinawa I
San Pablo
San Miguelito
Candelaria
Rio Piray
Montero
Okinawa II
Santa Maria
Santa Maria
Santa Rosario
San Antonio
Rio Yapacani
Parque
Nacional
Amboró
Warnes
Okinawa III
Texas
Pozo del Tigre
Rancho
Candelaria
Guapasal
San
Isidro
Santa Cruz
de la Sierra
Cotoca
Pailon
San Juan
San Francisco
Puerto
Quijarro
Rincón
del Tigre
Mataral
Samaipata
Poso Redondo
San José
de Chiquitos
Santiago
de Chiquitos
Santo
Corazón
Puerto
Isabel
El Fuerte
Puerto Izozog
Chochis
Roboré
Tucavaca
Vallegrande
Estancia
Florida
Bañados del Izozog
Parque Nacional
Kaa-Iya del Gran Chaco
Puerto
Suárez
La Higuera
Izozog
Rio Parapeti
Fortin Suarez
Arana
Naranjos
Pozo Yaré
El Carmen
Parque
Nacional
Otuquis
Corumb
Padilla
Ipita
Soledad
Fortin
Ravelo
Puerto
Busch
Gutierrez
Capitan
Ustarez
Lagunillas
La Herradura
Ipati
Fortin
Max Paredes
Vaca Guzmán
Camiri
Itatique
Fortin Vanguardia
Azurduy
Cuevo
General
Eugenio
A Garay
27 de Noviembre
CHUQUISACA
Boyuibe
Fortin
Villazón
PARAGUAY
Villamontes

Footprint picks

1 **Samaipata**, page 250
2 **El Fuerte**, page 251
3 **The Che Guevara Trail**, page 257
4 **Amboró National Park**, page 259
5 **Jesuit missions**, page 265
6 **Noel Kempff Mercado National Park**, page 277

Santa Cruz

Bolivia's largest city, gateway to one of the most fascinating parts of the country

Despite the city's rapid growth, the centre still retains a bit of its former air and the main plaza – 24 de Septiembre – is well cared for and a popular meeting place. The narrow, congested streets are lined with low, red-tiled roofs with overhanging eaves, giving pedestrians much-needed protection from the fierce sun or pouring rain.

Essential Santa Cruz and eastern lowlands

Finding your feet

The international **airport** is at **Viru-Viru**, 13 km from the centre of Santa Cruz, reached by taxi or micro. Regional flights operate from **El Trompillo** airport, south of the centre on the Segundo Anillo. Long-distance and regional **buses** leave from the combined bus/train terminal, **Terminal Bimodal**, Avenida Montes on the Tercer Anillo. There are two train lines, to Quijarro on the Brazilian border and to Yacuiba on the Argentine border.

Getting around

The city has eight ring roads, Anillos 1, 2, 3, 4 and so on, the first three of which contain most sites of interest to visitors. The neighbourhood of Equipetrol, where many upscale hotels, restaurants and bars are situated, is northwest of the centre in the Tercer (3rd) Anillo.

When to go

It is hot most of the year. The rainy season runs from December to March.

Time required

One or two days for Santa Cruz itself; two to four days for Samaipata, one week for Chiquitania, two to three weeks for remote areas.

Weather Santa Cruz

January	February	March	April	May	June
21°C 11°C 114mm	20°C 10°C 103mm	20°C 10°C 66mm	21°C 9°C 26mm	21°C 7°C 5mm	21°C 5°C .3mm

July	August	September	October	November	December
20°C 5°C 8mm	21°C 6°C 5mm	22°C 7°C 25mm	22°C 9°C 40mm	22°C 10°C 57mm	22°C 11°C 76mm

most sites of interest to visitors are in the first three anillos

El Casco Viejo, the heart of the city, with its arcaded streets and buildings with low, red-tiled roofs and overhanging eaves, retains a slight colonial feel, despite the profusion of modern, air-conditioned shops and restaurants. During the extended lunchtime hiatus, locals (who call themselves *cambas*) take refuge in their homes and the gridlock traffic eases.

Tip...
Dengue fever outbreaks are common during the wet season (December to March), take mosquito precautions.

The Plaza 24 de Septiembre is the city's main square with the huge **cathedral (Basílica de San Lorenzo)** ⓘ *Museum of Sacred Art, T03-332 4683, Mon-Sat 0730-1200, 1500-2030, Sun 0700-1200, 1500-2130, US$1.50.* You can climb to a mirador in the cathedral **bell tower** ⓘ *daily 0800-1200, 1500-1900, US$0.50,* with nice views of the city. The block behind the cathedral, **Manzana Uno** ⓘ *Tue-Sat 1000-1230, 1600-2100, Sun 1600-2100, www.manzanauno.org.bo,* has been set aside for rotating art and cultural exhibits. The **Museo de Historia** ⓘ *Junín 141, T03-336 5533, Mon-Fri 0800-1200, 1500-1830, free,* has several displays including archaeological pieces from the Chané and Guaraní cultures and explorers' routes. The **Museo de Arte Contemporáneo** ⓘ *Sucre y Potosí, T03-334 0926, Mon-Fri 1000-1200, 1500-1900, free,* houses contemporary Bolivian and international art in a nicely restored old house. By the Primer Anillo is the **Museo de Historia Natural Noel Kempff Mercado** ⓘ *Av Irala 565, between Velasco e Independencia, T03-337 1216, www.museonoelkempff. org, Mon-Fri 0800-1200, 1500-1830, US$0.15,* not only a museum, but also a zoological, botanical and geographical research centre. It is part of the Universidad Autónoma Gabriel René Moreno.

Around Santa Cruz

from tropical gardens to huge sand dunes

At Km 8 on the road east to Cotoca are the **Botanical Gardens** ⓘ *T03-362 3101, open Mon-Fri 0900-1700, entry US$0.50,* a bit run-down but with many walking trails, birds and several forest habitats. To get there, take a *micro* or *trufi* from Calle Suárez Arana (15 minutes).

Cotoca, 20 km east of the city, is where the church has a statue of the Virgin Mary thought to perform miracles, associated with which is a religious handicraft tradition. The town holds a fiesta on 8 December, with several hundred cruceños making the trip on foot – the more penitent on their knees.

*At Km 12.5 sou*th on Doble *Vía a La Guardia (taxi US$5)* **Parque Ecológico Yvaga Guazu** ⓘ *T03-352 7971, www.*

Tip...
Try the local snack, sonsos (mashed yucca or plátano mixed with cheese and toasted on a stick) in the market.

parqueyvagaguazu.org, daily 0800-1600, US$10 for 2-hr guided tour in Spanish (more for English-speaking guide), 14 ha of tropical gardens with native and exotic species, has plants for sale and a restaurant serving Sunday buffet lunch.

Santa Cruz

To ⑥ ⑨, Av San Martin & Barrio Equipetrol
To ③ ⑧ ⑩, Av Monseñor Rivero & Viru-Viru Airport

Where to stay 🛏
1 Bibosi B1
2 Copacabana B1
3 Cortez A2
4 Hostal Río Magdalena B3
5 Jodanga D3
6 Los Tajibos A1
7 Milan B2
8 Res Bolívar B2
9 Royal Lodge A1
10 Sarah B1
11 Senses B2
12 Villa Magna B3

Restaurants 🍴
1 Alexander Coffee B2
2 Café 24 & Café Lorca B2
3 El Chile A2
4 Fridolín B2
5 Horno Caliente D2
6 Horno Caliente D2
7 Ken B3
8 La Casona B2
9 La Creperie B2
10 Los Hierros A2
11 Los Lomitos B3
12 Michelangelo C2
13 Pizzería Marguerita B2
14 Rincón Brasilero B2
15 Su Salud B3
16 Tapekuá C2
17 Vegetarian Center B3

Bars & clubs 🍸
18 Café Irlandés B2

200 metres
200 yards

BACKGROUND

Santa Cruz

The original settlement of Santa Cruz, founded in 1561 by the Spaniard Ñuflo de Chávez, was some 250 km east (near the present-day town of San José de Chiquitos). It was moved in 1590 and again in 1595 to its present location, in response to attacks from indigenous tribes. A little over 50 years ago, what is now Bolivia's largest city (population 1,566,000) was still a remote backwater, but rail, road and air links ended its isolation. The exploitation of oil and gas in the Departments of Santa Cruz and Tarija and a burgeoning agribusiness sector, helped fuel rapid development. Since the election of Evo Morales in 2006, however, *cruceños* have been concerned about the impact of his economic policies, perceived as favouring the highlands. There is considerable local opposition to the national government and Santa Cruz has spearheaded the eastern lowland departments' drive for greater autonomy from La Paz.

Heading west out of the city, at Km 5 on the Camino a Porongo (taxi US$7), **Biocentro Güembé** ① *T03-370 0700, www.biocentroguembe.com, daily 0830-1800, US$18.75 includes guided tour in Spanish or English,* is a resort with accommodation ($$$ range), restaurant, butterfly farm, walk-in aviary, swimming pools and other family recreation.

Las Lomas de Arena del Palmar are huge sand dunes, 18 km to the south of the city, off the road to Palmasola. In some parts are small lagoons where you can swim. Head to the furthest ones; they are cleaner than the nearest, which are stagnant, even if the most popular. To get there take a 4WD from the bus terminal, especially in the wet season when the river crossing can be difficult. It may also be possible to hitch at weekends.

Listings Santa Cruz *map p243*

Tourist information

Municipal Tourism and Culture Office
Libertad 65, on Plaza 24 de Septiembre T03-337 8493, Mon-Sat 0900-1900, and at Plaza del Estudiante, Av Cañoto y Av Mons Rivero, Biblioteca Municipal, T03-337 8493, www.gmsantacruz.gob.bo, see also Dirección-Municipal-de-Cultura-Patrimonio-y-Turismo on Facebook.

InfoTur
Sucre y Potosí, inside the Museo de Arte, T03-336 9581. Mon-Fri 0800-1200, 1500-1900.

Departmental tourist desk
At Viru-Viru airport. Open 0700-2000.

APAC
Av Busch 552 (2nd Anillo), T03-333 2287, www.festivalesapac.com.
Has information about cultural events in the department of Santa Cruz. See also www.destinosantacruz.com.

Fundación Amigos de la Naturaleza (FAN)
Km 7.5 Vía a La Guadria, T03-355 6800, www.fan-bo.org.

SERNAP
Calle 9 Oeste 138, frente a la Plaza Italia,
Barrio Equipetrol, T03-339 4311. Mon-Fri
0800-1200, 1400-1800.

Where to stay

$$$$ Los Tajibos
Av San Martín 455, Barrio Equipetrol, T03-
342 1000, www.lostajiboshotel.com.
Set in 6 ha of lush gardens, one of several
hotels in this price bracket in the city
and the most traditional, all facilities
including business centre, art gallery,
restaurants and spa. Weekend discounts.

$$$ Cortez
Cristóbal de Mendoza 280 (2do Anillo),
T03-333 1234, www.hotelcortez.com.
Traditional tropical hotel with restaurant,
pool, gardens, meeting rooms, parking,
good for dining and nightlife.

$$$ Royal Lodge
Av San Martín 200, Equipetrol, T03-343
8000, www.royalhotel.com.bo.
With restaurant and bar, pool, airport
transfers. Excellent option for its location
and price range.

$$$ Senses
Sucre y 24 de Septiembre, just
off main plaza, T03-339 6666,
www.sensescorp.com.
Self-styled boutique hotel in the heart
of the city, minimalist decor, includes
all services.

$$$ Villa Magna
Barrón 70, T03-339 9700,
www.villamagna-aparthotel.com.
Fully furnished apartments with small
pool, Wi-Fi, parking, attentive owner and
staff, English and German spoken, from
daily to monthly rates.

$$-$ Hostal Río Magdalena
Arenales 653 (no sign), T03-339 3011,
www.hostalrio magdalena.com.
Comfortable rooms, downstairs ones
are dark, with a/c or fan, small yard and
pool, popular.

$$ Bibosi
Junín 218, T334 8548,
htlbibosi@hotmail.com.
Central, nothing fancy, electric shower,
a/c, cheaper with fan, Wi-Fi in lobby,
good value.

$$ Copacabana
Junín 217, T03-336 2770,
www.hotelcopacabanabolivia.com.
Very good, popular with European tour
groups, rooms cheaper without a/c,
restaurant.

$$-$ Jodanga
C El Fuerte 1380, Zona Parque Urbano,
Barrio Los Chóferes, T03-339 6542,
www.jodanga.com.
Good backpacker option 10 mins' walk
from Terminal Bimodal, cheaper with fan
and without bath, cheaper still in dorm,
kitchen, bar, swimming pool, billiards,
DVDs, nice communal areas, laundry,
helpful owner and multilingual staff.

$$-$ Residencial Bolívar
Sucre 131, T03-334 2500,
www.residencialbolivar.com.
Includes good breakfast, cheaper
with shared bath and in dorm, lovely
courtyard with hammocks, rooms can
get hot, alcohol prohibited, popular.

$ Milán
René Moreno 70, T03-339 7500.
Some rooms with a/c, hot water, central
location.

$ Sarah
C Sara 85, T03-332 2425,
HotelSarah on Facebook.
Simple rooms which cost less without
a/c, screened windows, small patio,
good value.

Restaurants

Santa Cruz has the best meat in Bolivia,
try a local *churrasquería* (grill). Av San
Martín in Barrio Equipetrol, and Av
Monseñor Rivero are the areas for
upmarket restaurants and nightlife. Both
are away from the centre, take a taxi at
night. Some restaurants close Mon.

$$$-$$ La Creperie
Arenales 135. Mon-Sat 1900-2400.
Serves crêpes, fondues and salads.

$$$-$$ Los Hierros
Av Monseñor Rivero 300 y Castelnau.
Daily 1200-1500, 1900-2400.
Popular upmarket grill with salad bar.

$$$-$$ Michelangelo
Chuquisaca 502. Mon-Fri 1200-1430,
1900-2330, Sat evenings only.
Excellent Italian cuisine, a/c.

$$ El Chile
Libertad y 2do Anillo, T03-336 8629.
Daily 1000-2345.
Mexican and Bolivian food, good set
lunch with salad bar, à la carte at night.

$$ Ken
Uruguay 730 (1er Anillo), T03-333 3728.
Open 1130-1430, 1800-2300, closed Wed.
Sushi and authentic Japanese
food, popular.

$$ La Casona
Arenales 222, T03-337 8495. Open
1130-1500, 1900-2400.
German-run restaurant, very good food.

$$ Los Lomitos
Uruguay 758 (1er Anillo), T03-332 8696.
Daily 0800-2400.
Traditional *churrasquería* with
unpretentious local atmosphere,
excellent Argentine-style beef, also
pastas, sandwiches and desserts.

$$ Pizzería Marguerita
Junín y Libertad, northwest corner of the
plaza. Open 0930-2400, from 1600 on
Sat-Sun.
A/c, good service, coffee, bar. Popular
with expats, Finnish owner speaks
English and German.

$$ Rincón Brasilero
Libertad 358. Daily 1130-1430, 1930-2330.
Brazilian-style buffet for lunch, pay by
weight, very good quality and variety,
popular; pizza and à la carte at night.
Recommended.

$$ Tapekuá
Ballivián y La Paz, T03-334 5905.
French and international food,
good service, live entertainment
some evenings.

$$-$ Vegetarian Center
Aroma 64, entre Bolívar y Sucre. Mon-Sat
1200-1500.
Set lunch or pay-by-weight buffet, wide
variety of dishes.

$ Pizzería El Horno
3er Anillo, frente a Hospital Oncológico,
Equipetrol; also Av Roque Aguilera 600,
Las Palmas; and Av Piraí diagonal al
Supermercado Slam, T03-358 0801.
Daily 1800-2330.
True Italian pizza, very popular.

$ Su Salud
Quijarro 115. Mon-Thu 0800-2100, Fri and
Sun 0800-1700.
Tasty vegetarian food, filling lunches,
sells vegetarian products.

Cafés

There are lots of very pleasant a/c cafés where you can get coffee, ice cream, drinks and snacks.

Alexander Coffee
Junín y Libertad near main plaza, and Av Monseñor Rivero 400 y Santa Fe.
For good coffee and people-watching.

Café 24
Downstairs at René Moreno y Sucre, on the main plaza. Daily 0830-0200.
Breakfast, juices, international meals, wine rack, nice atmosphere, Wi-Fi.

Café Lorca
Upstairs at Sucre 8 y René Moreno, on the main plaza. Open daily 0900-1600 for lunch, 1600-2300 for dinner.
Meals and drinks, Spanish wines, central patio, small balcony with views over plaza, live music most nights 2030-0130, lounge open Wed-Sat 1600-0300, part of a cultural project, see www.lorcasantacruz.org.

Fridolín
21 de Mayo 168, Pari 254, Av Cañoto y Florida, and Monseñor Rivero y Cañada Strongest.
All good places for coffee and pastries.

Horno Caliente
Chuquisaca 604 y Moldes, also 24 de Septiembre 653.
Salteñas 0730-1230, traditional local snacks and sweets 1530-1930. Popular and very good.

Bars and clubs

Bar Irlandés Irish Pub
3er Anillo Interno 1216, entre Av Banzer y Zoológico), www.irishpub.com.bo, Wed, Fri and Sat evenings.
Irish-themed pub, food available, Irish owner, live music.

Café Irlandés
Plaza 24 de Septiembre, Shopping Bolívar, overlooking main plaza.
Popular.

Kokopelli
Noel Kempff Mercado 1202 (3er Anillo Interno). Open from 2100.
Bar with Mexican food and live music.

Entertainment

Cinema Cine Center, *Av El Trompillo – 2do Anillo – entre Monseñor Santiesteban y René Moreno, www.cinecenter.com.bo.*

Cultural centres with events and programmes Centro Cultural Santa Cruz (*René Moreno 369, T03-335 6941, www.culturabcb.org.bo*); **Centro Simón I Patiño** (*Independencia y Suárez de Figueroa 89, T03-337 2425, www.fundacionpatino.org*), with exhibitions, galleries, and bookstore on Bolivian cultures; **Centro Boliviano Americano** (*Potosí 78, T03-334 2299, www.cba.com.bo*); **Centro Cultural Franco Alemán** (*24 de Septiembre 36, on main plaza, T03-335 0142, www.ccfrancoaleman.org*); **Centro de Formación de la Cooperación Española** (*Arenales 583, T03-335 1311, www.aecid-cf.bo*).

Festivals

Cruceños are famous as fun-lovers and their music, the *carnavalitos*, can be heard all over South America.
Feb Of the various festivals, the brightest is **Carnaval**, renowned for riotous behaviour, celebrated for the 15 days before Lent. There's music in the streets, dancing, fancy dress and the coronation of a queen. Water and paint throwing is common – no one is exempt.

Apr/May **Festival de Música Renacentista y Barroca Americana 'Misiones de Chiquitos'** is held in late Apr through early May every even year (next in 2016) in Santa Cruz and the Jesuit mission towns of the Chiquitania. It is organized by **Asociación Pro Arte y Cultura** (Av Busch 552, Santa Cruz, T03-333 2287, www.festivalesapac.com), and celebrates the wealth of sacred music written by Europeans and indigenous composers in the 17th and 18th centuries. APAC sells books, CDs and videos and also offers – in both Santa Cruz and the mission towns – a schedule of musical programmes. The festival is very popular: book hotels at least 2-3 weeks in advance.

Apr/May **Festival Internacional de Teatro**, also organized **APAC** (see above) is held every odd year (next in 2017).

Aug and Dec **Festival de la Temporada** in Santa Cruz and major towns of Chiquitania, featuring *música misional* with local performers.

24 Sep The local holiday of Santa Cruz city and department.

Shopping

Handicrafts

Bolivian Souvenirs, *Shopping Bolívar, local 10 and 11, on main plaza, T03-333 7805; also at Viru-Viru airport.* Expensive knitwear and crafts from all over Bolivia.
Paseo Artesanal La Recova, *off Libertad, ½ block from Plaza.* Many different kiosks selling crafts.
Vicuñita Handicrafts, *Ingavi e Independencia, T03-333 4711.* Wide variety of crafts from the lowlands and the altiplano, very good.

Jewellery

Carrasco, *Velasco 23, T03-336 2841, and other branches.* For gemstones.
RC Joyas, *Bolívar 262, T03-333 2725.* Jewellery and Bolivian gems.

Markets

Los Pozos, *between Quijarro, Campero, Suárez Arana and 6 de Agosto.* A sprawling street market for all kinds of produce.
Siete Calles, *Isabel la Católica y Vallegrande.* Mainly clothing.
Mercado Nuevo, *Sucre y Cochabamba.*

What to do

Bird Bolivia, *T03-356 3636, www. birdbolivia.com.* Specializes in organized birding tours, English spoken.
Forest Tour, *Junín y 21 de Mayo, Galería Casco Viejo, upstairs, No 115, T03-337 2042, www.forestbolivia.com.* Environmentally sensitive tours to Refugio los Volcanes, birdwatching, national parks, Chiquitania and Salar de Uyuni. English spoken.
Magri Turismo, *Velarde 49 y Irala, T03-334 4559, www.magriturismo.com.* Long-established agency for airline tickets and tours.
Misional Tours, *Los Motojobobos 2515, T03-360 1985, www.misionaltours.com.* Covers all of Bolivia, specializing in Chiquitania, Amboró, and Santa Cruz. Tours in various languages.
Nick's Adventures, *Equipetrol 8 Este, No 11, T7845 8046, www. nicksadventuresbolivia.com.* Australian/ Bolivian-owned company offering tours locally and throughout Bolivia, with a strong emphasis on wildlife conservation.
Ruta Verde, *21 de Mayo 318, T03-339 6470, www.rutaverdebolivia.com.* Offers national parks, Jesuit missions, Ruta

del Che, Amazonian boat trips, Salar de Uyuni, and tailor-made tours, Dutch/Bolivian-owned, English and German also spoken, knowledgeable and helpful.

Transport

Air
Viru-Viru, T03-338 5000, open 24 hrs, airline counters from 0600; *casa de cambio* changing cash US$ and euros at poor rates, 0630-2100; various ATMs; luggage lockers 0600-2200, US$5.50 for 24 hrs; ENTEL for phones and internet, plus a few eateries. Taxi US$10, micro from Ex-Terminal (see below), or El Trompillo, US$1, 45 mins. From airport take micro to Ex-Terminal then taxi to centre. Domestic flights with **Boliviana de Aviación** (BoA, T03-311 6247) and **TAM** (Bolivia, T03-352 9669), to **La Paz**, **Cochabamba**, **Sucre**, **Tarija** and **Cobija**. International flights to **Asunción**, **Buenos Aires**, **Salta**, **Lima**, **Madrid**, **Miami**, **Washington**, **Santiago** and **São Paulo**.

El Trompillo is the regional airport operating daily 0500-1900, T352 6600, located south of the centre on the 2do Anillo. It has a phone office and kiosk selling drinks, but no other services. Taxi US$1.50, many micros. **TAM** has flights throughout the country, different destinations on different days. **Aerocon**, T03-351 1010) flies via **Trinidad** to various towns in the northern jungle.

Bus
Regional buses and vans These leave either from behind the Terminal Bimodal (use pedestrian tunnel under the rail tracks) or from near the Ex-Terminal (the old bus station, Av Irala y Av Cañoto, 1er Anillo, which is no longer functioning).

Long distance Most long-distance buses leave from the combined bus/train terminal, **Terminal Bimodal**, Av Montes on the 3er Anillo, T03-348 8382; police check passports and search luggage here; taxi to centre, US$1.50. Terminal fee, US$0.50 , left luggage US$0.50, there are ATMs and *cambios*. To **Cochabamba**, via the lowland route, many depart 0600-0930 and 1630-2130, US$9-12. 75, *bus-cama* US$18.55, 8-10 hrs, also **Trans Carrasco** vans leave when full across the street from the Terminal Bimodal, US$20; via the old highland route, **Trans Carrasco**, depart from the main plaza in El Torno, 30 km west of Santa Cruz, daily at 1200 (from Mairana daily at 0800 and 1500), US$8, 14 hrs. Direct to **Sucre** via Aiquile, around 1600, US$13.50-18, 12-13hrs. To **Oruro**, US$15-21, 14-15 hrs, and **La Paz** between 1630-1900, US$15.50-22.75, *bus-cama* US$31.25, 15-16 hrs; change in Cochabamba for daytime travel. To **Camiri** (US$5, 4-5 hrs), **Yacuiba** (border with Argentina), US$8.50-13, 8 hrs and **Tarija**, US$18.75-27, 17-24 hrs. To **Trinidad**, several daily after 2000, 9 hrs, US$9-13. To **San José de Chiquitos**, US$7-10, 5 hrs, **Roboré**, US$7-10, 7 hrs, and **Quijarro** (border with Brazil), at 1030 and between 1700-2000, US$12-22, 8-10 hrs. Also vans to San José, leave when full, US$10, 4½ hrs. To **San Ignacio de Velasco**, US$10, 10 hrs; **Jenecherú** *bus-cama* US$18; also **Expreso San Ignacio** vans leave when full, US$20, 8 hrs.

International Terminal fee US$1.50 (for international journeys). To **Asunción**, US$52-64, 20-24 hrs via Villamontes and the Chaco, at 1930, with **Yacyretá**, T03-362 5557, Mon, Tue, Thu, Sat; **Stel Turismo**, T03-349 7762, daily; **Pycazú**, daily, and **Palma Loma**. Other companies are less reliable. See page 263 for the route to Paraguay across the

Chaco. To **Buenos Aires** daily departures around 1900, US$158, 36 hrs, several companies. To **São Paulo** via Puerto Suárez, with **La Preferida**, T03-364 7160, Mon, Wed, Fri, 2 days.

Car hire
Avis, Carretera al Norte Km. 3.5, T03-343 3939, www.avis.com.bo. **A Barron's**, Av Alemana 50 y Tajibos, T03-342 0160, www.abarrons.com. Outstanding service and completely trustworthy. **IMBEX**, 3er Anillo Interno, entre Bush y N Ortiz, T03-311 1000, www.imbex.com.

Taxi
About US$1-1.50 inside 1er Anillo (more at night), US$2 inside 3er Anillo, fix fare in advance. Use radio-taxis at night.

Train
Ferroviaria Oriental, at Terminal Bimodal, T03-338 7300, www.fo.com.bo, runs east to **San José de Chiquitos**, **Roboré** and **Quijarro** on the Brazilian border. The **Ferrobús** (a rail-car with the fastest most luxurious service) leaves Santa Cruz Tue, Thu, Sun 1800, arriving Quijarro 0700 next day, US$29.50; **Expreso Oriental** (an express train), Mon, Wed, Fri 1320, arriving 0602, US$12.50. There is also little-used weekly train service south to **Yacuiba** on the Argentine frontier, Thu 1530, arrives 0805 next day, US$6, returns Fri 1700; buses are much faster.

South of Santa Cruz

a perfect pit-stop and the biggest carved rock in South America

In times gone by, Samaipata was a 'pascana' or rest stop for people undertaking the arduous journey from Potosí, Sucre and Cochabamba to the tropical lowlands of Santa Cruz, and vice-versa. It remains today a most congenial spot for travellers to rest and acclimatize to changes in altitude and temperature. Samaipata is also popular among Cruceños, who flock here at weekends and holidays. Close by is El Fuerte, the easternmost outpost of the Inca Empire, with the largest sculpted rock in South America. Samaipata has a wonderful setting and climate and an excellent selection of hotels and restaurants. It also remains strategically located for those travelling from Santa Cruz to Cochabamba via the old mountain road, to Vallegrande and the Che Guevara Trail, as well as on to Sucre.

★Samaipata *Colour map 3, A5.*
From Santa Cruz the old mountain road to Cochabamba runs along the Piray gorge and up into the highlands. Some 100 km from Santa Cruz is Samaipata (population 10,470), a great place to relax midweek, with good lodging, restaurants, hikes and riding, and a growing ex-pat community. A two-hour walk takes you to the top of Cerro de La Patria, just east of town, with nice views of the surrounding valleys. Local *artesanías* include ceramics, paintings and sculpture. At weekends the town bursts into life as crowds of Cruceños come to escape the city heat and to party. See www.samaipata.info and www.guidetosamaipata.com. There is a Banco Unión ATM at Calle Campero s/n, between Warnes and Saavedra.

The **Museo de Arqueología** ⓘ *2 blocks east, 1 north from the plaza, Mon-Fri 0830-1200, 1400-1800, Sat-Sun 0830-1600, US$1 (for museum only, US$8 for El Fuerte and museum),* houses the tourist information office and a collection of ceramics with anthropomorphic designs, dating from 200 BC to AD 300, and provides information on the nearby pre-Inca ceremonial site commonly called El Fuerte.

★El Fuerte
Daily 0900-1630, US$8 for El Fuerte and Museum, ticket valid 4 days, Spanish- and English-speaking guides available, US$12.

El Fuerte is 9 km from Samaipata; 3 km along the highway to Santa Cruz, then 6 km up a rough, signposted road (taxi from Plaza Principal US$6 one way, US$13 return with two hours' wait); two to three hours' walk one way. Pleasant bathing is possible in a river on the way to El Fuerte.

This sacred structure (altitude 1990 m) consists of a complex system of channels, basins, high-relief sculptures, etc, carved out of one vast slab of rock. Some suggest that Amazonian people created it around 1500 BC, but it could be later. There is evidence of subsequent occupations and that it was the nethermost outpost of the Incas' Kollasuyo (their eastern empire).

> **Tip...**
> It is not permitted to walk on the rock, so visit the museum first to see the excellent model.

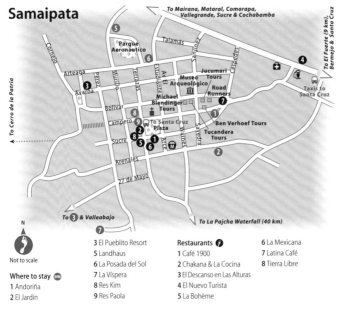

Samaipata

Not to scale

Where to stay
1 Andoriña
2 El Jardín
3 El Pueblito Resort
5 Landhaus
6 La Posada del Sol
7 La Víspera
8 Res Kim
9 Res Paola

Restaurants
1 Café 1900
2 Chakana & La Cocina
3 El Descanso en Las Alturas
4 El Nuevo Turista
5 La Bohème
6 La Mexicana
7 Latina Café
8 Tierra Libre

The **carved rock** will be your first stop. It is 240 m by 40 m and 10 m high; the biggest in South America. The main carvings are Inca. In front is a circular relief of a puma and alongside two others, badly eroded. The wall further back forms the remains of the temple of the jaguar. Also further back are the beautiful, 24-m-long patterned channels (which will be easier to see from the viewpoint). These are thought to symbolize rattlesnakes and sacrificial blood and, during Inca rituals, *chicha* (corn beer) released from the central temple would wriggle its way down the criss-cross rhombus carvings like a moving snake.

Walking around you'll first see what may have been carved seating for people to watch the ceremonies. Below are a series of niches (the first of which has been re-roofed in traditional style), which would have held mummies and gold offerings. The last eight or so were still being carved when the Spanish arrived and are incomplete. A wall at the eastern end may have been originally painted red with niches.

The route will take you past Inca agriculture terracing to Chinkana, a hole that may have been a well or an entrance to a labyrinth containing lost Inca treasure. The Spanish found nothing and the word Chinkana means 'lost'.

The rest of the site, sadly, is poorly restored. You'll pass the ruins of two Inca houses before passing into what was once the central plaza of a grand town (and now looks little better than a football pitch). Imagination is needed to conjure up the image of the large, 68-m by 16-m, 12-m-high **Kallanka**, which flanked the southern side. This had eight doors opening onto the plaza and was used for religious and military ceremonies.

The **Akllawasi** for Virgins of the Sun is mainly overgrown. Finish by climbing to the viewpoint from where the rock can be best appreciated. As this spot is the highest it is thought there may be another, even more important, carved rock below.

Around Samaipata

In addition to tours to El Fuerte and the Ruta del Che (see below), many other worthwhile excursions can be made in the Samaipata area. Impressive forests of

El Fuerte

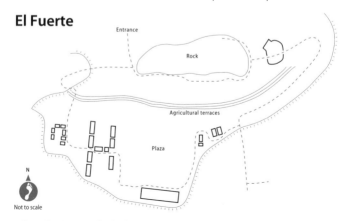

Entrance

Rock

Agricultural terraces

Plaza

N

Not to scale

Knight in shining armour

You may be surprised to discover that tiny Samaipata has a chess club built to international standards. It has produced teenage nationwide champions. Wolfgang Paulin was one of five foreign teachers who came to Samaipata, began building cabañas and changed the village for tourists. He realized there was little for the town's youth to do so he built a chess centre. Check it out, next to the museum; it also has a snack bar. You may even want to give one of them a game. Be prepared for a thrashing.

giant ferns can be visited around **Cerro La Mina** and elsewhere in the Amboró buffer zone. Also **Cuevas**, 20 km east of town, with waterfalls and pools, often visited together with El Fuerte. Further east are forest and sandstone mountains at **Bella Vista/Codo de los Andes**. There is a wonderful hike up to the **Mirador de Cóndores**, with many condors and nearby the the 25-m-high **La Pajcha** waterfall, 40 km south of Samaipata. **Postrervalle** is a quaint hamlet with many interesting walks and mountain bike trails. There is good birdwatching throughout the region, especially around Mataral (see below). Tour operators in Samaipata can arrange all of the above trips.

The little village of **Bermejo**, 40 km east of Samaipata on the road to Santa Cruz, provides access to the strikingly beautiful **Serranía Volcanes** region, abutting on Parque Nacional Amboró. Here is the excellent **Refugio Los Volcanes** ⓘ *T7688 0800, or 03-337 2042, www.refugiovolcanes.net*, a small lodge with a 15-km trail system, with good birdwatching, orchids and bromeliads. Ginger's Paradise, some 2 km from Bermejo (T6777 4772, www.gingersparadise.com), offers an organic, communal alternative, popular with backpackers (you can work to offset some room costs).

Listings South of Santa Cruz *map p251*

Where to stay

Samaipata
Rooms may be hard to find at weekends in high season.

$$$$-$$ El Pueblito Resort
camino a Valle Abajo, 20 mins' walk uphill from town, T03-944 6383, www.elpueblitoresort.com.
Fully equipped cabins and rooms, pool, restaurant and bar set around a mock colonial plaza, with shops and meditation chapel.

$$ Landhaus
C Murillo uphill from centre, T03-944 6033, www.samaipata-landhaus.com.
Cabins and rooms in nice ample grounds, small pool, hammocks, parking, sauna (extra), craft shop, good breakfast available. Older rooms are cheaper and good value.

$$ La Posada del Sol
C Arteaga, 3 blocks north of plaza, T03-944 6366, www.laposadadelsol.net.
Most rooms with bath, electric shower, nice grounds, restaurant, views, US/Bolivian-run.

$$ La Víspera
1.2 km south of town, T03-944 6082,
www.lavispera.org.
Dutch-owned organic farm with
accommodation in 5 cosy cabins with
kitchen, camping US$4-7 pp, breakfast
and lunch available in **Café-Jardín**
(0800-1500 daily), book exchange,
maps for sale. A peaceful slow-paced
place; owners Margarita and Pieter are
very knowledgeable and can arrange
excursions and horse riding. They also
sell medicinal and seasoning herbs.
Highly recommended.

$ Andoriña
C Campero, 2½ blocks from plaza, T03-
944 6333, www.andorinasamaipata.com.
Tastefully decorated hostel, cheaper
without bath, good breakfast,
kitchen, bar, good views, volunteer
opportunities. Dutch/Bolivian-run,
enthusiastic owners Andrés and Doriña
are very knowledgeable, English spoken.

$ El Jardín
C Arenales, 2 blocks from
market, T7311 9461,
www.eljardinsamaipata.blogspot.co.uk.
With electric shower, cheaper in dorm,
ample grounds, camping US$2.50 pp,
kitchen facilities, Belgian/Bolivian-run.

$ Paola
C Terrazas, diagonal to the plaza,
T03-944 6093.
Simple rooms, cheaper without bath,
electric shower, restaurant serves set
meals, internet (extra), kitchen and
laundry facilities.

$ Residencial Kim
C Terrazas, near plaza, T03-944 6161.
Cheaper than Paola, with shared bath,
family-run, spotless, good value.

Restaurants

Samaipata

$$ El Descanso en Las Alturas
C Arteaga, uphill from plaza, opens
mostly on weekends.
Wide choice including good steaks
and pizzas.

$$ La Mexicana
C Rubén Terrazas near the plaza. Tue-Sun
1100-1500 and 1800-2300.
Nice restaurant/bar with very good
Mexican food. Also serves breakfast
Sat-Sun.

$$ Latina Café
Bolívar, 3 blocks from plaza. Fri-Tue 1800-
2200, Sat-Sun also 1200-1430.
Nice upmarket restaurant/bar with very
good Bolivian and international food
including vegetarian. French/Bolivian-
run and recommended.

$$-$ Chakana
Terrazas on plaza. Daily 0800-2300.
Bar/restaurant/café serving *almuerzos*,
good snacks, salads, cakes and ice
cream, outside seating, book exchange,
Dutch-owned.

$$-$ Tierra Libre
Sucre ½ block from plaza. Open 1200-
2200, Sun 1200-1500, closed Wed.
Nice terrace with outdoor seating,
good meat and vegetarian, pleasant
atmosphere.

$ Café 1900
Sucre on plaza. Daily 0800-2300.
Good set lunch, sandwiches and crêpes.

$ El Nuevo Turista
opposite the gas station on the highway.
Good local dishes.

$ La Boheme
Sucre y Terrazas, diagonal to plaza.
Daily 1200-2400.
Trendy Australian-run bar for drinks
and snacks.

$ La Cocina
Sucre by the plaza. Tue-Sat 1900-2200.
Middle Eastern and Mexican fast food
with home-made breads.

What to do

Samaipata
Massage
Samaipata Spa, *at the end of C Bolivar,*
T7263 6796, samaipata.spa on Facebook.
Daily 0900-1200, 1500-2000. Offers
massage, yoga and alternative therapies.

Tour operators
Samaipata has many tour operators,
more than we can list. Except as noted,
all are on C Bolívar near the museum.
Most day trips cost about US$20-25 pp
in a group of 4.
Ben Verhoef Tours, *Campero 217, T03-
944 6365, www.benverhoeftours.com.*
Dutch-owned, English, German and
Spanish also spoken. Offer tours along **La
Ruta del Che** and throughout the area.
Jucumari Tours, *T944 6129, erwin-am@
hotmail.com.* Run by Edwin Acuña, who
has a 4WD vehicle.
Michael Blendinger, *T03-944 6227,
www.discoveringbolivia.com.* German
guide raised in Argentina who speaks
English, runs fully equipped 4WD
tours, short and long treks, horse rides,
specialist in nature and archaeology.
Road Runners, *T944 6193/6294, www.
hosteltrail.com/roadrunners.* Olaf and
Frank speak English, German and

Dutch, enthusiastic, lots of information
and advice.
Tucandera Tours, *T7316 7735,
tucandera.tours@hotmail.com.* Saul Arias
and Elva Villegas are biologists, excellent
for nature tours and birdwatching,
English spoken, competitive prices.
Recommended.

Wine tasting
2 bodegas located outside Samaipata
are **Uvairenda** (*www.uvairenda.com*)
and **Vargas** (*www.vitivinicolavargas.com*).

Transport

Samaipata
Bus
From **Santa Cruz** to Samaipata, only
Sucre-bound buses leave from the
Terminal Bimodal. **Taxis Expreso
Samaipata** in Santa Cruz at Av Omar
Chávez 1147 y Soliz de Holguín, T03-333
5067 (Samaipata T03-944 6129), leave
when full Mon-Sat 0530-2030 (for Sun
book in advance), US$3.75 per person
shared; or US$15 in private vehicle,
2½ hrs. Returning to Santa Cruz,
they pick you up from your hotel in
Samaipata. See hotel websites and www.
guidetosamaipata.com for more services.
Buses leaving Santa Cruz for **Sucre** and
other towns pass through Samaipata
between 1800 and 2100; tickets can be
booked with 1 day's notice through **El
Nuevo Turista** (see Restaurants, above).
To get to **Samaipata** from **Sucre**, buses
leave at night and arrive 0500-0600 (set
your alarm in case the driver forgets
to stop for you), stopping in Mataral
or Mairana for breakfast, about ½ hr
before Samaipata.

Past Samaipata the road from Santa Cruz continues west 17 km to Mairana, a hot dusty roadside town where long-distance buses make their meal stops and there is daily service to Cochabamba (see Transport, page 249). It is 51 km further to Mataral, where there are petroglyphs and a cactus desert (ask for a guide in the town). The paved road to Vallegrande (51 km, see below) branches south here. At La Palizada, 32 km west of Mataral, a road branches west towards Aiquile (see page 233), on the main bus route between Santa Cruz and Sucre.

Soon after the turn-off, left, is the lovely, friendly old village of Saipina, with colonial houses around its plaza. Saipina sits in the valley of the Río Grande, an agricultural centre where, they say, "the only thing that doesn't grow is that which isn't planted." Buses can get stuck here in the rainy season as the river is subject to flash flooding. In the village is a **museum** ① *1000-1200, 1430-1700, closed Sat, US$1,* which displays local archaeological finds. Three hours away by horse is the well-preserved hilltop Inca fortress of **Pukara**, where you can camp. Trips to Pukara, and other interesting local sites, can be arranged at the museum.

Comarapa *Colour map3, A4.*

Another 57 km west is Comarapa (population 15,875, altitude 1800 m), a tranquil agricultural centre halfway between Santa Cruz and Cochabamba. The town provides access to several lovely natural areas including **Laguna Verde** (12 km, taxi US$11.50 with two hours' wait, or walk back over the hills), surrounded by cloudforest bordering Parque Nacional Amboró (see below); and the **Jardín de Cactáceas de Bolivia**, where the huge *carpari* cactus and 25 other endemic species may be seen (entry US$0.75, take a *trufi* from Comarapa to Pulquina Abajo, US$1). The Jardín itself is run-down but there are many more impressive cacti, good walking and birdwatching throughout the area. The tourist office at El Parquecito in Comarapa can arrange local guides. Beyond Comarapa the road is unpaved and very scenic. It climbs through cloudforest past the village of **La Siberia** to the pass at El Churo and enters the department of Cochabamba, heading for Pojo and Epizana (see page 233).

Vallegrande and La Higuera *Colour map3, A5.*

Some 115 km south of the Santa Cruz–Cochabamba road is La Higuera, where Che Guevara was killed. On 8 October each year, visitors, most from outside Bolivia, gather there to celebrate his memory. La Higuera is reached through the town of Vallegrande (population 17,200) where, at **Hospital Nuestro Señor de Malta** ① *no fee, but voluntary donation to the health station,* you can see the old laundry building where Che's body was shown to the international press on 9 October 1967. The old laundry, now an abandoned shed behind the main building, is an evocative place, the walls covered in signatures and slogans scratched into the plaster. One of the most poignant is actually on the adobe wall of the public telephone office. It reads: "Che – alive as they never wanted you to be". Near Vallegrande's airstrip

ON THE ROAD

★Band on the run

Band on the run One of the most enduring images of youthful rebellion is that of Che Guevara staring proud, implacable and defiant under that trademark black beret. It is an image that has graced many a student's wall. But how did this great 20th-century icon come to die in a miserable little hamlet in the Bolivian wilderness? Ernesto Guevara de la Serna, or Che as he became known, was born in Argentina on 14 June 1928 to wealthy middle-class parents. However, his eyes were soon opened to the plight of South America's poor during a journey around the continent on a beat-up old motorcycle, chronicled in The Motorcycle Diaries. He met Fidel Castro in Mexico in 1956 and together they planned the overthrow of the harshly repressive dictatorship of Fulgencio Batista in Cuba. This was achieved in January 1959, after an extraordinary and heroic three-year campaign with a guerrilla force reduced at one point to 12 men. Che worked tirelessly to create the ideal socialist model in Cuba as well as establish links with other, sympathetic nations, but his overriding ambition had always been to spread the revolutionary word and take the armed struggle to other parts of Latin America. Impoverished Bolivia seemed the obvious choice. He left Cuba for Bolivia in November 1966 and, after a brief stay in La Paz (at the Hotel Copacabana), Che travelled to the guerrilla base at Ñancahuazú, a farm 250 km south of Santa Cruz where they began their preparations. But their constant movements aroused suspicion and Che and his group were on the run from April 1967 when the army began looking for them. There was little sympathy from the Bolivian peasantry, as the government had successfully played on their patriotism in the face of this 'foreign invasion'. Che and his band were now very much on their own and worse was to come. One of his men had been captured and, under interrogation, confirmed Che's presence in the country, contrary to the CIA belief that he had been killed a few years earlier in the Congo. The USA immediately despatched a group of Special Forces to create a counterinsurgency battalion, the Bolivian Army Rangers, and stop Che gaining a foothold. By August, Che was sick and exhausted, as were many of his dwindling force. On 31 August he lost one-third of them in an army ambush. The army had enlisted the help of local peasants to inform them of the guerrillas' movements, so they were ready and waiting when Che and his men made their way slowly north towards Vallegrande, the Argentine now crippled by his chronic asthma and travelling by mule. They reached the tiny village of La Higuera, where they faced the US-trained Army Rangers in what would be their final battle. On 8 October the surviving guerrillas were trapped in a ravine. A prolonged gun battle ensued during which a wounded Che was caught while trying to escape. He was held prisoner overnight in the village schoolhouse, under the supervision of a Cuban-American CIA agent, and executed the following day, 9 October, aged 39. Che's body was dumped in a secret grave, the precise whereabouts of which had remained a mystery, until it was finally discovered in July 1997. He now lies in peace in his beloved Cuba.

you can see the results of excavations carried out in 1997 which finally unearthed his physical remains (now in Cuba); ask an airport attendant to see the site. Vallegrande has a small **archaeological museum** ① *on the plaza, Mon-Fri 1000-1200, 1400-1700, US$1.50, see www.santacruz.gob.bo, Museos page for information on archaeological sites*, above which is the **Che Guevara Room** ① *free*.

The schoolhouse in La Higuera (60 km south of Vallegrande via the village of Pucará) where Che was executed is now a museum. Another **museum** ① *T03-942 2003*, owned by René Villegas, is open when he is in town. Guides, including Pedro Calzadillo, headmaster of the school, will show visitors to the ravine of El Churo (or Yuro), where Che was captured on 8 October 1967.

A **'Che Guevara Trail'**, following the last movements of Che and his band as they tried to flee the pursuing Bolivian Army, is an ambitious 815-km circuit, winding its way along dirt roads in the subtropical area bordering Santa Cruz and Chuquisaca departments. It was officially inaugurated in 2004 but to do the entire route by public transport, arranging local guides, is difficult. La Ruta del Che tours organized by agencies in Santa Cruz (three days, two nights) and Samaipata (two days, one night) follow some of the last movements of Che and his band and are an easier option.

Listings Highland road to Cochabamba

Where to stay

Comarapa

$ El Paraíso
Av Comarapa 396 (main road to Cochabamba), T03-946 2045.
Pleasant economical hotel, electric shower, nice garden, parking, decent restaurant, popular.

Vallegrande and La Higuera

$ Hostal Juanita
M M Caballero 123, Vallegrande, T03-942 2231.
Cheaper without bath, electric shower, good value, Doña Juanita is kind.

$ La Casa del Telegrafista
La Higuera, T7493 7807/6773 3362, casadeltelegrafista@gmail.com.
Small, welcoming French-owned

posada, rooms with shared bath, lovely garden, great views, meals on request, camping (US$2), horseback and mountain-bike tours, US$15, also bikes for hire.

$ Residencial Vallegrande
on the plaza, Vallegrande.
Basic accommodation.

Transport

Comarapa
Bus
To/from **Santa Cruz** with **Turismo Caballero** (T03-350 9626) and **Trans Comarapa** (T7817 5576), both on Plazuela Oruro, Av Grigotá (3er Anillo), 3 daily each, US$4.50, 6 hrs. To **Cochabamba**, 2 buses a day pass through from Mairana.

Vallegrande and La Higuera
Bus
Flota Vallegrande has 2 daily buses morning and afternoon from Santa Cruz to **Vallegrande** via **Samaipata** (at 1130 and 1630), 5 hrs, US$5. Best to book in advance. Samaipata–Vallegrande

US$3.25. From Vallegrande market, a daily bus departs 0815 to **Pucará** (45 km, US$2.50), from where there is transport (12 km) to La Higuera.

Taxi
Vallegrande–La Higuera US$30-35.

Lowland road to Cochabamba

you can visit Amboró from Samaipata or Buena Vista

The 465-km lowland road from Santa Cruz to Cochabamba first passes through the fertile lowlands north of the city. The route goes past Viru-Viru airport, through **Warnes** (a satellite of Santa Cruz, district population 96,400), then a further 37 km north to **Montero** (population 109,520). Montero is named after Independence hero Marceliano Montero and is an important agricultural centre. Just north of Montero the road branches west through Buena Vista and past the northern edge of Amboró National Park towards Villa Tunari. Another branch runs east to the incongruously named town of **Okinawa I** (population 12,480), located 80 km northeast from Santa Cruz. Japanese immigrants settled here in the aftermath of the Second World War and Okinawa is now a rich agricultural area. There are other settlements called Okinawa II and III.

★Parque Nacional Amboró

This vast protected area lies only three hours west of Santa Cruz. Of its total 637,600 ha, 442,500 ha (or roughly 70%) is set aside as exclusive parkland, while the remaining 195,100 ha is an integrated-use area or buffer zone where most tours operate. Amboró encompasses four distinct major ecosystems – the rainforests of the Amazon, the forests and grasslands of the Andes, the dry plains of the Chaco and

Tip...
The best time of year to visit the park is between April and October.

the savannahs of the Cerrado – and 11 life zones and is home to thousands of animal, plant and insect species (it is reputed to contain more butterflies than anywhere else on earth). The park is home to over 850 species of bird, including the blue-horned curassow, quetzal and cock-of-the-rock, red and chestnut-fronted macaws, hoatzin and cuvier toucans, and 130 mammals, many native to Amazonia, such as capybaras, peccaries, tapirs, several species of monkey and the spectacled bear, as well as jungle cats like the jaguar, ocelot and margay. There are over 100 reptiles and almost 3000 known plant species, including mahogany, giant ferns and many orchids. There are also numerous waterfalls and cool, green swimming pools, moss-ridden caves and large tracts of virgin rainforest.

You cannot enter the park without a guide, either from a tour operator, or from a community-based project. Note that there are many biting insects so take repellent, long-sleeved shirts, long trousers and good boots. There are two places to base yourself: Samaipata (see above) to access the southern highland areas of the park, and Buena Vista (see below) for northern lowland sections.

Essential Parque Nacional Amboró

Park information

The park is administered by SERNAP (Calle 9 Oeste 138, frente a la Plaza Italia, Barrio Equipetrol, T03-339 4311, Monday-Friday 0800-1200, 1400-1800, see www.sernap.gob.bo and www.biobol.org). There are also park offices in Samaipata and Buena Vista.

Finding your feet

From Samaipata Park entrances include the following: **Bermejo**, 44 km east on the road to Santa Cruz, from where you have a guided riverbed-crossing hike, two to three hours to Comunidad Los Volcanes. **Abra de los Toros/Barrientos**, touching on the highest points in the park and the un-excavated Inca fortress of Pucará. You enter via Achira and Barrientos, which are about 15 km from Samaipata and are accessed by jeep. **Las Lauras**, with steep hiking with beautiful giant ferns. **La Yunga** is a popular access, but loggers destroyed many of the giant ferns here up until the 1960s. Local trucks and shared taxis run from Mairana (see page 256) to this little village, which has basic community-run cabins ($ shared bath, no shower). Local guides may be available in La Yunga for treks into Amboró, but take all your own trekking gear and provisions. There is also access to Amboró from Mataral (page 256), where there is a guest hut, directly from Samaipata (9 km from park

boundary, a 4WD is essential in rainy season) and Comarapa (page 256). Tour operators in Samaipata and Santa Cruz offer a variety of tours.

From Buena Vista There are five tourist sites for entering the national park from Buena Vista: **Villa Amboró** (T03-343 1332, www.probioma.org.bo), good for hiking; the community can also arrange horse riding. Get there either by 4WD, or take a *trufi* to Las Cruces (35 km from Buena Vista) and then hike to the refuge (about two hours). **Macuñucu**, about 2 km from Villa Amboró, is an entrance favoured by tour operators. **La Chonta** (T6773 5333, www.lachontaamboro.wordpress.com, a community-based ecotourism lodge, offers tours to the forest and to farming communities with local guides. Take a *trufi* via Haytú to the Río Surutú and from there, walk or horse ride (2½ hours). Further along the road to Cochabamba is **Mataracú**, used by the operators, with natural pools, waterfalls and dinosaur fossils. It has the private **Mataracú Tent Camp** (T03-342 2372), and other camping options. At **Cajones de Ichilo** (T7630 2581, 0600-0900, 1800-2200), a community lodge 70 km west from Buena Vista in Cochabamba department in mountainous scenery with a large river, there are trails which offer a good chance of seeing mammals and, with luck, the horned currassow, one of the most endangered species of bird in Bolivia.

Buena Vista *Colour map 3, A5.*

This sleeply little town is 100 km northwest of Santa Cruz by paved road (see www.buenavistabolivia.com). The mission church dates from 1694 (most recently rebuilt in 1970) and was built to hold more than 700 Chiriguanos who had been converted to Christianity. The stores in town are well stocked with basic supplies and there are also craft shops as well as several tour operators. No ATM in town, but US dollars cash can be changed. There is an Amboró interpretation office one block from the plaza, T03-932 2055. Three kilometres from town is **Eco-Albergue Candelaria** ① *T7668 7071, ecocandelaria@anditradecoffee.com, or contact in advance through Hacienda El Cafetal (page 261),* a community-tourism project offering cabins in a pleasant setting, activities and tours.

Listings Lowland road to Cochabamba

Where to stay

Buena Vista

$$$-$$ Hacienda El Cafetal
5.5 km south of town (taxi from plaza US$3), T03-935 2067,
www.haciendaelcafetal.com.
Comfortable suites for up to 5 people, double rooms, restaurant, bar, birdwatching platform, on a working coffee plantation (tours available), with shade forest.

$$ Buenavista
700 m out of town, T03-932 2104,
buenavista.hotel@hotmail.com.
Pretty place with rooms, suites and cabins with kitchen, viewing platform, pool, sauna, very good restaurant, horse riding.

$ La Casona
Av 6 de Agosto at the corner of the plaza,
T03-932 2083.
Small simple rooms with fan, shared

Buena Vista

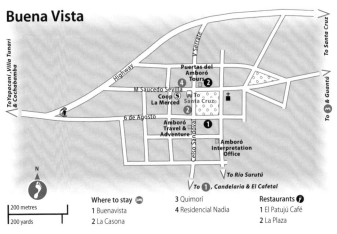

Where to stay	3 Quimorí	Restaurants
1 Buenavista	4 Residencial Nadia	1 El Patujú Café
2 La Casona		2 La Plaza

bath, electric shower, courtyard in hammocks, plants and birds, good value.

$ Quimori
1 km east of Buena Vista, T03-932 2081.
Includes breakfast, other meals with advance notice, pool, nice grounds, tours in dry season, family-run.

$ Residencial Nadia
C M Saucedo Sevilla 186, T03-932 2049.
Cheaper without bath, simple, small, family-run.

Villamontes

$$$-$$ El Rancho Olivo
Av Méndez Arcos opposite the train station, 15 blocks from the centre, T04-672 2059, www.elranchoolivo.com.
Lovely rooms, frigobar, nice grounds and pool, parking, excellent restaurant.

$ Gran Hotel Avenida
Av Méndez Arcos 3 blocks east of Plaza 15 de Abril, T04-672 2828.
Helpful owner, parking.

$ Residencial Raldes
Cap Manchego 171, 1½ blocks from Plaza 15 de Abril, T04-672 2088, fernandoarel@gmail.com.
Well maintained, family-run, electric shower, cheaper with shared bath and fan, nice courtyard, small pool, parking.

Restaurants

Buena Vista

$$-$ La Plaza
on the plaza.

Elegant restaurant/bar with a terrace, wide range of international dishes, good service.

$ El Patujú
on the plaza.
The only café in town, serving excellent local coffee, teas, hot chocolate and a range of snacks. Also sells local produce and crafts.

What to do

Buena Vista
Amboró Travel & Adventure, *C Celso Sandoval, ½ block from the plaza, T7663 2102, amborotravel@hotmail.com.* Prices include transport to and from the park, guide and meals. Recommended.
Puertas del Amboró, *corner of the plaza, T03-932 2059.* They also offer full packages.

Transport

Buena Vista
Sindicato 10 de Febrero in Santa Cruz at Izozog 668 y Av Irala, 1er Anillo behind ex-terminal, T03-334 8435, 0730-1830, US$3 pp (private vehicle US$15), 1¾ hrs. Also another shared taxi company nearby, *micros* from Av Banzer y 3er Anillo and 'Línea 102' buses from regional section of Terminal Bimodal, US$1.50, 3 hrs. From Buena Vista, the access to the Amboró park is by gravel road, 4WD jeep or similar recommended as rivers have to been crossed. All operators and community ecolodge coordinators offer transport.

South of Santa Cruz a good paved road passes through Abapó, Camiri (Hotel Premier, Avenida Busch 60, T03-952 2204, is a decent place to stay), Boyuibe, Villamontes – access for the Trans-Chaco route to Paraguay – and Yacuiba, on the border with Argentina.

Villamontes *Colour map 3, C5.*

Villamontes, 500 km south of Santa Cruz, is renowned for fishing. It holds a Fiesta del Pescado in August. It is a hot, friendly, spread-out city on the north shore of the Río Pilcomayo, at the base of the Cordillera de Aguaragüe. The river cuts through this range (Parque Nacional Aguaragüe) forming **El Angosto**, a beautiful gorge. The road to Tarija, 280 km west, is cut in the cliffs along this gorge. At Plaza 6 de Agosto is the **Museo Héroes del Chaco** ① *Tue-Sun 0800-1200, 1400-1800, US$0.30*, with photographs, maps, artefacts, and battle models of the 1932-1935 Chaco War. There are a couple of ATMs. **Prodem** and various *cambios* are on Avenida Méndez Arcos.

From Villamontes, the road to Paraguay, almost all paved, runs east to **Ibibobo** (70 km). Motorists and bus travellers should carry extra water and some food, as climatic conditions are harsh and there is little traffic in case of a breakdown. Bolivian exit stamps are given at Ibibobo. If travelling by bus, passports are collected by driver and returned on arrival at Mcal Estigarribia (Paraguay), with Bolivian exit stamp. Paraguayan immigration and thorough drugs searches take place in Mcal Estigarribia. There are Paraguayan consulates in Santa Cruz (Avenida San Martín, Equipetrol Norte, Calle H Este Casa 8, T03-344 8989, scruzcongralpar@mre.gov.py), and Villamontes (Avenida Ingavi entre Héroes del Chaco y Cochabamba, T4672 3648, villamontesconsulpar@mre.gov.py). See Santa Cruz Transport (page 249) for international bus services. From Ibibobo to the Bolivian frontier post at Picada Sucre is 75 km, then it's 15 km to the actual border and another 8 km to the Paraguayan frontier post at **Fortín Infante Rivarola**. There are customs posts, but no police, immigration nor any other services at the border.

Yacuiba *Colour map 3, C5.*

Yacuiba is a prosperous city at the crossing to Pocitos in Argentina. The train service from Santa Cruz is slow and poor, road travel is a better option, or **Aerocon** flights to Santa Cruz (T901-10-5252, www.aerocon.bo). In Yacuiba, there are ATMs on Campero. The Argentine consul is at Santa Cruz 1540, entre Sucre y Crevaux (T04-682 2062). Passengers leaving Bolivia must disembark at Yacuiba, take a taxi to Pocitos on the border (US$0.50, beware unscrupulous drivers) and walk across to Argentina.

Where to stay

Villamontes

$$$-$$ El Rancho Olivo
Av Méndez Arcos opposite the train station, 15 blocks from the centre, T04-672 2059, www.elranchoolivo.com.
Lovely rooms, frigobar, nice grounds and pool, parking, excellent restaurant.

$ Gran Hotel Avenida
Av Méndez Arcos 3 blocks east of Plaza 15 de Abril, T04-672 2828.
Helpful owner, parking.

$ Residencial Raldes
Cap Manchego 171, 1½ blocks from Plaza 15 de Abril, T04-672 2088, fernandoarel@gmail.com.
Well maintained, family-run, electric shower, cheaper with shared bath and fan, nice courtyard, small pool, parking.

Yacuiba

Hotels include **$$ Valentín** (*San Martín 3271, T04-682 2645, www. valentinhotelbolivia.com*) and **$$ París**, (*Comercio 1175 y Campero, T04-682 2182*).

Transport

Villamontes
Bus
To **Yacuiba**, **Coop El Chaco**, Av Méndez Arcos y Ismael Montes, hourly 0630-1830, US$1.35, 1½ hrs. Cars from Av Montenegro y Cap Manchego, hourly or when full, 0630-1830, US$2, 1½ hrs. Long-distance buses from terminal on Av Méndez Arcos, 13 blocks east of Plaza 15 de Abril (taxi US$0.40 pp). To **Tarija** via Entre Ríos, mostly unpaved (sit on the right for best views), US$6, 10-11 hrs, several companies 1730-1930; for day travel, **Copacabana** may depart at 1030, 2-3 per week from the terminal; **Guadalupana**, Wed and Sat at 0930, from Coop El Chaco office. To **Santa Cruz**, several companies daily, US$5-8.50, some *bus-cama*, 7-8 hrs.

To **Asunción**, buses from Santa Cruz pass through 0200-0300, reserve a day earlier, US$35, about 15 hrs. 5 companies, offices all on Av Montenegro, either side of Av Méndez Arcos. Best are **Stel**, T04-672 3662, or Vicky Vides T7735 0934; **Yaciretá**, T04-672 2812, or Betty Borda, T7740 4111.

Yacuiba
Bus
To **Santa Cruz**, about 20 companies, mostly at night, 14 hrs, US$8.50-13. To **Tarija**, daily morning and evening.
Eastern Bolivia

Eastern Bolivia

The vast and rapidly developing plains to the east of the Eastern Cordillera are Bolivia's richest area in natural resources. For the visitor, the beautiful churches and rich traditions of the former Jesuit missions of Chiquitos are well worth a visit. Here too are some of the country's largest and wildest protected natural areas. This combination of natural beauty, living indigenous culture and Jesuit heritage make the region one of Bolivia's hidden gems.

Jesuit missions of Chiquitos

six dusty little towns, each boasting a beautiful colonial church

★Of the series of Jesuit missions established east of Santa Cruz between 1691 and 1760, six survive: San Javier, Concepción, San Rafael, Santa Ana, San Miguel and San José de Chiquitos. All have churches which are UNESCO World Heritage Sites. Many of these were built by the Swiss Jesuit, Padre Martin Schmidt (see Box, The Renaissance priest) and his pupils. As rich as the region is in cultural heritage, it is still very much a frontier and one of the best regions outside of the altiplano to sample true Bolivian culture. Tours can also be organized from Santa Cruz (see page 248).

San Javier (San Xavier) *Colour map 4, A2.*

The first Jesuit mission in Chiquitos (1691), San Javier's church was built by Padre Schmidt between 1749 and 1752. Some of the original wooden structure has survived more or less intact and restoration was undertaken between 1987 and 1992 by the Swiss Hans Roth, himself a former Jesuit. Subtle designs and floral patterns cover the ceiling, walls and carved columns. One of the bas-relief paintings on the high altar depicts Martin Schmidt playing the piano for his indigenous choir. It is a fine 30-minute walk (best in the afternoon light) to **Mirador El Bibosi** and the small **Parque Piedra de Los Apóstoles**. There is also good walking or all-terrain cycling in the surrounding countryside (no maps, ask around), thermal swimming holes at **Aguas Calientes**, and horse riding from several hotels. Tourist guides' association has an office in the **Alcaldía** ① *T7761 7902, or 7763 3203 for a guide.* Information also from the **Casa de Cultura** ① *on the plaza, T963 5149.*

Essential Jesuit missions of Chiquitos

Finding your feet

Two main routes encompass the Jesuit missions, both heading east from Santa Cruz as separate parts of Bolivia's share of the Pacific-to-Atlantic Interoceanic Highway (Carretera Bioceánica). The more southerly route is the completed section of the highway running from the Chilean and Peruvian borders through Cochabamba and Santa Cruz to Puerto Suárez, into Brazil at Corumbá, thence to the Atlantic. The more northerly road gives access to most of the mission towns, with a branch heading to Cuiabá (Brazil), via the border at San Matías.

Getting around

Southern route On the southern route there is plenty of public transport and you can start a tour of the missions by getting off the bus or train at San José de Chiquitos and heading north to San Rafael and the other towns.

Northern route Bus transport on the northern route is less frequent, but you can explore the area in a hired vehicle, preferably 4WD. From Santa Cruz head east on Avenida Virgen de Cotoca to **Cotoca** (18 km). About 1 km before the entrance to the town, turn right on an unsigned road after a petrol station to **Puerto Pailas** (27 km from Santa Cruz) where it crosses the Río Grande and continues to **Pailón** (another 18 km). Pay a US$3 toll and take the road north towards Trinidad (don't turn right to Puerto Suárez) to **Los Troncos** (120 km from Santa Cruz), **San Julián** (another 30 km) and **San Ramón** (another 30 km), where the road branches

northwest to Trinidad and northeast – the road you want – to **San Javier**, 220 km from Santa Cruz. The road is paved, but bumpy in parts.

The road then heads east for 60 km to **Concepción**, passing the turn-offs to Parque Nacional Noel Kempff Mercado, and on to **San Ignacio de Velasco**, 160 km, four hours from Concepción. Thirty kilometres out of Concepción the pavement gives way to packed earth for the rest of the way. Two roads from San Ignacio head south to **San Rafael**; one via **San Miguel** and the other via **Santa Ana** (these three mission settlements are best visited as day trips from San Ignacio; otherwise, if in private transport doing the circuit, the shortest route is from San Ignacio to San Miguel and San Rafael – a good, fast road – then up to Santa Ana and back down again). The road east from San Ignacio to San Matías and the Brazilian border, 323 km, can be a taxing trip on barely passable roads. From San Rafael, 68 km from San Ignacio, the road heads south to **San José de Chiquitos** (142 km). From here you can complete the circuit by catching a bus or the Quijarro–Santa Cruz train back to Santa Cruz.

When to go

The best time to visit is from January onwards, when the fruit is in season, but September, after the spring rains begin, is also nice. The months when most rain falls are October to March.

Time required

You should spend at least five days on the Jesuit missions route.

Concepción *Colour map 4, A2.*

The lovely town is dominated by its magnificent **cathedral** ① *0700-2000, tours 1000, 1500, donation invited*, completed by Padre Schmidt and Juan Messner in 1756 and totally restored by Hans Roth (1975-1986). The interior of this beautiful church has an altar of laminated silver. In front of the church is a bell-cum-clock tower housing the original bells and behind it are well-restored cloisters. On the plaza, forming part of the Jesuit complex, is the **Museo Misional** ① *Mon-Sat 0800-1200, 1430-1830, Sun 1000-1230, US$3.50*, which has an *artesanía* shop. The ticket also gives entry to the **Hans Roth Museum**, dedicated to the restoration process. Visit also the **Museo Antropológico de la Chiquitania** ① *16 de Septiembre y Tte Capoblanco, 0800-1200, 1400-1800, free*, which explains the life of the indigenous peoples of the region. It has a café and guesthouse. The **Municipal tourist office** ① *Lucas Caballero y Cabo Rodríguez, one block from plaza, T03-964 3057*, can arrange trips to nearby recreational areas, ranches and communities. An **Asociación de Guías Locales** ① *south side of plaza, contact Ysabel Supepi, T7604 7085; or Hilario Orellana, T7534 3734*, also offers tours to local communities many of which are developing grass-roots tourism projects: eg **Santa Rita**, **San Andrés** and **El Carmen**. With a week's advance notice, they can also organize private concerts with 30 to 40 musicians. There are various restaurants in town and many places sell wood carvings, traditional fabrics and clothing.

San Ignacio de Velasco *Colour map 4, B3.*

This is the main commercial and transport hub of the region, with road links to Brazil. A lack of funds for restoration led to the demolition of San Ignacio's replacement Jesuit church in 1948, the original having burnt down in 1808. A modern replica contains the elaborate high altar, pulpit and paintings and statues of saints. Tourist information office at **Casa de la Cultura** ① *La Paz y Comercio, on the plaza, T03-962 2056 ext 122, culturayturismo.siv@gmail.com, Mon-Fri 0800-1200, 1430-1830*, can help organize guides and visits to local music schools. The **Centro Artesanal** ① *Santa Cruz entre Bolívar y Oruro, Mon-Sat 0800-1930, Sun 0800-1200*, sells lovely textile and wood crafts. There is community tourism in the villages of **San Juancito**, 18 km from San Ignacio, where organic coffee is grown, and **San Rafael de Sutuquiña**, 5 km; both have artisans. **Laguna Guapomó** reservoir on the edge of San Ignacio is good for swimming and fishing. There is only one ATM in town, best take some cash.

Santa Ana, San Rafael and San Miguel de Velasco *Colour map 4, B3.*

These three small towns are less visited than some others along the missions circuit. Allow at least two days if travelling independently from San Ignacio: you can take a bus to Santa Ana in the afternoon, stay overnight, then continue to San Rafael the next afternoon and return to San Ignacio via San Miguel on Tuesday, Thursday or Sunday (see Transport, page 275). A day trip by taxi from San Ignacio costs about US$65

> **Tip...**
> Santa Ana, San Rafael and San Miguel de Velasco are best visited as day trips from San Ignacio.

BACKGROUND

The Jesuits in Bolivia

The Jesuits first arrived in Lima, Peru, in 1569 and were assigned to the religious instruction of the Aymaras on Lake Titicaca. They moved to Paraguay where they set up an autonomous religious state. It was from there that they expanded northwards to the vast unexplored region of the eastern lowlands of Bolivia, reaching Santa Cruz only in 1587.

The Jesuits then set about the seemingly impossible task of converting the various indigenous communities to Christianity and persuading them first to build and then live together in self-sufficient settlements. These settlements of 2000-4000 inhabitants, known as *reducciones*, were organized into productive units, headed by two or three Jesuit priests. Architects, sculptors and musicians were enlisted to help construct the churches and communities. They also formed military units which, for a time, were the strongest and best trained on the continent. These armies provided a defence against the slave-hunting Portuguese in Brazil and the more aggressive native groups.

Politically, the settlements were ruled by the Audiencia de Charcas and ecclesiastically by the Bishop of Santa Cruz, but in reality, due to their isolation, they enjoyed a considerable degree of independence. The internal administration was the responsibility of a council of eight indigenous people, each of whom represented an ethnic group, and who met daily to receive the orders of the priests.

In 18th-century terms the *reducciones* were run on remarkably democratic principles. The land and the workshops were the property of the community and work was obligatory for all able-bodied members. Nevertheless, the Jesuits' prime concern was to save souls, therefore the indigenous customs and beliefs were largely suppressed. So effectively were Christian values imposed on the people that little is known about the indigenous cultures of this region except what symbolism the natives were sometimes able to express in their ingenious carvings, replicas of which still decorate the mission churches today.

In saying that, however, the establishment of the *reducciones* brought economic advantages to this previously barren corner of Bolivia. Such was the success of the Jesuits' commercial network with the Quechuas and Aymaras of the highlands that a surplus was sent in the form of money to Europe as well as being used to enhance the splendour of the churches. These massive temples were the biggest and most beautiful in the Americas, each one built by hand by the *indígenas* under the supervision of the priests. Because of the distances between the mission settlements, each church is distinctive from the others.

The Jesuits also trained the *indígenas* to become great craftsmen in wood and precious metals. They even taught them to make and play unfamiliar musical instruments such as the violin and the harp. Each settlement had its own orchestra, which performed concerts and even Italian baroque operas. The orchestral music fascinated the indigenous peoples and was a factor in persuading them to partake in the Jesuit experiment. More important than that, though, in ensuring their full cooperation was the fact that those who formed part of the *reducciones* remained free from the system of *encomiendas*, whereby groups of labourers were sent to the mines of Potosí.

The expulsion of the Jesuits

Despite the economic and religious success of the Jesuit settlements and the fact that they played a large part in limiting the territorial ambitions of Portuguese Brazil, in 1767 the missions were dismantled by royal and papal decree and the Jesuits expelled from the continent.

There were various reasons given for the expulsion, some less than credible. Basically, the Spanish Crown came to believe the Jesuits had usurped too much power from the state. Furthermore, this was the age of enlightenment and the militant Jesuits were seen as a major obstacle to the progress of reason. Finally, the Jesuits' success caused jealously amongst some of the older religious orders, many of whom wanted to establish inroads themselves in the new continent.

Whatever the real motivation, many of the settlements were abandoned and the inhabitants suffered the consequences. The priests who replaced the Jesuits treated the indigenous peoples badly, fomenting war and hatred among the disparate groups while prospering from the livestock that had been introduced to the region. Even after independence the exploitation of the local people continued during the years of the rubber boom. Scarcely 50 years after the expulsion of the Jesuits, the missions had become decrepit shanty towns.

Restoration of the mission churches

More than a century of isolation followed. But the mission buildings' survival was precarious at best, and the tropical climate meant they deteriorated badly. By the 1950s, all of them were well on the way to ruin, although each continued to function as a church. Their salvation came in the form of a Swiss architect, Hans Roth, who dedicated 27 years to the restoration of the churches built by his fellow countryman, Father Martin Schmidt (see box, page 271), more than two centuries before. Sadly, he developed lung cancer and died in 1999 in Austria, aged 65, before he could see the restoration work completed. At the time, he was still looking for an expert to translate the missionaries' baroque music.

Fortunately, in recent decades, much has been done to carefully promote the heritage of these Jesuit mission churches and their towns. A bi-annual Festival de Música Renacentista y Barroca Americana is held every even year in the city of Santa Cruz and throughout the region (see Festivals, page 248), the astonishing sacred art of Chiquitania is displayed in museums all over the world, and a Hans Roth Museum has been opened in Concepción. Church services are exceptionally well attended, with Chuiquitano musicians and choirs sometimes performing at Sunday Mass. The centres of the towns have been beautifully refurbished and are a pleasure to stroll around. Along with Parque Nacional Noel Kempff Mercado, one could argue that the Jesuit missions are the best-preserved and most 'authentic' patrimonies to be found in Bolivia.

or an all-inclusive tour can be arranged by **Parador Santa Ana** (see Where to stay, page 273). Local guides are available, US$10.

The church in Santa Ana (town founded 1755, church constructed 1773-1780, after the expulsion of the Jesuits), is a lovely wooden building. It is the most authentic of all the Jesuit *templos* and Santa Ana is a particularly authentic little village. The tourist office on the plaza can provide guides. Simple economical accommodation is available (see below).

San Rafael's church was completed by Padre Schmidt in 1748. It is one of the most beautifully restored, with mica-covered interior walls and frescoes in beige paint over the exterior. There are restaurants near the plaza. For the tourist information office, call T03-962 4022.

The frescoes on the façade of the church (1752-1759) at San Miguel depict St Peter and St Paul; designs in brown and yellow cover all the interior and the exterior side walls. The mission runs three schools and a workshop; the sisters are very welcoming and will gladly show tourists around. There is a **Museo Etnofolclórico**, off the Plaza at Calle Betania; next door is the Municipalidad/Casa de la Cultura, with a tourist information office, T03-962 4222. San Miguel has many workshops and rivals San Ignacio for the quality of its Jesuit-inspired art.

San José de Chiquitos *Colour map 4, B3.*

One complete side of the plaza is occupied by the superbly restored frontage of the Jesuit mission complex of four buildings and a bell tower, begun in the mid-1740s. Best light for photography is in the afternoon. The stone buildings, in baroque style, are connected by a wall. They are the workshops (1754); the church (1747) with its undulating façade; the four-storey bell tower (1748) and the mortuary (*la bóveda* – 1750), with one central window but no entrance in its severe frontage. The complex and **Museo** ① *Mon-Fri 0800-1200, 1430-1800, Sat-Sun 0900-1200, 1500-1800, entry US$3,* are well worth visiting. Behind are the *colegio* and workshops, which house the **Escuela Municipal de Música**; visits to rehearsals and performances can be arranged by the tourist office. **InfoTur** ① *in the Municipio, C Velasco, ½ block from plaza, T03-972 2084, Mon-Fri 0800-1200, 1430-1830,* which has information and arranges various tours; there is internet upstairs. On Mondays, Mennonites bring their produce to San José and buy provisions. The colonies are 50 km west and the Mennonites, who speak English, German, Plattdeutsch and Spanish, are happy to talk about their way of life. There is only one ATM in town, best take some cash.

About 2 km south from San José is the 17,000 ha **Parque Nacional Histórico Santa Cruz la Vieja** ① *www.biobol.org.* It has a monument to the original site of Santa Cruz (founded 1561) and a *mirador* with great views. The park's heavily forested hills contain much animal and bird life. There are various trails for hiking; guides can be organized by the tourist office in San José. It gets very hot so start early, allow over one hour to get there on foot (or hire a vehicle) and take plenty of water and insect repellent. There is also good walking with lovely views at **Cerro Turubó** and the **Serranía de San José**, both outside San José.

ON THE ROAD

The Renaissance priest

The majority of the Jesuits naturally came from Spain, but one of the factors in the efficiency of their methods may have been the many priests who also came from the countries of northern and central Europe. One of these was Father Martin Schmidt, a Swiss musician and architect, born in 1694. Father Schmidt began his education with the Jesuits in Lucerne and in 1728 travelled from Cádiz to Buenos Aires. Later he travelled through Bolivia before settling in Santa Cruz. Despite having no formal training, he made all kinds of instruments for the communities and even built organs for the churches. He also taught indigenous people to play them and wrote music, some of which is still played today on traditional instruments. As if that wasn't enough, Father Schmidt also built the churches of San Rafael, San Javier and Concepción and the altars of some of the others. He even published a Spanish-Chiquitano dictionary based on his knowledge of all the dialects of the region. By the time of the expulsion of the Jesuits in 1767 he was 73 years old. He died in Lucerne in 1772.

East of San José de Chiquitos

Paving of the highway from Santa Cruz east to Brazil in 2011 opened up this once-isolated region of friendly villages surrounded by natural wonders. The village of **Chochís**, 90 km east of San José de Chiquitos, is known for its sanctuary of the Virgen Asunta built by Hans Roth in 1988 (one of his few major works not connected with restoring Jesuit missions). The large sanctuary is built at the foot of an impressive red sandstone outcrop called **La Torre**, 2 km from town. Along the rail line from Chochís toward La Torre is a signed trail leading to the **Velo de Novia** waterfall, a pleasant one- to two-hour walk. A much more challenging hike climbs 800 m to the flat top of **Cerro de Chochís**, where you can camp or return to town in a long day; guide required.

Chochís is at the western end of the **Serranía de Chiquitos**, a flat-topped mountain range running east–west, north of the highway and railroad. It is filled with rich vegetation, caves, petroglyphs, waterfalls, birds and butterflies. These hills are part of the 262,000-ha **Reserva Valle de Tucavaca** (www.biobol.org) which protects unique Chiquitano dry forest and offers great hiking opportunities. Various community tourism projects are underway in the area and local guides are available in the towns.

Forty kilometers east of Chochís is **Roboré**, the regional centre and transport hub. The **Oficina de Turismo** ⓘ *Av Ejército, Parque Urbano, T7761 8280, http:// turismoenrobore.com,* has information about local excursions including **Los Helechos** and **Totaisales**, two lovely bathing spots in the forest, Chochís and Santiago de Chiquitos. Roboré is an old garrison town dating back to the Chaco War and retains a strong military presence. The local fiesta is 25 October.

Seven kilometres east of Roboré, a paved road branches northeast and in 14 km reaches the particularly friendly village of **Santiago de Chiquitos**, within the Reserva Valle de Tucavaca. Founded in 1754, Santiago was one of the last missions built in Chiquitania. There are good accommodations and more good walking to a fine mirador, natural stone arches and caves with petroglyphs; guides are available in town. A poor road continues 150 km past Santiago to **Santo Corazón**, a still-isolated Jesuit mission town (the last one built, 1760) inside **Área Natural de Manejo Integrado San Matías** ⓘ www.biobol.org.

Aguas Calientes is 15 km east of Roboré along the rail line and highway to Brazil. The hot little village is unimpressive but nearby is a river of crystal-clear thermal water, teeming with little fish and bird life. There are several spots with facilities for bathing and camping, which is preferable to the basic accommodations in town. There are many tiny biting sand-flies, so your tent should have good netting. Soaking in the thermal water amid the sights and sounds of the surrounding forest at dawn or on a moonlit night is amazing.

Listings Jesuit missions of Chiquitos

Where to stay

San Javier

$ Alojamiento San Xavier
C Santa Cruz, T03-963 5038.
Cheaper without bath, electric shower, garden, nice sitting area. Recommended.

$ Residencial Chiquitano
Av Santa Cruz (Av José de Arce), ½ block from plaza, T03-963 5072.
Simple rooms, fan, large patio, good value.

Concepción

$$ Gran Hotel Concepción
On plaza, T03-964 3031, www.granhotelconcepcion.com.bo.
Excellent service, buffet breakfast, pool, gardens, bar, very comfortable. Highly recommended.

$$ Hotel Chiquitos
End of Av Killian, T03-964 3153, hotel_chiquitos@hotmail.com.

Colonial style construction, ample rooms, frigobar, pool, gardens and sports fields, orchid nursery, parking. Tours available. Recommended.

$$-$ Oasis Chiquitano
S Saucedo 225, 1½ blocks from plaza, T03-964 3223/7602 5442.
Buffet breakfast, pool, nice patio with flowers.

$ Colonial
Ñuflo de Chávez 7, ½ block from plaza, T03-964 3050.
Economical place, hammocks on ample veranda, parking, breakfast available.

$ Residencial Westfalia
Saucedo 205, 2 blocks from plaza, T03-964 3040.
Cheaper without bath, German-owned, nice patio, good value.

San Ignacio de Velasco

$$$ La Misión
Libertad, on plaza, T03-962 2333, www.hotel-lamision.com.

Upmarket hotel, restaurant, meeting rooms, pool, parking, downstairs rooms have bath tubs.

$$ Apart Hotel San Ignacio
24 de Septiembre y Cochabamba, T03-962 2157, www.aparthotel-sanignacio.com.
Comfortable rooms, nice grounds, pool, hammocks, parking. Despite the name, no apartments or kitchenettes.

$$ Parador Santa Ana
Libertad entre Sucre y Cochabamba, T03-962 2075, www.paradorsantaana.blogspot.com.
Beautiful house with small patio, tastefully decorated, 5 comfortable rooms, good breakfast, knowledgeable owner arranges tours, credit cards accepted. Recommended.

$$ San Ignacio Miguel Areiger
Plaza 31 de Julio, T03-962 2283.
In a beautifully restored former episcopal mansion, non-profit (run by diocese, funds support poor youth in the community), breakfast.

$ Residencial Bethania
Velasco y Cochabamba, T03-962 2307.
Simple rooms with shared bath, electric shower, small patio, economical and good value.

Santa Ana
Simple economical accommodation is available at **Comunidad Valenciana**, T03-980 2098.

San Rafael
Hotel Paradita, T03-962 4008, and others ($).

San José de Chiquitos

$$$ Villa Chiquitana
C 9 de Abril, 6 blocks from plaza, T7315 5803, www.villachiquitana.com.
Charming hotel built in traditional style, restaurant open to public, frigobar, pool (US$3 for non-guests), garden, parking, craft shop, tour agency. French-run.

$ Turubó
Bolívar on the plaza, T03-972 2037, hotelturubo on Facebook.
With a/c or fan, electric shower, variety of different rooms, ask to see one before checking-in, good location.

East of San José de Chiquitos
Chochís
$ Ecoalbergue de Chochís
1 km west of town along the rail line, T7263 9467; Santa Cruz contact: **Probioma**, *T03-343 1332, www. probioma.org.bo.*
Simple community-run lodging in 2 cabins, shared bath, cold water, small kitchen, screened hammock area, camping US$3.50 pp, meals on advance request.

$ El Peregrino
on the plaza, T7313 1881.
Simple rooms in a family home, some with fan and fridge, shared bath, electric shower, ample yard, camping possible.

Roboré

$$ Anahí
Obispo Santiesteban 1½ blocks from plaza, T03-974 2362.
Comfortable rooms with electric shower, nice patio, parking, kitchen and washing facilities, owner runs tours.

$$ Choboreca
Av La Paz 710, T03-974 2566,
www.hotelchaboreca.com.
Nice hotel, rooms with a/c. Several other
places to stay in town.

Santiago de Chiquitos
There are various *alojamientos familiares*
around town, all simple to basic.

$$ Beula
On the plaza, T03-313 6274,
http://hotelbeula.com.
Comfortable hotel in traditional style,
good breakfast, frigobar. Unexpectedly
upmarket for such a remote location.

$ El Convento
on plaza next to the church, T7890 2943.
Former convent with simple rooms, one
has private bath, lovely garden, hot and
no fan but clean and good value.

$ Panorama
1 km north of plaza, T03-313 6286,
katmil@bolivia.com.
Simple rooms with shared bath and a
family farm, friendly owners Katherine
and Milton Whittaker sell excellent
home-made dairy products and jams,
they are knowledgeable about the area
and offer volunteer opportunities.

Aguas Calientes
$$ Cabañas Canaan
Across the road from Los Hervores baths,
T7467 7316.
Simple wooden cabins, cold water, fan,
restaurant, rather overpriced but better
than the basic places in town.

$ Camping El Tucán
1 km from town on the road to Los
Hervores baths, T7262 0168, www.
aguascalientesmiraflores.com.bo.
Lovely ample grounds with clean

bathrooms, electric showers, barbecues,
small pier by the river.

Restaurants

San Javier

$$ Ganadero
In Asociación de Ganaderos on plaza.
Excellent steaks. Other eateries around
the plaza.

Concepción

$ El Buen Gusto
North side of plaza.
Set meals and regional specialities.

San Ignacio de Velasco

$ Club Social
Comercio on the plaza. Daily 1130-1500.
Decent set lunch.

Panadería Juanita
Comercio y Sucre.
Good bakery.

Mi Nonna
C Velasco y Cochabamba.
1700-2400, closed Tue. Café serving
cappuccino, sandwiches, salads
and pasta.

San José de Chiquitos

$$ Sabor y Arte
Bolívar y Mons Santisteban, by the plaza.
Tue-Sun 1800-2300.
International dishes, for innovation try
their coca-leaf ravioli, nice ambience,
French/Bolivian-run.

$$-$ Rancho Brasilero
by main road, 5 blocks from plaza. Daily
0900-1530.
Good Brazilian-style buffet, all you can
eat grill on weekends.

East of San José de Chiquitos
Roboré
Several restaurants around the plaza,
including:

$ Casino Militar
on the plaza, daily for lunch and dinner.
Set meals and à la carte.

Santiago de Chiquitos

$ Churupa
½ block from plaza.
Set meals (go early or reserve your meal
in advance) and à la carte. Best in town.

Festivals

The region celebrates the **Festival
de Música Renacentista y Barroca
Americana** every even year (next in
2016). Many towns have their own
orchestras, which play Jesuit-era music
on a regular basis. **Semana Santa** (Holy
Week) celebrations are elaborate and
interesting throughout the region.

San Javier
29 Jun **Feast of St Peter and St Paul**,
best for viewing traditional costumes,
dances and music.
3 Dec **Patron saint's fiesta**.

Concepción
2nd week Oct **Orchid festival**.
8 Dec **Fiesta de la Inmaculada
Concepción**.

San Ignacio de Velasco
31 Jul **Patron saint's day**, preceded by
a cattle fair.

Santa Ana
26 Jul **Fiesta de Santa Ana**.

San Rafael
24 Oct **Patron saint's day**, with
traditional dancing.

San Miguel de Velasco
29 Sep **Patron saint's day**.

San José de Chiquitos
1 May **Fiesta de San José**, preceded by
a week of folkloric and other events.

Transport

San Javier
Bus and trufi
Línea 102, T03-346 3993, from Santa
Cruz Terminal Bimodal regional
departures area, 2 a day, 4 hrs, US$3,
continue to **Concepción**. Also Flota 31
del Este (poor buses, T03-334 9390, same
price) and **Jenecherú**, T03-348 8618,
daily at 2000, US$4.25, *bus-cama* US$5,
continuing to Concepción and, on Tue,
Thu, Sat, **San Ignacio**. Various taxi-*trufi*
companies also operate from regional
departures area, US$5, 3½ hrs.

Concepción
Bus
To/from **Santa Cruz**, companies as
above, US$3.55, 6½ hrs, and **Jenecherú**,
as above, US$5-5.75. To **San Ignacio de
Velasco**, buses pass though from Santa
Cruz (many at night); **31 del Este** leaves
from C Germán Busch in Concepción.
Concepción to **San Javier**, 1 hr, US$1.50.

San Ignacio de Velasco

Bus and trufi
From **Santa Cruz**, companies as above,
plus Trans Bolivia (daily, T03-336 3866),
from Terminal Bimodal depart 1830-
2000, including **Jenecherú** (Tue, Thu,
Sat, most luxurious buses, see above),

US$7, *bus-cama* US$7.75, 10 hrs; returning 1800-1900. For daytime services, *trufis* from regional departures area 0900 daily (with minimum 7 passengers), US$15, 8 hrs. To **San José de Chiquitos**, see San José Transport, below. To **San Rafael** (US$2, 2½ hrs) via **Santa Ana** (US$1, 1 hr) **Expreso Baruc**, 24 de Septiembre y Kennedy, daily at 1400; returning 0600. To **San Miguel**, *trufis* leave when full from Mercado de Comida, US$1.75, 40 mins, bus US$0.75. Trans Bolivia and Jenecherú services also go to San Miguel and San Rafael (US$6.50-7.75 from Santa Cruz). To **San Matías** (for Cáceres, Brazil) several daily passing through from Santa Cruz starting 0400, US$12, 8 hrs. To **Pontes e Lacerda** (Brazil), **Rápido Monte Cristo**, from Club Social on the plaza, Wed and Sat 0900, US$22, 8-9 hrs; returning Tue and Fri, 0630. All roads to Brazil are poor. The best option to Pontes e Lacerda is via Vila Bela (Brazil), used by **Amanda Tours** (T7608 8476 in Bolivia, T65-9926 8522 in Brazil), from **El Corralito** restaurant by the market, Tue, Thu, Sun 0830, US$28; returning Mon, Wed, Fri 0600.

San José de Chiquitos
Bus and trufi

To **Santa Cruz** many companies pass through starting 1700 daily, US$7-10.55. Also *trufis*, leave when full, US$10, 3½ hrs. To **Puerto Suárez**, buses pass through 1600-2300, US$10, 4 hrs. To **San Ignacio de Velasco** via San Rafael and San Miguel, **Flota Universal** (poor road, terrible buses), Mon, Wed, Fri, Sat at 0700, US$5, 5 hrs, returning 1400; also **31 de Julio**, Tue, Thu, Sun from San Ignacio at 0645, returning 1500.

Train
Westbound, the **Ferrobús** passes through San José Tue, Thu, Sat at 0150, arriving Santa Cruz 0700; **Expreso Oriental**, Tue, Thu, Sun 2305, arriving 0540. Eastbound, the **Ferrobus** passes through San José Tue, Thu, Sun 2308, arriving Quijarro 0700 next day; **Expreso Oriental** Mon, Wed, Fri 1930, arriving 0602 next day. See Santa Cruz Transport (page 249) and www.fo.com.bo for fares and additional information.

East of San José de Chiquitos
Bus and trufi

To **Chochís** from San José de Chiquitos, with **Perla del Oriente**, daily 0800 and 1500, US$3, 2 hrs; continuing to **Roboré**, US$1, 1 hr more; Roboré to San José via Chochís 0815 and 1430. Roboré bus terminal is by the highway, a long walk from town, but some buses go by the plaza before leaving; enquire locally. From **Santiago de Chiquitos** to Roboré, Mon-Sat at 0700, US$1, 45 mins; returning 1000; taxi Roboré–Santiago about US$15. Buses to/from Quijarro stop at **Aguas Calientes**; taxi Roboré–Aguas Calientes about US$22 return. From Roboré to **Santa Cruz**, several companies, from US$7, 7-9 hrs; also *trufis* 0900, 1400, 1800, US$14.50, 5 hrs. From Roboré to **Quijarro** with **Perla del Oriente**, 4 daily, US$4, 4 hrs; also *trufis* leave when full, US$8, 3 hrs.

Train
All trains stop in Roboré (see www. fo.com.bo), but not in Chochís or Aguas Calientes. Enquire in advance if they might stop to let you off at these stations.

Parque Nacional Kaa-Iya del Gran Chaco

the ultimate destination for die-hard adventurers

Larger than Belgium and not much smaller than Switzerland, the enormous Parque Nacional Kaa-Iya del Gran Chaco, is in southeastern Santa Cruz department. At 3,441,115 ha, it the largest national park in the country and possibly the continent, if not the entire hemisphere and is among the most difficult to access. San José de Chiquitos to the north of the park and Camiri to the west are the only places from which tracks lead into the park, but there is no organized transport of any sort. A 4WD vehicle may get in in the dry season.

Tip...
GPS, absolute self-sufficiency and careful planning of your expedition are essential as there are no facilities of any kind.

Founded in 1995 by a consortium of local indigenous peoples in conjunction with several environmental non-profit organizations, this is about as far off the beaten track as one can get. It is also the only national park in the world whose administration is entrusted to indigenous peoples who live within its borders, the Izoceño-Guaraní Capitanía del Alto y Bajo Izozog (CABI). So remote is Kaa-Iya that anthropologists speculate that areas within it have never seen even native tribes, let alone latter-day explorers. The majority of the park is uncharted and unknown except by local peoples, although parts of it were a battleground during the Chaco War between Bolivia and Paraguay. The mysterious **Bañados del Izozog** wetlands, where the sizeable Río Parapeti simply disappears, are within the park, and it plays host to over 1500 species of bird and animal, including jaguar, puma, and a large number of rare desert-habitat creatures. It also contains a unique desert forest ecosystem that has drawn considerable scientific interest. For further information, contact **SERNAP** ① *Calle 9 Oeste 138, Barrio Equipetrol in Santa Cruz, T03-339 4310, www.sernap.gob.bo, or www.biobiol.org.*

Parque Nacional Noel Kempff Mercado

remote, pristine park with uparalleled wildlife spotting

★In the far northeast corner of Santa Cruz Department, Parque Nacional Noel Kempff Mercado (named after a Bolivian conservation pioneer who was killed while flying over the park), is one of the world's most diverse natural habitats. This World Heritage Site covers 1,523,446 ha and encompasses seven ecosystems. Highlights include the Huanchaca or Caparú Plateau, which with its 200-500 m sheer cliffs and tumbling waterfalls is a candidate for Sir Arthur Conan Doyle's *Lost World* (Colonel Percy Fawcett, who discovered the plateau in 1910, was a friend of Conan Doyle).

The southwestern section of the park is reached from the village of **Florida**, where there is a ranger station and a community tourism project offering basic accommodation and guides (guide compulsory, US$25 per day). It is 65 km from Florida to the trailhead (pickup US$60 one way), which provides access to the

80-m-high **El Encanto** waterfall and the climb to the plateau; allow five to six days for the return excursion. In the northeastern section of the park are the great **Arco Iris** and **Federico Ahlfeld** waterfalls, both on the Río Paucerna and accessible mid-December to May when water levels are sufficiently high. Access is either from the Bolivian village of **Piso Firme** or the Brazilian town of **Pimenteiras do Oeste**; in all cases you must be accompanied by a Bolivian boatman/guide, available in Piso Firme and organized by the park office in San Ignacio. It is six to seven hours by motorized canoe from Piso Firme to a shelter near the Ahlfeld waterfall, and a full day's walk from there to Arco Iris.

The wildlife count in the Noel Kempff Mercado park is astounding – so far over 620 bird species have been identified, which is approximately one-quarter of all the birds in the neotropics. These include nine types of macaw such as the blue and yellow, scarlet, golden-collared, and chestnut-fronted; over 20 species of parrot; crimson-bellied parakeets; red-necked aracari; the Amazonian umbrella bird; the pompadour cotinga; helmeted manakin; curl-crested jays; hoatzin and harpy eagles. Among the many large mammals frequently sighted are the tapir, grey and red brocket deer, silvery marmoset, and spider and black howler monkeys. Giant otter and capybara are relatively common along the Iténez and Paucerna rivers, as are jabiru and the maguari stork. Giant anteaters, marsh deer and the rare maned wolf inhabit the western grasslands and the endangered pampas deer roam the dry twisted forest of the Huanchaca Plateau. There's also a chance of seeing jaguars where the narrow Río Paucerna winds its way through dense towering rainforest on its way to join the Río Iténez. Also present are 74 species of reptile and 110 species of orchid.

ON THE ROAD

Discovering the Lost World

The first to discover the Huanchaca Plateau was the legendary British explorer Colonel Percy Fawcett. He did so in 1910 while exploring the Río Verde and demarcating the border for the Bolivian government. Colonel Fawcett was the archetypal early 20th-century explorer. Disappearing into the heart of the Amazon on his last expedition in 1925, never to be seen again, he became almost as much of a legend as the lost city for which he tirelessly searched. His life of jungle exploration was an inspiration to many. It is claimed that Arthur Conan Doyle, who was a friend of the colonel's, wrote *The Lost World* as a result of a conversation about the flat-topped Huanchaca when he was shown photographs of the apparently unscaleable cliffs and imagined an isolated plateau inhabited by dinosaurs. From the descriptions given in *The Lost World*, this link appears to be real, as the details closely match the landscape of the park. Despite various other theories, notably that of Mount Roraima (located at the intersection of Brazil, Venezuela and Guyana), Huanchaca is accepted by most Doyle scholars. For a detailed account of Colonel Fawcett's adventures see *Exploration Fawcett* (Century, 1988).

Listings Parque Nacional Noel Kempff Mercado

Transport

Road/bus

All overland journeys are long and arduous, take supplies. The unpaved roads to the park turn off the Concepción–San Ignacio road at Santa Rosa de la Roca, 79 km before San Ignacio (the better route, well signed, petrol at the turn-off), or Carmen Ruiz, 47 km before San Ignacio. Florida is 200 km northeast. Paso Firme is a further 129 km, via Porvenir, on an abysmal road. A bus runs **Santa Cruz–Piso Firme** (via Santa Rosa de la Roca, not San Ignacio), **Trans Bolivia**, C Melchor Pinto entre 2do y 3er Anillo, T03-336 3866, once a week (schedule changes often), US$24, 16 hrs minimum, very rough and exhausting. Otherwise the park can be reached by hired 4WD vehicle (US$100 a day) or on a tour. For **Pimenteiras do Oeste** (Brazil) see San Ignacio Transport (above) to Pontes e Lacerda and make connections there via Vilhena. This route is no easier than on the Bolivian side. Even hiring a 4WD vehicle to get to the park via Brazil is hard-going.

There are four routes from Santa Cruz: by air to Puerto Suárez, by rail or road to Quijarro (fully paved), by road to San Matías (a busy border town reported unsafe due to drug smuggling), and via San Ignacio de Velasco to either Vila Bela or Pontes e Lacerda (both in Brazil). Parque Nacional Otuquis and Parque Nacional San Matías can both be reached on tours from Puerto Suárez.

Puerto Suárez is near Quijarro and this route leads to Corumbá on the Brazilian side, from where there is access to the southern Pantanal. The San Matías and Vila Bela/Pontes roads both link to Cáceres, Cuiabá and the northern Pantanal in Brazil. There are immigration posts of both countries on all routes except Vila Bela/Pontes. If travelling this way get your Bolivian exit stamp in San Ignacio (immigration office near Jenecherú bus station) and Brazilian entry stamp in Cáceres or Vilhena. There may be strict customs and drugs checks entering Brazil, no fresh food may be taken from Bolivia.

Parque Nacional Otuquis *Colour map 4, C5.*

SERNAP office: final Av Adolfo Rau, T03-976 3270, Puerto Suárez. Entry to the park is free but all visitors must register. Ask around Puerto Suaréz to see if any tours are being offered.

Carved out of the southern Pantanal in 1997, this 1,005,950 sq-km park is one of Bolivia's most remote habitats. Until recently, it was virgin wilderness at every turn except for a small enclave near Puerto Suárez, separate from the main park, the **Zona Río Pimiento**, which is easily reached from the city.

Otuquis' large southern sector potentially offers everything a trip to the Brazilian Pantanal does, only without any of its better-known counterpart's amenities. Wildlife abounds, especially aquatic mammals and reptiles, and the species count is said to rival that of Amboró in some areas. Caimans, tigers, jaguars, otters, egrets, even rare river dolphins have been spotted, along with some of the world's largest flocks of toucans and parrots. It is a RAMSAR site.

> **Tip...**
> Be sure to carry all food and gear with you as there are no services within the park itself.

It does, however, lie close to the world's largest iron ore deposit of **Cerro Mutún**, on the border with Brazil. Attempts to exploit the mineral had, until 2014, been unsuccessful for various reasons, but in September of that year the Bolivian government signed an accord with China to finance the project. If not managed properly, this poses a major threat to the local habitat, on both sides of the Bolivia–Brazil border.

Access to Otuquis is by road to **San Juan** near Cerro Mutún. Minibuses run the 29 km from Puerto Suárez to San Juan at weekends (US$2, 30 minutes) or take a taxi (US$10). **Puerto Busch**, at the south end of the park, is about 200 km further south on the Río Paraguay. It is connected to San Juan by a rough track that is sometimes passable in the dry season.

Parque Nacional San Matías *Colour map 4, B5.*
Information can be found at the SERNAP office in Santa Cruz (see page 245)

North of the Zona Río Pimiento is Parque Nacional San Matías, at 2,918,500 ha, Bolivia's second-largest park. Owing to its remoteness it is one of the least known. The flora and fauna of San Matías largely resemble that of Otuquis and Noel Kempff Mercado. Visitors will find the climate slightly drier than that of the southern Pantanal, but the primary attractions are definitely aquatic fowl and sub-Amazonian animals, including the increasingly rare jaguar. San Matías's three big lakes – Mandiore, La Gaiba, and Liberaba – and its Río Curiche Grande are favourites for fishermen. Access to the park is problematic at best: there are no roads and only one dirt airstrip at Santo Corazón. Tours may be arranged from Puerto Suárez, and a few visitors have made the trip in a 4WD vehicle from Santiago de Chiquitos (near Roboré) during the dry season, but the main attraction of visiting is to see it in the wet season when everything springs to life. An alternative route is a vague path that heads south from the border town of San Matías for approximately 120 km. There are no signs, official entrance posts nor services of any kind.

Quijarro and Puerto Suárez *Colour map 4, C6.*
The eastern terminus of the Bolivian road and railway is **Quijarro**. It is quite safe by day, but caution is recommended at night. The water supply is often unreliable. Prices are much lower than in neighbouring Brazil and there are some decent places to stay. ATMs and banks are at the border.

On the shores of Laguna Cáceres, 8 km west of Quijarro, is **Puerto Suárez**, with a shady main plaza. There is a nice view of the lake from the park at the north end of Avenida Bolívar.

Border with Brazil
The neighbourhood by the border is known as Arroyo Concepción. You need not have your passport stamped if you visit Corumbá for the day. Otherwise get your exit stamp at Bolivian immigration (see below), entry stamp at Brazilian border complex. Yellow fever vaccination is compulsory to enter Bolivia and Brazil; have your certificate to hand when you go for your entry stamp, otherwise you may be sent to get revaccinated. Bolivian immigration is at the border at Arroyo Concepción (0800-1200, 1400-1730 daily), or at Puerto Suárez airport, where Bolivian exit/entry stamps are also issued. There is one ATM at Arroyo Concepción, at the Hotel Pantanal. Money changers right at the border offer the worst rates, better to ask around in the small shops past the bridge. There are Brazilian consulates in Puerto Suárez (Avenida R Otero Reich y H Suárez Abrego, T03-976 2040, cg.psuarez@itamaraty.gov.br) and Santa Cruz (Avenida Noel Kempff Mercado, Calle 9A Norte, casa 9, T03-344 7575, geral@consbras.org.bo). See Transport, below, for taxis from the border.

Quijarro

$$$-$$ Jardín del Bibosi
Luis Salazar 495, 4½ blocks east of train station, T978 2044, www.hotelbibosi.com.
Variety of rooms and prices, some with a/c, fridge, cheaper with fan and shared bath, breakfast, pool, patio, restaurant, upscale for Quijarro.

Willy Solís Cruz
Roboré 13, T7365 5587,
wiland_54@hotmail.com.
For years Willy has helped store luggage and offered local information and assistance. His home is open to visitors who would like to rest, take a shower, do laundry, cook or check the internet while they wait for transport; a contribution in return is welcome. He speaks English, very helpful.

Puerto Suárez

$ Beby
Av Bolívar 111, T03-976 2700.
Private bath, a/c, cheaper with shared bath and fan, no frills, very basic.

$ Casa Real
Vanguardia 39, T03-976 3335.
A/c, frigobar, Wi-Fi and internet, parking, tours, a decent choice.

Transport

Quijarro and Puerto Suárez
Air
Puerto Suárez airport is 6 km north of town, T03-976 2347; airport tax US$2. Flights to **Santa Cruz** with **TAM**, 3 times a week. Don't buy tickets for flights originating in Puerto Suárez in Corumbá, these cost more.

Bus
Buses from Quijarro pick up passengers in Puerto Suárez en route to **Santa Cruz**, many companies, most after 1800 (**Trans Bioceánico** at 1030), US$12-20, 8-10 hrs.

Taxi
Quijarro to the border (**Arroyo Concepción**) US$0.70 pp; to **Puerto Suárez** US$1 pp, more at night. If arriving from Brazil, you will be approached by Bolivian taxi drivers who offer to hold your luggage while you clear immigration. These are the most expensive cabs (US$5 to Quijarro, US$15 to Puerto Suárez). Instead, keep your gear with you while your passport is stamped, then walk 200 m past the bridge to an area where other taxis wait (US$0.70 pp to Quijarro). Colectivos to Puerto Suárez leave Quijarro when full from Av Bolívar corner Av Luis de la Vega, US$1.

Train
With paving of the highway from Santa Cruz train service is in less demand, but it remains a comfortable and convenient option. Ticket office in Quijarro station Mon-Sat 0730-1200, 1430-1800, Sun 0730-1100. Purchase tickets directly at the train station (passport required; do not buy train tickets for Bolivia in Brazil). The **Ferrobus** leaves Quijarro Mon, Wed, Fri 1800, arriving Santa Cruz 0700 next day; **Expreso Oriental**, Tue, Thu, Sun 1300, arriving 0540 next day. See Santa Cruz Transport (page 249) and www.fo.com.bo for fares and additional information.

Northern lowlands

Bolivia's largely untamed Amazon region

Beyond and beneath the great cordilleras, Bolivia's Amazon lies in the north of the country. This vast region, covered by steamy jungles and flat savannah lands, is bursting with all manner of wildlife. Beni department alone has 53% of the country's birds and 50% of its mammals. This natural paradise is threatened by colonization and logging but, although destruction of forest habitat is proceeding at an alarming rate, parts of the region have embraced ecotourism as an alternative.

Rurrenabaque is the single most popular destination. It can be reached from La Paz by road or, more conveniently, by air, and provides access to two large and spectacularly diverse protected natural areas: Madidi National Park and the Pilón Lajas Biosphere Reserve. Here are several highly regarded and successful community tourism projects that allow visitors to experience life in the jungle and on the pampas. Vast as they are, Rurrenabaque's surroundings represent but a small fraction of the immense and sparsely populated area that stretches north and east to the Brazilian border. Largely ignored by tourists to date, this region offers opportunities for exploration and demands the utmost respect if its natural treasures are to survive.

Best for
Jungle lodges ■ River trips ■ Wildlife

Footprint
picks

★ **Flight from La Paz to Rurrenabaque**, page 287
Outstanding views of the dramatic Cordillera Real.

★ **Community tourism in Madidi National Park**, page 288
One of the world's most diverse regions with pristine
jungle and abundant wildlife.

★ **Pampas tours from Rurrenabaque**, page 290
Vast swampy grasslands rich in wildlife, best spotted along
the Río Yacuma.

★ **Cruise on the Río Mamoré**, page 298
Sail up the Río Mamoré on the *Flotel Reina de Enín*
or on a cargo boat to Guayaramerín.

★ **Fiesta del Santo Patrono de Moxos**, page 298
Colourful parades in San Ignacio de Moxos accompanied
by several days of drinking, dancing and fireworks.

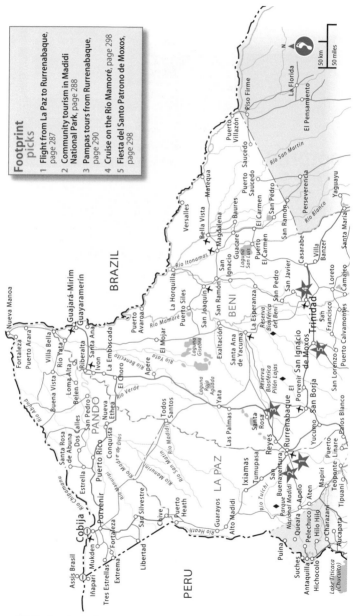

Footprint picks

1 Flight from La Paz to Rurrenabaque, page 287
2 Community tourism in Madidi National Park, page 288
3 Pampas tours from Rurrenabaque, page 290
4 Cruise on the Río Mamoré, page 298
5 Fiesta del Santo Patrono de Moxos, page 298

Caranavi to San Borja *Colour map 2, B2, A3.*

From Caranavi (see page 113), a road runs north to Sapecho, where a bridge crosses the Río Beni. Beyond Sapecho (7 km from the bridge), the road passes through Palos Blancos (several cheap lodgings). The road between Sapecho and Yucumo, three hours from Sapecho *tránsito*, is a good all-weather gravel surface. There are basic *hospedajes* and restaurants in **Yucumo** where a road branches northwest, fording rivers several times on its way to Rurrenabaque. Taking the eastern branch from Yucumo it is 50 km (one to two hours) to San Borja (see page 298).

Essential Northern lowlands

Finding your feet

Rurrenabaque, Trinidad and the far northern towns have airports. All are served by bus as well, but roads are rough, journeys long and, in the wet season, frequently disrupted.

When to go

The weather is hot and humid all year round. The wettest season is December to March when severe flooding can occur.

Time required

Five to seven days for Rurrenabaque, two to four weeks for remote areas.

Weather Rurrenabaque

Jan	Feb	Mar	Apr	May	Jun
31°C	31°C	31°C	31°C	29°C	28°C
23°C	22°C	22°C	21°C	19°C	18°C
256mm	222mm	211mm	141mm	120mm	106mm
☁️	☁️	☁️	☁️	☁️	☁️

Jul	Aug	Sep	Oct	Nov	Dec
28°C	31°C	31°C	32°C	32°C	31°C
16°C	17°C	19°C	21°C	22°C	22°C
73mm	72mm	82mm	141mm	144mm	225mm
☁️	☁️	☁️	☁️	☁️	☁️

★**Rurrenabaque** *Colour map 2, A2.*

The charming, picturesque jungle town of Rurre (as the locals call it), on the Río Beni, is the main jumping-off point for tours in the Bolivian Amazon and pampas, from two- to four-day trips through to full expeditions. It is hemmed in by the river and a range of forested hills, the last vestiges of the sierras before the seemingly endless plains that spread north to the Amazon. Across the river is the smaller town of **San Buenaventura** (canoe US$0.15). Despite its growth as a trading, transport and ecotourism centre, Rurre (population 19,195, altitude 200 m) is a pleasant town to walk around, although the climate is usually humid. Market day is Sunday. There are two ATMs, both on Comercio near the intersection with Aniceto, but don't rely on either of them.

> **Tip...**
> When walking in town, watch out for the deep gullies between the pavement and street.

Jungle tours

There are two types of tours from Rurrenabaque, jungle and pampas tours. See below for the latter. Jungle

ON THE ROAD

Wildlife of the Beni

The **tapir** is a shy animal that confines itself to an intricate network of trails in the forests of the marshy lowlands of Bolivia, Brazil, Colombia, Venezuela, Ecuador, Peru and the north of Argentina. Water is essential for its survival; it drinks a great deal and is an excellent swimmer. It is herbivorous, eating water plants and the leaves and twigs of trees. Its only enemies are jaguars and alligators; it runs fast through very dense undergrowth and dives into water as a defence.

Jaguars are the largest of the New World cats. They are great wanderers, roaming even further than pumas. Usually they haunt forests where they hunt for deer, agoutis and especially peccaries. They follow the herds of these South American swine and pounce on the stragglers. They also attack capybara. Unlike most cats, jaguars are often found beside rivers and frequently enter the water. Jaguars attack tapir that come down to the water to drink and will even scoop fish from the water with their paws. The jaguar is referred to as the *tigre* to distinguish it from the ocelot, called *tigrillo* or *tigrecillo*.

The **ocelot** is the next-largest South American cat after the puma and jaguar. It inhabits forests and while its spotted buff-brown coat assists in hunting it has also made it an attractive target for man. When left undisturbed it is diurnal, but becomes nocturnal in areas where it is hunted. Though it can climb it hunts on the forest floor, making good use of its acute sight and hearing. It preys on agoutis and pacas (which are large rodents), peccaries, brocket deer, birds and some reptiles. It has even been known to kill large boas.

tours normally involve travelling by boat on the **Río Beni** and **Río Tuichi**. Lodging is either in purpose-built camps on higher-end tours, or tents at the budget end. Tours are long enough for most people to get a good feeling for life in the jungle and to experience community-run lodges. In the rainy season the jungle is very hot and humid with more biting insects and fewer animals to be seen. All journeys pass the **Estrecho de Bala**, a natural gateway where the Beni passes between two escarpments to a more open landscape, with the river heading into the jungle beyond.

★Parque Nacional Madidi *Colour map 1, C2.*
Headquarters in San Buenaventura, C Libertad, about 4 blocks upriver from the plaza, T03-892 2540. US$16 entry is collected near the dock in San Buenaventura. All visitors must disembark to have their permit checked on entry to the park, just past the Estrecho de Bala. Insect repellent and sun protection are essential. See www.sernap.gob.bo.

Parque Nacional Madidi is quite possibly the most bio-diverse of all protected areas on the planet. It is the variety of habitats, from the freezing Andean peaks of the Cordillera Apolobamba in the southwest (reaching nearly 6000 m), through cloud, elfin and dry forest to steaming tropical jungle and pampas (neotropical

The **giant otter** is found along the tributaries of the Amazon. It can measure up to 2 m in length. They are active by day when they hunt for food, often in small groups. They are not rare but are rarely seen as they are shy and submerge quickly at the slightest hint of danger. They feed on fish, molluscs and crustaceans, as well as small mammals and birds. They can be tamed easily and are often raised as pets by some tribes.

The **capybara** is a large aquatic rodent that looks like a cross between a guinea pig and a hippopotamus. It is the largest of all the rodents at over 1 m long and weighing over 50 kg. They live in large groups along the river banks, where they graze on the lush grasses. They come out onto dry land to rest and bask in the sun, but at the first hint of danger the whole troop dashes into the water. Its greatest enemies are the jaguar and puma. They are rather vocal for rodents, often emitting a series of strange clicks, squeaks and grunts

Caiman are South American alligators. Black caiman can reach up to 6 m in length but other varieties are usually no more than 2.5 m. They are found in areas of relatively still water, ranging from marshland to lakes and slow-flowing rivers. Youngsters feed mainly on small fish while adults also take larger prey, including wild pigs and small travellers. During the dry season when pools dry up caimans can stop feeding altogether and burrow into the mud at the bottom of a pool waiting for the rains. There are also several species of forest caiman.

Pink river dolphins are excellent at fishing and will sometimes rip fishermen's nets and steal their catch. Adults can grow to nearly 3 m in length. The pink colouring is more marked in older dolphins, young dolphins being born a more conventional grey-blue colour. They are thought to be an ancient species and are endangered.

savannah) in the north and east, that account for the array of flora and fauna within the park's boundaries. In an area roughly the size of Wales or El Salvador (1,895,750 ha) are an estimated over 1100 bird species, 10 species of primate, five species of cat (with healthy populations of jaguar and puma), giant anteaters and many reptiles. Madidi is at the centre of a bi-national system of parks that spans the Bolivia–Peru border, the **Corredor de Conservacíon Vilcabamba–Amboró** (Vilcabamba, Peru, to Parque Nacional Amboró, Bolivia, page 259), which aspires to be the largest and most varied conservation corridor in South America. To the southwest the Area Protegida Apolobamba protects extensive mountain ecosystems. It is easiest to visit the lowland areas of Madidi through Rurrenabaque.

The park has three major river systems. The Ríos Beni, Madidi and Heath provide potential arteries for river transport, but only the Río Beni and its tributary the Río Tuichi are visited by most tours from Rurrenabaque.

On the **Río Beni** at the edge of the national park, **San Miguel del Bala** is a small indigenous Tacana community (some 32 families) located only 45 minutes upriver from Rurrenabaque by motorized canoe. In 2005, the community opened a tourist lodge (see Where to stay, below). San Miguel can easily be visited on a day-trip but a longer stay is recommended.

About six hours upriver from Rurre along the **Río Tuichi** is **San José de Uchupiamonas**, a Quechua-Tacana community that operates the highly regarded **Chalalán Ecolodge** (see page 294), also built with international aid. Further upriver on the Río Tuichi lie significant areas of Grade IV whitewater. Rafting or kayaking from the mountains to the jungle here would be an epic river adventure.

Harder to access is Madidi's namesake, the **Río Madidi** in the park's centre, which is reported to have families of giant otters. Access is also via the Río Tuichi above San José. Then it would be a tough hike across the dividing range of hills that separate the Tuichi and Madidi river basins. The third leg of the journey would involve a descent of the Madidi by raft or canoe and a return to Rurrenabaque via Ixiamas. This wild and remote route is not part of the usual jungle tours and would require organizing a private expedition.

Some 300 km northwest of Rurrenabaque, the **Río Heath** is the most distant of the park's major rivers. It lies in a frontier zone not only between Peru and Bolivia but also between the pampas and the rainforest. The pampas near the Rio Heath support unique and varied wildlife, including the highly endangered maned wolf (imagine a wolf on stilts) and the toco toucan, largest of the toucans. Access to the Heath River is difficult and the best way to reach it is via **Puerto Maldonado** in Peru, from where several hours up the **Río Madre del Dios**, the Heath joins it on the border.

★Pampas tours

In the more open terrain of the pampas you will see a lot of wildlife: howler, squirrel and capuchin monkeys, caiman, capybara, pink dolphins and a huge variety of birds. These will be seen in the gallery forest as you travel on boat trips on the slow-moving river. To see anacondas, not very likely these days, you may have to wade through knee-deep water in the wide-open pampas; wear appropriate footwear (boots may be provided). Community tourism is being developed at **Santa Rosa de Yacuma**, 100 km northeast of Rurre (for information contact **FAN**, page 244). There is a fee of US$18.75 to enter the Area Protegida Municipal. All pampas tours involve a four-hour jeep ride to El Puerto de Santa Rosa, 7 km beyond Santa Rosa on the Río Yacuma. There is an albergue at El Puerto and boats to other lodges depart from here.

Pilón Lajas Biosphere Reserve and Indigenous Territory

Headquarters at Campero y Germán Busch, Rurrenabaque, T03-892 2246, crtmpilonlajas@yahoo.com, www.sernap.gob.bo, entrance fee US$18.75.

Beyond the Beni River in the southeast runs the Pilón Lajas Biosphere Reserve and Indigenous Territory (400,000 ha), home to the Tsimane and Mosetene peoples. Together with Madidi, it constitutes approximately 60,000 sq km, one of the largest systems of protected land in the neotropics. Unfortunately, much of this land is under pressure from logging interests, especially along the western border of the reserve. Set up under the auspices of UNESCO, Pilón Lajas has one of the continent's most intact Amazonian rainforest ecosystems, as well as an incredible array of tropical forest animal life. NGOs have been working with the people of La Unión, Playa Ancha, Nuevos Horizontes and El Cebú to develop sustainable forestry, fish farming, cattle ranching and *artesanía*.

ON THE ROAD
The debonair dolphin

One of the most bizarre examples of the wide diversity of flora and fauna in the Bolivian Amazon is a strange, prehistoric-looking mammal that can transform itself into a suave gentleman in a white linen suit. Or so local legend would have it. But the Amazonian river dolphin is a strange creature indeed. Part myth, part real, this beast can change its skin colour from a pale grey to a bright, luminescent pink. The indigenous people of the Amazon rainforest have long revered what they call the *bufeo*, and even today, unwanted pregnancies within indigenous communities are sometimes blamed on this magical animal with an impressive line in seduction techniques.

Stories about the *bufeo* have been passed down from generation to generation. One such tale is of an underwater city where the *bufeo* walk on pavements made from turtle shells and lie in hammocks strung from anacondas.

Another common belief serves to protect the dolphins from being hunted by local fishermen. This stems from the analogy between dolphins and witchdoctors. The *bufeo* can be a malevolent creature if hunted, and will avenge the death of one of their own. To kill a dolphin, then, is the same as killing a powerful witchdoctor, with the same inevitable consequences.

In 1987 Jacques Cousteau astounded TV viewers around the world with the first-ever pictures of pink dolphins frolicking in the waters of the Amazon. Now visitors to the Río Yacuma and to jungle rivers can see the *bufeo* in the flesh – be it grey, or pink, or even dressed in a white suit. But women travellers should beware any charming, smartly dressed gentlemen in these parts.

Wildlife

The diversity of life in these parks, both on the pampas and in the jungle, is truly impressive, but creatures don't sit around waiting for you to see them. Patience is a real virtue when it comes to sighting wildlife. Even on the best tour, your experiences will be unpredictable; the only guarantee is that the surprises will be genuine and all the more unforgettable.

In addition to caiman, fish, monkeys and turtles – all of which are easily spotted – the observant visitor can see a plethora of unique bird and insect life. There are vast numbers of armadillos, deer, sloths, squirrels, peccary and tapirs that roam the area, as well as river otters, dolphins and anacondas.

Some jungle creatures, such as the increasingly rare jaguar and many varieties of deer, are nocturnal and are not likely to be sighted on day trips. There are also, however, numerous animals that keep normal office hours, such as the giant anteater, capybara, peccary and tapir. Overhead are macaws, parrots and toucans, while flying squirrels and monkeys flit from tree to tree. Among this dazzling array of fauna must be included the innumerable insects – over 200 species of butterfly alone – and rodents, as well as fish of every description. For more information about some of these species, see the boxes above as well as pages 288 and 305.

Tourist information

Rurrenabaque

Infotur municipal tourist office
Abaroa y Vaca Díez, turismorurre@
hotmail.com. Mon-Fri 0800-1200,
1430-1830, Sat 0900-1100.
General information and information on
tours, operators, hotels and restaurants
in Spanish, English and French. Kiosks
may open at the bus station and airport.

Regional tourist office
Abaroa casi Santa Cruz.
Mainly for statistics and records, but they
can give general information.

Where to stay

Rurrenabaque

$$-$ Hostal Pahuichi
Comercio y Vaca Díez, T03-892 2558.
Some big rooms, cheaper with shared
bath, electric shower, fan, breakfast
extra, rooftop views, good.

$ Beni
Comercio y Arce, along the river,
T03-892 2408.
Best rooms have a/c and TV, hot
showers, cheaper with fan and without
bath, kitchen facilities. Spacious,
good service.

$ El Ambaibo
Santa Cruz entre Bolívar y Busch, T03-892
2107, hotel_ambaibo@hotmail.com.
Includes breakfast and airport transfer,
private and shared rooms, large pool
(US$2.50 for non-guests), parking, also
has dorms at Tuky, also on Santa Cruz,

T03-892 2686, Ambaibo Backpackers
Hotel on Facebook.

$ El Curichal
Comercio 1490, 7 blocks
from plaza, T03-892 2647,
www.newgenerationbolivia.com.
Nice courtyard, rooms with and without
bath, dorms, lockers, hammocks, laundry
and small kitchen facilities, pool, book
exchange, games, helpful staff. Popular
economy option.

$ Hostal Lobo
Upstream end of Comercio, no fixed
phone.
Cheap rooms in large breezy building
overlooking the river, shared bath, some
double rooms, with breakfast and Wi-Fi,
laundry service, *parrillada*.

$ Los Tucanes de Rurrenabaque
Arce y Bolívar, T7153 4521,
www.hotel-tucanes.com.
Big place with thatched structures,
hammocks and an open communal
area, rooms with and without bath. Also
has **$$ La Isla resort**, on the outskirts
between Av Bolívar and Av Amutari,
T03-892 2127, www.islatucanes.com.

$ Oriental
Pellicioli, on plaza, T03-892 2401.
Hot showers, fan, small breakfast
included, quiet, hammocks in peaceful
garden, family-run, Wi-Fi in public areas.
A good option.

$ Santa Ana
Abaroa entre Vaca Díez y Campero,
T03-892 2399.
A variety of rooms, all cheap and simple,
laundry, pleasant hammock area in
garden, no breakfast.

Jungle trips

San Miguel del Bala
45-min boat trip upriver from Rurre (office at C Comercio entre Vaca Díez y Santa Cruz), T03-892 2394, www.sanmigueldelbala.com.

This award-winning community lodge gives a good taste of the jungle, offers day trips, well-laid-out trails and has en suite cabins in a delightful setting, good restaurant with typical dishes, including vegetarian, attentive staff, bar

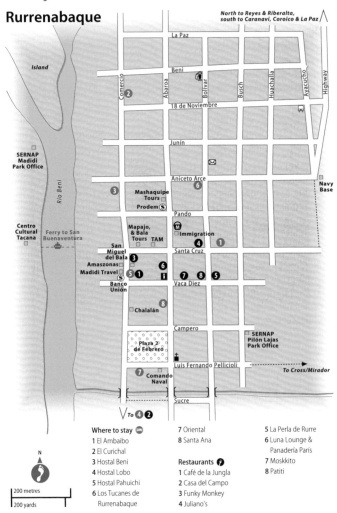

Rurrenabaque

Where to stay 🛏
1 El Ambaibo
2 El Curichal
3 Hostal Beni
4 Hostal Lobo
5 Hostal Pahuichi
6 Los Tucanes de Rurrenabaque
7 Oriental
8 Santa Ana

Restaurants 🍴
1 Café de la Jungla
2 Casa del Campo
3 Funky Monkey
4 Juliano's
5 La Perla de Rurre
6 Luna Lounge & Panadería París
7 Moskkito
8 Patiti

and a pool fed by a waterfall. It is owned and operated by the indigenous Tacana community. They have a 2nd lodge in Madidi with similar attention, walks, community visits. 3 days/2 nights cost US$240 pp. Advance booking required. Highly recommended.

Parque Nacional Madidi

Berraco del Madidi
6 hrs upriver from Rurrenabaque (office Comercio y Vaca Díez, T03-892 2966, www.berracodelmadidi.com).
This lodge is run by members of the San José de Uchupiamonas community. Fully enclosed tents with mosquito screens on covered platforms, good mattresses, clean toilets, cold showers, good kitchen with excellent food, well-run, professional, plenty of activities, US$480 for 3 days/2 nights, also longer programmes and specialist trips.

Chalalán Ecolodge
5 hrs upriver from Rurrenabaque, at San José de Uchupiamonas, in Madidi National Park. La Paz office: Sagárnaga 189, Edif Shopping Doryan, of 23, T02-231 1451; in Rurrenabaque, C Comercio entre Campero y Vaca Díez, T03-892 2419, www.chalalan.com.
This is Bolivia's top ecotourism project, founded by the Quechua Tacana community, Conservation International and the Interamerican Development Bank, and now has a well-deserved international reputation. Accommodation is in thatched cabins, and activities include fantastic wildlife-spotting and birdwatching, guided and self-guided trails, river and lake activities, and relaxing in pristine jungle surroundings. 3-day/2-night packages cost US$410 pp (US$380 with shared bath).

Madidi Jungle Eco Lodge
3½ hrs from Rurre (office Av Comercio entre Vaca Díez y Campero, T7128 2697, www.madidijungle.com).
Also run by families from the San José de Uchupiamonas community. Rooms around a central garden, comfortable cabins in the forest, with and without shower, hammocks, good regional food, 11 trails to explore with expert guides, other activities include tubing, handicraft-making, piranha fishing. Programmes from 1 to 5 days, US$250-280 pp for 3 days, 2 nights, flexible, responsible and excellent service.

Pilón Lajas Biosphere Reserve and Indigenous Territory

Mapajo
Mapajo Ecoturismo Indígena, Santa Cruz entre Abaroa y Comercio, Rurrenabaque, T7113 8838, http://mapajo-ecoturismo-indigena.blogspot.co.uk.
A community-run ecolodge 3 hrs by boat from Rurrenebaque has 6 cabañas without electricity (take a torch), shared cold showers and a dining room serving traditional meals. You can visit the local community, walk in the forest, go birdwatching, etc. Take insect repellent, wear long trousers and strong footwear.

Restaurants

Rurrenabaque
$$ Casa del Campo
Comercio, opposite El Lobo. Daily 0730-1400, 1800-2130.
Restaurant in a thatched building with flowers around the terrace.

$ Juliano's
Santa Cruz casi Bolívar. Daily 1200-1430, 1800-late.

French and Italian food. Good presentation and service. Recommended.

$$ Paititi
Vaca Díez casi Bolívar.
Good Mediterranean-influenced dishes, friendly service.

$$-$ Luna Lounge
Abaroa entre Santa Cruz y Vaca Diez.
Open 0800-2200.
International meals, pizza, snacks and drinks, also pool table and sports TV.

$$-$ Funky Monkey
Comercio entre Santa Cruz y Vaca Díez.
Open 0900-0100.
Big pizzas, imaginative pastas, vegetarian options, grilled meats and fish, bar, lively crowd.

$$-$ The Angu's
Comercio entre Santa Cruz y Vaca Díez.
Pizzas, pastas, meat dishes, burgers soups and veggie options. Wi-Fi, music and sports, happy hour 1900-2200.

$ La Perla de Rurre
Bolívar y Vaca Díez. Open daily
0730-2100.
Set lunch and à la carte, also breakfast and sandwiches in the morning, good food, eating outside under the mango trees.

Cafés
Café de la Jungla
Comercio y Vaca Díez. Mon-Sat
0800-1630.
Neat little café serving breakfasts, sandwiches, salads, snacks and juices, mostly local produce, Wi-Fi.

Moskkito Bar
Vaca Díez casi Abaroa.
Cool bar for tall jungle tales. Burgers, pizzas, rock music and pool tables. Open in the evening only.

Panadería París
Abaroa entre Vaca Díez y Santa Cruz.
Mon-Sat 0600-1200.
Delicious croissants and *pain au chocolat*, get there early, also quiches and pizzas.

What to do

Rurrenabaque
Jungle and pampas tours cost about US$80 pp plus the park fee for a typical 3-day tour by a responsible operator. Prices and quality both vary but booking in Rurre is usually cheaper than in La Paz. Much effort is being put into ensuring that all companies adhere to codes of practice that do not permit hunting, feeding animals, especially monkeys, catching caiman or handling anaconda, but there are still a few that do so. If you do not want to encourage such activities, ask in advance what is offered on the tour. Before signing up for a tour, check the Municipal Infotur office for updates and try to talk to other travellers who have just come back. Guides who belong to Agnatur (Asociación de Guías Naturalistas de Turismo Responsable), from the same community as Chalalán, have pioneered respect for wildlife here, first in Madidi and recently in the pampas. Ask for a member, or for an operator who uses them.

Some operators pool customers, so you may not go with the company you booked with. There are many more agencies in town than those listed below. Shop around and choose carefully.

Tour operators
Bala Tours, *Av Santa Cruz y Comercio,*
T03-892 2527, www.balatours.com.
Arranges pampas and jungle tours, singly or combined, with their own

lodge in each (with bath and solar power), also specialist programmes, visits to local communities and the Guanay-Rurrenabaque route. English-speaking guides. Award-winning, services and lodges recently upgraded, top-class service. Recommended.

Donato Tours, *Vaca Díez entre Abaroa y Comercio, T7126 0919, www.donatotours. com*. Regular tours plus the opportunity to stay in a community in Pilón Lajas for 1 to 20 days.

Lipiko Tours, *Av Santa Cruz entre Bolívar y Abaroa, T02-231 5408, http://lipiko.com*. Rurre office of a company offering tours throughout Bolivia.

Madidi Expeditions, *Comercio entre Vaca Díez y Campero, T7199 8372, www. madidiexpeditions.com*. Responsible tours to Madidi and the pampas, chief

guide Norman is very experienced, knowledgeable and professional. Good staff. Recommended.

Madidi Travel, *Comercio y Vaca Díez, T03-892 2153, in La Paz, Linares 947, T02-231 8313, www.madidi-travel.com*. Specializes in tours to the private Serere Sanctuary in the Madidi Mosaic (details on website), minimum 3 days/2 nights, good guiding. Recommended.

Mashaquipe Tours, *Abaroa entre Pando y Arce, T03-892 2704, www. mashaquipeecotours.com*. Jungle and pampas tours run by an organization which works with communities, with lodges in both locations. They offer combined jungle and pampas tours (eg 5 days US$390 pp), also short tours. Small groups, safe, most guides speak English, a popular company.

Caranavi to San Borja
Bus

See page 115 for buses in Caranavi. **Yucumo** is on the La Paz–Caranavi–Rurrenabaque and San Borja bus routes. Rurrenabaque–La Paz bus passes through about 1800. If travelling to Rurrenabaque by bus take extra food in case there is a delay (anything from road blocks to flat tyres to high river levels). **Flota Yungueña** daily except Thu at 1300 from San Borja to **La Paz**, 19 hrs via Caranavi. Also San Borja to **Rurrenabaque**, **Santa Rosa**, **Riberalta**, **Guayaramerín** about 3 times a week. Minibuses and *camionetas* normally run daily between San Borja and **Trinidad** throughout the year, US$15, about 7 hrs including 20 mins crossing of Río Mamoré on ferry barge (up to 14 hrs in wet season). Fuel available at Yolosa, Caranavi, Yucumo, San Borja and San Ignacio.

Rurrenabaque
Air

Several daily flights to/from **La Paz** with **Amaszonas** (Comercio entre Santa Cruz y Vaca Diez, T03-892 2472), US$97; and 3 a week with **TAM** (Santa Cruz y Abaroa, T03-892 2398/7113 2500). Both also fly to **Trinidad**, but not daily. Book flights as early as possible and buy onward ticket on arrival. Check flight times in advance; they change frequently. Delays and cancellations are common. Airport taxes total US$2.75 (airport and municipal taxes). Airlines provide transport to/from town, US$1.25; confirm flight 24 hrs in advance and be at airline office 2 hrs before departure.

Bus

A new bus terminal is being built near the airport. To/from **La Paz** via Caranavi with **Flota Yungueña**, **Totaí** and **Vaca Díez**; 18-20 hrs, US$10, daily at 1030 and Sat-Mon also at 1900. See under Sorata and Cocoico, Transport, for alternative routes to Rurre. Some La Paz buses continue to **Riberalta** (US$19, 13 hrs from Rurre), **Guayaramerín** (US$20, 15 hrs) or **Cobija** (US$35, 30 hrs). Rurrenebaque–**Riberalta** may take 6 days or more in the wet season. Take lots of food, torch and be prepared to work. To **Trinidad**, with **Trans Guaya** (buses) or **Trans Rurrenabaque** (minibuses) daily, **Flota Yungueña** Mon, Wed, via **Yucumo** and **San Borja**, US$20, check that the road is open.

San Borja and the Estación Biológica del Beni
C 4 Sul esq Trinidad, T03-895 3898, www.sernap.gob.bo; advance arrangements required in order to visit.

San Borja, a relatively wealthy cattle-raising centre (population 40,865) with simple hotels and restaurants clustered near the plaza, is 50 km east of Yucumo. In the town is the headquarters of the Estación Biológica del Beni (also called Reserva Biológica del Beni).

This 135,000-ha reserve is situated along the Río Maniqui, about 150 km east of Rurrenabaque. It is home to the Chimane people, as well as more than 500 species of bird and 200 different mammals. There are thought to be more than 1500 plant species and 900 species of fauna in all. It also contains **Laguna Normandia**, which has large numbers of the endangered black caiman.

The road east from San Borja to Trinidad passes through part of the Pilón Lajas Reserve (see above). There are five or six river crossings and, in the wetlands, a multitude of waterfowl. At times the road can be flooded out. Another route into Beni Department is from the lowland road between Cochabamba and Santa Cruz and then by river from Puerto Villarroel (see page 232).

★San Ignacio de Moxos *Colour map 1, C4.*
San Ignacio de Moxos, 90 km west of Trinidad, is known as the folklore capital of the Beni Department. It's a quiet town (population 22,165) with a mainly indigenous population; 60% are *Macheteros*, who speak their own language. San Ignacio still maintains the traditions of the Jesuit missions with big fiestas, especially during Holy Week and the **Fiesta del Santo Patrono de Moxos** (see Festivals, below).

> **Tip...**
> Come in July/ August for the most important and colourful festival in the Bolivian Amazon.

Trinidad *Colour map 1, C5.*
The hot and humid capital of the lowland Beni Department is a dusty city in the dry season, with many streets unpaved. Primarily a service centre for the surrounding ranches and communities, most travellers find themselves in the area for boats up and down the ★Río Mamoré. There are two ports, Almacén and Varador, check at which one your boat will be docked. **Puerto Varador** is 13 km from town on the Río Mamoré on the road between Trinidad and San Borja; cross the river over the main bridge by the market, walk down to the service station by the police checkpoint and take a truck, US$1.75. **Almacén** is 8 km from the city. The main mode of transport in Trinidad is the motorbike (even for taxis, US$0.50 in city); rental on plaza from US$2.50 per hour, US$10 per half day. There are several ATMs on or near the central Plaza Ballivián.

About 5 km from town is the **Laguna Suárez**, with plenty of wildlife; swimming is safe where the locals swim, near the café with the jetty (elsewhere there are stingrays and alligators). Motorbike taxi from Trinidad, US$1.50.

Magdalena and around *Colour map 1, B5.*

A road from Trinidad heads north to **San Ramón** (population 4955) and then turns east to Magdalena (population 11,275), a charming little town on the banks of the Río Itonama. It was founded by Jesuit missionaries in 1720, made a city in 1911 and is now the capital of the province of Iténez. Beef is the main product of the region and the river is the means of transporting cattle and other agricultural produce. Some 7 km upriver is the **Laguna La Baíqui**, which is popular for fishing. There is an abundance of wildlife and birds in the surrounding area. The city's main festival, Santa María Magdalena, is held on 22 July and attracts many groups and visitors from all over Beni and beyond.

East of Magdalena on the Río Blanco, **Bella Vista** is considered by many to be one of the prettiest spots in northeast Bolivia (see www.faunagua.org/bellavista/index.html). Lovely white sandbanks line the Río San Martín, which is 10 minutes

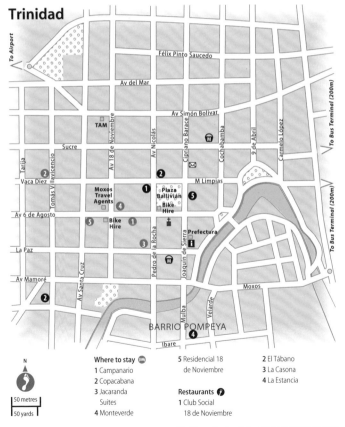

Trinidad

N
50 metres
50 yards

Where to stay 🛏
1 Campanario
2 Copacabana
3 Jacaranda Suites
4 Monteverde
5 Residencial 18 de Noviembre

Restaurants 🍴
1 Club Social 18 de Noviembre
2 El Tábano
3 La Casona
4 La Estancia

by canoe from the boat moorings below town. Local boatmen will take you there, returning later by arrangement. The sandbanks are also accessible by motorcycle.

Check that the sand is not covered by water after heavy rain. Other activities are swimming and canoeing in the Río San Martín, and the countryside is good for cycling. There are a few places to stay and some well-stocked shops on the plaza. There is no bank.

Tip...
Bring your own mosquito repellant as none is available and there are many mosquitoes at the beginning of the wet season.

Listings San Borja to Trinidad *map p299*

Tourist information

Trinidad

Beni Department Tourist offices
Prefectura building, Joaquín de Sierra y La Paz, ground floor, T03-462 4831, www.trinidad.gob.bo, see also TurismoBeniBolivia on Facebook.

Municipal Tourism offices
Félix Pinto Saucedo y Nicolás Suárez, T03-462 1322.

Where to stay

San Ignacio de Moxos
There are some cheap *alojamientos* on and around the main plaza.

Trinidad

$$$ Campanario
6 de Agosto 80, T03-462 4733, www.hotel-campanario.com.
Rooms with a/c and frigobar, meeting room, restaurant, bar, pool.

$$ Jacaranda Suites
La Paz entre Pedro de la Rocha y 18 de Noviembre, T462 2400.
Good services, restaurant, pool, meeting rooms, internet.

$ Copacabana
Tomás M Villavicencio, 3 blocks from plaza, T03-462 2811.
Good value, some beds uncomfortable, cheaper with shared bath, helpful staff.

$ Monteverde
6 de Agosto 76, T03-462 2750.
With a/c (cheaper with fan), frigobar, owner speaks English. Recommended.

$ Residencial 18 de Noviembre
6 de Agosto 135, T03-462 1272.
With and without bath, welcoming, laundry facilities.

Magdalena

$$ Internacional
near the airport, T03-886 2210, http://hotelmagdalena.hwz-inc.com.
The best hotel in Magdalena with gardens, a pool and excellent restaurant.
There are other, more modest places to stay.

Restaurants

Trinidad
There are several good fish restaurants in **Barrio Pompeya**, south of the plaza across river.

$$ Club Social 18 de Noviembre
N Suárez y Vaca Díez on plaza.
Good-value lunch, lively, popular
with locals.

$$ El Tábano
*Villavicencio entre Mamoré y Néstor
Suárez.*
Good fish and local fare, relaxed
atmosphere.

$$ La Estancia
*Barrio Pompeya, on Ibare entre
Muiba y Velarde.*
A good choice for excellent steaks.

$ La Casona
Plaza Ballivián. Closed Tue.
Good pizzas and set lunch.

Heladería Oriental
On plaza.
Good coffee, ice cream, cakes, popular
with locals.

Festivals

San Ignacio de Moxos
**Jul/Aug Fiesta del Santo Patrono de
Moxos**, at the end of Jul and beginning
of Aug, is the most important and
colourful fiesta in the Bolivian Amazon
and features many traditional elements
of Beni culture, with sports, food and
drink and, above all, processions and
dances with feather headdresses,
masked participants and others with
wooden machetes and huge wind
instruments.

What to do

Trinidad
Most agents offer excursions to
local *estancias* and jungle tours.
Most *estancias* can also be reached

independently in 1 hr by hiring a
motorbike.
Flotel Reina de Enín, *Av Comunidad
Europea 624, T7391 2965, http://
amazoncruiser.com.bo.* Cruises on the
Mamoré River within in the Ibare-
Mamoré Reserve. Floating hotel with
comfortable berths with bath, US$455
pp for 3-day/2-night cruise includes
all activities: dolphin watching, horse
riding, visiting local communities, jungle
walks, swimming and piranha fishing.
La Ruta del Bufeo, *T7281 8317, laruta.
delbufeo on Facebook.* Specializes in river
tours for seeing dolphins.
Moxos, *6 de Agosto 114, T03-462 1141.*
Multi-day river and jungle tours with
camping. Recommended.
Paraíso Travel, *6 de Agosto 138,
T03-462 0692, paraiso@entelnet.bo.*
Offers excursions to Laguna Suárez,
Rio Mamoré, camping and bird-
watching tours.

Transport

San Ignacio de Moxos
Bus
The Trinidad to San Borja bus stops at
the **Donchanta** restaurant for lunch,
otherwise difficult to find transport to
San Borja. Minibus to Trinidad daily at
0730 from plaza, also *camionetas*, check
road conditions and times beforehand.

Trinidad
Air
Daily flights with **Aerocon** (6 de
Agosto y 18 de Noviembre, T03-462
4442) to **La Paz**, **Santa Cruz**, **Cobija**,
Riberalta and **Guayaramerín**. TAM
(Bolívar 42, T02-268 1111) to **La Paz**,
Santa Cruz, **Cochabamba**, **Riberalta**,
Guayaramerín and other northern
destinations. To La Paz and Santa Cruz

with Ecojet (Av 6 de Agosto 146, T03-465 2617). **Amaszonas** (18 de Noviembre 267, T03-462 2426) Mon, Wed, Fri to **Rurrenabaque**. Airport (T03-462 0678). Mototaxi to airport US$1.50.

Boat

Cargo boats down the Río Mamoré to **Guayaramerín** take passengers, 3-4 days, assuming no breakdowns, best organized from Puerto Varador (speak to the Port Captain). **Argos** is recommended as friendly, US$25 pp, take water, fresh fruit, toilet paper and ear-plugs; only for the hardy traveller.

Bus

Bus station is on Rómulo Mendoza, between Beni and Pinto, 9 blocks east of main plaza. Motorbike taxis will take people with backpacks from bus station to centre for US$0.50. To **Santa Cruz** (10 hrs on a paved road, US$9-13, *bus-cama* US$20) and **Cochabamba** (US$14-20, 20 hrs), with **Copacabana**, **Mopar** and **Bolívar** mostly overnight (*bus-cama* available). To **Rurrenabaque**, US$20, 12-20 hrs. Enquire locally what services are running to San Borja and **La Paz**. Similarly to **Riberalta** and **Guayaramerín**.

Magdalena and around

Air

To get to this area, ask for flight schedules of Itonama air-taxis at Trinidad airport, usually daily.

Bus

Trinidad–Magdalena (10-12 hrs) and **Magdalena–Bella Vista** (1 hr) only run in the dry season, end Jul-Nov.

Riberalta to Brazil

east via Guayaramerín

This northern outpost region is one of the least-visited areas of the Bolivian Amazon and as such has relatively little tourist infrastructure. This is the wettest part of Bolivia, receiving more than 1770 mm of rain annually. The rainy season is November to April; the rest of the year is dry and hot. Temperatures average 29°C but can reach 40°C, or fall to 15°C when the cold southerly *surazo* wind blows.

The region attained temporary importance during the natural-rubber boom of the late 19th century. But this collapsed, as it did throughout South America, in the second decade of the 20th century when cheaper Asian rubber cornered the world market. It is now the centre for Brazil nut production. Logging is another mainstay of the local economy and threatens to destroy the area's rainforests. There are attempts to promote sustainable timber management and the extraction of non-traditional rainforest products for use in foods, cosmetics and pharmaceuticals.

Because of the remoteness of the area and the precarious state of its roads, air service is very important. There are several flights a week from La Paz to Cobija, as well as service from Trinidad to smaller jungle communities. An 'all-weather' road does lead from La Paz via Rurrenabaque and Santa Rosa to Cobija, Riberalta and Guayaramerín, a gruelling multi-day journey at the best of times, often impossible in the rainy season. See also Transport, below.

Riberalta *Colour map 1, A4.*

At the confluence of the Madre de Dios and Beni rivers, Riberalta (population 97,982 altitude 175 m) is off the beaten track and a centre for Brazil nut production. It's very laid back, but take care if your bus drops you in the middle of the night and everything is closed. There are places to eat on the plaza and near the airport. Change cash in shops and on street.

Guayaramerín and border with Brazil *Colour map 1, A4.*

Guayaramerín, 84 km from Riberalta by paved road, is a cheerful, prosperous little town (population: 39,010) on the bank of the Río Mamoré, opposite the Brazilian town of Guajará-Mirim. There are several restaurants and cafés around the plaza. It has an important Zona Libre. Passage between the two towns is unrestricted; boat trip US$1.75 (more at night).

Bolivian immigration Avenida Costanera near port; open 0800-1100, 1400-1800. Passports must be stamped here when leaving, or entering Bolivia. On entering Bolivia, passports must also be stamped at the Bolivian consulate in Guajará-Mirim. The Brazilian consulate is on 24 de Septiembre 28, Guayaramerín, T03-855 3766, open 0900-1300, 1400-1700; visas for entering Brazil are given here. To enter Brazil you must have a yellow fever certificate, or be inoculated at the health ministry (free). Exchange cash at the dock on the Bolivian side where rates are written up on blackboards (no traveller's cheques), although there is an ATM at the Banco do Brasil in Guajará-Mirim; no facilities for cash.

Listings Riberalta to Brazil

Where to stay

Riberalta
Ask for a fan and check the water supply.

$$ Colonial
Plácido Méndez 745, T03-852 3018.
Charming colonial *casona*, large, well-furnished rooms, no singles, nice gardens and courtyard, comfortable, good beds, helpful owners.

$$ Jomali
Av Nicolás Suárez, beside Banco Ganadero, T03-852 2398,
www.hoteljomali.com.
Central, smart hotel with big rooms and suites, a/c, comfortable, central patio.

$ Alojamiento Comercial Lazo
NG Salvatierra 244, T03-852 2380.
With a/c, cheaper with fan, comfortable, laundry facilities, good value.

Guayaramerín

$$ San Carlos
6 de Agosto 347, 4 blocks from port,
T03-855 3555.
With a/c, hot showers, changes dollars cash, TCs and reais, swimming pool, reasonable restaurant.

$ Santa Ana 25 de Mayo 611
Close to airstrip in town, T03-855 3900.
With bath, fan, cheap and recommended.

What to do

Riberalta
Riberalta Tours, *Av Sucre 634, T03-852 3475, www.riberaltatours.com.* Multi-day river and jungle tours, airline tickets, very helpful.

Transport

Riberalta
Air
Flights to **Trinidad** and **Cobija** with **Aerocon** (at airport, T03-852 4679). To La Paz and Santa Cruz with Ecojet (Av Bernardino Ochoa 966, T03-852 4837). **TAM** (Av Chuquisaca y Salvatierra, T03-852 2646) to **Trinidad**, **Santa Cruz**, **Cochabamba** and **La Paz**. Expect cancellations in the wet season.

Boat
Cargo boats carry passengers along the **Río Madre de Dios**, but they are infrequent. There are no boats to Rurrenabaque.

Bus
Roads to all destinations are appalling, even worse in the wet season. Several companies (including **Yungueña**) to **La Paz**, via **Rurrenabaque** and **Caranavi**

daily, 35 hrs to 3 days or more, US$30. To **Trinidad** via Rurrenabaque and San Borja, 25-35 hrs. To **Guayaramerín** 7 daily, US$5, 1 hr, paved road. To **Cobija** several companies, none with daily service, 10-11 hrs.

Guayaramerín
Air
Daily flights to **Trinidad**, with onward connections, with **Aerocon** (Oruro entre Sucre y 25 de Mayo, T03-855 5035). To La Paz with Ecojet (Sucre entre Beni y 16 de Julio, T03-855 9176). **TAM** has same services as for Riberalta. Airport is southwest of centre.

Boat
Check the notice of vessels leaving port on the Port Captain's board, prominently displayed near the immigration post on the riverbank. Boats sailing up the Mamoré to **Trinidad** are not always willing to take passengers.

Bus
Buses leave from General Federico Román. Same long-haul services as Riberalta, above. To **Riberalta** 1 hr, US$5, daily 0700-1730.

Cobija *Colour map 1, A1.*

go (Brazil) nuts in Bolivia's wettest region

The capital of the lowland Department of Pando lies on the Río Acre which forms the frontier with Brazil. Roughly 500 km northwest of La Paz, and once accessible only by air or river, Cobija (population 55,692) is opposite Brasiléia and is also only 80 km east of the border with Perú.

Founded in 1906 as Bahía, Cobija was settled during the rubber boom. As production declined, so did the town's importance. Cobija has grown rapidly in recent years but still retains an outpost feel. It does not follow a standard street grid, but has a number of roads that meander through the town. The church, with

ON THE ROAD
Killer fish

The much-maligned piranha has a fearsome reputation as a frenzied flesh-eating monster who will tear any unsuspecting tourist to shreds within seconds of setting foot in a tropical river. But is this infamous fish really so bad? Or is it merely the victim of bad publicity?

There are over 30 types of piranha in South America but only two types are meat eaters. Some feed on other fish and some are even vegetarians. The red-bellied piranhas, though, are real flesh eaters. These 20-cm-long fish with razor-sharp teeth hunt in shoals in the many rivers that intersect the Beni flood-plains.

They breed early in the wet season, when both sexes turn black and the female is swollen with eggs. Then begins the courtship ritual, which can last several nights, as the female takes her time in deciding on her potential partner's suitability as a father. Once her mind is made up they mate and the female takes off, leaving the male to guard the eggs.

Although as many as 4000 fry hatch from a single batch of eggs, only a handful survive the first few months. Their greatest test comes in the dry season when there is a danger of becoming isolated from the main rivers and food becomes scarce. The weaker piranhas then become victims as they fall prey to the stronger ones in a frenzy of cannibalism. Birds also join in, feeding on the dying fish. The fabled killer now has no defence against the elements. Those that are too large to be swallowed by the storks are picked off by vultures. Caiman also feed on dying piranhas, attracted by the birds. Piranhas are their favourite snack. But when the rains come the savannah is turned into a huge inland sea and the tables are turned. The piranhas prey on the great white egrets, which nest in the trees, attracted by the young egrets' constant pleading for food. In their desperate attempts to find more food than their parents can supply the clumsy chicks leave the nest and fall into the rivers where they are grabbed by the piranhas.

interesting primitive art, and other public buildings are located around the plaza. In the centre are a few original wooden buildings from the rubber boom era, and on the outskirts is a modern Brazil nut processing plant.

Border with Brazil

A single-tower suspension bridge crosses the river to Brasiléia. As a duty-free zone, shops in centre have a huge selection of imported consumer goods at bargain prices. Brazilians and Peruvians flock here to stock up. As this is a border area, watch out for scams and cons. **Bolivian immigration** ① *Miguel Farah 41 esq Av Internacional, T03-842 2081, open daily 0900-1800.* **Brazilian consulate** ① *Av René Barrientos s/n, T03-842 2110, Mon-Fri 0830-1230.* There are *casas de cambio* on Avenida Internacional and Avenida Cornejo. Most shops will accept dollars or reais, and exchange money. Entry/exit stamps (free) are necessary and yellow fever vaccination certificate also, when crossing into Brazil.

To Peru

Bolivia, Brazil and Peru meet about 80 km west of **Cobija**, upriver on the Río Acre. The Bolivian town is called Bolpebra, but travel from Cobija to Peru is via Brazil. Cross the international bridge to Brasiléia (see above), from where a road leads west to Assis Brasil at the triple frontier. On the Peruvian side is **Iñapari**, from where a road runs 230 km west to Puerto Maldonado. There is no Peruvian consulate in Cobija. Enquire locally about road conditions to Assis Brasil. From there, east and west, the road is part of the Carretera Interoceánica, so there is plenty of traffic into Brazil and Peru.

Listings Cobija

Where to stay

$$ Diana
Av 9 de Febrero 123, T03-842 2073.
A/c, TV, safe, buffet breakfast, pool.

$$ Nanijos
Av 9 de Febrero 147, T03-842 2230.
Includes breakfast, a/c, TV, *comedor* does good lunch, helpful.

$$ Triller
Av Internacional 640, T03-842 2024.
With a/c (cheaper with fan) and bath, restaurant.

Transport

Air
Daily flights to **Riberalta** and **Trinidad**, with onward connections, with **Aerocon**, at airport, T03-842 4600. To La Paz and Santa Cruz with Ecojet. **TAM** (Av 9 de Febrero 49, T02-268 1111), to **La Paz** or **Trinidad** on alternating days.

Bus
Flota Yungueña and **Flota Cobija** to **La Paz** via Riberalta and Rurrenabaque, 2-3 days or more, US$30-40. To **Riberalta** with several bus companies, depart from 2 de Febrero, most on Wed, Fri, Sun at 0600; good all-weather surface; 2 river crossings on pontoon rafts, takes 10-11 hrs.

Taxi
Taxis charge US$0.75 in centre, but more expensive beyond, according to time and distance. Besides taxis there are motorbike taxis (US$0.75).

Border with Brazil
Taxis over the international bridge to **Brasiléia** are expensive. Brasiléia can also be reached by canoe, US$0.50. The bridge can be crossed on foot as well. Dress neatly when approaching Brazilian customs. From Brasiléia, **Real Norte**, has buses to **Rio Branco** and **Assis Brasil**, and **Taxis Brasileiros** run to Rio Branco.

Background
Bolivia

History & politics

The barren, windswept atiplano, the highest plateau in Latin America, has been home to various indigenous cultures from the earliest times. Artefacts found on the altiplano date the first human occupation at around 7000-8000 BC, but a much older fossilized human footprint discovered in the department of La Paz in 2007 has challenged prevailing theories. Early man followed a seasonal cycle of hunting and gathering around the shores of Lake Titicaca, travelling as far as the eastern valleys and the desert coast of southern Peru and northern Chile.

One of the most important developments of life on the altiplano was the domestication of the llama and alpaca, which centred around Lake Titicaca and developed in conjunction with farming. The llama was of crucial importance to the altiplano people. It provided protein to supplement their basic diet as well as wool for weaving and was also a beast of burden. The combination of the domestication of camelids and the development of agriculture helped give rise to the great Andean civilizations.

Tiwanaku

The greatest of the pre-Inca civilizations is at Tiwanaku, or Tiahuanaco (see page 77). Most visitors are aware of this mysterious site just south of Lake Titicaca but few people understand the extent of this culture's influence throughout the South Central Andes and the reason for its sudden demise. The remains of Tiwanaku culture show that the inhabitants reached a high degree of development and organization. Remains of a huge ceremonial and urban centre with palaces, temples and pyramids, elaborate textiles and beautiful pottery suggest a sophisticated culture.

Sustained by innovative forms of intensive farming, the Tiwanaku region became one of the most densely populated areas of the altiplano. The influence of the culture gradually spread to other areas, through military conquest or trade. After around AD 500 its influence was felt in almost all parts of Bolivia, southern Peru, northern Chile and northwest Argentina. Civilization reached its high point here around AD 1000, after which a period of decline set in, leading to its complete collapse around AD 1100-1200. The cause of its sudden demise remains a mystery.

Aymara kingdoms

After the fall of Tiwanaku a proliferation of distinct political groups evolved to control the vast territory formerly under the influence of the great empire. These independent Aymara Kingdoms, which shared a common language and many cultural patterns, played a leading role on the altiplano for 300 years until the arrival of the Spaniards. Each kingdom boasted a powerful organization based on a collective and military model.

BACKGROUND
Bolivia fact file

Population: 10.6 million
Urban population: 66.8%
Population density:
  9.5 inhabitants per sq km
Population growth rate:
  1.6% per year (2014 estimate)

Infant mortality: 38.6 per 1000
  live births
Life expectancy: 68.6 years
GDP per capita: US$5500 (2013)
Minimum wage: US$210 a month
Literacy: 91.2%

At the centre of Aymara society were the *ayllus*, groups based on kinship which owned and worked the land collectively. The Aymaras cultivated potatoes and cereal crops and kept llamas and alpacas for meat, milk and wool and used them as pack-animals. Indeed, the kingdoms' wealth was measured in the number of alpacas and llamas. Like the Tiwanaku Empire before them, the Aymara maintained important connections with communities in the eastern valleys and on the Pacific coast. They exchanged potatoes, meat and wool from the cold, barren plateau for fruit, vegetables, maize and coca from the subtropical valleys.

The most powerful kingdoms were the Lupaca, based at Chuquito, southwest of Lake Titicaca, and the Colla, with their capital at Huatuncolla, near present-day Puno. These two kingdoms were in constant warfare until around 1430, when the Lupaca conquered the Colla.

The Incas

While the Aymara were fighting among themselves to establish territorial rights to lands around the Titicaca basin, the Quechua-speaking Incas from Cuzco were preparing to invade the kingdoms and incorporate them into their expanding empire. Despite the fact that they were divided, the Aymara resisted obstinately and were not finally conquered until the latter part of the 15th century in the reign of Inca Túpac Yupanqui (1471-1493).

The origins of the Inca Dynasty are shrouded in mythology. The best-known story reported by the Spanish chroniclers talks about Manco Capac and his sister, Mama Ocllo, rising out of Lake Titicaca, created by the Sun as divine founders of a chosen race. A more down-to-earth version suggests that the inhabitants of the valleys around Cuzco began their rise to prominence around AD 1200. Over the next 300 years they grew to supremacy as leaders of Tawantinsuyo, the largest empire ever known in the Americas.

At its peak, just before the Spanish Conquest, the Inca Empire stretched from the Río Maule in central Chile, north to the present Ecuador-Colombia border, containing most of Ecuador, Peru, western Bolivia, northern Chile and northwest Argentina. Typical of the Inca method of conquest was to assimilate the skills of their defeated enemies into their own political and administrative system.

Though the Incas respected the languages and cultures of the subjugated peoples and only insisted on imposing their religion, a certain amount of

Quechuanization did occur. Around Lake Titicaca, Aymara language and culture remained practically intact but the cultural and linguistic traditions of other peoples of the altiplano were almost completely displaced, especially as groups of Quechua-speaking Incas were brought from Peru to live and work in Collasuyo. But Inca culture was tied to the highlands and they never succeeded in annexing all of the peoples of Bolivia. Their powerful armies could not defeat the semi-nomadic peoples in the lower-lying valleys and the eastern plains, such as the Guaraníes.

Although the Incas left a great impression on the country in the shape of an extensive road system, architecture, ceramics and metal artefacts and established their own language in many parts, the duration of their stay in Bolivia may have been no more than 80 years.

Conquest and colonial rule

The end of the Inca Empire was signalled by the landing of Francisco Pizarro in Peru in 1532. The imperial capital, Cuzco, fell in 1535 and soon afterwards the Spanish began the conquest of Bolivia. Diego de Almagro travelled south with an army of Spanish and native forces through Bolivia to the Chilean coast and in 1542 the entire area was annexed as the Audencia of Charcas of the Viceroyalty of Peru.

During the Spanish colonization, towns were founded and grew rapidly. In 1538 La Plata, now Sucre, was founded and, in 1559 became capital of the Audiencia de Charcas (it is still the official capital of Bolivia). Another administrative centre, La Paz, was founded in 1548. In the eastern lowlands the colonization process was rather different. Like the Incas before them, the Spaniards experienced enormous difficulties in conquering the native peoples of this region. Apart from a number of Jesuit mission settlements (see page 265), the Spanish presence here remained limited to the town of Santa Cruz.

At first the Spanish left the existing socio-economic structure more or less intact. They also adopted the system of compulsory labour (*mita*) which the Incas had imposed, though much more forcefully. Spanish colonial rule was always motivated by greed and over time became more and more aggressive. The barter economy and communal working of the land were replaced by a society based on the extraction and exportation of wealth through the ownership of haciendas (large estates) and mining.

Bolivia's destiny was shaped in 1545 with the discovery of silver at Cerro Rico (Rich Mountain) in Potosí (see page 188). Charcas became one of the most important centres of the Spanish colonial economy, sending a constant supply of silver to Spain. The mining town of Potosí grew rapidly and by 1610 had a population of over 160,000, making it for a long time, by far the largest city in Latin America. Potosí's opulent extravagance became legendary and for decades a favourite Spanish description for untold wealth was 'vale un Potosí' (worth a Potosí).

Together with precious metals from smaller mining centres such as Oruro, silver from Cerro Rico was crucial to the maintenance of the Spanish empire and financed their wars in Europe. Many hundreds of thousands of local indigenous people were forced to work in the mines, in the workshops of the crown mint or on the haciendas.

The Spaniards regarded the local peoples as inferior and cared little for their welfare. The suppression of indigenous culture went as far as making it compulsory to wear Spanish-style dress. According to popular belief this is the origin of many of Bolivia's distinctive hats and the *cholas'* skirts (see page 40). The mortality rate among the indigenous people was high, because of appalling working conditions in the mines and the arrival of European infectious diseases. By the mid-17th century the indigenous population had been almost halved.

During the 18th century many of Potosí's rich silver veins became exhausted and the colony of Alto Perú (as Bolivia was known) lost much of its influence.

Independence

Resistance to Spanish colonial rule had been less intense in Bolivia than neighbouring Peru. The most notable uprising took place in 1781 and was led by **Túpac Katari**, who successfully laid siege to La Paz for eight months, but was eventually crushed. Inspired by the French and American revolutions at the end of the 18th century, the *criollos*, descendants of Spaniards born in Latin America, became increasingly frustrated by trade restrictions and high taxes imposed by the Spanish bureaucracy in the interests of Spain.

While Spain was occupied defending its borders against Napoleon's armies between 1808 and 1810, the University of San Francisco Xavier, at Sucre, called for the independence of all Spain's American colonies. When Spain tried to restore its rule in the following years the *criollo* commercial elites rebelled and took up arms against the Spanish authorities, under the leadership of the Venezuelan **Simón Bolívar**. On 9 December 1824 Simón Bolívar's general, **Antonio José de Sucre**, won the decisive battle of Ayacucho in Peru and invaded Alto Perú, defeating the Spaniards finally at the battle of Tumusla on 2 April 1825.

On 9 February 1825, when he first entered La Paz, Sucre had already promulgated the decree of independence, but his second in command, **Andrés Santa Cruz**, was for retaining links with Peru. Bolívar was of two minds, but Sucre had his way and Bolivia was declared independent on 6 August. In honour of its liberator and first president, the country was named República de Bolívar, soon to be changed to Bolivia. La Plata became the capital and Sucre became the second president.

The Republic

For most of the period since independence, three main features have dominated Bolivian history: the importance of mining; the loss of territory through disputes and wars with neighbouring countries; and chronic political instability.

The noble principles of revolution were soon forgotten as the *caudillos* (military 'strongmen') revealed themselves to be defenders of the political and economic status quo. Although in the 19th century the army was small, officers were key figures in power-struggles, often backing different factions of the *criollo* land-owning elite, whose interests had replaced those of the former colonial rulers. At the end of the 19th century the political elite ended the existence of the *ayllus*, the indigenous communal lands, which were swallowed up into the huge ranches

BACKGROUND
War of the Pacific

One of the major international wars in Latin America since independence, this conflict has its roots in a long-running dispute between Chile and Bolivia over the ill-defined frontier in the Atacama desert.

There had already been one conflict, in 1836-1839, when Chile defeated Peru and Bolivia, putting an end to a confederation of the two states. The discovery of nitrates in Atacama complicated relations. Nitrates were exploited by Anglo-Chilean companies in the Bolivian province of Antofagasta.

In 1878 the Bolivian government, short of revenue, attempted to tax the Chilean-owned Antofagasta Railroad and Nitrate Company. When the company refused to pay, the Bolivians seized the company's assets. The Chilean government claimed that the Bolivian action broke an 1874 agreement between the two states. When Peru announced that it would honour a secret alliance with Bolivia by supporting her, the Chilean president, Aníbal Pinto, declared war on both states.

Chile won the war and even captured Lima, but Bolivia had already signed a cease-fire as early as 1880, giving up its coastal province. Apart from souring relations between Chile and her two northern neighbours to this day, the war gave Chile a monopoly over the world's supply of nitrates and enabled her to dominate the southern Pacific coast.

Bolivia had lost its access to the sea and many still blame their country's under-development on this event. Ever since 1880, recovering an outlet to the Pacific has played an important part in foreign policy, but endless negotiations have produced little more than token sympathy.

Bolivia was eventually compensated for the loss of her sea-coast by the construction of a railway from La Paz to Arica. The line is currently out of service but a good paved highway links the two cities and there is a great deal of commercial traffic between the ports of northern Chile and Bolivia. Bolivian vacationers also frequent the Chilean seaside but never without a twinge of sadness and resentment over the loss of their precious Litoral. In April 2014, Bolivia lodged a claim at the International Court of Justice in The Hague to regain access to the Pacific Ocean through territory it lost to Chile in the War of the Pacific. Lawyers from both sides began to present their arguments to the Court in May 2015.

(*latifundios*) of the landowners. The *indígenas*, who had suffered under the *mita*, the system of compulsory labour, now became serfs, as their lives and labour were owned by the estate owners.

For much of the 20th century the Bolivian economy depended on tin exports. The construction of railways and the demand for tin in Europe and the USA led to a mining boom after 1900. In 1902 export earnings from tin exceeded those of silver for the first time. By the 1920s the industry was dominated by three 'tin-barons',

Simón Patiño, Mauricio Hochschild and the Aramayo family, who exercised great influence over national politics.

Political instability

Bolivian politics have been even more turbulent than elsewhere in Latin America. When the governing class was not engaged in conflicts with neighbouring countries, internal power struggles consumed all its energies. Between 1825 and 1982 there were no fewer than 188 coups d'état, earning the country a place in the Guinness Book of Records. The longest lasting government of the 19th century was that of Andrés Santa Cruz (1829-1839), but when he tried to unite Bolivia with Peru in 1836, Chile and Argentina intervened to overthrow him.

An 1899 revolt called the **Guerra Federal**, led by business groups from La Paz and the tin-mining areas, defeated Sucre and made La Paz the centre of government. This has never been forgiven or forgotten by Sucre which, to this day, hopes to regain full capital status.

Since independence Bolivia has suffered continual losses of territory, partly because of communications difficulties and the central government's inability to control distant provinces. Following its rapid defeat in the **War of the Pacific** (1879-1883, see box, page 313) Bolivia lost her costal provinces. Chile later agreed to build a railway between La Paz and Arica. When Brazil annexed the rubber-rich **Acre Territory** in 1903, Bolivia was compensated with another railway, but this Madeira–Mamoré line, which cost a life for every rail-tie, never reached its intended destination of Riberalta. And there was no railway at all to compensate Bolivia for its great loss in the **Chaco War** (1932-1935, see box, page 315).

Modern Bolivia

The Chaco War was a turning point in Bolivian history. The political influence of the army increased and in 1936 it seized power for the first time since the War of the Pacific. Defeat in the Chaco War bred nationalist resentment among junior army officers and among the *indígenas* who had been used as cannon-fodder. After demobilization thousands of *indígenas* refused to return to serfdom. Instead they settled in towns where they played a significant part in the political radicalization of the population, particularly the peasants and miners.

This growing national malaise among different sectors of society led to a group of young intellectuals setting up a nationalist party, the **Movimiento Nacional Revolucionario** (MNR) headed by **Víctor Paz Estenssoro**, Hernán Siles Zuazo, Walter Guevara Arce and Juan Lechín Oquendo. Their anger was directed against the mine owners and the leaders who had controlled Bolivian politics, and they claimed to stand for the emancipation of the poor masses.

In 1944 Víctor Paz Estenssoro succeeded in taking the MNR into the radical government of young army officers led by Major **Gualberto Villaroel**. However, in 1946 Villaroel was overthrown and publicly lynched in Plaza Murillo, and Paz Estenssoro had to flee to Argentina.

BACKGROUND
The Chaco War

In the 1920s the US Standard Oil Company was drilling for oil in the Bolivian Chaco. The company and the Bolivian government intended to transport the oil to the Atlantic coast on the Río Pilcomayo. It also seemed likely that there were further reserves in other parts of the inaccessible wilderness.

The problem was, however, that the Bolivian frontier with Paraguay had never been well defined. From 1928 there were border clashes with Paraguayan army patrols and in 1932 the Chaco War broke out. The Paraguayan forces knew the terrain much better than the Bolivian soldiers, who were mostly from the Andes and unused to the intense heat. By 1935 Bolivia had lost the war, practically the whole of the Chaco and 56,000 lives. Another 36,000 Paraguayans perished in equally hideous conditions, more dying of thirst than in combat.

The war marked a turning point in the history of both nations. Oil was eventually discovered on the Bolivian side of the border, and the reserves around Camiri exploited and exhausted. More recently, multinational oil companies have again cast their eyes on what is today the Paraguayan Chaco, where almost 100,000 people met a horrible and futile end.

The 1952 revolution

The 1951 elections were won by Víctor Paz Estenssoro, as the MNR candidate. However, the incumbent government refused to recognize the result and transferred power to a military junta. The organized and radicalized miners reacted immediately and revolution broke out on 9 April 1952, backed by sections of the police as well as *campesinos*, urban factory workers and the lower middle classes. Two days later the army surrendered to the MNR's militias and the National Revolution was a fact.

Paz Estenssoro became president and his MNR government nationalized the mines, introduced universal suffrage and began the break-up and redistribution of large estates under the Agrarian Reform programme, which ended the feudal economic conditions of rural Bolivia. In the aftermath of the revolution, the **Central Obrera Boliviana** (COB, or Bolivian Workers Central), under the leadership of **Juan Lechín Oquendo**, became a major political force in the country. The giant mineral barons, Patiño, Hochschild and Aramayo, lost their political and economic influence and a new leadership class developed that would dominate Bolivia's political life for almost the next 40 years.

As the Bolivian constitution did not permit a second successive term of office, Paz Estenssoro stood down in 1956 in favour of the more pragmatic Vice-President **Hernán Siles Zuazo**. Faced with a drastic fall in the price of tin, Bolivia's main source of foreign income, and galloping inflation, Siles Zuazo accepted a 'stabilization' plan designed by the International Monetary Fund (IMF). Hardest hit by the policy of freezing wages and scrapping basic food subsidies were the working class and the MNR became increasingly distanced from its original power base. The rank and file of the MNR split into peasants on the one side and miners and the urban proletariat on the other.

Víctor Paz Estenssoro, who had by now become leader of the centre-right faction within the MNR, was re-elected president in 1960, with Juan Lechín Oquendo as vice-president. Growing ideological divides were tearing the party apart and by 1964 it disintegrated into factional warfare. The constitution had to be changed to allow Paz Estenssoro to stand again, which he did with the support of the charismatic General **René Barrientos**. Shortly afterwards, however, Paz Estenssoro was overthrown by his vice-president, who relied on the support of the army and the peasants to defeat the miners.

Military coups

As in many other Latin American countries, the 1960s and 1970s were dominated in Bolivia by coups d'état and military governments. The many military dictatorships of this period were very different in nature. Some were authoritarian and repressive while others were populist. Under the Barrientos regime (1964-1969) political opponents and trade union activists were brutally persecuted and miners' rebellions were put down violently, just as they had been before the 1952 Revolution. The death of Barrientos in a mysterious air crash in 1969 was followed by three brief military governments. The third, led by General **Juan José Torres**, pursued left-wing policies which alarmed many army officers and business leaders.

In August 1971 Torres was overthrown by the right-wing General **Hugo Banzer**, whose rule lasted until 1978. During those years tens of thousands of Bolivians were imprisoned or exiled for political reasons. Political parties and trade unions were banned, state universities were subject to military supervision and there was strict censorship. In 1974 the MNR left the government and Paz Estenssoro, who had returned in 1971, went back into exile. The Banzer regime continued to rule in an even more authoritarian manner, though mild by comparison with contemporary dictatorships in Argentina and Chile. In 1978 Banzer was forced to call elections, partly as a result of the pressure which US President Jimmy Carter exerted on the military government because of its human rights abuses.

There followed another period of chronic instability, political unrest and military violence between 1978 and 1982, with three presidential elections and five coups. Civilian rule returned in 1982 when Hernán Siles Zuazo once again took office, but not before the notoriously brutal military coup led by General **Luis García Meza** (1980-1981). In August 1982 the military returned to barracks and Siles Zuazo assumed the presidency in a leftist coalition government with support from the communists and trade unions. Under this regime inflation spiralled out of control, reaching an annual rate of 24,000%, with banknotes of up to 10,000,000 pesos bolivianos in common circulation.

The neo-liberal era

The 1985 elections were won by Víctor Paz Estenssoro, but only by forming a coalition with **Jaime Paz Zamora** of the **Movimiento de la Izquierda**

Revolucionaria (MIR). In an attempt to save the economy, Paz Estenssoro enlisted the help of Dr Jeffrey Sachs, a Harvard professor who imposed a radical programme of structural adjustment.

Perhaps no one could have predicted it would be so tough, or maybe those that could did not care about the hardship they were creating. One of the main thrusts was the radical dismantling of the state sector which Víctor Paz had set up 30 years before. Under Professor Sach's neo-liberal economic model, the first sacrificial targets were the by-now outdated mines of the state-owned Corporación Minera Boliviana (Comibol). By the end of 1985, 23,000 miners had lost their jobs. Some remained to form so-called mining cooperatives but most left in search of livelihoods in coca-growing regions like Chapare, or in larger cities. In the elections of 1989 a new character appeared on the political stage, **Gonzalo Sánchez de Lozada** of the MNR, one of the chief proponents of the neo-liberal reforms. Sánchez de Lozada, or 'Goni' as he was known, won most votes but the result was so close that Congress had to choose a president from the three leading contenders. Paz Zamora, who came third in the elections, won-out after making an unlikely alliance with former military dictator General Hugo Banzer.

The presidential election of 1993 was finally won by Sánchez de Lozada. In a shrewd move to gain the support of the Indian population, Goni formed an alliance with **Víctor Hugo Cárdenas**, leader of the **Movimiento Revolucionario Túpac Katari de Liberación** (MRTKL), one of Bolivia's two indigenist parties at the time. Goni implemented across-the- board capitalization (privatization) of state enterprises which, opponents claimed, in effect awarded many companies to government cronies for a fraction of their real value.

The 1997 presidential elections were won by former dictator General Hugo Banzer and his **Acción Democrática Nacionalista** (ADN) party. Banzer and his advisors immediately took a flight to Washington DC to secure approval from the US. Ironically, it was former US president Jimmy Carter who had brought about Banzer's downfall in 1978.

Banzer supported many of the previous government's policies. During his first two years in office, he pursued economic austerity and the US-backed policy of forcibly eradicating coca plantations, both of which led to widespread hardship and popular unrest. With the country's economic and social problems growing steadily worse, Banzer was forced to resign in 2001 because of cancer. His replacement, Vice-President **Jorge (Tuto) Quiroga**, had just a year left of Banzer's term to serve before new elections were held.

In 2002 Gonzalo Sánchez de Lozada was elected president for the second time. However, another new political personality was making his appearance: **Evo Morales**, indigenous leader of the coca-growers, and now head of the opposition. The following year, tension between the government and its opponents boiled over on several occasions, with more than 100 people killed and hundreds injured in violent protests which forced Goni from office and into exile in the USA.

Sánchez de Lozada was succeeded by his deputy, **Carlos Mesa**, but he fared no better in the face of what became a full-fledged national uprising against decades of neo-liberal economic policies, US-sponsored coca eradication, and private exploitation of the country's rich natural gas resources. Mesa held office for less than two years before being replaced by Supreme Court President **Eduardo Rodríguez**, who became interim president until new elections were held in December 2005.

Movement toward socialism

Evo Morales and his **Movimiento al Socialismo** (MAS, Movement Toward Socialism) party won the 2005 elections with a clear majority, marking a watershed in Bolivian and Latin American history (see box, page 319). Morales' rise to power was precipitated by the continued opposition to gas exports, mass protests by the inhabitants of El Alto calling for a more equal society and his support for coca growers. Morales soon announced elections to a new constituent assembly and, in May 2006, sent troops into the gas fields, provoking foreign hydrocarbon companies to renegotiate their contracts with Bolivia. The Constituent Assembly eventually approved a new socially oriented constitution in November 2007, but the process was marred by procedural irregularities and violence. After a year and a half of fruitless debate, the charter was voted in a single marathon session from which some opposition delegates were forcibly barred.

Despite adhering to other campaign promises such as ending forced coca eradication, nationalizing the strategic natural gas sector and implementing new social programmes, the Morales government failed to include a broad cross-section of Bolivians in its vision of the future. While he had originally received the support of many non-indigenous, urban middle-class voters seeking a genuine change in the country's leadership, this fell away in the face of the government's own ethnocentric outlook. Morales also failed to appreciate the depth of regionalist sentiment in Bolivia's eastern lowland departments or the local sensitivities of Sucre (Bolivia's official capital) and needlessly aroused antagonism among many sectors that might otherwise have continued to support him.

With the usual protagonists of social unrest – indigenous leaders, coca-growers and trade unionists – now in the Presidential Palace and with traditional political parties largely discredited, political opposition took on a new form. In 2008, wealthy landowners, business leaders and local politicians backing autonomy for northern and eastern lowland departments (dubbed **La Media Luna**, the Half Moon, for their geographic location) tried to gain the upper hand over the La Paz government. **Estatutos Autonómicos** (Statutes of Autonomy) were drawn up in the departments of Santa Cruz, Tarija, Beni and Pando, and approved by ample majorities in local referendums. Following this opposition victory, the Morales government offered to negotiate a mechanism whereby increased departmental autonomy could be incorporated in the new constitution. Leaders of the Media Luna refused to participate in negotiations. In the face of these apparently irreconcilable positions, the Senate called another nationwide referendum for August 2008, in which voters could either ratify or revoke the mandates of both the president and their *prefecto* (departmental governor). Voters ratified President Morales' leadership by a 67% majority nationwide and the most important opposition *prefectos* were also ratified in office. Nothing substantial

BACKGROUND
Evo Morales

21 January 2006 was an emotional dayby anyone's standards. A tearful 46-year-old Juan Evo Morales Ayma stood before tens of thousands of his countrymen to be ceremonially invested with Bolivia's leadership at Tiwanaku, archaeological symbol of the nation's ancient grandeur. He had become the first indigenous president in the history of Bolivia and South America, and only the second inall of Latin America (after Mexico's Benito Juárez, 1858-1872).

Born on 26 October 1959 in Isallavi, a tiny native community in the vicinity of Lago Poopó in the department of Oruro, he was one of seven children, only three of whom survived infancy. Evo grew up in an adobe house with a straw roof and herded llamas on the altiplano. At age 16 he moved to the city of Oruro to attend high school, working as a baker,a bricklayer and a trumpet-player in a band; the latter gave him the opportunity to travel the country. After graduation, the remainder of his education was, by his own account, "in the university of life".

In 1980, when Evo was 21 years old, drought and famine forced his family to migrate from the altiplano to the subtropics of Chapare where, like so many other *campesinos*, they grew coca. He became involved in the *cocaleros* federation and rose rapidly in its ranks. During the many conflicts with successive Bolivian governments who attempted to carry out US-sponsored coca eradication programmes in the 1980s and 90s, Morales led numerous marches from Chapare to La Paz. He was arrested, beaten and, in 1989, nearly killed by government forces.

In 1995 he tried to found a new political party and, although this proved unsuccessful, he was elected to Congress in 1997. His political following eventually gelled into the Movimiento al Socialismo (MAS) party, for whom he ran and came second in the 2002 presidential elections. Then, in 2005 he captured 54% of votes and became president of Bolivia – the difficult part of his career had just begun.

had changed, but the results convinced the Morales government that the time was ripe for yet another referendum, this time to approve the controversial new constitution in December 2008. The constitution was approved by a 61% majority, but predictably voters in the eastern states rejected it. Despite these profound divisions, presidential and congressional elections in December 2009 revealed greater unity as Morales became the first Bolivian president to be democratically reelected (with a 63% majority) and his MAS party won outright majorities in both houses of the legislature.

For most Bolivians, day-to-day concerns revolved around sudden increases in the cost of basic foods, blamed by the government on business leaders seeking to destabilize the administration, and blamed by the opposition on government economic mismanagement. Other examples of popular ire were transport strikes which led to the reversal of an increase in fuel prices by 73-83% in December 2010 and month-long mass demonstrations in early 2012 over the government's refusal to raise wages after increasing working hours. Later in the year strikes over low levels of pay for police and army officers led to violence. The government also climbed down over a proposed road through the Isiboro Sécure national park following protests by indigenous people in late 2011, only to change its mind, reopen the project and stimulate more protests in 2012.

In July 2013 the case of the US whistleblower, Edward Snowden, briefly enveloped Bolivia as the plane that was carrying President Morales home from Moscow was forced to land in Vienna after France, Italy, Spain and Portugal were reported to have refused to let it enter their airspace. Rumours that Snowden was on board were unfounded; likewise, accusations that Washington had pressurized the European countries were denied. Many Latin American governments supported Bolivia's assertion that the action was unjustified.

In 2014, the economy was registering positive growth (6.5% estimated for GDP for 2013, with slightly less estimated for 2014) and prudent use of the income from sales of natural gas and other commodities gave the country healthy foreign reserves equivalent to about half of GDP. Acute poverty was being reduced, the minimum wage increased and a law to ensure food security, passed in 2011 after demonstrations over food shortages, led to a decline in hunger and undernourishment of children. Small-scale infrastructure projects were being allocated to many communities, providing medical centres, schools and gymnasiums. Inflation was limited to less than 10% and the foreign debt was also cut drastically.

In this upbeat climate, opinion polls in 2014 showed that President Morales was receiving support from over 40% of voters, way more than that for any of his rivals in the divided opposition. This gave a boost to the president as his bid to run for a third term in office in October 2014 was approved by the Constitutional Court. The court stated that his first term started before the new constitution of 2009 came into force, so elections in 2014 would mark his second consecutive term, not third. Morales won the presidential vote by 61%, compared with 25% for his nearest rival, Samuel Dora Medina of the Concertación Unidad Demócrata. Morales' Movimiento al Socialismo (MAS-IPSP) also won majorities in both houses of congress.

In January 2015 President Morales took office for his third term, due to run until 2020. He vowed to follow the same path as the previous two terms, concentrating on reducing still further poverty and deprivation and maintaining fiscal discipline. The strength of this commitment would be largely determined by international prices for gas, since the economy is heavily dependent upon exports of natural gas. Prices were falling in early 2015 because of weak demand, but the search for new deposits continued. Morales also made a pledge to a reform of the judicial system.

Economy

With GDP of about US$31 billion (2013 estimate, World Bank), Bolivia is one of the smaller economies in South America. Its fossil fuel resources however, especially **natural gas**, of huge importance to the much larger economies of its neighbours: Brazil and Argentina.

This gas industry provides the government with its largest single source of income and is perhaps the most important hope for Bolivia's economic future. Natural gas has also generated much controversy. For years, Bolivia has refused to sell gas to Chile, potentially one of its most important customers, because of lingering resentment over the War of the Pacific (see box, page 313). Brazil and Argentina, on the other hand, were considered friends and allies and at one time received Bolivian gas at below market prices. Then Argentine companies allegedly sold the gas to Chile at market rates, thus turning a quick profit and ridiculing Bolivia, who had gone out of its way to help the Argentines.

Outraged by such multinational scheming, and ever mindful of what happened to 62,000 tonnes of silver mined from Potosí's Cerro Rico since colonial times, which disappeared overseas without the Bolivian people seeing any benefit, many Bolivians demanded the re-nationalization of the gas sector which had been partially privatized during the presidency of Gonzalo Sánchez de Lozada. A publicly owned natural gas industry became one of Evo Morales' most important campaign promises and, following his election in 2005, this was started in 2006. Since the nationalization of the gas sector, the focus has been on production rather than exploration. In 2014 annual output was 500 billion cubic feet. There is, however, some debate over how long Bolivia's gas reserves will last. Some state estimates say they will last until 2023, with probable reserves of over 20 trillion cubic feet. Other analysts give lower estimates, from 8 to 13 trillion cubic feet with exhaustion set at 2017. Either way, the government is seeking to invest in gas exploration in order to ensure the future of this dominant sector.

Agriculture is also an important sector of the economy, contributing 9.2% of GDP and employing just under a third of the population. Subsistence farming of traditional products takes place mostly in the highlands, where excess produce is sold in local markets. In the east, however, there is very fertile land. The most productive area is in the province of Santa Cruz, where the fluvial plains are extremely rich in nutrients. Here the tropical climate allows two crops a year of soya beans and farmers achieve yields of around three tonnes a hectare, compared with 1½-2 tonnes in neighbouring countries. Investors have bought large estates to grow soya and other crops, such as cotton, sunflower and sugarcane, and export-oriented agro-industry is booming. Soya is also pertinent to global interest in **bio-fuels** but, along with several other nations, the current Bolivian government opposes bio-fuels on principle, asserting that it is immoral to feed cars in preference to people. Sources of biofuel production other than soya are being studied.

Despite its great historical importance, **mining** contributed about 5.5% to GDP in 2014, although this figure fluctuates with world mineral prices. Bolivia is a major producer of tin, antimony, wolfram, bismuth, boron, silver, lead, zinc and gold, while there are large reserves of iron, lithium and potassium. The Kori Kollo gold mine, near Oruro, is the second largest in Latin America and the San Cristóbal silver mine, in the Lípez region of Potosí, is the largest of its kind on the continent. Some mineral deposits are in especially sensitive ecological areas, such as lithium in the Salar de Uyuni and iron at Cerro Mutún in the Pantanal. To date they have not been extensively worked.

The production of **coca and cocaine** is also one of Bolivia's important sources of employment and income. It is estimated that about 10% of the working population are directly dependent on the coca industry for their livelihoods. Coca cultivation provides a much higher return for *campesinos* than any other crop. It can continue on the same land for at least 15 years and can be harvested four times a year, whereas other crops can exhaust the soil within as little as three years. It is for these reasons as well as traditional distrust of the authorities, that farmers in Chapare are reluctant to abandon coca cultivation in favour of the proposed crop substitution programmes. See also box, page 234.

Tourism is a growing sector of the Bolivian economy but remains highly focused on a few well-know attractions like Lake Titicaca and the Salar de Uyuni.

The informal economy

Bolivia has, for centuries, neglected its indigenous majority yet they have always found ways to eke out a livelihood. This informal sector of the economy includes armies of *vendedores ambulantes* or **street merchants**, and many small workshops – often just a sewing machine on the sidewalk. Because of a shortage of 'real jobs', poorer families have created their own work, often demonstrating remarkable inventiveness and making use of family networks and contacts. **Contraband** is another important aspect of the informal economy, with thriving smugglers' markets on many borders. As a result, there are shortages of subsidised products like petrol and domestic natural gas in border areas.

Economic necessity has also led to growing numbers of working women and children. According to UNICEF in 2014, more than 500,000 children worked in Bolivia, with almost 60% under 14. This explosion of child labour is most obvious in cities and towns, with the swelling ranks of shoe-shiners (*lustrabotas*), lottery ticket sellers, beggars, cigarette and sweet vendors and street musicians. Despite international labour conventions advising that the minimum age for work should be 15, Bolivia passed a new law in 2014 allowing 10-year-olds to work as long as they attend school, are under parental supervision and are self-employed.

But it is the **rural population** which bears the brunt of Bolivian poverty. Although the level of those living below the poverty line stood at 45% in 2011, the percentage of the rural population in acute poverty was over 60%. This can be seen most clearly on the altiplano. Scenes of llamas grazing on the shores of Lake Titicaca under the snow-capped Mount Illimani are misleadingly idyllic; life on the altiplano can be exceptionally harsh.

Migration

The departments of Bolivia show remarkable differences in patterns of population growth, caused mainly by migration from the countryside to the large towns and cities. Apart from urban centres, newly colonized regions in the Yungas and northern or eastern lowlands also attract migrants. The department of Santa Cruz, for example, has grown twice as fast as the national average in recent decades. The rural altiplano, in particular, has been rapidly depopulated since the collapse of tin mining.

Migration further afield is also common, with many Bolivians going to live and work – often illegally and in precarious conditions – in Argentina, Brazil, Spain or the USA. The money they send back to their families in Bolivia is an increasingly important part of the economy, with US$1.3 billion sent home by overseas workers in 2013, compared with US$172 million in 2000 (World Bank figures).

As in the rest of Latin America, urbanization is increasing rapidly, having grown from 26% to 67% between 1950 and 2011. Bolivia has changed drastically from a predominantly rural society to an urban one. El Alto is the best example of this phenomenon. Once little more than a railway station on the desolate altiplano above La Paz, it is today the second-largest city in Bolivia; for a time it was the fastest-growing city in South America. It is home to a thriving and politically powerful *cholo* (urban indigenous) society, many of whose members make a decent income in the wholesale or retail trades.

Culture

Arts and crafts

The wealth of Bolivian crafts draws on many centuries of skills and traditions from diverse peoples who were first incorporated into the Inca Empire and later into the Spanish colony. Though much of this artistic heritage was destroyed by the Spanish conquest, the traditions adapted and evolved in numerous ways, absorbing new methods, concepts and materials from Europe while maintaining ancient techniques and symbols.

Textiles and costumes

Some of the most beautifully woven and dyed textiles to be found anywhere were produced by the Aymara people of the Bolivian altiplano up until the late 19th century. These reflect the incredibly rich textile tradition which flourished in the Lake Titicaca basin since ancient times.

Originally, textile production arose out of the simple need for clothing. Gradually, though, more complicated techniques and designs evolved. Far from being merely of utilitarian purpose, Andean textiles played major political, social and religious roles. Woven cloth was the most highly prized possession and sought-after trading commodity in the Andes in pre-Columbian times and was used to establish and strengthen social and political relationships. It also played a role in all phases of the life cycle.

The Incas inherited this rich weaving tradition from the Aymara and forced them to work in *mitas* or textile workshops. The largest quantities of the finest textiles were made specifically to be burned as ritual offerings – a tradition which still survives. The Spanish, too, exploited this wealth and skill by using the *mitas* and exporting the cloth to Europe.

Spanish chroniclers reported that, upon retreating from battle, Inca soldiers sometimes left behind thousands of llamas and prisoners, and even gold and silver, but chose to burn entire warehouses filled with cloth rather than leave them for the *conquistadores*. Indeed, in the *Quipus*, the string knot recording system of the Incas, only people and camelids ranked above textiles.

It is, therefore, not surprising that ancient weaving traditions survived the conquest while other social and cultural traditions disappeared. Textiles continue to play an important part in society in many parts of Bolivia. They are still handed down from one generation to the next and used specifically for ritual ceremonies. As a result, the finest textiles have survived until today. However, the influence of modern technology has reached even remote highland areas. Rural people have begun to wear machine-made clothes and many aspects of the ancient art of weaving are now lost.

Costumes

Prior to Inca rule Aymara men wore a tunic (*llahua*) and a mantle (*llacata*) and carried a bag for coca leaves (*huallquepo*). The women wore a wrapped dress (*urku*) and mantle (*iscayo*) and a belt (*huaka*); their coca bag was called an *istalla*. The *urku* was fastened at shoulder level with a pair of metal *tupu*, the traditional Andean dress-pins.

Probably in imitation of the Aymara, the Inca men had tunics (*unkus*) and a bag for coca leaves called a *ch'uspa*. The women wore a blouse (*huguna*), skirts (*aksu*) and belts (*chumpis*), and carried foodstuffs in large, rectangular cloths called *llicllas*, which were fastened at the chest with a single pin *(tupu)* or a smaller clasp called a *ttipqui*.

In isolated Andean villages and communities women still wear the traditional *aksu*, a skirt over two pieces of cloth overlapping at the sides and held up by a belt. The women of Tarabuco and Potolo, near Sucre, for example, commonly wear *aksus*, while Tarabuco men wear red and orange striped ponchos, and hats similar to crash helmets, possibly inspired by the Spanish army helmets. Tarabuco women's hats are small white *monteras* decorated with sequins. One item of costume which plays a particularly important role in the lives of the native population is the belt. The Aymara devote much of their lives to making belts for different occasions.

During the post-conquest period native dress was modified to satisfy Spanish ideas of propriety. Spanish policy concerning dress demanded that the indigenous population should be fully and properly dressed at all times and that each person must be dressed according to his/her class. Spanish dress was restricted to the upper-class *indígenas*.

The last century of the colonial period was disturbed by numerous indigenous uprisings. The Spanish rulers believed that by restricting the natives' traditional clothing it could diminish their identification with their ancestors and that discontent would, therefore, be reduced. Thus the native male costume became pants, jacket, vest and poncho. In the less accessible parts, people were able to preserve their customs to a certain extent. While the Spanish influence is still evident in much of the dress, indigenous garments are also worn, forming a costume that is distinctly Andean.

Textile materials and techniques

The Andean people used mainly alpaca or llama wool. The former can be spun into fine, shining yarn when woven and has a lustre similar to that of silk, though sheep's wool came to be widely used following the Spanish conquest.

A commonly used technique is the drop spindle. A stick is weighted with a wooden wheel and the raw material is fed through one hand. A sudden twist and drop in the spindle spins the yarn. This very sensitive art can be seen practised by women while herding animals in the fields.

Spinning wheels were introduced by Europeans and are now prevalent due to increased demand. Pre-Columbian looms were often portable and those in use today are generally similar. A woman will watch over her animals while weaving, perhaps on a backstrap loom, or waist loom, so-called because the weaver controls the tension on one side with her waist with the other side tied to an upright or tree. These looms can't be used on the treeless altiplano so the Aymara people use four sticks set in the ground to hold the loom in place. The pre-Columbian looms are usually used for personal costume while the treadle loom is used for more commercial pieces in textile centres such as Villa Ribera, near Cochabamba, as it provides greater efficiency and flexibility.

Most weaving occurs during the winter, after the harvest and before the next year's planting. The women spend much of their day at the loom while also looking after the children and carrying out daily chores. A complex piece of textile can take up to several months to complete and, because of the time taken, is built to last many years.

Today, there is increasing pressure on indigenous people to desert their homes and join the white and mestizo people in the cities. Furthermore, *indígenas* in native costume are often looked down on and considered uncivilized. There is a danger of the traditional textiles of the Andes becoming museum pieces rather than articles of daily use and wear. In some areas foreign aid and leadership of experts is proving effective. In Sucre, for example, a group of anthropologists has successfully brought about the revival of traditional village weaving.

Knitting

Knitting has a relatively short history in the Andes. Fibres commonly used are alpaca, llama and sheep's wool. During the past two decades though, much of the alpaca and llama wool has been bought by larger companies for export. Today, much of the wool for knitting is bought ready-spun from factories.

Outside the towns the majority of knitting is still done by hand. Traditionally many of the *chullos*, knitted hats with ear flaps worn on the altiplano, are knitted with four small hooked needles. In the Andes the more traditional pieces still have patterns with llamas, mountains and other scenic and geometric designs.

Dyeing

The skills of dyeing were still practised virtually unchanged even after the arrival of the Spaniards. Nowadays, the word *makhnu* refers to any natural dye, but originally was the name for cochineal, an insect which lives on the leaves of the nopal cactus. These dyes were used widely by pre-Columbian weavers. Vegetable dyes are also used, made from the leaves, fruit and seeds of shrubs and flowers and from lichen, tree bark and roots. Although the high price for cochineal in the use of food colouring has discouraged its use for textiles, it is still widely combined with man-made dyes in textile centres such as Villa Ribera and around Lake Titicaca.

Symbolism

Symbolism plays an important role in weaving. Traditionally every piece of textile from a particular community had identical symbols and colours which were a source of identity as well as carrying specific symbols and telling a story. In the Andean world the planet Venus *(Chaska)* played an important role in mythology and agricultural pattern. Its appearance was used to forecast the coming year's rainfall. This symbol and that of the Sun (*Inti*) predominated in textile decoration and were universal to the *ayllus*, the self-sufficient and self-governing communities. The Jalq'a people of Sucre weave bizarre animal motifs on their *aksus*, or overskirts. These symbols perhaps represent *chulpas*, creatures that inhabited the Earth before the birth of the Sun.

The arrival of the Spaniards in the 16th century initiated a new era of symbolism as old and new elements appeared side by side. Symbols such as *Inti* may be found together with a horse figure introduced after the conquest. Sometimes the meanings of motifs have multiplied or been superseded. The cross, for example, in prehispanic times signified the constellation of Cruz del Sur, the Southern Cross, or Cruz de la Siembra, guardian of the fields. Both have been eclipsed by the Christian symbol.

Buying textiles
Bolivia is an excellent source of textiles, which vary greatly from region to region in style, technique and use. For *mantas* the best place is in the shops behind San Francisco church in La Paz (see page 39). Prices are lower if you buy direct from the Tarabuco people who carry their loads of textiles up and down the steep streets. Other good places to find textiles are the market in Tarabuco and at ASUR, a textile project based in Sucre which works closely with rural communities.

Among the many villages dotted throughout the Andes, the following produce textiles which are particularly sought after and, therefore, more expensive: **Calcha**, in southern Potosí; **Tarabuco**, near Sucre; **Charazani**, in the Apolobamba mountains in the north of La Paz department; **Sica Sica**, between La Paz and Oruro; **Calamarca**, south of La Paz on the road to Oruro; **Challa**, halfway between Oruro and Cochabamba. In the northern part of the Potosí department, southeast from Oruro and northwest of Sucre, are the villages of **Llallagua**, **Sacaca**, **Bolívar** and **Macha**. Here, traditional weaving is maintained more than in any other part of Bolivia and the textiles are the most widely sold, especially in La Paz.

If you are asked to pay US$200-300 for a *manta*, which usually takes around two months to weave, this a more realistic price than US$10-20. If a *manta* has old stains on it, it may be better to leave them, as cleaning it may damage the textile. In general, though, Andean weavings are tough and can cope with washing, though at cool temperatures. If buying a newly woven piece, check that the dyes are properly fixed before washing. Wet a small part then wipe it on white paper to see if any of the colours appear.

Hats
Hats were an important element of much prehispanic costume and Bolivia has perhaps a greater variety than any other region in South America, with over 100 different styles. One reason for this is the high altitude of the Andes, where the sun's rays are more intense, making hats a necessity. Another is the survival of traditional costume among the country's indigenous majority. The hat is the most important piece of the *indígena's* outfit and accompanies the wearer everywhere.

The reason it is so important is because it is worn on the head, the most sacred part of the body and spirit.

One of the most familiar features of La Paz are the Aymara women with their brown or grey bowler, or derby hats, locally called a *bombín*. While the vast majority of the hats are made of felt, some are still made from rabbit hair, as they all were originally. Another style, worn by the residents of Tarija, near the Argentine border, is based on those worn by their colonial ancestors from Andalucía. In Potosí, the women's hat is like a 'stove-pipe', though these are becoming increasingly rare.

In Cochabamba, Quechua women wear a white top hat of ripolined straw, decorated with a black ribbon. According to legend, a young unmarried Quechua woman in the city was reprimanded by a Roman Catholic priest for living with her boyfriend, a practice common among indigenous couples intending to marry. As a punishment, she was made to wear a black ribbon around the base of the hat. The next day at Mass, much to the priest's chagrin, all the women were wearing the black ribbon and the style stuck.

Pottery

In all their variety, the prehispanic ceramics found in burial sites across the Americas have emphasized the extent to which the potters were concerned with imbuing their work with religious or magical symbolism. Their skill was not merely required to produce utilitarian objects necessary for daily life but was evidently a specialized, sometimes sanctified, art which required more than technical expertise.

Inca ceramic decoration consists mainly of small-scale geometric and usually symmetrical designs. One distinctive form of vessel which continues to be made and used is the *arybola*. This pot is designed to carry liquid, especially *chicha*, and is secured with a rope on the bearer's back. It is believed that *arybolas* were used mainly by the governing Inca elite and became important status symbols.

With the Spanish invasion many indigenous communities lost their artistic traditions, others remained relatively untouched, while others still combined Hispanic and indigenous traditions and techniques. The Spanish brought three innovations: the potter's wheel, which gave greater speed and uniformity; knowledge of the enclosed kiln; and the technique of lead glazes. The enclosed kiln made temperature regulation easier and allowed higher temperatures to be maintained, producing stronger pieces. Today, many communities continue to apply prehispanic techniques, while others use more modern processes.

Jewellery and metalwork

The Incas associated gold with the Sun. However, very few examples of their fine goldwork remain as the Spaniards melted down their amassed gold and silver objects and then went on to extract more precious metals from the ground. The surviving *indígenas* were forced to work in barbaric conditions in gold and silver mines, where the death toll was horrifically high, most notoriously at Potosí.

During the colonial period gold and silver pieces were made to decorate the altars of churches and houses of the elite. Metalworkers came from Spain and Italy to develop the industry. The Spanish preferred silver and strongly influenced the evolution of silverwork during the colonial period. A style known as Andean baroque developed embracing both indigenous and European elements. Silver bowls in this style – *cochas* – are still used in Andean ceremonies.

Part of the Inca female costume was a large silver pin with a decorative head, the *tupu*, worn at the neck of the cloak, or *lliclla*, to hold it in place. Today, it continues to be made and used by the majority of Quechua-speaking people in Bolivia, though its form has changed over the centuries. In Inca times the decorative head was usually disc or fan-shaped, thought to derive from the *tumi* knife used for surgery. During colonial times Western emblems superseded the Inca forms. When in the 19th century uprisings caused native costume to be strictly authority-regulated, the *tupu* developed an oval, spoon-shaped head, sometimes incised, and had charms suspended on silver chains.

In the Amazon Basin seeds, flowers and feathers continue to be used as jewellery by many peoples. The Western fashion for natural or ethnic jewellery has encouraged production, using brightly coloured feathers, fish bones, seeds or animal teeth.

Woodcarving

Carved religious figures, usually made from hardwoods, were a central influence in the development of woodcarving. In Eastern Bolivia, as in Paraguay, the tradition of carving and painting religious figures originates with the Jesuits, whose missions, or *reducciones*, gathered the indigenous people into settlements (see page 265). They were set to work to build churches and produce handicrafts, such as earthenware pots, paintings and woodcarvings to adorn the churches. After the Jesuits' expulsion the **indígenas** were left to fend for themselves. They kept their techniques and traditions that had been passed on to them and from these evolved the style of woodcarving today.

Good examples of indigenous woodcarving can be found in La Paz and Cochabamba. Images of Indians, mountains, condors and Tiahuanaco are carved on wooden plaques. In La Paz, carvers specialize in male and female heads.

Music

When people talk of Bolivian music they are almost certainly referring to the music of the Quechua- and Aymara-speaking people of the high altiplano which provides the most distinctive Bolivian sound. The music of the Andes has become very well known throughout Europe and North America ever since the Bolivian song *El Cóndor Pasa* was recorded with English lyrics by Simon and Garfunkel and became an international hit. Now the distinctive sound of the Andes can be heard echoing around shopping malls and pedestrian precincts from London to Los Angeles.

The origins

The music of Bolivia can be described as the very heartbeat of the country. Each region has its own distinctive music that reflects its particular lifestyle, its mood and its physical surroundings. The music of the altiplano, for example, is played in a minor key and tends to be sad and mournful, while the music of the lowlands is more up-tempo and generally happier.

Pre-Columbian music, which is still played today in towns and villages throughout the Andes, sounds very different from the music normally associated with that region now. The original uninfluenced music can sound unusual and even unpleasant to Western ears with its shrillness and use of scales and notes to which we are unaccustomed. Pre-Columbian music consisted of a five-note (pentatonic) scale, supposedly based on the five notes ancient people discovered in the wind. With the arrival of the Spaniards Andean music changed and took on Western forms, notably the seven-note scale. As more notes became available, so more varied themes could be played and the music we understand today as being Andean began to evolve.

Musical instruments

Before the arrival of the Spaniards in Latin America, the only instruments were wind and percussion. Although it is a popular misconception that Andean music is based on the panpipes, guitar and *charango*, anyone who travels through the Andes will realize that these instruments only represent a small aspect of Andean music. Bolivian music itself has more Amerindian style and content than that of any other country in South America. It is rare to find an indigenous Bolivian who cannot play an instrument and it is these instruments, both wind and percussion, that are quintessentially Bolivian.

The *quena* is a flute, usually made of reed, characterized by not having a mouthpiece to blow through. As with all Andean instruments, there is a family of *quenas* varying in length from around 15 to 50 cm. The *siku* is the Aymara name for the *zampoña*, or panpipes. It is the most important prehispanic Andean instrument, formed by several reed tubes of different sizes held together by knotted string. Traditionally they are played singly, one person having one row of pipes. *Tarkas* are a type of flute made from the wood of the taco tree, from which their name derives. They are used a lot in festivals and have a shrill sound. *Pinquillos* are bamboo flutes with three octaves manufactured in Patacamaya, between Oruro and La Paz, and *moseños* are long, thick bamboo instruments played from the side.

Phututos were prehispanic trumpets originally made from seashells, wood or ceramics. Now the horn of a bull is used to produce the deep sound used by rural communities to call meetings. In Tarija, bulls' horns are also used to make *erkes*, which are very similar to *phututos* but are tied to long reeds and played collectively.

Among the percussion instruments are the *bombo*, a drum of various sizes, originally made from a hollowed-out tree trunk with the skins of llama or goat. *Chaj'chas* are made from sheep's hooves, dried in the sun, oiled and sewn onto a wrist cloth. Virtually the only instrument of European origin is the *charango*, which is traditionally made in the village of Aiquile, near Cochabamba. When stringed instruments were first introduced by the Spanish, the indigenous people liked them but wanted something that was their own and so the *charango* was born. Originally, they were made of clay, condor skeletons and armadillo or tortoise shells. Now, though, they are almost always made from wood. One of the main production centres is Oruro. In the Chuquisaca region it's traditional to have groups playing three or even four sizes of *charango* with different voices.

Where to hear music
During periods of military dictatorship many folk musicians used their performances in *peñas* to register their opposition to repression and censorship in protest songs. *Peñas* became a focus of resistance to military rule. In recent years, though, with the return to democracy and the rise of more contemporary varieties of youth culture, *peñas* have been losing their attraction. Every town in Bolivia has its own *peña*, where you can hear popular Bolivian folk music, but today *peñas* are more likely to attract tourists than native young Bolivians.

Bolivia's many festivals are also good places to hear traditional music. For example, La Fiesta del Gran Poder in La Paz, the carnival in Oruro, or the Luzmilla Patiño festival in Cochabamba. The Fiesta de la Cruz takes place all over the Andes on 3 May, when thousands of musicians come together to play all shapes and sizes of instruments, including the *toyos*, which are huge panpipes over one metre long and hail from the Titicaca region.

The region of Tarija near the Argentine border has a musical tradition of its own, based on religious processions that culminate with that of San Roque on the first Sunday in September. The influence is Spanish and the musical instruments are the *caña*, *erke* and violin *chapaco*. The *caña* is a long bamboo tube with a horn at the end.

There are many professional folk groups on record. The most popular, **Los Kjarkas** (also known for a time as **Pacha**), wrote the original song *Llorando se fue*, but the hit version was recorded by a French group under the famous title *Lambada*. Other well-known folk groups are **Wara**, **Los Masis**, **Los Quipus** and **Rumillajta** who have built up a considerable following in Europe. The greatest exponent of the *charango* is the legendary **Ernesto Cavour**, who can be heard at some of the best-known *peñas* in La Paz (see page 91).

Dance

Just as music is the heartbeat of the country, so dance conveys the rich and ancient heritage that typifies much of the national spirit. Bolivians are tireless dancers and dancing is the most popular form of entertainment. Unsuspecting travellers should note that once they make that first wavering step there will be no respite until they collapse from exhaustion.

Organized group dances
Comparsas are organized groups of dancers who perform dances following a set pattern of movements to a particular musical accompaniment, wearing a specific costume. These dances have a long tradition and some of them still parody the ex-Spanish colonial masters. The most famous *comparsas* are those from the Oruro carnival (see page 128).

Another notable *comparsa* is the comical *Auqui Auqui* (*auqui* is Aymara for old man). The dance satirizes the solemnity and pomposity of Spanish gentlemen from the colonial period. The dancers' dignified dress and manners make them appear old, and a humped back is added to emphasize age. These little old men have long pointed noses, flowing beards and carry crooked walking sticks. They dance stooped, regularly pausing to complain and rub aching backs, at times even stumbling and falling, to the accompaniment of *pinquillos*.

A number of dances replicate hunting scenes, the origins of which are thought to lie in the *chacu*, the great annual Inca hunt which involved 20,000-30,000 people forming a huge circle and then closing in until the animals could be caught by hand. The main protagonist in most of the hunting dances is the *K'usillu*, a mischievous character, half monkey half devil. He wears a bright costume, a horned crown and carries a whip, tambourine or *pinquillo*. The *Liphi* dance, or vicuña hunt, often involves the *K'usillu* carrying a stuffed vicuña while being chased by an old man representing the *achachila* or spirit of the mountains. When the *K'usillu* is caught, an old woman, the spirit of the earth, beheads the vicuña and the body is then carried off by a condor.

In the Wititis the *K'usillu* carries a live partridge, singing out in imitation of the bird. He is accompanied by men dressed as young women and condors. Other dancers try to lasso the fleeing partridge but often hook the young women instead. In the *Chokelas*, or fox hunt, the *K'usillu* carries a stuffed fox and chases the women relentlessly, mimicking the Spaniards' pursuit of native women.

Dances for everyone

Many dances for couples and/or groups are danced spontaneously at fiestas throughout Bolivia. These include indigenous dances which have originated in a specific region and ballroom dances that reflect the Spanish influence.

One of the most popular of the indigenous dances is the *huayño* which originated on the altiplano but is now danced throughout the country. It involves numerous couples, who whirl around or advance down the street, arm-in-arm, in a '*pandilla*'. During fiestas, and especially after a few drinks, this can develop into a kind of uncontrolled frenzy.

Similar to the *huayño* is the *chovena* from the Beni and Santa Cruz regions. The *chovena* originated from tribal dances, as did the *machetero*, another folkloric dance from the lowlands. The *chapaqueada* is a dance from Tarija which is performed at religious festivals such as Christmas and Easter. The name derives from the word *chapaco*, a person from Tarija. The dance is accompanied by typical Tarijan instruments (see above). There are countless other indigenous dances, far too many to list here.

Of the ballroom dances, the *cueca* is perhaps the best known. The Bolivian *cueca* is a close relative of the Chilean national dance of the same name and they share a mutual origin in the *zamacueca*, itself derived from the Spanish fandango. Today the *cueca* is very representative of Bolivia, as typical of this country as the Tango is of Argentina. Similar to the *cueca* is the *Bailecito Chuquisaqueño*, though it is more delicate, without the emphasis on provocative mannerisms. Other regional

BACKGROUND
Behind the mask

One of the most striking features of the Bolivian fiesta is the fantastic variety of wildly imaginative masks worn by the dancers.

The indigenous peoples of the Andes believe that masks transform individuals – not only into characters from popular folklore but also into spirits of another time and place and defenders of a sacred knowledge.

This can be explained by the legend of the *amaut'as*, or wisemen. The *amaut'as* are the keepers of the wisdom and values of the Andean civilization. They are said to personify the indigenous cultural identity and reaffirm its rebellion against foreign domination. Upon hearing of the death of the last Inca, Atahuallpa, the *amaut'as* were so horrified that, instead of rebelling, they retreated into themselves and stoically endured the injustices of a world that had ceased to be theirs.

In the same way, the *indígenas* adapted to the oppression of daily life under a mask of submission and indifference. It is only during ceremonies of rebellion and remembrance that they come back to life. Crucial to the success of such ceremonies – fiestas in other words – is the excessive consumption of alcohol, food and coca as well as repetitive, incessant dancing. This collective altered state draws the community together until the individual members are indistinguishable from one another. In this way, the community communes with itself and with its surroundings, thus affirming its will to live.

So, when the indigenous people put on their masks and costumes they cover their psychological masks of obstinate passivity, which allows them to show their true faces. Only by covering themselves up can the indigenous people uncover their repressed energies and desires and hidden resentments. These pent-up emotions overflow during the wild, excessive and colourful celebrations of the fiesta; the awakening of a sleeping culture.

---

dances include the *Khaluyo Cochabambino* and *Rueda Tarijeña* from the southeast and *Carnavalito Cruceño* and *Taquirari Beniano* from the tropical lowlands.

Outside of the fiestas, the most popular dances are not of Bolivian origin: salsa, merengue, Caribbean soca, Brazilian samba and Colombian cumbia.

Festivals *For a list of the main festivals, see page 18.*

Fiestas are a fundamental part of life for most Bolivians, taking place the length and breadth of the country and with such frequency that it would be hard to miss one, even during the briefest of stays. This is fortunate because arriving in any town or village during these frenetic celebrations is one of the great Bolivian experiences.

Bolivian fiestas range from the elaborately choreographed processions of Oruro to a simple llama sacrifice in a tiny rural community. Some are highly Catholicized, particularly in the more Spanish dominated towns of Tarija and Santa Cruz, while

BACKGROUND

Origins of Oruro's carnival

The origins of Oruro's carnival go back to 1789, when an image of the Virgen de la Candelaria was found painted on Cerro Pie de Gallo. There are several related legends involving a repentant outlaw called Nina Nina or Chiru Chiru, who as a devotee of the Virgin was saved from his sins.

Miners started worshipping this image and danced for her festival, February 2, which that year was also the Saturday of carnival. This became a yearly tradition.

Gradually the image became known as Virgen del Socavón or Mamita del Socavón (Beloved Mother of the Mineshaft). A century later, the Santuario was built on the spot where the image was found.

Over time, the worship of the Virgen del Socavón and the cult of *Supay*, the devil, merged in the carnival celebrations. In the 19th century, in an attempt to counter indigenous myths and deities, a Spanish priest introduced the *relato*, the depiction of the struggle of the Archangel Michael against the Seven Deadly Sins. Hence the prominent place of the Archangel at the head of the procession of devils in the *Diablada*.

Like so many other expressions of Bolivian culture, Oruro's carnival is a complex, often inscrutable, mixture of indigenous and Catholic elements.

others incorporate Spanish colonial themes into predominantly ancient rituals.

Carnival in most areas involves much throwing of water, paint, oil – anything, in fact, that people can get their hands on. The more paranoid travellers may assume that they are being picked on, but to someone from the altiplano, a six-foot tall, blond-haired gringo makes an easy target. So, arm yourself with a waterproof jacket, plenty of water bombs, a good sense of fun and have a great time.

Who pays?

A lot a careful organization and preparation goes into a community's fiesta, and a lot of expense. The brass bands, the food, the beer, the pipe bands, the decorations, are all laid on free for the participants and someone has to foot the bill.

Every fiesta needs a patron, or a sponsor. It's an honour to bear the *cargo* (cost) of a fiesta. So great is the prestige that it's impossible to rise in the community without sponsoring fiestas. But how does a patron pay for it all? There are two ways: one is to save, the other is to get help from friends. They will lend the money on the understanding that when they have a *cargo* the favour will be returned. This bond of mutual assistance is known as an *ayni*. A man may spend lots of money on other people's fiestas before he can sponsor one himself. But the more *ayni* bonds he can accrue by helping others, the more money he'll be able to raise when it's his turn. Thus, the principle of the *cargo* is that the more you do for the community, the more it'll do for you. Lay on a good fiesta and you'll rise in the hierarchy.

BACKGROUND

The history of Alasitas

The roots of Alasitas appear to go as far back as the Tiwanaku culture. A small stone sculpture found in the ruins is believed to be the forefather of the contemporary Ekeko. During the Aymara Kingdoms period, people carried with them miniature coca leaves, seeds, shells and sculptures of houses and animals. At the summer solstice (21 December), the start of the rainy season, these miniatures or *illas* were taken out so they would be blessed by the rays of the sun, in order for them to multiply. At the same time, people exchanged *illas*, part of the concept of reciprocity so ingrained in Andean cultures. The festival was called Chhalasita, which means 'exchange with me'.

The tradition continued after the arrival of the Spanish and gradually evolved. If in the past on the solstice the god Inti (sun) blessed the miniatures and people asked Pachamama (mother earth) for plentiful rains and a good harvest, today, on 24 January, day of the Virgen de Nuestra Señora de la Paz (the date was moved by decree in colonial times), people ask for money or a car. If in the past the miniatures were exchanged as a sign of reciprocity and good wishes, today they are sold as merchandise ... a sign of our times. The festival changed from Chhalasita, 'exchange with me'; to Alasita, 'buy from me'.

Over time, Ekeko also evolved and the god of fertility gradually became the god of consumerist abundance. In colonial times he carried a pick and axe, around the time of the 1952 revolution he carried a rifle. Miniature potatoes and maize have been replaced by a tiny diploma, computer, vehicle or stacks of mini-euros are more coveted than US dollars.

Literature

Pre-independence

The absence of a written language in prehispanic Bolivia means that there is no recorded literature from this period, though there was an oral tradition of story-telling which still survives today. The primary function of early Spanish literature in Bolivia, then known as Alto Perú, was to spread Catholicism through the newly conquered empire. One of the earliest known of these works was the *Crónica de Perú*, by Pedro Cieza de León (1518-1560). The Spaniards' fear of the unknown culture of the indigenous people meant that these early chronicles lacked much local detail, focusing more on the religion and the activities of the conquerors themselves. Even the early texts by native Bolivian authors showed the extent of their indoctrination with colonial ideas.

The only area in which the *indígenas* were allowed to maintain their own culture was in theatre and poetry. One of the few texts to survive, *La Tragedia de Atahuallpa*, indicates that plays were passed orally from generation to generation. Poetry in the Quechua and Aymara languages also continued to flourish, again orally, throughout the colonial era. Not until the early 18th century does a text appear which takes the religious chronicle into the realms of literature: Bartolomé Arzán's *Historia de la Villa Imperial de Potosí*, written between 1700 and 1736, is an epic account of most of the colonial period. Unlike any other text produced until then, it mixes fact and fantasy, the author even immersing himself in a fictional context into phases of history hundreds of years earlier. It is a remarkable Baroque example of what later came to be known as *Lo Real Maravilloso*.

The transformation of Bolivia into a republic is recorded by a native of La Paz, Vicente Pazos Kauki (1779-1853) in *Memorias Histórico-políticas*, in which he defends the notion of Latin American independence from the Spanish. The literary qualities of this work bring the skill of fictional narrative to the sections based on historical fact.

Post-independence

The birth of Bolivia as an independent nation in 1825 coincided with the beginning of Romanticism in Latin America. European Romantic fiction was widely read and local authors developed a similar style to create tales of contemporary life in Bolivia. The sentimental novel was popularized primarily by Vicente Ballivián (1816-1891) with *Recreos juveniles* in 1834. Julio Lucas Jaimes, a Bolivian Romantic writing in the mid-19th century, gained the admiration of the well-known Nicaraguan writer, Rubén Darío, who dedicated part of his *Prosas profanas* to him.

European-influenced Romanticism came to an end with the birth of Latin American Modernism at the turn of the century. Ricardo Jaimes Freyre was one of the forerunners of the movement. His *La Villa Imperial de Potosí*, published in 1905, examined the pervading mood in Latin America and sought inspiration from past events, such as the French Revolution of 1789, which he saw as an example of positive rational action distinctly lacking in his homeland. Jaimes Freyre went on to found an important literary review in Buenos Aires with Rubén Darío and gained an international reputation with his poetry, plays, novels and critical essays.

Nataniel Aguirre's 1885 *Juan de la Rosa* was another landmark literary work. In this highly original novel, he subverts the whole concept of the 19th-century novel by placing the narrative in the hands, or voice, of one of his characters, thus relinquishing the privileged position of the author/narrator.

A major contribution to Feminism was made by the modernist poet Adela Zamudio (1854-1928). She formed a Latin American triad of Romantic-Modernist poets with José Martí in Cuba and Manuel González Prada in Peru, all of whom used their innate spirit of rebellion as an inspiration for their poetry. Zamudio dedicated her life and work to the struggle against the oppression of women.

The Bolivian Modernist movement continued to flourish with the publication of *Odas* in 1898 by Franz Tamayo (1880-1956). His analysis of post-colonial Latin America saw the huge divide between the ruling minority and the anonymous, voiceless majority. He was nominated president of the Republic in 1935, but a military coup prevented him from assuming the post.

Early 20th-century prose reflected the injustices of the *latifundista* system. Alcides Arguedas (1879-1946) began his fictional account of the inequality of

Bolivian society with *Wata Wara*, which he later incorporated in his 1919 *Raza de bronze*. This is one of the major novels in Bolivian letters, examining the life of the *indígena* in a society dominated by a white ruling class. Jaime Mendoza's (1874-1939) novels also denounced the exploitation of the indígenas, in particular their conditions in the tin mines and rubber plantations. His best-known work is *En las tierras de Potosí* (1911). The extreme politicization of his work has led some critics to refer to him as the Bolivian Gorky.

The literature of the Chaco War (1932-1935) was mainly by those who had fought in it, documenting a national sense of despair at having been forced to fight a protracted and futile war. Augusto Céspedes (1904-1997) was one of the key figures of this era, both in politics and literature. He had already founded the Nationalist Party of Bolivia by the time he published his account of the Chaco War, *Sangre de mestizos*, in 1936. This collection of short stories saw that for the first time whites and *indígenas* had shared the same plight, fighting alongside each other and united in bitter disappointment at the outcome. This book is now considered a classic and Céspedes went on to become a major literary and political figure until his death at the age of 94.

The revolution of 1952 did not produce any significant literature, but this can be explained by the fact that a revolutionary consciousness had already been established by writers and intellectuals in the 20 years after the Chaco War. The pressing issues of exploitation of the *indígenas* and conditions in the tin mines, criticized in fiction since the early 1930s, had finally been addressed by the revolution. Some writers also gave up their craft to work in politics. The few novels that did emerge just after the revolution, such as *Cerco de penumbras* by Oscar Cerruto (1912-1981) and *Los deshabitados* by Marcelo Quiroga (1931-1980), broke with the tradition of social realism and began experimenting with a more abstract, existential kind of work, mirrored by the dark poetry of Jaime Sáenz and Gonzalo Vázquez Méndez.

The next significant change in Bolivia to be marked by literature was the guerrilla uprising led by Che Guevara, and his subsequent execution in 1967. The key novels in this new subversive literature were *Los fundadores del alba*, by Renato Prado de Oropeza, which won the coveted Cuban Casa de las Américas prize in 1969 and *Los deshabitados* by Marcelo Quiroga Santa Cruz (1959). Many poets from this period, the most important being Pedro Shimose (born 1940), denounced the violence that was then shaping society in all of Latin America. Another writer from this period was Yolanda Bedregal (1916-1999), after whom the country's most prestigious poetry prize is named

Literature in the 1970s and 1980s continued to criticize Bolivian society, though the presence of various military dictatorships restricted the writers' freedom to chronicle the injustices around them with such blatant acrimony as before. However, an important collection of short stories, *Antología del terror político*, was published in 1979, combining the work of established figures like Raul Leyton with younger writers like René Bascope and Roberto Laserna. All the stories are concerned with the restrictions placed on all levels of life by dictatorship. Other writers of the same period avoided social realism altogether, turning to experimentation and poetic writing. The fantasies and myths of indigenous culture have also been a source of inspiration for many contemporary writers, reflecting a common trend throughout Latin American literature in general.

Among better-know Bolivian authors of the 1990s and beyond are the poet Blanca Garnica (1944-) and the novelists Ramón Rocha Monroy (1950-), René Poppe (1943-), Adolfo Cárdenas Franco (1950-) and multifaceted Ruber Carvalho (1938-). The latter offers a fresh eastern Bolivian perspective on the country and its history.

Painting and sculpture

Pre-independence
As a result of the discovery of the fabulously rich silver mines of Potosí in 1544 Bolivia, then part of the Viceroyalty of Peru, was one of the major commercial and cultural centres of colonial Spanish America. Artists and craftsmen followed the merchants, churchmen, colonial administrators and adventurers along the trade route from the Viceregal capital of Lima to Potosí via Cuzco, La Paz and Sucre. The demand for paintings, sculptures and altarpieces was met first by Europeans such as the itinerant Italian Jesuit Bernardo Bitti (1548-1610?) who, after a spell in Lima, moved on to Lake Titicaca, La Paz, Sucre and Potosí, and the influence of his delicate mannerist style can be traced through several subsequent generations. Another mobile and important Jesuit painter but in this case of Flemish origin, was Diego de la Puente (1586-1663) who worked in towns and cities throughout the Viceroyalty. His paintings were often based on engravings after works by Rubens, an influence that was to persist in Bolivian painting until late in the 18th century. The work of Gregorio Gamarra, active 1601-1630, is typical of the first generation of Bolivian-born artists in combining elements of the Italianate style of Bitti and the Flemish tradition of Puente, as in his *Adoration of the Kings* in the Museo Nacional de Arte in La Paz.

Colonial sculpture, however, has its stylistic roots in Spain. Andalusian sculptors were attracted by lucrative commissions for altarpieces and choirstalls. Several workshops were established in highland Bolivia by the 1570s, and Spanish-born craftsmen continued to be influential into the 17th century. The Sevillian Gaspar de la Cueva (active 1613-1640) settled in Potosí where many of his best works are still preserved in the churches for which they were made. His *Christ at the Column* in the church of San Lorenzo, for example, is elegantly dignified despite the numerous bleeding lacerations on his white skin. This powerful colonial tradition of silent suffering in the face of physical abuse continues to reverberate in Bolivian art.

The work of painter Melchor Pérez Holguín (1660?-1733, his likeness appears on the 50 boliviano banknote) combines Flemish, Spanish and Andean elements, and is typical of the cultural heterogeneity of later colonial painting. The composition of his *Rest on the Flight into Egypt* in the Museo Nacional de Arte in La Paz is based on a Flemish engraving; the style, however, is reminiscent of Zurbarán, while the anecdotal detail owes much to Andean traditions. While the infant Jesus sleeps, the Virgin, dressed in a *manta* and travelling hat, washes nappies in a portable wooden basin. This 'Americanization' of subject matter owes much to the Cuzco school of painting and although Holguín largely resisted the typical Cuzco hallmark of applying gold to the painted surface, the next generation of Bolivian artists did not. The painting of San Francisco de Paula (Museo Nacional de Arte, La Paz) by Holguín's follower Manuel de Córdoba (active 1758-1787) is a striking example of the resulting tension between the real and the divine. The saint's hands and face are painted with close attention to every vein, tendon and wrinkle in the tradition of Caravaggio and Ribera while his habit is overlaid with a flat wallpaper pattern in gold. The effect is simultaneously to emphasize and deny the figure's corporeality. Another follower of Holguín, Gaspar Miguel de Berrio (active 1706-1762) uses gold to emphasize the divinity of the principal figures in his impressive *Coronation of the Virgin* (Museo Nacional de Arte, La Paz). He is also remembered for his detailed documentary view of Potosí (c1760, Museo Charcas, Sucre) which shows the distinctive triangular mountain, the colonial city below it, and in the surrounding hills the elaborate system of dams and canals which channelled water to the mine-workings.

Initially European craftsmen worked mainly for the creole elite while indigenous workshops developed to meet the needs of the newly Christianized 'Indians', often with remarkable results. In 1582 Francisco Tito Yupanqui, a native of Copacabana who claimed descent from the Incas, wanted to make an image of the Virgin for his parish church and travelled to Potosí to learn to carve. The fame of the resulting sculpture derives from the tradition that after two years' work and still unable to finish the piece to his own satisfaction, Yupanqui appealed to the Virgin for help whereupon she kindly obliged. Once installed in Copacabana the miraculously completed statue quickly became the focus of a popular cult, so perpetuating the sacred significance Lake Titicaca had had under the Incas. Native Andean beliefs include the veneration of important geographical features, and the rigid triangular representations of the Virgin can often be related to mountain peaks. The Virgin of Sabaya (Museo de la Moneda, Potosí) by the Indian Luis Niño (18th century) is associated with the Sabaya volcano in Oruro, while in the anonymous painting of the Virgin of Potosí (in the same museum) the Virgin's body is the mountain: her head and hands, radiating silvery light, are superimposed on the landscape making her the Christian embodiment of Pachamama, the Andean earth mother goddess. Other indigenous divinities reappeared in Christian garb in the 18th century, most famously the forces of nature. These were transformed by Andean artists into richly dressed archangels with *arquebuses*: powerful, unpredictable intermediaries between celestial and earthly realms. Examples can be seen in many rural churches as well as in the major museums.

Post-independence

In the years following independence in 1825 itinerant artists of diverse origins played an important role, as they had in the early colonial period. The Peruvian José Gil de Castro (died 1841), the Ecuadorean Manuel Ugalde (1817-1881) and the Austrian Francisco Martín Drexel (1792-1863) helped to meet the new demand for portraits of military leaders and society hostesses. Bolivian-born Antonio Villavicencio (born 1822) trained in a conventional academic manner in Paris before returning in 1858 to head the Escuela de Dibujo in La Paz. The interest of the works of this period, including Villavicencio's monumental series of presidential portraits in the Museo Charcas, Sucre, lies less in their artistic merit than in the historical personalities they represent.

Portraiture was the dominant form of artistic expression. Nineteenth-century political nationalism was not parallelled by a strong school of landscape painting although Zenón Iturralde (born 1838) and Melchor María Mercado (19th century), both self-taught, painted interesting topographical scenes. José García Mesa (1851-1905), despite extensive studies in Europe, returned to paint city views which sometimes seem closer to the colonial topographical tradition of, for example, Berrio's Potosí, than to the Impressionism of his French contemporaries (for example 'Plaza de Cochabamba', 1889, Casa de Cultura, Cochabamba).

Popular religious artistic expression was largely unaffected by the political changes. In the later colonial period many rural churches had been decorated with brightly coloured and iconographically complex murals, a practice which persisted throughout the 19th century, and artists such as Juan de la Cruz Tapia (1830?-1892), a sculptor as well as a painter, continued to produce devotional images in the tradition of Holguín.

Twentieth-century art

Art in Bolivia during the early 20th century, dominated by figurative styles and local subject matter, is scarcely touched by developments in Europe. Cecilio Guzmán de Rojas (1900-1950) presents himself in his self-portrait of 1919 as a bohemian dandy (Museo de la Moneda, Potosí) but, although he spent the 1920s in Europe, the modern movements passed him by. In Madrid he painted sentimental visions of the Andes using naked or semi-naked indigenous figures in questionable taste (for example *El Beso del Idolo/The Idol's Kiss*, 1926, Museo de la Moneda, Potosí). On his return to Bolivia in 1930 he saw his country afresh and used more sensitive if politically anodyne indigenist modes. But his real importance lies in the way in which, as Director of the Escuela de Bellas Artes of La Paz, he promoted the land, landscape and peoples of Bolivia as serious subjects for painters and sculptors. Other practitioners include Juan Rimsa (c1898-c1975), Gil Coimbra (1908-1976) and Jorge de la Reza (1901-1958).

The success of the revolution of 1952 inspired artists of the younger generation of '52' to add a much-needed social and political dimension to Bolivian art. As in Mexico, murals offered a way of reaching a wide audience and during the 1950s the government sponsored numerous narrative and allegorical works in schools, hospitals and the offices of nationalized companies. Two major exponents were Miguel Alandia Pantoja (1914-1975) and Walter Solón Romero (1925-1999), their work can be seen at the Museo de la Revolución Nacional and other places in La Paz; Solón's art is also seen in the murals and stained-glass windows of the Catholic University in Sucre. The euphoria was short-lived and after the military coup of 1964 artists had to find alternative means of expression. The *indígenas*

Gil Imana (born 1933) paints in the 1970s are no longer folkloric and rural, as in the generation of Guzmán de Rojas, nor inspired by Marxist optimism, but simply hungry and oppressed. Enrique Arnal (born 1932) paints faceless indigenous porters in ragged Western clothes; they inhabit not a traditional picturesque landscape but an abstract, lonely no-man's land of blank planes.

The two best-known artists of 20th-century Bolivia were both women, the painter, María Luisa Pacheco (1919-1974), and the sculptor Marina Núñez del Prado (1910-1996). Both worked in a predominantly abstract mode, but with a distinctively Bolivian flavour. In her mixed-media canvases Pacheco used a cubist vocabulary and coarsely textured surface to evoke to the peaks, crags and sharply faceted rocks of the Andean landscape. Núñez del Prado, by contrast, carved iron-hard native wood and stone into softly curving, often feminine forms.

In recent decades Bolivia has seen the growth of numerous different artistic tendencies, dominated by a continued preoccupation with figuration. The Museo Nacional de Arte in La Paz has a very good collection of contemporary art and there are several new commercial galleries. Look out for Gastón Ugalde (born 1944), Edgar Arandia (born 1950) and particularly Roberto Valcárcel (born 1951), who produced powerful indictments of political repression in the 1970s and has gone on to explore different aspects of Bolivian iconography including a fascinating series in which he dissects and reworks the colonial image of the archangel.

People

Bolivia is a culturally diverse country. Its population can be roughly divided into three distinct ethnic categories: about 60% are indigenous (comprising over 30 different native groups, many living in the jungle lowlands); about 30% are *mestizo* (people of mixed European and indigenous ancestry); and the remainder are of European origin. The racial composition varies from place to place: almost entirely indigenous around Lake Titicaca; more than half indigenous in La Paz; three-quarters *mestizo* or European in the Yungas, Cochabamba and Santa Cruz, and Tarija, which is the most European of all.

The Highland *indígenas* are composed of two main groups: those in the north of the altiplano who speak the guttural Aymara (an estimated 1.6 million), and those elsewhere, who speak Quechua, the Inca tongue (2.3 million). Both cultures were dominated by the Incas but the Aymara were allowed to keep their own language. Both have kept their languages and cultures distinct. Outside the big cities some 11% of the populatin speak no Spanish, but knowledge of Spanish is on the increase. About 43% of Bolivians are Aymara, Quechua or Tupi-Guaraní speakers. Under the 2009 constitution, all native languages, as well as Spanish, are offical.

The Aymara

The Aymaras, who populate the Titicaca region, are descendants of the ancient Tiwanaku people. They are a squat and powerfully built race who have developed huge chests and lungs to cope with the rarefied air of the altiplano. Since the agrarian revolution of 1952 the Aymara *campesinos* own the land on which they live, but still live in extreme poverty.

Though introduced to Catholicism by the Spaniards, the Aymara remain grudging converts. They are a deeply religious people who may observe Christian rituals but also continue to worship the ancient animist spirits and celebrate rituals which date from the Tiwanaku period. Aymara culture is permeated with the idea of the sacred. They believe that God, the Supreme Being, gives them security in their daily lives and this God of Life manifests him/herself through the deities, such as those of the mountains, the water, the wind, the sun, the moon and the *wa'qas* (sacred places). As a sign of gratitude, the Aymara give *wax'ta* (offerings), *wilancha* (llama sacrifices) and *ch'alla* (sprinkling alcohol on the ground) to the *achachilas* (the protecting spirits of the family and community), the *Pachamama* (Mother Earth), *Kuntur Mamani* and *Uywiri* (protecting spirits of the home).

The remote mountains of the bleak altiplano are of particular importance for the Aymara. The most sacred places are these high mountains, far from human problems. It is here that the people have built their altars to offer worship, to communicate with their God and ask forgiveness. The community is also held important in the lives of the Aymara. The *achachila* is the great-great grandfather of the family as well as the protector of the community, and as such is God's representative on earth.

The offerings to the sacred mountains take place for the most part in August and are community celebrations. Many different rituals are celebrated: there are those within the family; in the mountains; for the planting and the harvest; rites to ask for rain or to ask for protection against hailstorms and frosts; and ceremonies for Mother Earth.

All such rituals are led by *Aymara Yatiris*, who are male or female priests. The *Yatiri* is a wise person – someone who knows – and the community's spiritual and moral guide. Through a method of divination that involves the reading of coca leaves, they guide individuals in their personal decision-making.

The Quechua

The Quechua language was imposed by the Incas on several culturally and linguistically divergent groups and, to this day, many of these groups have maintained separate social identities. The Quechua language, much more than the Aymara, is divided by many variations in regional dialect. Geographically, they are more varied, too. There are Quechua speakers in the fertile valleys of Cochabamba, on the high plateaux of Potosí, in Chuquisaca and parts of Oruro. Some Quechua communities have lived free from outside influence for centuries. Others, such as those of the Cochabamba valley, have long been in close contact with *cholos*, a term used to describe indigenous people who have abandoned the traditional rural way of life and moved to the towns. These people have always been bilingual and have adapted easily to the *cholo* way of life, thus weakening their own ethnic distinctiveness. Their religious life lacks the specialized rituals of the Aymara and the music and dance also shows considerable *cholo* influence.

Other ethnic groups

There are other smaller ethnic groups, such as the Uru and the Chipaya of the altiplano. The Chipaya, who inhabit the inhospitable Carangas region of the western Oruro department and speak their own language, are now so small numerically that they are in danger of disappearing. A similar fate could befall the Uru, a fishing and herding people who live in the swamps of the Río Desaguadero on the edge of Lake Titicaca.

In the lowlands are some 30 ethnic groups, including the Chiquitano (numbering about 220,000), Guaraní (about 150,000), Ayoreo, Chiriguano, Guaravo, Chimane and Mojo. Each group has its own language and, though the Jesuits settled missions in some of these remote areas over 300 years ago, have only recently been assimilated into Bolivian culture. There are also about 17,000 blacks, descendants of slaves brought from Peru and Buenos Aires in the 16th century, who now live in the Yungas and the department of Santa Cruz.

Religion, customs and beliefs

Although some 97% of the population ostensibly belong to the Roman Catholic religion, in reality religious life for the majority of Bolivians is a mix of Catholic beliefs imported from Europe and indigenous traditions based on animism, the worship of deities from the natural world, such as mountains, animals and plants.

Pachamama

Ecotourism is a buzzword on the lips of all self-respecting travellers and tour operators. But though ecology may be a relatively new concept in the West, to the people of the bleak northern Bolivian altiplano, this idea is absolutely fundamental to their culture and almost as old as the land itself.

Pachamama, or Mother Earth, occupies a very privileged place in indigenous culture because she is the generative source of life. The Aymara believe that Man was created from the land, and thus he is tied to all the living beings that share the earth. According to them, the earth is our mother, and it is on the basis of this understanding that all of human society is organized, always maintaining the cosmic norms and laws.

Women's and men's relationship with nature is what the Aymara call ecology, harmony and equilibrium. The Aymara also believe that private land ownership is a social sin because the land is for everyone. It is meant to be shared and not used only for the benefit of a few.

Vicenta Mamani Bernabé of the Andean Regional Superior Institute of Theological Studies explains: "Land is life because it produces all that we need to live. Water emanates from the land as if from the veins of a human body, there is also the natural wealth of minerals, and pasture grows from it to feed the animals. Therefore, for the Aymaras, the *Pachamama* is sacred and since we are her children, we are also sacred. No one can replace the earth, she is not meant to be exploited, or to be converted into merchandise. Our duty is to respect and care for the earth. This is what white people today are just beginning to realize, and it is called ecology. Respect for the *Pachamama* is respect for ourselves as she is life. Today, she is threatened with death and must be liberated for the sake of her children's liberation."

Day of the Dead

One of the most important dates in the indigenous people's calendar is 2nd November, the 'Day of the Dead'. This tradition has been practised since time immemorial. In the Inca calendar, November was the eighth month and meant Ayamarca, or land of the dead. The celebration of Day of the Dead, or 'All Saints' as it is also known, is just one example of religious adaptation or syncretism in which the ancient beliefs of ethnic cultures are mixed with the rites of the Catholic Church.

According to Aymara belief, the spirit (*athun ajayu*) visits its relatives at this time of the year and is fed in order to continue its journey before its reincarnation. The relatives of the dead prepare for the arrival of the spirit days in advance. Among the many items necessary for these meticulous preparations are little bread dolls, each one of which has a particular significance. A ladder is needed for the spirit to descend from the other world to the terrestrial one. There are also figures which represent the grandparents, great grandparents and loved ones of the person who has 'passed into a better life'. Horse-shaped breads are prepared that will serve as a means of transport for the soul in order to avoid fatigue.

Inside the home, the relatives construct a tomb supported by boxes over which is laid a black cloth. Here they put the bread, along with sweets, flowers, onions and sugar cane. This last item is an indispensable part of the table as it symbolizes the invigorating element which prevents the spirit from becoming tired on its journey towards the Earth. The union of the flowers with the onion is called *tojoro* and is a vital part of the preparations. It ensures that the dead one does not become disoriented and arrives in the correct house.

The tomb is also adorned with the dead relative's favourite food and drink, not forgetting the all-important glass of beer as, according to popular tradition, this is the first nourishment taken by the souls when they arrive at their houses. Once the spirit has arrived and feasted with his/her living relatives, the entire ceremony is then transported to the graveside in the local cemetery, where it is carried out again, together with the many other mourning families.

This meeting of the living and their dead relatives is re-enacted the following year, though less ostentatiously, and again for the final time in the third year, the year of the farewell.

Land & environment

Geology and landscape

Bolivia is the fifth largest of the 13 South American countries in size (1,098,581 sq km) and the eighth largest in population. The most recent census took place in 2012 and counted 10.0 million Bolivians. Estimates for 2014 population are close to 10.6 million. They are based on the 2001 to 2012 annual growth rate of 1.7%, as are the population figures given throughout this book. That makes Bolivia about the same size as France and Spain together but with less than 10% of their population. This low population density – the lowest in the continent except for the Guianas – is explained by the high altitude and aridity of much of the terrain in the west and south, and the remoteness of the wetter, forested areas of the northeast.

Bolivia is bounded by Chile and Peru to the west, Brazil to the north and east, and Argentina and Paraguay to the south. It is, like Paraguay, landlocked, although the latter has access to the sea via the Paraná. Bolivia had a Pacific coastline until 1880 when it was lost to Chile in the War of the Pacific (1879-1883, see box, page 313). Since then its principal surface link to the rest of the world has been the railway and road to Arica built by the Chileans. The road linking the capital, La Paz and Arica is now paved and in good condition, while the rail line on the Bolivian side is out of service.

Bolivia also lost territory to Brazil (Acre was lost under the treaty of Petrópolis in 1903), and to Argentina and Paraguay, notably in the Chaco War (1932-1935, see box, page 315). The country lies wholly between the Tropic of Capricorn and the Equator.

Structure

The Andes are at their widest in Bolivia. They are formed of two main ranges (*cordilleras*), of which the most westerly is the frontier with Chile, and stretch for 250 km across Bolivia. The formation of the Andes began at the end of the Cretaceous geological period about 80 million years ago and has continued to the present day. To the east are much older structures of granite and crystalline rocks belonging to the South American Plate which comes to the surface further east in Brazil.

In Bolivia, however, these rocks are overlain with thick, geologically recent deposits of alluvium brought down from the mountains by rivers and glaciers over millions of years of widely differing climates. During the most recent ice age (Pleistocene), a continuous ice-cap extended from the Antarctic to southern Bolivia, with a much lower snow line on the mountains to the north. With heavy precipitation and vast quantities of meltwater, the deep valleys were gouged out to the east and vast lakes were formed on the plateau, the most notable of which remains today as Lake Titicaca.

The altiplano

The altiplano is one of the largest interior basins in the world extending from northern Argentina some 900 km into southern Peru, and is nearly 10% of Bolivia. It is between 100 and 200 km wide throughout its length. The high Andes rise on either side of the altiplano, the Cordillera Occidental to the west which includes the highest mountain in Bolivia, Nevado Sajama, 6542 m, and the Cordillera Oriental to the east, whose highest point is Nevado de Illampu, 6485 m. There are many snow-capped peaks, mostly volcanic in origin, in both these ranges, between 5000 m and 6500 m.

The altiplano itself lies at around 3500-4000 m, and being in the rain shadow from both east and west, has very little direct precipitation. It is a bleak, almost treeless area – just a few introduced eucalyptus in sheltered spots in the north near villages – the southern part is practically uninhabited desert. The winds can be strong and are often violent, stirring up dust clouds and compounding the discomforts of the cold dry climate. Much of the time, however, the air is unbelievably clear and the whole plateau is a bowl of luminous light.

There are no passes out of the altiplano below 4000 m. The easiest exit, that is the least mountainous, is to the southeast, across the plateau and *salar* (salt desert) to Argentina through Villazón. To the southwest is a remote area of volcanic activity, which gives rise to some unusual saline lakes where certain algae create the colourful Laguna Colorada (bright red) and Laguna Verde (green), among other exquisite natural wonders.

In spite of this hostile environment, almost 70% of the population of the country live on the altiplano, one of the highest inhabited areas of the world. Half are in the mining towns and the cities of La Paz and El Alto, and the other half live in the north on or near the shores of Lake Titicaca.

Lake Titicaca

This is the largest lake in South America (ignoring Lake Maracaibo in Venezuela which is linked to the sea) and, at 3812 m, is the highest regularly navigated body of water in the world. It covers about 8300 sq km, running a maximum of 190 km from northwest to southeast and 80 km across. The average depth is over 100 m with the deepest point recorded at 281 m. The border with Peru passes north-south through the lake and about half is in each country.

Over 25 rivers, most from Peru, flow into the lake and a small outlet leaves the lake at Desaguadero on the Bolivia-Peru border. This takes no more than 5% of the inflow, the rest is lost through evaporation and hence the waters of the lake are slightly brackish, producing the *totora* reeds used to make the mats and balsa boats for which the lake dwellers are famed.

The lake level fluctuates seasonally, normally rising from December to March and receding for the rest of the year but extremes of 5 m between high and low levels have been recorded. This can cause problems and high levels in the late 1980s disrupted transport links near the shoreline. The night-time temperature occasionally falls as low as -25°C but high daytime temperatures ensure the surface average is about 14°C which in turn modifies the extremes of winter and night temperatures of the surrounding land. One of the reasons for the relatively high population around the lake are the rich volcanic soils of which good use is made where water is available.

The outflow from the lake, called the Río Desaguadero, continues intermittently for 250 km to Lake Uru Uru, and the larger Lake Poopó, which has no surface outlet and indeed often dries up in the summer.

Titicaca, Uru Uru, Poopó and other intermittent lakes are the remnants of a vast area of water formed in the last ice age known as Lake Ballivián. This extended at least 600 km south from Lake Titicaca and included Lake Poopó and the salt flats of Salar de Coipasa and Salar de Uyuni. Its surface was estimated to have been over 100 m above the present Lake Titicaca level and 225 m above Poopó.

The Yungas and the Puna

La Paz is built in several layers, starting on the altiplano and going east down a steep, narrow valley which may have been one of the ice age exits of Lake Ballivián. Northeast from La Paz, the road to Coroico goes through a section of the Eastern Andes chain called the Cordillera Real. Immediately after the pass at La Cumbre (4725 m), the descent towards the interior plains begins. This area of precipitous valleys and mountain spurs is called the Yungas, has considerable rainfall and is heavily forested.

The escarpment stretches northeast to the frontier with Peru, and in spite of the difficulty of the terrain, is one of the most fertile parts of the country. South from this point, the escarpment, now facing east, falls less steeply towards the interior of the continent, backed by a plateau at around 4000 m, called the Puna, whose western edge also overlooks the Antiplano between the high peaks of the Cordillera Oriental. The eastern slopes become drier to the south, but are still important crop growing areas. The name Yungas is used for all the semi-tropical mountain valleys. Most of this sector drains north into the Madeira river system and thence to the Amazon, but from 20° south to the border with Argentina, the rivers flow east into the Paraná basin. Between these two great watersheds lies the Río Parapeti, whose waters never reach the sea but instead disappear into the mysterious Bañados de Izozog.

The Oriente

Beyond the Yungas and the Puna are the lowlands that stretch northwards and eastwards to Brazil and Paraguay and represent more than 70% of the territory of Bolivia. Similar to Peru and Colombia that also have extensive provinces east of the Andes, Bolivia's Oriente was until recently remote, sparsely inhabited and poorly served by roads and other communications. In the northeast of this region there is dense tropical forest and wetlands. In the extreme east, the border runs close to the Río Paraguay and the Pantanal of Brazil. In the centre, the land is drier, more open with rough pasture and scrub, while in the south close to the Paraguayan and Argentine frontiers, there is still less rain and more arid savannah – part of the immense Gran Chaco.

Climate

The main factors controlling the climate of Bolivia are the trade wind systems and the Andes. The rising of the hot air in the tropical centre of the continent draws in the southeast Trade Winds from the south Atlantic, which are not significantly impeded by the eastern highlands of Brazil. As these moist winds rise up the lower slopes of the Andes, the rain falls. Humidity is high and temperatures high also, but not excessive: 27°C on the lower slopes, 19°C in the upper valleys of the Yungas. Rainfall is higher in the summer (November-March) as the Trades are less active in the winter months. Nevertheless, there is some precipitation all year round in the north of the country as far west as Titicaca.

In the Andes and the altiplano, different conditions prevail. By the time the Trades have crossed the Cordillera Oriental, they have lost almost all their moisture. On the Pacific side, air is also drawn inwards over the Cordillera Occidental. However, because of the cold Humboldt current off the west coast, the air does not absorb moisture from the sea and is dry when it rises over the land. There is therefore no regular source of rain for this region. Violent local storms do produce snowfalls on the highest peaks and rain lower down from time to time.

Temperature in the altiplano is a function of altitude, both in average levels and daily ranges. The average of 10°C at 4000 m can be 20°C at midday often falling to -15°C at night. Arctic conditions prevail at 6000 m. Although there can be considerable day-to-day fluctuations in climatic conditions, there are no noticeable seasonal changes apart from the tendency for rain to fall in the summer months.

There is one other factor which affects the south of the country. Winds originating in the south of the continent blow up the eastern side of the Andes across Argentina and push the southeast Trades northwards. This reduces the rainfall in the south of Bolivia particularly in the altiplano resulting in near desert conditions. On the eastern slopes too, the land gets progressively drier to the south to become the semi-arid scrubland of the Chaco.

National parks

About 15% of Bolivia's territory – over 17 million hectares – is made up of legally protected natural areas of one form or another, the second-highest percentage of any country in the Western Hemisphere. In reality, however, only about 4% is actually maintained as parkland. In 2015, there were 22 areas of varying sizes designated as national parks, integrated use areas, fauna reserves, indigenous territories, and the like. Most people visit only a very few of these areas, generally as part of guided tours from major cities or popular tourist towns. The parks nonetheless represent an outstanding opportunity for the more patient and

BACKGROUND

Bolivian national parks *(All fees under review and subject to change)*

Map key	Name	Access
1	**Aguaragüe**	Villamontes
2	**Amboró**	Samaipata, Buena Vista
3	**Apolobamba**	La Paz
4	**Carrasco**	Cochabamba, Villa Tunari
5	**Cordillera de Sama**	Tarija, Villazón
6	**Cotapata**	La Paz
7	**Eduardo Avaroa**	Uyuni, Tupiza
8	**El Palmar**	Sucre, Tarabuco
9	**Estación Biológica del Beni**	Rurrenabaque, Trinidad
10	**Iñao**	Padilla, Monteagudo
11	**Isiboro-Sécure (TIPNIS)**	Villa Tunari, Trinidad
12	**Kaa-Iya**	San José de Chiquitos
13	**Madidi**	Rurrenabaque
14	**Manuripi**	Cobija
15	**Noel Kempff Mercado**	Santa Cruz, San Ignacio de Velasco
16	**Otuquis**	Puerto Suárez
17	**Pilón Lajas**	Rurrenabaque
18	**Sajama**	La Paz, Oruro
19	**San Matías**	San Matías, Puerto Suárez
20	**Tariquía**	Tarija, Entre Ríos
21	**Torotoro**	Cochabamba
22	**Tunari**	Cochabamba

adventurous traveller, so long as he or she is prepared to face the challenges involved. Access to most parks is difficult and time-consuming (often outright impossible in the rainy season), there are very few if any services available within the parks themselves and no assistance in case of a mishap. You must be self-sufficient in all regards.

You should also be sensitive to the political and social atmosphere surrounding some of the parks. Much of Isiboro-Sécure, for example, is considered dangerous at present because of cocaine production in the area. Other parks, like **Amboró** and **Estación Biológica del Beni** are under constant pressure from *campesinos*, loggers, miners, and others seeking ever more land to sustain their activities.

Habitat/features	Year created	Size (Ha)	Page in text
forest, upland and lowland Chaco	2000	108,307	212
cloud- and rainforest	1984	637,600	259
glacier to jungle	1972	483,743	105
cloud- and rainforest	1991	622,600	232
puna, forest	1991	108,500	213
Cordillera Real, yunga	1993	40,000	111
desert puna, coloured lakes, geysers	1973	714,745	153
dry forest, upland Chaco	1997	59,484	180
jungle, pampa	1982	135,000	298
forest, upland Chaco	2004	263,090	180
jungle, pampa	1965	1,236,296	350
chaco, Bañados de Izozog	1995	3,441,115	277
yunga, jungle, pampa	1995	1,895,750	288
jungle	1973	747,000	353
jungle, tablelands, waterfalls	1979	1,523,446	277
pantanal	1997	1,005,950	280
yunga, jungle, pampa	1992	400,000	290
glaciers, puna, queñua forest, hot springs	1939	100,230	136
pantanal, dry forest, grassland	1995	2,918,500	281
forest, upland Chaco	1989	246,870	214
dry forest, canyons, dinosaur prints	1989	16,570	231
puna, yunga	1962	300,000	228

Outsiders may not be received with open arms in such areas, where it is prudent to keep a low profile.

Finally, keep in mind that many of Bolivia's supposedly protected areas are in fact particularly vulnerable to the impact of tourism, precisely because they are so pristine. This is where being a responsible tourist matters most.

National parks are administered by **Servicio Nacional de Areas Protegidas (SERNAP)** ① *Fransisco Bedregal 2904 y Víctor Sanjinés, Sopocachi, La Paz, T02-242 6272, www.sernap.gob.bo*, which can provide limited tourist information. Better are SERNAP's regional offices in departmental capitals and/or the most important access towns for each park; contact information is given in the corresponding text.

All are basically administrative rather than tourist information offices. Some staff may go out of their way to help you but your expectations should be reasonable. SERNAP charges entry fees for many parks, but prices and policies vary. Local communities may also charge their own separate fees.

Fundación para el Desarrollo del Sistema Nacional de Areas Protegidas (FUNDESNAP) ① *Prolongación Cordero 127, La Paz, T02-211 3364, www.fundesnap. org*, is an NGO working for the development on Bolivia's national parks system. **Fundación Amigos de la Naturaleza (FAN)** ① *Km 7.5 Vía a La Guadria, Santa Cruz, T03-355 6800, www.fan-bo.org*; **Probioma** ① *Calle 7 Este 29, Equipetrol, Santa Cruz, T03-343 1332, www.probioma.org.bo*. See also **www.biobol.org**, a portal with information on Bolivia's protected areas, and the **World Conservation Society's site** (*www.wcs.org/international/latinamerica/amazon_andes*) with information on the Gran Chaco and on northwestern Bolivia. See also **Ramsar's site**, *www. ramsar.org*, for protected wetlands, including the Llanos de Moxos (Ríos Blanco, Matos and Yata), at 6.9 million ha the largest protected wetland in the world.

National parks

① See key on previous page

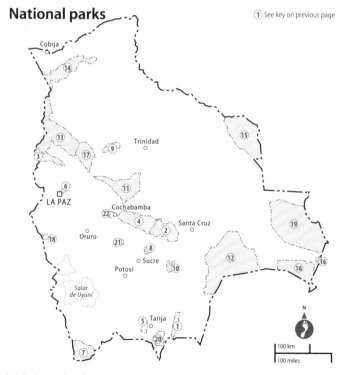

Bolivia is a land of superlatives. It contains part of the most extensive tropical rainforest in the world; the Amazon, to which Bolivia contributes important tributaries, has by far the largest volume of any river in the world and the Andes is the longest uninterrupted mountain chain. The fauna and flora are to a large extent determined by the influence of those mountains and the great rivers, particularly the Amazon. In Bolivia there are vast forests carpeting the lowlands and ascending the slopes of the Andes. Equally spectacular are the huge expanses of open, tree-covered savannahs and dry deserts of the altiplano. It is this immense range of habitats which makes Bolivia one of the world's greatest regions of biological diversity.

This diversity arises not only from the wide range of habitats available, but also from the history of the continent. South America has essentially been an island for some 70 million years joined only by a narrow isthmus to Central and North America. Land passage played a significant role in the gradual colonization of South America by species from the north. When the land-link closed these colonists evolved to a wide variety of forms free from the competitive pressures that prevailed elsewhere. When the land-bridge was re-established some four million years ago a new invasion of species took place from North America, adding to the diversity but also leading to numerous extinctions. Comparative stability has ensued since then and has guaranteed the survival of many primitive groups like the opossums.

Bolivia is a complex mosaic of more than 40 well-defined ecological regions and the transition zones between them. Each has its own characteristic geology, soil, flora and fauna. There are seven major habitats worth considering here: descending from the Puna and the high Andes there are the narrow subtropical valleys or Yungas, the inter-Andean valleys, the dry Chaco, semi-humid woodlands, savannahs and lowland rainforest.

The lowland forests

Situated between latitudes 10° and 15° south and below 250 m altitude the great lowland forests of Bolivia encompass the entire department of Pando and parts of those of La Paz, Beni, Cochabamba and Santa Cruz. Bisected by the great tributary rivers of the Amazon – the Madeira, Mamoré, Madre de Dios, Manuripi and Beni – the area appears at first sight to be in pristine condition. But past and ongoing activities of timber operators extracting mahogany and South American cedar, latex tappers, Brazil nut gatherers, and mineral extraction have had a major impact on the larger species of mammals. These were extensively hunted and the result is an impoverished fauna in many areas.

Notable exceptions are the 1.8 million hectare Pando and the Noel Kempff Mercado National Park. Here in the relatively constant climatic conditions animal and plant life has evolved to an amazing diversity over the millennia. It has been estimated that 2 sq km of lowland rainforest can harbour some 1200 species of vascular plants, 600 species of tree, and 120 species of woody plants.

In the lowland forests, many of the trees are buttress rooted, with flanges extending 3-4 m up the trunk of the tree. Among the smaller trees stilt-like prop roots are also common. Frequently flowers are not well developed, and some emerge directly from the branches and even the trunk. This is possibly an adaptation for pollination by the profusion of bats, giving easier access than if they were obscured by leaves. Lianas are plentiful, especially where there are natural clearings resulting from the death of old trees. These woody vines reach the tops of all but the tallest trees, tying them together and competing with them for space and light. Included here are the strangler figs. These start life as epiphytes, their seeds germinating after deposition by birds. Aerial roots develop and quickly grow down to the ground. These later envelop the trunk, killing the host and leaving the hollow 'trunk' of the strangler.

In the canopy epiphytes are also common and include bromeliads, orchids, ferns, mosses and lichens. Their nutrition is derived from mineral nutrients in the water and organic debris they collect often in specialized pitcher-like structures. Animals of the canopy have developed striking adaptations to enable them to exist in this green wilderness, for example, the prehensile tails of the opossums and many of the monkeys, and the peculiar development of the claws of the sloth.

Many of the bird species which creep around in the understorey are drab coloured, for example tinamou and cotingas, but have loud, clear calls. Scuttling around on the ground are the elusive armadillos, their presence marked by burrows. Pock-marked areas may be indicative of the foraging activities of pacas or peccaries, where their populations have not been exploited by over-hunting.

The forest is at its densest along the river margins; here the diffused light reduces the density of the understorey plant community. The variety of trees is amazing. The forest giants are the kapok and the Brazil nut or *castaña*. These river corridors are often the best places to observe wildlife. Caiman and turtles are commonly seen basking on the river banks. Neotropical cormorants, Roseate spoonbills and Jabiru storks are commonly observed fishing in the shallow waters. The swollen rivers of the lowland forest are home to perhaps 2000 species of fish including piranha, sting ray and electric eel. Many species provide an important source of protein for the native communities, for example, giant catfish. River dolphins also frequent these waters.

The vast river basin of the Amazon is home to an immense variety of species. The environment has largely dictated the lifestyle. Life in or around rivers, lakes, swamps and forest depends on the ability to swim and climb; amphibious and tree-dwelling animals are common. Once the entire Amazon Basin was a great inland sea and the river still contains mammals more typical of the coast, for example manatees and dolphins.

The best way to see the wildlife is to get above the canopy. Ridges provide elevated view points from which excellent views over the forest are obtained. From here, it is possible to look across the lowland flood plain to the very foothills of the Andes, possibly some 200 km away. Flocks of parrots and macaws can be seen commuting between fruiting trees and noisy troupes of squirrel monkeys and brown capuchins come tantalizingly close.

The savannah

The savannah habitat comprises grass and low shrub criss-crossed with rivers and contrasts greatly with the lowland rainforest. It is more obviously seasonal, dry in August and verdant with profuse new growth in December. Small palm groves are characteristic and provide nesting opportunities for macaws.

In the Beni region the savannahs are seasonally flooded, and the mammal fauna then has to congregate on high ground. Impressive aggregations of birds flock to feed on the fish stranded in the withering pools. Large anacondas and caiman abound and herds of russet-coloured capybara and swamp deer may be seen from roads that intersect the area. Small isolated fragments of dry deciduous forest are found interspersed among the flooded plains, and these hold a characteristic fauna in refuges from the ingress of cattle ranching and the burning of grassland associated with it.

In the northwestern part of the Beni region and southeastern Santa Cruz there are also permanently flooded savannahs which are swampy and have characteristic floating mats of vegetation (some with trees), that are shifted around by the wind.

The well-drained soils and moderate climate of the region of Santa Cruz provide conditions for the growth of semi-humid forests from about 300 m to 1200 m above sea level. The altitudinal and climatic range experienced provides for a wealth of flora and fauna which has been exploited by man.

The Chaco

This is a dry region with an annual precipitation of usually less than 300 mm and an average temperature of 26°C, but characterized by cold fronts that on occasion kill new growth in the forest leaving bare trunks. Somewhat surprisingly many species of larger mammals are found here including tapir, jaguar, brocket deer, peccary, and even an unusual lowland guanaco.

The Chaco consists of a variety of habitat types ranging from a mixture of thorny chapparal, with natural grasslands, palms and dry deciduous forests. Due to the intense heat and sun, most of the animals are nocturnal, giving the impression of a low density of mammals. The Bolivian Chaco is perhaps the last refuge for the Chacoan peccary and guanacos. The saó dwarf palm used in the manufacture of the traditional straw hats from Santa Cruz is also found here.

Some of the drier valleys have a mesothermic vegetation (for example cactuses) as they are in the rain shadow of the surrounding mountains. The valleys have a very rich bird fauna, including the military and golden macaw. Rare mammals such as the spectacled bear, taruca (a deer), and the pacarana (a large rodent) are found here. At higher altitudes the cloudforests contain tree ferns and epiphyte clad trees, including birch (aliso) and podocarpus.

The Yungas

The Yungas comprise a belt of very humid forests at altitudes ranging up to 3600 m. The headwaters of many of Bolivia's major rivers rise here and flow as clear, rapid streams through deep canyons. The vegetation ranges from that typical of lowland forest through to cloudforest and, at the tree line, elfin forest with ferns and bamboo. The great diversity of habitats has led to a great diversity of fauna, likely to be the richest in the country. The spectacled bear, and exotic birds such as the Andean cock of the rock and the horned currasow are denizens of this habitat.

The highlands

Life is rare in the puna and high mountains. The climate is dry and cold, particularly in the altiplano where there is little or no vegetation except for a few shrubs, cacti and dry grass. The vast climatic range, from 15°C during the day to -25°C during the night, impose severe limits on life. An exception to this is the Laguna Colorada where a vast lake warmed by fumaroles is home to thousands of flamingos and other water birds. Vicuñas, vizcachas, rheas and Andean wild cats survive in a delicate balance within this fragile environment.

The pantanal

The Bolivian pantanal is an ecologically diverse zone continuous with that in Brazil. When flooded from December to March, it creates the largest area of wetlands in the world. It also includes dry savannahs or *cerrado*, Chaco scrublands as well as gallery rainforest. The area is very flat and flooded by the rising rivers leaving isolated islands (*cordilheiras*) between vast lakes (*bahías*) which become saline as the waters evaporate.

This mixed ecosystem supports a highly diverse fauna characteristic of the constituent habitat types which includes 200 species of mammal. Capybara, tapir and peccary are common along the water's edge, as are marsh deer. Jaguar, more commonly associated with the forest, prey on these herbivores and the cattle and feral pigs which graze here. Spectacular numbers of wading birds – egrets, jabiru storks, ibises and herons – prey on the abundant invertebrate and fish fauna. Anacondas and caiman are still common, although the black caiman has been hunted out.

Practicalities
Bolivia

Getting there

Air

International flights to Bolivia arrive either at **La Paz (LPB)** or **Santa Cruz (VVI)**. There are frequent domestic flights between La Paz and Santa Cruz, as well as plentiful bus services. For airport tax, see page 373.

From Europe

Air Europa (www.aireuropa.com) and **BoA (Boliviana** – www.boa.bo) offer direct flights from Europe to Bolivia, four times a week each from Madrid to Santa Cruz and, in the latter case, on to La Paz. Alternatively, connections can be made in Miami, São Paulo, Buenos Aires, Santiago or Lima.

From North America

Miami's international airport is the only air transport gateway linking Bolivia with North America. **American** (www.aa.com) flies daily to La Paz and Santa Cruz. **LAN** (www.lan.com) has services from Miami to Bolivia via Lima. From other North American cities, change in Miami.

From Australia and New Zealand

There are three options: 1) To Los Angeles (USA) with **Qantas/American Airlines** (code share, www.qantas.com.au), or **Air New Zealand** (www.airnewzealand.co.uk), continuing to Bolivia via Miami (see above) or via Bogotá with **Avianca** (www.avianca.com); 2) From Auckland to Santiago, Chile, continuing to La Paz with **LAN**; 3) To Buenos Aires (Argentina) from Sydney and Auckland with **Aerolíneas Argentinas** from December 2015 (www.aerolineas.com.ar), continuing to Bolivia with various South American carriers. These are all expensive long-haul routes; round-the-world and Circle Pacific fares may be convenient alternatives.

From South America

There are direct flights to La Paz and/or Santa Cruz from Asunción, Bogotá, Buenos Aires, Cuzco, Iquique (Chile), Lima, Santiago, Salta (Argentina) and São Paulo. **Amaszonas'** (www.amaszonas.com) daily flight between La Paz and Cuzco is convenient for tourists visiting Bolivia and Peru.

Road, rail, lake and river

Bolivia has numerous borders with Argentina, Brazil, Chile, Paraguay and Peru, and they are heavily used, see Border crossings box, page 360.

Getting around

Air

All of the following offer internal air services: **Boliviana de Aviación (BoA)** ⓘ *T901-105010*, *www.boa.bo*, has a growing international network. **Aerocon** ⓘ *T901-105252*, *www.aerocon.bo*, serves mostly the northern jungle, Oruro, Potosí, Tarija and Yacuiba (note that **Aerocon** has had a few accidents since 2010). **Amaszonas** ⓘ *T901-105500*, *www.amaszonas.com*, flies to all main cities and between La Paz and Rurrenabaque, Trinidad and Uyuni; its international network is also increasing. **Ecojet** ⓘ *T901-105055*, *www.ecojet.bo*, based in Cochabamba, flies from Cochabamba, La Paz and Santa Cruz to the main lowland destinations, Sucre and Tarija. **TAM** ⓘ *T901-105510*, *www.tam.bo*, the civilian branch of the Bolivian Air Force, flies to main cities as well as Puerto Suárez, Yacuiba and several smaller and more remote destinations. Many flights radiate from La Paz, Santa Cruz or Cochabamba. Make sure you have adequate baggage insurance.

TRAVEL TIP
Border essentials

Land crossings
A direct international bus service connects several Bolivian cities with Peru, Chile, Argentina and Paraguay. In addition, tour agencies offer transport (in buses and vans) between La Paz and Puno (Peru), with connections to Cuzco and beyond. It is usually much cheaper however, to buy bus tickets only as far as the nearest border town, cross on foot or by taxi, and then purchase tickets locally in the country you have just entered. If entering Bolivia by car, customs procedures are described in the Driving in Bolivia box, page 362. For train service from the Brazilian and Argentine borders, see page 365.

Lake/river crossings
Crillon Tours and Transturin (see La Paz tour operators, page 65) combine their boat services on Lake Titicaca with onward transport in Peru. Full details can be obtained from the respective companies.

Although Bolivia's larger jungle rivers are navigable and flow to the Amazon, there is no international river-boat service to Brazil.

Bolivia–Argentina
There are three official border crossings between Bolivia and Argentina. See page 160 for Villazón–La Quiaca, and page 214 for Bermejo–Aguas Blancas and page 263 for Yacuiba Pocitos.

Road

A relatively small (but growing) percentage of Bolivian roads is paved, the rest being gravel-surfaced or earth. Any road, whatever its surface, may be closed in the rainy season (December-March). The main paved road axis of Bolivia runs from the Peruvian border at Desaguadero (also Copacabana) via La Paz and Oruro to Cochabamba and Santa Cruz, continuing to the Brazilian border at Arroyo Concepción. Some sections, such as La Paz–Oruro, are dual carriageway; others are being dualled. Other paved roads connect the La Paz–Oruro highway with Tambo Quemado on the Chilean border, continuing paved to Arica. From Potosí there are paved, or soon-to-be-paved roads to Uyuni, to Villazón (on the Argentine border) via Tupiza and to Aguas Blancas (also on the Argentine border) via Camargo and Tarija. As well as the main route to Brazil mentioned above, paved routes from Santa Cruz go to Trinidad and to Yacuiba on the Argentine border. The Trans-Chaco highway, from Santa Cruz to Asunción (Paraguay) branches off the Yacuiba road at Villamontes; it is mostly paved. Road-improvement projects continue in many areas. The remainder of Bolivia's roads are either gravel or earth, notoriously narrow and tortuous in the highlands, notoriously prone to wash-outs in the lowlands.

Bolivia–Brazil

There are several border crossings from the far east of Bolivia to neighbouring Brazil. By far the most convenient border point is Arroyo Concepción–Corumbá (Brazil), see page 281. North of this crossing are the routes from San Ignacio de Velasco to San Matías and Cáceres and to Pontes e Lacerda, see page 280. For Cobija–Brasiléia, see page 305, and for Guayaramerín–Guajará–Mirim, see page 303.

Bolivia–Chile

There are five official border crossings between Bolivia and Chile: three northern and two southern. For the northern border crossings of Tambo Quemado–Chungará, Charaña–Visviri and Pisiga–Colchane, see page 139. For the southern borders of Avaroa–Ollagüe and Hito Cajones–Hito Cajón, see page 155.

Bolivia–Paraguay

The crossing is at Picada Sucre–Fortín Infante Rivarola, see page 263. Customs posts are 60 km beyond, on either side of the actual border, but these are just place names, not towns.

Bolivia–Peru

There are three main border crossings to Peru, plus a fourth via Brazil. The route most commonly used by tourists is the Kasani–Yunguyo crossing. See page 95 for Kasani–Yunguyo, for Desaguadero–Desaguadero, and for Puerto Acosta–Tilali. See page 306 for the Bolpebra–Iñapari crossing, via Brazil.

TRAVEL TIP
Road travel tips

Bus

▪ For international service it's cheaper to take a bus to the border, cross and then take another to your final destination.

▪ Make sure you see your gear being loaded on the correct bus, especially at busy terminals. 'Mistakes', intentional or innocent, are not uncommon.

▪ Try to reserve and pay for a seat in advance and arrive in time, as buses may depart when full. Confirm where the bus leaves from.

▪ Long-distance buses usually make meal stops and it is often possible to buy some food on the roadside; have small Boliviano notes at hand. It is a good idea to also carry a little food and water with you.

▪ Always keep your valuables with you, even when leaving the bus at a meal stop. Never leave a day-pack to hold a seat.

▪ On overnight trips, especially in the highlands, you will appreciate extra clothing or a blanket as many buses do not have any form of heating.

▪ Always take toilet paper. Toilets on cheaper buses are non-existent but drivers can be asked to stop in an emergency.

▪ If your bus has a TV, don't expect to see any scenery by day, and don't expect to get any sleep at night.

▪ Avoid the back seats at all costs. On unpaved roads you will spend more time airborne than seated, and the windows will be jammed open, causing you to cough your lungs up from the exhaust fumes and clouds of dust, as well as freeze to death at night in the mountains.

Car

▪ When hiring a car check exactly what the insurance policy covers. In many cases it will only protect you against minor bumps and scrapes and not major accidents. Ask if extra coverage is available. Beware of being billed for scratches that were on the vehicle before you hired it.

▪ Never leave a car unattended except in a locked garage or guarded parking space. Street children will generally protect your car in exchange for a tip. Lock the clutch or accelerator to the steering wheel with a heavy, obvious chain or lock.

▪ You cannot take a hire car across international borders.

Bus

Buses ply most of the main roads. Inter-urban buses are called *flotas*, inter-urban minibuses are minivans or *surubíes*; urban buses are *micros* or *minibuses* (vans); *trufis* are shared taxis. Larger bus companies run frequent services and offer a/c, and TV. You can usually buy tickets with reserved seats a day or two in advance. Savings may sometimes be obtained by bargaining for fares at the last minute, although not at peak travel times like national holidays. Companies with the best reputation are Bolívar and Copacabana. *Surubíes* and *trufis* leave when full; sometimes you have no choice but to take them, but they drive very fast and dangerously. A small charge is made for use of bus terminals; payment is before departure.

In the wet season, bus travel is subject to long delays and detours, at extra cost, and cancellations are not uncommon. At any time of year, though, journey times are approximate. On all journeys, take some food, water and toilet paper. It is best to travel by day, not just to enjoy the scenery and avoid arriving at night, but also for better road safety (also see Road safety, page 362). It is not always possible to travel by day. Often buses leave in the early to mid-evening, with the result that you will arrive at your destination in the early hours of the morning if the journey is not too long. Bus companies are responsible for any items packed in the luggage compartment or on the roof, but only if they give you a ticket for each bag.

Car

Road tolls These vary from US$0.50 to US$2.45 for journeys up to 100 km. On toll roads you are given a receipt at the first toll; keep it at hand as it is asked for at subsequent toll posts. The **Administradora Boliviana de Carreteras** (ABC, Av Mcal Santa Cruz, Edif Centro de Comunicaciones p 8, T02-215 9800) maintains a useful website, www.abc.gob.bo, with daily updates of road conditions, including any roadblocks due to social unrest. ABC also has a toll-free phone for emergencies and to report road hazards, T800-107222.

Safety Always carry spare petrol/gas and supplies and camping equipment if going off major roads. Your car must be able to cope with high altitude and below-freezing temperatures. Take great care on the roads, especially at night. Too many truck drivers are drunk and many vehicles drive with faulty headlights. Stalled trucks without lights are a common cause of accidents.

Documents To bring a private vehicle into Bolivia you need an International Driving Permit, the vehicle's registration document (in your name, or with a notarized letter of authorization from the owner plus approval from the Bolivian consulate in the country of origin) and your passport. On entry you get temporary admission from customs (free of charge) and surrender the document on departure; maximum 90 days. Details are available at www.aduana.gob.bo. A *carnet de passages en douane* is required according to www.aduana.gob.bo and insurance is compulsory. It is called SOAT and can be bought locally. Generally the police are helpful to foreign motorists, but stop you often and ask to see your documents, a complete first-aid kit, triangle and fire extinguisher.

TRAVEL TIP
Don't forget your toothbrush

▪ Pack light. Take clothes that are quick and easy to wash and dry. Loose-fitting clothes are more comfortable in hot climates and can be layered if it gets cooler. The highlands can get very cold.

▪ You can cheaply and easily buy things en route, but musts to take are: good walking shoes, a money belt, a sun hat and sunglasses and the chargers and adapters for all your electronic kit.

▪ Other useful items are a handkerchief or bandana, pocket-knife, flip flops, a headtorch/flashlight, the smallest alarm clock you can find, a padlock, dental floss and a basic medical kit.

▪ Pack photocopies of essential documents like passport and visas just in case you lose the originals. Also leave a copy with someone at home and an electronic version somewhere safe that you can access easily.

▪ Photographers should take all film and memory sticks required for the trip. Keep them in a waterproof bag.

▪ Don't load yourself down with toiletries. They're heavy and can be bought everywhere. Contact lens solution and tampons may be harder to find; stock up in major cities.

Note There are restrictions on which vehicles may drive in La Paz, depending on license plate number and day of the week.

Organizations Automóvil Club Boliviano, C 12 de Calacoto esq Inofuentes, La Paz, T02-279 1755, www.acbbolivia.com.bo.

Car hire The minimum age for hiring a car is 25. Rental companies may only require your licence from home, but police ask to see an international licence. Rental of a medium-sized car costs about US$370 per week; a small 4WD vehicle US$505-550 per week.

Fuel Especial, 85 octane containing lead, US$0.54 per litre (may cost more in remote areas). **Diesel** costs about the same. Higher-octane **Premium**, US$0.70 per litre, is only available in La Paz, if at all. There may be fuel shortages, especially in border areas, so keep your tank full.

Train

The western highland railway is operated by **Ferroviaria Andina (FCA)** ⓘ *T02-241 6545, www.fca.com.bo.* There are passenger trains to Villazón from Oruro, via Atocha, Tupiza and Uyuni. There are plans to reopen to passengers the La Paz to Arica line (2015). The eastern lowland line is run by **Ferroviaria Oriental** ⓘ *www.fo.com.bo*, with services from Santa Cruz east to the Brazilian border and south to the Argentine border at Yacuiba.

Maps

Good maps of Bolivia are few and far between, and maps in general can be hard to find. **Instituto Geográfico Militar** (IGM, see page 63). Many IGM maps date from the 1970s and their accuracy is variable; prices also vary, US$4.50-7 a sheet. **Walter Guzmán Córdova** makes several travel and trekking maps, available from some bookshops in La Paz. The **German Alpine Club (Deutscher Alpenverein)** ⓘ *www.alpenverein.de*, produces two maps of Sorata-Ancohuma-Illampu and Illimani, but these are not usually available in La Paz.

Essentials A-Z

Accident and emergency

Contact the relevant emergency service and your embassy in La Paz. Make sure you obtain police/medical reports in order to file insurance claims.

Emergency services A-Z
Ambulance T165 nationwide, T161 in El Alto. **Police** T110 nationwide. Fire T119 nationwide. Robberies should be reported to the **Policía Turística**, they will issue a report for insurance purposes but stolen goods are rarely recovered. In cities which do not have a Policía Turística report robberies to the **Fuerza Especial de Lucha Contra el Crimen (FELCC)**, Departamento de Robos. In La Paz, see safety, page 31.

Children

Travel with children can bring you into closer contact with Bolivian families and, generally, presents no special problems – in fact the path may even be smoother for family groups. Officials are sometimes more amenable where children are concerned and they are pleased if your child knows a little Spanish.

Transport Remember that a lot of time can be spent waiting for and riding buses, which are sometimes crowded and uncomfortable. On long-distance buses you pay for each seat, and there are no half-fares. For shorter trips it is cheaper, if less comfortable, to seat small children on your knee. Sometimes there are spare seats that children can occupy after tickets have been collected.

On domestic flights in Bolivia, children under 2 pay 10% of the adult fare; 2-12 year-olds pay about 75%. Make sure that children accompanying you are fully covered by your travel insurance policy.

Food Most Bolivian food is spicy, which can be a problem for children. It is easier to take food with you on longer trips than to rely on meal stops where the food may not be to taste. Best stick to simple things like bread, bananas and tangerines, while you are the road. Biscuits, packaged junk food and bottled drinks abound. A small immersion heater and jug for making hot drinks is invaluable. In restaurants, you may be able to buy a *media porción* (half portion), or divide a full-size helping between 2 children.

Disabled travellers

Unfortunately, there are very few facilities for disabled travellers in Bolivia. This is compounded by the particularly steep streets and narrow sidewalks of many highland cities. Santa Cruz, while it has no special facilities, may be a little more accessible just because of its level topography. Visually or hearing-impaired travellers are also poorly catered for but some travel companies outside South America specialize in holidays that are tailor-made for the individual's level of disability. For general information, the **Global Access – Disabled Travel Network** website, www.globalaccessnews.com/index. htm, is useful. Another informative site, with lots of advice on how to travel with specific disabilities, plus listings and links belongs to the **Society for Accessible Travel and Hospitality**, www.sath.org.

Drugs

Illegal drugs are the most common way for foreigners to get into serious trouble in Bolivia. Some people come specifically to consume or buy drugs, especially cocaine, and may have the false impression that the country is permissive in this regard. This is not the case. Although coca leaves are legal, and the government of Evo Morales promotes their traditional and medicinal uses, it is making an international point of continuing the fight against cocaine without the involvement of the US Drug Enforcement Agency (DEA). Anyone caught in possession will automatically be assumed to be a drug trafficker, punishable by up to 15 years' imprisonment. If you are asked to have your bags searched, insist on having a witness present at all times. Be aware of tricks to plant drugs on you and never answer offers by anyone selling drugs on the street. Even if you are not personally involved with drugs, you place yourself at risk by associating with Bolivians or foreigners who are.

Electricity

220 volts 50 cycles AC. Sockets usually accept both continental European (round) and US-type (flat) 2-pin plugs. Also some 110-volt sockets, when in doubt, ask.

Embassies and consulates

For all Bolivian embassies abroad and all foreign embassies and consulates in Bolivia, see http://embassy.goabroad.com.

Festivals and public holidays

Festivals

2 Feb Virgen de la Candelaria, in rural communities in Copacabana, Santa Cruz departments.

Feb/Mar Carnaval, especially famous in Oruro, is celebrated throughout the country. There are parades with floats and folkloric dances, parties, much drinking and water throwing even in the coldest weather and nobody is spared. Many related festivities take place around the time of Carnaval. 2 weeks beforehand is **Jueves de Compadres** followed by **Jueves de Comadres**. In the altiplano Shrove Tuesday is celebrated as **Martes de Challa**, when house owners make offerings to Pachamama and give drinks to passers-by. **Carnaval Campesino** usually begins in small towns on Ash Wednesday, when regular Carnaval ends, and lasts for 5 days, until **Domingo de Tentación**. Palm Sunday (**Domingo de Ramos**) sees parades to the church throughout Bolivia; the devout carry woven palm fronds, then hang them outside their houses.

Mar/Apr Semana Santa in the eastern Chiquitania is very interesting, with ancient processions, dances, and games not found outside the region.

3 May Fiesta de la Invención de la Santa Cruz, various places.

May/Jun Corpus Christi is another colourful festival.

2 Jun Santísima Trinidad in Beni Department.

24 Jun San Juan, bonfires throughout all Bolivia.

29 Jun San Pedro y San Pablo, at

Tiquina, Tihuanaco and throughout Chiquitania.

25 Jul Fiesta de Santiago (St James), altiplano and lake region.

14-16 Aug Virgen de Urkupiña, Cochabamba, a 3-day Catholic festivity mixed with Quechua rituals and parades with folkloric dances.

16 Aug San Roque, patron saint of dogs; the animals are adorned with ribbons and other decorations.

1 and 2 Nov: All Saints and All Souls, any local cemetery.

Public holidays

Some dates may be moved to the nearest weekend.

1 Jan, New Year's Day; Carnaval Week, Mon, Shrove Tuesday, Ash Wednesday; Holy Week: Thu, Fri and Sat; 1 May, Labour Day; Corpus Christi (movable May/Jun); 16 Jul, La Paz Municipal Holiday; 5-7 Aug, Independence; 24 Sep, Santa Cruz Municipal Holiday; 2 Nov, Day of the Dead; Christmas Day.

Health

See your GP or travel clinic at least 6 weeks before departure for general advice on travel risks and vaccinations. Try phoning a specialist travel clinic if your own doctor is unfamiliar with health conditions in Bolivia. Make sure you have sufficient medical travel insurance, get a dental check, know your own blood group and if you suffer a long-term condition such as diabetes or epilepsy, obtain a **Medic Alert** bracelet/necklace (www.medicalert.co.uk). If you wear eye glasses, take a copy of your prescription.

Vaccinations

It is advisable to vaccinate against polio, tetanus, typhoid, hepatitis A, yellow fever if visiting the lowlands, and rabies if going to more remote areas. Malaria is a danger in the northern jungle and parts of the eastern lowlands. Specialist advice should be taken on the best anti-malarials to use.

Health risks

Altitude sickness is a common but usually mild affliction of most visitors to Bolivia's highlands, especially if you arrive by plane and therefore do not have time to acclimatize. Smokers and those with underlying heart or lung disease are often hardest hit. Take it easy for the first few days, rest-up from your trip and drink plenty of water, you will feel better soon. It is essential to get acclimatized before undertaking long treks or arduous activities. The altitude of the altiplano also means that strong protection from the sun is essential regardless of how cool it may feel; always use sunglasses, sun block and a hat.

The major health risks in lower parts of the country are those **diseases carried by insects** such as mosquitoes and sandflies. These include **Chagas disease** (endemic in parts of rural Bolivia), **leishmaniasis**, **malaria** and **dengue fever**. In 2015 cases of the **chikungunya** virus, transmitted by the same mosquito that carries dengue, had been confirmed in Bolivia. Long trousers, a long-sleeved shirt and insect repellent, all offer protection. Mosquito nets dipped in permethrin provide a good physical and chemical barrier at night. The *vinchuca* insect, which carries Chagas disease, usually lives in the thatch roofs of houses and is active at night. If sleeping in such a setting, use a tent or mosquito net.

A bout of **stomach upset** is almost inevitable on a longer visit to Bolivia.

Consider it part of the travel experience and don't get scared or overreact. If diarrhoea persists for several days or you develop additional symptoms, then see a doctor. The standard advice for prevention is to be careful with drinking water and ice; all tap water in Bolivia must be purified before being consumed but bottled water is easily available. In a restaurant, ask what water drinks are prepared with. Also be wary of raw salads and undercooked meat. **Tuberculosis** is a hazard and it is best to avoid unpasteurized dairy products and try not to let people cough and splutter all over you.

If you get sick

Contact your embassy or consulate or the tourist office for a list of doctors and dentists who speak your language, or at least some English. Good-quality health care is available in the larger centres of Bolivia but it can be expensive, especially hospitalization. Make sure you have adequate insurance (see below). Your hotel may also be able to recommend good local medical services.

La Paz

Laboratorios Illimani, Edif Alborada p 3, of 304, Loayza y Juan de la Riva, T02-231 7290, www.laboratoriosillimani. com. Open 0900-1230, 1430-1700. Fast, efficient, hygienic.
Ministerio de Desarrollo Humano, **Secretaría Nacional de Salud**, Av Arce, near **Radisson Plaza**. Yellow fever shot and certificate, rabies and cholera shots, malaria pills, bring your own syringe.
Pharmacies Daily papers list pharmacies on duty (*de turno*).
Sumaya (Dr Orellana), Linares 339 esq Sagárnaga, T02-242 2342, or 7065 9743. Good English-speaking doctor; for more

severe cases the same doctor runs the **Clínica Lausanne**, Av Los Sargentos,esq Costanera in Bajo LLojeta, close to upper side of Obrajes. Very helpful, recommended.

Santa Cruz

Santa Cruz is an important medical centre with many hospitals and private clinics.
Clínica Foianini, Av Irala 468, T03-336 2211,www.clinicafoianini.com. Among the better-regarded and more expensive hospitals.
San Juan de Dios, Cuéllar y España. The public hospital.

Sucre

Hospital Cristo de las Américas, Av Japón s/n, T04-643 7804, www.hsjd.org. Private hospital.
Hospital Santa Bárbara, Ayacucho y R Moreno, Plazuela Libertad, T04-645 1900, Hospital-Santa-Barbara on Facebook. Public hospital.

Useful websites

www.cdc.gov Centres for Disease Control and Prevention (USA).
www.nhs.uk/nhsengland/ Healthcareabroad/pages/ Healthcareabroad.aspx Department of Health advice for travellers.
www.fitfortravel.scot.nhs.uk Fit for Travel (UK), a site from Scotland providing a quick A-Z of vaccine and travel health advice requirements for each country.
www.itg.be Institute for Tropical Medicine, Antwerp.
www.nathnac.org National Travel Health Network and Centre (NaTHNaC).
www.who.int World Health Organisation.

Insurance

Travel insurance is a must for all visitors to Bolivia. Always take out insurance that covers both medical expenses and baggage loss and read the small print carefully before you set off. Check that all the activities you may end up doing are covered. Mountaineering, for example, is excluded from many policies; also make sure that coverage is not excluded at high altitude, the cut off may be below the height of most altiplano cities! Also check if medical coverage includes air ambulance and emergency flights back home. Mind the payment protocol: in Bolivia you will have to have to pay out of pocket and later request reimbursement from the insurance company. Before paying for any medical services, insist on getting a fully itemized invoice. In case of baggage loss, have the receipts for expensive personal effects like cameras and laptops on file, take photos of these items, note the serial numbers and be sure to leave unnecessary valuables at home. Keep the insurance company's telephone number with you and get a police report for any lost or stolen items (see La Paz Tourist Police, page 31).

Language

The official languages of Bolivia are **Spanish**, **Aymara** and **Quechua**. In the highland countryside many people do not speak Spanish, only their native tongue, although you can usually find someone in most villages who speaks at least a little Spanish. **English**, or any other foreign language, is absolutely useless off the beaten track. With even a modest knowledge of Spanish you will be able to befriend Bolivians, to interchange ideas and insights with them. Without any language skills, you will feel like someone trying to peep through the keyhole at Bolivia. So learn some Spanish before you come to Bolivia or begin your travels in Bolivia with a period of language study. Sucre has several language schools where you can study Spanish or Quechua, and there are others in Cochabamba and La Paz. See language schools listed in the What to do sections of this book. The following companies also organize language training and, in some cases, homestays and activities:

AmeriSpan, *T1-215-531 7917 (worldwide), T1-800-511 0179 (USA), www.amerispan. com.* Spanish immersion programmes, educational tours, volunteer and internship positions throughout Latin America.

Cactus, *T0845-130 4775 (UK), +44-1273-830960 (international), www. cactuslanguage.com.*

Spanish Abroad, *3219 East Camelback Rd No 806, Phoenix, AZ 85339, USA, T1-888-722 7623, or T602-778 6791, www. spanishabroad.com.*

LGBT

Bolivia is still quite intolerant of homosexuality. La Paz and Santa Cruz are perhaps the most liberal places in the country, while smaller cities and rural areas tend to be very conservative. It is therefore prudent to respect local sensibilities and avoid provoking a reaction. For local information see the website of **Adesproc Libertad GLBT**, www.libertadglbt.org (in Spanish).

Money

US$1 = Bs6.9. €1 = Bs7.6. £1 = Bs10.6
(Jul 2015)

Currency

The currency is the boliviano (Bs),
divided into 100 centavos. There
are notes for 200, 100, 50, 20 and 10
bolivianos, and 5, 2 and 1 boliviano
coins, as well as 50, 20 and (rare) 10
centavos. Bolivianos are often referred
to as pesos; expensive items, including
hotel rooms, may be quoted in dollars.

ATMs and credit cards

Many *casas de cambio* and street
changers (but among banks only **Banco
Nacional de Bolivia**, BNB, www.bnb.
com.bo) accept cash euros as well as
dollars. Large bills may be hard to use
in small villages, always carry some
20s and 10s.

ATMs (**Enlace** network T800-103060)
are common in all departmental capitals
and some other cities but not in all small
towns, including several important
tourist destinations. Sorata, for instance,
has no ATM. Don't rely on ATMs in small
towns with few machines, for example
Rurrenabaque; they frequently run out
of cash. **Banco Unión**, has most ATMs
in small towns, see www.bancounion.
com.bo for locations. ATMs are not
always reliable and, in addition to plastic,
you must always carry some cash.
Most ATMs dispense both Bs and US$.
Debit cards and Amex are generally less
reliable than Visa/MC credit cards at
ATMs. Note that Bolivian ATMs dispense
cash first and only a few moments later
return your card. In small towns without
banks or ATMs, look for **Prodem**, which
changes US$ cash at fair rates, and
gives cash advances at tellers on Visa/

MC credit – not debit – cards for about
5% commission. (Prodem ATMs do not
accept international cards.) **Banco Fie**
is also found throughout the country,
changes US$ cash at all branches and
gives cash advances at some locations.
ATM scams are worst in La Paz, but may
occur elsewhere. For lost Visa cards
T800-100188, MasterCard T800-100172.

Cost of travelling

Bolivia is cheaper to visit than most
neighbouring countries. Budget
travellers can get by on US$20-25 per
person per day for 2 travelling together.
A basic hotel in small towns costs about
US$6-12 pp, breakfast US$1.50-2, and
a simple set lunch (*almuerzo*) around
US$2.50-3.50. For around US$35-40,
though, you can find much better
accommodation, more comfortable
transport and a wider choice in food.
Prices are higher in the city of La Paz; in
the east, especially Santa Cruz and Tarija;
and in Pando and the upper reaches of
the Beni. The average cost of using the
internet is US$0.50 per hr.

Opening hours

Banks and offices: normally open Mon-
Fri 0900-1600, Sat 0900-1300, but may
close for lunch in small towns.
Shops: Mon-Fri 0830-1230, 1430-1830
and Sat 0900-1200. Opening and closing
in the afternoon are later in lowland
provinces.

Police and the law

You are required to carry your passport
at all times, although this is seldom
asked for outside border areas. In the
event of a vehicle accident in which
anyone is injured, all drivers involved are
usually detained until blame has been

TRAVEL TIP
Safe travel checklist

- Keep valuables out of sight.
- Keep documents/money secure.
- Split up your main cash supply and hide it in different places.
- Lock your luggage, even in your hotel room.
- At night, take a taxi between transport terminals and your hotel.
- Use the hotel safe deposit box and keep an inventory of what you have deposited.
- Look out for tricks to distract your attention and steal your belongings.
- Notify the police of any losses and make sure you get a written report for insurance claims.
- Avoid hiking alone in remote areas.
- Avoid travelling at night.
- Don't fight back – it is better to hand over your valuables rather than risk injury.

established, which may take several weeks. Never offer to bribe a police officer; you don't know the rules so don't try to play the game. If an official suggests that a bribe must be paid before you can proceed on your way, be patient and they may relent. In general however, there are few hassles and most police are helpful to travellers. For La Paz **tourist police**, see page 31.

Post and couriers

The main branches of post offices in La Paz, Santa Cruz and Cochabamba are best for sending parcels. DHL and FedEx have offices in major cities.

Safety

Compared with some other parts of South America, Bolivia has less violent crime, but tricks and scams are common. The countryside and small towns are generally safe while the largest cities (Santa Cruz, El Alto, La Paz and Cochabamba) call for the greatest precautions. Fake police, narcotics police and immigration officers – usually plain-clothed but carrying forged ID – have been known to take people to their 'office' and ask to see documents and money; they then rob them. Legitimate police do not ask people for documents in the street unless they are involved in an accident, fight, etc. If approached, walk away and seek assistance from as many bystanders as possible. Never get in a vehicle with the 'officer' nor follow them to their 'office'. Many of the robberies are very slick, involving taxis and various accomplices. Take only radio taxis, identified by their dome lights and phone numbers. Always lock the doors, sit in the back and never allow other passengers to share your cab. If someone else gets in, get out at once. Also if smeared or spat-on, walk away, don't let the good Samaritan clean you up, they will clean you out instead.

Civil disturbance, although less frequent in recent years, remains part of Bolivian life. It can take the form of strikes, demonstrations in major cities and roadblocks (*bloqueos*), some lasting a few hours, others weeks. Try to be flexible in your plans if you encounter disruptions and make the most of nearby attractions if transport is not running. You can often find transport to the site of a roadblock, walk across and get onward transport on the other side. Check with locals first to find out how tense the situation is.

Road safety

This should be an important concern for all visitors to Bolivia. Precarious roads, poorly maintained vehicles and frequently reckless drivers combine to cause many serious, at times fatal, accidents. Choose your transport judiciously and don't hesitate to pay a little more to travel with a better company. Look over the vehicle before you get on; if it doesn't feel right, look for another. If a driver is drunk or reckless, demand that he stop at the nearest village and let you off. Also note that smaller buses, although less comfortable, are often safer on narrow mountain roads.

Student and teacher travellers

If you are in full-time education you are entitled to an International **Student Identity Card** (**ISIC**), which is sold by student travel offices and agencies in 70 countries. The ISIC may give you special prices on transport and access to a variety of other concessions and services in some countries, although these are relatively uncommon in Bolivia. Teachers are entitled to an International **Teacher Identity Card** (**ITIC**). Both are available from www.isic.org. In Bolivia, the ISIC is sold by The **Spitting Llama Bookstore**, with branches in Cochabamba (page 226) and La Paz (see page 62).

Taxes

Airport tax International departure tax (US$25) is included in tickets at La Paz, Cochabamba and Santa Cruz airports. Domestic tax is also included in tickets at these airports, but at all others an airport tax of US$1-2.50, depending on airport, is charged.
IVA/VAT 13%.

Telephone and Wi-Fi

Country code +591.
Equal tones with long pauses: ringing. Equal tones with equal pauses: engaged. IDD prefix: 00. Calls from public *cabinas* are expensive. Cellular numbers have no city code, but carry a 3-digit prefix starting with 7 or, less commonly, 6.

Mobile phone service is offered by 3 main companies, **Entel**, **Tigo** and **Viva**. They have shops everywhere and you can by a SIM card (un chip) for your phone or tablet if you would rather use local services than your home provider. Ask at a shop if a local SIM is compatible with your device and what the best package will be. There are call centres as well if you wish to make a call on a phone or local mobile.

Wi-Fi coverage is best in major towns and cities and where the service is available. Free Wi-Fi is standard from the most basic hostel to the best hotels. In more out of the way places, Wi-Fi may be slow and limited to a public area in the hostel or hotel. Many places, such as cafés and restaurants in tourist areas, have Wi-Fi. Just ask for the code.

Time

GMT-4 all year.

Tipping

Up to 10% in restaurants is very generous, Bolivians seldom leave more than a few coins. Tipping is not customary for most services (eg taxi driver) though it is a reward when service has been very good. Guides expect a tip as does someone who has looked after a car or carried bags.

Tourist information

InfoTur offices are found in most departmental capitals (addresses given under each city), at international arrivals in El Alto airport (La Paz) and Viru Viru (Santa Cruz). In La Paz at Mariscal Santa Cruz y Colombia and other sites (see La Paz listings).
Ministerio de Culturas y Turismo, *www.minculturas.gob.bo.*

Viceministerio de Turismo, *C Mercado, Ed Ballivián, p 18, T02-211 5380, www. bolivia.travel.*

Useful websites
www.bolivia.com (Spanish) News, tourism, entertainment and information on regions.
www.bolivia-online.net (Spanish, English and German) Travel information about La Paz, Cochabamba, Potosí, Santa Cruz and Sucre.
www.boliviaentusmanos.com (Spanish) News, entertainment, hotel and restaurant guide, tourist information and more.
www.presidencia.gob.bo Presidential website.
http://lanic.utexas.edu/la/sa/ bolivia Excellent database on various topics indigenous to Bolivia, maintained by the University of Texas, USA.
www.noticiasbolivianas.com All the Bolivian daily news in one place.

Tour operators

Andean Trails, *33 Sandport St, Leith, Edinburgh, EH6 6EP, UK, T0131-467 7086, www. andeantrails.co.uk.* Small group trekking, mountain biking and jungle tours in the Andes and Amazon.
Audley Travel, *New Mill, New Mill*

Lane, Witney, Oxfordshire, OX29 9SX, UK, T01993-838000, www.audleytravel.com. Tailor-made holidays to South America (and elsewhere).

Condor Travel, *Armando Blondet 249, San Isidro, Lima 27, T01-615 3000, www. condortravel.com. In USA T1-855-926 2975.* A full range of tours, including custom-made, and services in Bolivia and other South American countries, with a strong commitment to social responsibility.

Discover South America, *T01273-921655 (UK), www.discoversouthamerica. co.uk.* British/Peruvian-owned operator offering tailor-made and classic holidays in South America.

Dragoman, *Camp Green, Debenham, Suffolk, IP14 6LA, UK, T01728-861133, www. dragoman.co.uk.* Overland adventures.

Exodus Travels, *Grange Mills, Weir Rd, London SW12 0NE, T020 8772 3747, www. exodus.co.uk.*

Explore, *Nelson House, 55 Victoria Rd, Farnborough, Hampshire, GU14 7PA, UK, T01252-883687, www.explore.co.uk.*

Fairtravel4u, *Jan van Gentstraat 35, 1755 PB Petten, The Netherlands, T+31-61-5292565; in Ecuador T593-09-9569 3342, www.fairtravel4u.org, www.amazon-rainforest-tours.org.* Sells tours in Bolivia as well as Ecuador and Peru, specializing in economy trips.

HighLives Travel, *1 Empire Mews,* London, SW16 2BF, T020-8144 2629, www. highlives.co.uk. Organized luxury, tailor-made tours in Latin America.

Journey Latin America, *401 King St, London, W6 9NJ, UK, T020-8747 3108/3432 1590, www.journeylatinamerica.co.uk.* The specialists.

Last Frontiers, *The Mill, Quainton Rd, Waddesdon, Bucks, HP18 0LP, UK, T01296-653000, www.lastfrontiers.com.* South American specialists offering tailor-made itineraries plus family holidays, honeymoons, Galápagos and Antarctic cruises.

Latin American Travel Association, *www.lata.org.* For useful country information and listings of all UK tour operators specializing in Latin America. Also has the **LATA Foundation**, www. latafoundation.org, supporting charitable work in Latin America.

Neblina Forest Tours, *Puembo PO Box 17 17 12 12 Quito, Ecuador, T+539-2-239 3014, www.neblinaforest.com.* Birdwatching and cultural tours in Bolivia and other Latina American countries.

Oasis Overland, *The Marsh, Henstridge, Somerset, BA8 0TF, UK, T01963-530113, www.oasisoverland.co.uk.* Small group trips to Bolivia and Peru and overland tours throughout South America.

Select Latin America, *3.51 Canterbury Court, 1-3 Brixton Rd, Kennington Park*

Business Centre, London, SW9 6DE, UK, T020-7407 1478, www.selectlatinamerica. co.uk. Tailor-made holidays and small group tours.

Steppes Latin America, *51 Castle St, Cirencester, Glos, GL7 1QD, T01285-880980, www.steppestravel.co.uk.* Tailor-made itineraries for destinations throughout Latin America.

Tambo Tours, *USA, T1-888-2-GO-PERU (246-7378), www.tambotours.com.* Long-established adventure and tour specialist with offices in Peru and the US. Customized trips to the Amazon and archaeological sites of Bolivia, Peru and Ecuador.

Visas and immigration

A passport only, valid for 6 months beyond date of visit, is needed for citizens of Western European countries (except Romania), Japan, Canada, South American countries (except Guyana and Suriname), Mexico, Costa Rica, Panama, Australia and New Zealand. These countries are in Group 1. Most others are in Group 2, which require a visa, but it can be obtained on arrival at the airport or border post if not acquired at a consulate in advance. Group 3 countries must obtain a visa in advance at a Bolivian consulate, must show flight and hotel reservations, prove financial solvency and pay a fee. These include US and Israeli citizens, for whom the fee is US$135. A yellow fever vaccination certificate may be also be asked for. Some nationalities must gain authorization from the Bolivian Ministry of Foreign Affairs, which can take 6 weeks. It is best to check current requirements before leaving home. Tourists are usually granted 90 days stay on entry at airports, less at land borders.

You can apply for a free extension (*ampliación*) at immigration offices in all departmental capitals, up to a maximum stay of 90 days per calendar year (180 days for nationals of Andean nations). If you overstay, the current fine is Bs20, roughly US$3 per day. Be sure to keep the white (sometimes green) paper with entry stamp inside your passport, you will be asked for it when you leave. Information, including for student and work visas, from **Dirección General de Migración** in La Paz (see below).

Immigration offices
Cochabamba
Av Ballivián 722 y La Paz, T452 4628. Mon-Fri 0830-1230, 1430-1830.

La Paz
Bolivia at Camacho 1480, T02-211 0960, www.migracion.gob.bo. Mon-Fri 0830-1230, 1430-1830, go early. To renew a visa. Allow 48 hrs for visa extensions.

Potosí
Calama 118 entre Av Arce y Av Cívica, T02-622 2745. Mon-Fri 0830-1230, 1430-1830.

Rurrenabeque
Abaroa entre Pando y Santa Cruz, just off street, T800-10-0004. Mon-Fri 0830-1230, 1430-1830.

Santa Cruz
Av Omar Chávez Ortiz y Ana Barba, T03-351 9576. Mon-Fri 0830-1200, 1430-1800. Busy office, give yourself extra time.

Sucre
Bustillos 284 entre La Paz y Azurduy, T04-645 5640. Mon-Fri 0830-1230, 1430-1830.

Tarija

C Ingavi esq Rojas 789, Barrio El Molino, T04-664 3450. Mon-Fri 0830-1230, 1430-1830. Visa renewals in 48 hrs.

Weights and measures

Bolivia officially uses the metric system but some old Spanish measures, like the *quintal* (hundredweight), *arroba* (25 lbs) and *cuartilla* (6 lbs), are used for produce in markets.

Women travellers

Unaccompanied foreign women may be objects of much curiosity. Don't be unduly scared – or flattered. Avoid arriving anywhere after dark. Remember that for a single woman a taxi at night can be as dangerous as wandering around alone. If you accept a social invitation, make sure that someone knows the address and the time you left. Ask if you can bring a friend (even if you do not), although saying you have a boyfriend will not necessarily discourage an aspiring suitor. As elsewhere, watch your alcohol intake at parties with locals, especially if you are on your own. A good general rule is to always to act with confidence, as though you know where you are going, even if you do not. Do not tell strangers where you are staying.

Index → Entries in **bold** refer to maps

FOOTPRINT

Features

Acknowledgements

The previous five editions of this book were researched and written first by Alan Murphy with the assistance, at various times, of Roger Perkins, Kate Hannay, Julius Honnor, Geoffrey Groesbeck, Jean Brown and Yossi Brain, and then by Robert and Daisy Kunstaetter. This sixth edition of the Bolivia Handbook was prepared and researched by Ben Box, under the guidance of Robert and Daisy Kunstaetter. We should like to thank the entire Footprint editorial and production team, in particular Patrick, Felicity, Kevin, Kirsty, Liz and Angus.

Ben also wishes to thank the following correspondents for their most welcome assistance: Geoffrey Groesbeck; Martin Stratker (Copacabana); Derren Patterson and Jill Benton (La Paz); Saúl Arias Cossío (Samaipata); Petra Huber (Sorata); and Fabiola Mitru (Tupiza).

In September and October 2014 Ben travelled in Bolivia, accompanied and assisted by Sarah Cameron. They should both like to thank most warmly the following, who helped to make the trip so memorable: in Tarija, Soraya Sánchez Ferreira and family, and Viviana Ugarte Martínez of *Bolivian Wine Tours*, Virgilio Avila, Martín and Luisa of *Altiplano Hotel*, Don Benjamín Aramayo Sivila (Camargo), Doña Zulma of *Hostal Cepas de Mi Abuelo* (Villa Abecia), Jaime and Carmen Rosa Rivera (*Cepa de Oro*); in Cochabamba, Remy van den Berg of *El Mundo Verde Travel* and Bastian Müller of *Creative Tours*, and Vivian Meruvia of *Hotel Monserrat*; in Torotoro, José Pérez, and Mariana Sánchez Mitru; in Quime, Marleny Mamani Limachi of *InfoTur*, and Marko Lewis, Hermana and Franz of *Rancho Colibrí*; in La Paz, Cecilia Morales and the staff at *Hotel Mitru*; Darius Morgan, Mirjam Kennedy and Judith Hoffmann of *Crillon Tours*, Derren Patterson, Jill Benton and Alistair Matthew of *Gravity Bolivia*; in Rurrenabaque, Norman Valdez and the team at *Madidi Expeditions*, Alex Villca and the staff of *Madidi Jungle Ecolodge*, and Irene of *Madidi Travel*. For their advice at TMLA in Salta: Sebastian Grisi (*Magri Turismo*), Juan R Luzio (*Transturin*), Juan Gabriel Quesada (*Hidalgo Tours*), Aldrin Poma (*Pure! Bolivia*) and Bram Evers, and, in London, Bibiana Tellez-Garside (*High Lives*). Finally we are most grateful to Chris Rendell-Dunn of *Journey Latin America* for sorting out all the travel arrangements.

We are also most grateful to the readers and travellers who have written to us. In addition to those already acknowledged in the 2015 *South American Handbook*, the following persons contributed their experiences and insights to the current edition: Solene Limet (Switzerland); Alan and Jan Midgley (UK); Gwen von Bargen; Jami Schorling; Heinz Friedrich (Germany).

About the authors

Robert and Daisy Kunstaetter

In this edition Robert and Daisy have taken on co-authorship of the Peru Handbook for the first time but their experience with the country goes back over 25 years. Even so, it was not until they spent 12 months trekking and travelling in Peru between 2013 and 2014 that they began to really feel comfortable with it. Daisy hails from neighbouring Ecuador, Robert from Canada, and they had regularly travelled in Peru for work and play. But it was in both their natures as well as the nature of Peru that they had to walk the country in order to get a grip on it. Over the preceding years and miles, Robert and Daisy had become regular correspondents for Footprint, helping to update annual editions of the *South American Handbook*. Based in Ecuador since 1993, they have been closely involved with tourism there as well as in Peru and Bolivia. They are authors, co-authors, contributors to and cartographers for numerous Footprint guidebooks. They are also authors of a trekking guide to Ecuador and are currently writing one for Peru.

Ben Box

One of the first assignments Ben Box took as a freelance writer in 1980 was subediting work on the South American Handbook. The plan then was to write about contemporary Iberian and Latin American affairs, but in no time at all the lands south of the Rio Grande took over, inspiring journeys to all corners of the subcontinent. Ben has contributed to newspapers, magazines and learned tomes, usually on the subject of travel, and became editor of the South American Handbook in 1989. He has also been involved in Footprint's Handbooks on Central America & Mexico, Caribbean Islands, Brazil, Peru, Cuzco & the Inca Heartland, Bolivia, Peru, Bolivia and Ecuador and Jamaica. On many of these titles he has collaborated with his wife and Footprint Caribbean expert, Sarah Cameron.

Having a doctorate in Spanish and Portuguese studies from London University, Ben maintains a strong interest in Latin American literature. In the British summer he plays cricket for his local village side and year round he attempts to achieve some level of self-sufficiency in fruit and veg in a rather unruly country garden in Suffolk.

Credits

Footprint credits
Editor: Felicity Laughton
Production and layout: Patrick Dawson
Maps: Robert Kunstaetter, Kevin Feeney
Colour section: Angus Dawson

Publisher: Patrick Dawson
Managing Editor: Felicity Laughton
Administration: Elizabeth Taylor
Advertising sales and marketing:
John Sadler, Kirsty Holmes, Debbie Wylde

Photography credits
Front cover: Galyna Andrushko/Shutterstock.com
Back cover: Top: Simon Dannhauer/Shutterstock.
com. Bottom: abc7/Shutterstock.com.
Colour section Inside front cover: Galyna
Andrushko/Shutterstock.com. Page 1: Galyna
Andrushko/Shutterstock.com. Page 2: Takuji Oishi/
Shutterstock.com. Page 4: javarman/Shutterstock.
com, Rafal Cichawa/Shutterstock.com, Free Wind
2014/Shutterstock.com. Page 5: Noamfein/
Dreamstime.com, Chris Howey/Shutterstock.
com, Steffen Foerster/Shutterstock.com, Jess
Kraft/Shutterstock.com. Page 6: Free Wind 2014/
Shutterstock.com, Cory Smith/Shutterstock.com,
Ben Box. Page 7: Jess Kraft/Shutterstock.com,
Jürgen Ritterbach/SuperStock, Pyty/Shutterstock.
com, J.Enrique Molina/Album, Jearu/Shutterstock.
com. Page 10: Elzbieta Sekowska/Shutterstock.
com. Page 11: Eduardo Rivero/Shutterstock.com.
Page 12: Paul Clarke/shutterstock.com, Jess Kraft/
Shutterstock.com. Page 13: MP cz/Shutterstock.
com. Page 14: Yongyut Kumsri/Shutterstock.
com, Andrea Izzotti/Shutterstock.com. Page 15:
Andre Dib/Shutterstock.com, Magiturismo, Eye
Ubiquitous/SuperStock. Page 16: Ian Trower/
SuperStock.
Duotones Page 28: gary yim/Shutterstock.com,
Page 74: flocu/Shutterstock.com, Page 122:
Andrey Gpntarev/Shutterstock.com, Page 166:
Jess Kraft/Shutterstock.com, Page 216: Jess
Kraft/Shutterstock.com, Page 238: Jess Kraft/
Shutterstock.com, Page 284: Elzbieta Sekowska/
Shutterstock.com

Printed in Spain by GraphyCems

Publishing information
Footprint Bolivia
6th edition
© Footprint Handbooks Ltd
September 2015

ISBN: 978 1 909268 66 1
CIP DATA: A catalogue record for this
book is available from the British Library

® Footprint Handbooks and the
Footprint mark are a registered
trademark of Footprint Handbooks Ltd

Published by Footprint
6 Riverside Court
Lower Bristol Road
Bath BA2 3DZ, UK
T +44 (0)1225 469141
F +44 (0)1225 469461
footprinttravelguides.com

Distributed in the USA by
National Book Network, Inc.

Every effort has been made to ensure
that the facts in this guidebook are
accurate. However, travellers should still
obtain advice from consulates, airlines,
etc about travel and visa requirements
before travelling. The authors and
publishers cannot accept responsibility
for any loss, injury or inconvenience
however caused.

Footprint Mini Atlas
Bolivia

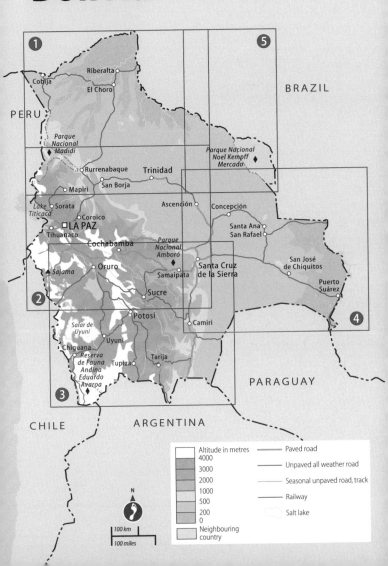

Map 2

PERU

A

B

C

CHILE

Ixiamas
Tumupasa
Santa Rosa
Río Yacuma
Río Tuichi
Parque Nacional Madidi
Río Amatola
Puerto Salinas
San Buenaventura
Reyes
Rurrenabaque
Reserva Biosférica Pilon Laja
El Porvenir
Chaupi Orco (6044m)
Lago Suches
Puina
Queara
Apolo
Aten
San Borja
Yucumo
Río Camata
Río Atén
Suches
Pelechuco
Antaquilla
Hichocolo
Ulla Ulla
Curva
Hilo Hilo
Área Protegida Apolobamba
Akamani
Canisaya
Charazani
Iskanwaya
Aucapata
Chuma
Río San Cristóbal
Río Llica
Mapiri
Consata
Río Mapiri
Río Kaka
Río Alto Beni
Santa Ana
Teoponte
Guanay
Puerto Linares
Palos Blanco
San Miguel de Huachi
Puerto Acosta
Escoma
Carabuco
Ancoraimes
Ancoma
Camino del Oro
Ocara
Sorata
Illampu (6380m)
Ticumbaya
Lili
Tipuani
Alcoche
Río Tipuani
Río Challana
Río Zongo
Caranavi
NOR YUNGAS
San Pedro
Río Boopi
Covendo
Lake Titicaca (Chucuito)
Isla del Sol
Isla de la Luna
Ancohuma (6427m)
Warisata
Achacachi
Challana
Zongo
El Choro
Yolosa
Unduavi
Coroico
Arapata
Coripata
Chulumani
SUD YUNGAS
Yampupata
Copacabana
Straits of Tiquina
San Pablo
Huarina
Puerto Pérez
Condoriri
Huayna Potosí (6088m)
Chacaltaya
La Cumbre
Milluni
Ventilla
Yanacachi
Mururata
Irupana
Chicaloma
Chuñavi
Lambate
Coripata
Isla de la Luna
San Pedro
Lago Huiñamarca
Pata Manta
Pucarani
Batallas
Lago Milluni
LA PAZ
Mallasa
Palca
Illimani (6402m)
Desaguadero
Taraco
Tiahuanaco
Guaqui
Tambillo
Laja
Viacha
Tirate
Río La Paz
Sapahaqui
Las Juntas
Suri
Collana
Calamarca
Quime
Santiago de Machaca
Vilchaya
Caquiviri
Ballivian
Comanche
Urmiri
Ayo Ayo
Luribay
Caxata
Cavari
Independencia
Cerro Tunari (5200m)
Achiri
Calacoto
Topohoco
Cordillera Quimza Cruz
LA PAZ
Berengula
Gral Campero
Corocoro
Cañaviri
Cañaviri
Patacamaya
Sica Sica
Puchini
Colquiri
Morochata
Quillacollo
Sipe Sipe
Inola
Gral Camacho
Ulloma
Puerto Japonés
Chacarilla
Umala
Panduro
Caracollo
Tapacari
Challa
Parotani
Charaña
San Pedro
La Joya
Soledad
Paria
Capachos
Arque
Totora
Curahuara de Carangas
Papelpampa
Oruro
Sacaca
Llanquera
Lago Uru Uru
Machacamarca
Parque Nacional Sajama
Sajama (6520m)
Turco
Toledo
Huanani
Llallagua
Poopó
Uncia
Sajama
Tambo Quemado
Lagunas
Cosapa
Corque
Pazña
Huancané
Galacala
Challapata
Sacabaya
San Juan de Kala
Andamarca
Lago Poopó
Huari
Huachacalla
Escara
Chipaya
ORURO
Sabaya
Concepción
Quillaca
Sevaruyo
Pisiga
Coipasa
Lago Coipasa
Tambillo
Salinas de Garci Mendoza
Río Mulatos

50 km
50 miles

N

1

2

3

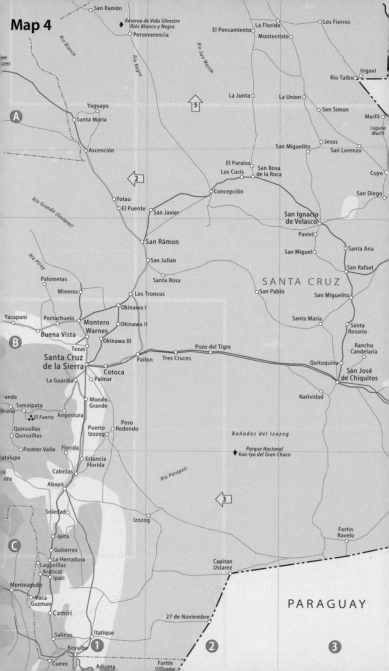

Map 4

San Ramón

Reserva de Vida Silvestre
Riós Blanco y Negra
Perseverancia

El Pensamiento
La Florida
Los Fierros
Montecristo

Rio Taibo
Ingavi

A

Yaguayu
Santa María

La Junta
La Union
San Simon

Marfil

Laguna
Marfil

Ascención

Jesus
San Miguelito
San Lorenzo

Cuyo

El Paraiso
Los Cusis
San Rosa
de la Roca

San Diego

Yotau
El Puente
San Javier
Concepción

San Ignacio
de Velasco

Pavivi

San Miguel
Santa Ana

San Rámon
San Rafael

San Julian

SANTA CRUZ

Santa Rosa
San Pablo
San Miguelito

Palometas
Mineros
Los Troncos
Santa Maria

Yacapaní
Portachuelo
Okinawa I
Santa
Rosario

B
Buena Vista
Montero
Warnes
Okinawa II
Rancho
Candelaria

Texas
Okinawa III
Pozo del Tigre
Quituquina

Santa Cruz
de la Sierra
Pailon
Tres Cruces
San José
de Chiquitos

Cotoca
Palmar

La Guardia
Mondo
Grande

anda
Samaipata
irana
El Fuerte
Angostura
Poso
Redondo

Natividad

Quirusillas
Quirusillas
Puerto
Izozog

Bañados del Izozog

Postrer Valle
Florida

Parque Nacional
Kaa-Iya del Gran Chaco

dalupe
Estancia
Florida

á
Cabezas
Rio Parapeti

era
Abapó

3

Soledad
Izozog

C
Ipita

Fortín
Ravelo

Gutierrez
La Herradura
Lagunillas
Arátical
Ipati

Capitan
Ustarez

Monteagudo

Vaca
Guzman
Camiri

PARAGUAY

Salinas
Itatique
1

Boyuibe
27 de Noviembre
2
3

Cuevo
Aduana
Fortín

Map 5

N

50 km

50 miles

BRAZIL

A

B

Versalles

Matequa

Rio Guaporé

Bella Vista

ena

Guacare

Baures

Puerto
Villazon

Piso Firme

Saucedo

El Carmen

Puerto
Saucedo

Rio Paragua

en

San Pedro

C

San
Ramón

Reserva de Vida Silvestre
Riós Blanco y Negra

4

La Florida

Los Fierros

Parque
Nacional Noel
Kempff
Mercado

Perseverencia

El Pensamiento

Montecristo

Rio Blanco

Rio Negro

Rio San Martin

Ingavi

Rio Taibo

1

Yaguayu

Santa María

2

La Junta

La Union

San Simon

3

El Marfil

Map index

Footprint story

It was 1921
Ireland had just been partitioned, the British miners were striking for more pay, and the Federation of British Industry had an idea. Exports were booming in South America – how about a handbook for businessmen trading in that far-away continent? The Anglo-South American Handbook was born that year, written by W Koebel, the most prolific writer on Latin America of his day.

1924
Two editions later, the book was 'privatized', and in 1924, in the hands of Royal Mail, the steamship company for South America, it became The South American Handbook, subtitled 'South America in a nutshell'. This annual publication became the 'bible' for generations of travellers to South America and remains so to this day. In the early days travel was by sea and the Handbook gave all the details needed for the long voyage from Europe. What to wear for dinner; how to arrange a cricket match with the Cable & Wireless staff on the Cape Verde Islands, and a full account of the journey from Liverpool up the Amazon to Manaus: 5898 miles without changing cabin!

1939
As the continent opened up, the South American Handbook reported the new Pan Am flying boat services and the fortnightly airship service from Rio to Europe on the Graf Zeppelin. For reasons still unclear but with extraordinary determination, the annual editions continued throughout the Second World War.

1970s
Many more people discovered South America and the backpacking trail started to develop. All the while the Handbook was gathering fans, including literary vagabonds such as Paul Theroux and Graham Greene (who once sent some updates addressed to "The publishers of the best travel guide in the world, Bath, England").

1990s
During the 1990s the company set about developing a new travel guide series using this legendary title as the flagship. By 1997 there were over a dozen guides in the series and the Footprint imprint was launched.

2000s
The series grew quickly and there were soon Footprint travel guides covering more than 150 countries. In 2004, Footprint launched its first thematic guide: *Surfing Europe*, packed with colour photographs, maps and charts. This was followed by further thematic guides such as *Diving the World*, *Snowboarding the World*, *Body and Soul Escapes*, *Travel with Kids* and *European City Breaks*.

2015
Today we continue the traditions of the last 92 years that have served legions of travellers so well. We believe that these help to make Footprint guides different. Our policy is to use authors who are genuine experts and who write for independent travellers; people possessing a spirit of adventure, looking to get off the beaten track.

footprinttravelguides.com